AF541062

NOONOMY

THE TRAJECTORY OF SOCIETAL TRANSFORMATION

NOONOMY

The Trajectory of Societal Transformation

Sergey Bodrunov

PENTAGON PRESS LLP

First published in 2025 by
PENTAGON PRESS LLP
206, Peacock Lane, Shahpur Jat
New Delhi-110049, India
Contact: 011-26490600

Typeset in AGaramond, 11.5 Point
Printed by Thomson Press India Limited.

ISBN 978-81-984458-5-8 (HB)

www.pentagonpress.in

Contents

PART TWO
NOONOMY AS REALITY TO BE AND THEORY ABOUT SOCIETY AND ITS DEVELOPMENT

A Note to Readers

The author has devoted many years of his life to the study of the processes of social development, the dynamics, causes, features and types of social structure, the search for the causes of the transformation processes occurring in society. The result of this work was the development of the theory of Noonomy, which absorbed many layers of fundamental ideas of predecessors, an analysis of the development trends in social processes, their philosophical generalisation and much more.

At the same time, the theory of Noonomy is not some static construct. The theory is developing – including in the course of further research not only by the author, but also by many of his followers and students. Books and articles on the theory of Noonomy are published in many countries in dozens of languages; elements of the theory of Noonomy are included in the curricula of many universities. However, the author believes that this is only the beginning of its development, and for this purpose he supports the publication of this book in such a scientifically advanced country as India.

Definitely, one can find many shortcomings, omissions, unexplained topics, etc., in this theory. We will leave their "revision" to you, dear Reader!

The advantages of the theory of Noonomy, as it seems to the author, include not only its practical focus, but also our very unusual authorial approach to shaping a holistic scientific basis for the prospects of global socio-economic development. It is this approach that allows us to involve new researchers in the work – despite the fact that the main provisions of this theory have already been set out in a number of major works (Bodrunov, 2016a, 2018a, 2019, 2020b, 2023*) and in a number of articles by the author that elicited response in the domestic and foreign expert communities, the ideas of Noonomy continue to be incessantly supplemented and developed.

One of the results of the evolution of the theory of Noonomy was this book, conceived by us as a kind of guide to its basic concepts and areas of research over time. The thesis statement allows us to briefly and succinctly present the logic of the author's approach and analysis. Following the key arguments and findings, the reader is invited to take a mental "journey" along the entire trajectory of social transformation, beginning with the prerequisites and starting point of this process and ending with the development of Noonomy and noosociety. In addition, this book prepared on the basis of a broad range of the author's developments over many years of intense intellectual work, will help significantly reduce the likelihood of the reader getting fragmentary or distorted insight into the theory of Noonomy.

One of the main objectives of this publication is to substantiate and illustrate the fundamental processes of global development in the fullest possible extent of their interaction and interrelation; this approach allows for a broad coverage and a more in-depth analysis of global trends.

The reader is invited not only to take a look at the theory of Noonomy and become aware of the stages of its development, but also to assess the relevance and demand for this work at the present stage of the history of human civilisation and socio-economic relations. By submitting his thoughts and research results to an impartial reader's judgment, the author of the book willingly shares his accumulated knowledge, is open to discussions and constructive feedback, and sincerely hopes that such "co-creation" with the audience will expedite the fruitful and progressive global transformation of society.

Introduction

When referring to the concept of "trajectory", we usually mean a certain line of movement of a specific object of study from a given starting state to a certain position or type.

In this case, according to the title of the book, the author offers an idea of the trajectory of transformation (or conversion, transformation, transition to a new state and quality) of such a multifaceted object as society.

To form this large-scale trajectory (or at least to outline its contours) indicating the exact direction of travel, stages and time frames for their completion, factors and prerequisites for efficiency, etc., means to recreate a true picture of the future social structure, based on the fundamental laws of its development, and to propose a certain plan for progressive socio-economic development which can and should be efficiently managed. This is the outline of the main objectives of this work.

It should be noted that in the book title the word "trajectory" is used in the singular, while in fact we are talking about a whole "bundle" of such lines with co-directional movement. Among them, we will include, first of all, the general trajectory of global transformation, outlined and analyzed in the first section based on the monograph of the same name (Bodrunov, 2020b, 2023*). Here are listed specific steps subject to the implementation of a favourable scenario for the development of human civilisation towards the transition from the current economic state to noo-intensive production and Noonomy, taking into account the change in technological modes, growing importance of nooneeds, the emerging role of culture and creative self-actualisation of a human.

The second branch of the "bundle of trajectories" in this work is the line formed by the so-called "Quadriga of Noonomy", thanks to which its genesis can already be observed today (see Parts 1 and 2). It is the four key processes (scientific and technical progress, diffusion of ownership, socialisation of society and solidarism) that serve as a guide to the main events of the future and testify to the validity of the author's forecast about the trajectory of global development.

Another branch from the "bundle of trajectories" represents the line of evolution of the theory of Noonomy itself and, accordingly, is associated with the expansion of the scope of the author's research in the field of transition to Noonomy as the future of human civilisation. The second part of this book is devoted to a greater extent to this topic, presenting the distinctive features and parallels of the theory of Noonomy with a number of other widely known theories and concepts, detailing the trajectory of the global nootransition, presenting the ideas and stages of noointegration, etc. In addition, the practical focus of developments in Noonomy is emphasised, which can serve as the basis for the development of strategic projects and programs at all possible levels of management.

Finally, the most important line in the "bundle of trajectories", used by the author in the title of the book, is the line of transformation of society from its current state through the development of a New Industrial Society of the Second Generation (NIS.2) to the noo-level. In fact, the entire book is devoted to this topic, with a special emphasis on the third part, which contains not only the results of building the image of the noosociety itself and highlighting its key characteristics and features, but also significant features of the noopersonality and the conditions for its creation and upbringing.

It is essential that this book itself, which is based on the revised texts of a number of fundamental monographs and a number of articles by the author, reflects the development trajectory of the author's research in the field of Noonomy and introduces the reader to the intimate process of the author's individual creative scientific activity associated with the search for answers to the most complex questions of our reality, many of which were identified and continue to be identified during the presentations of the author's reports at various congresses, in discussions with colleagues, etc. The author considered it possible and useful to open his mind to the readers, letting them into his personal creative laboratory. The author may be a bit presumptuous, but he remains convinced that walking the path to the ideas of Noonomy together with the reader will allow us to establish a deeper connection, to look at these ideas with an interested and unbiased gaze.

PART ONE

Nooapproach and the Trajectory of Global Transformation[1]

How does one open a door to the future? After all, not all motion signifies movement towards the future: we might be treading water, going in circles, or even turning back, without finding the road that would lead us to a new world, a genuine (and better) future. "If a person does not know to which port they are sailing, no wind is favourable" – this phrase from Seneca is worth remembering every time we think about long-term strategic prospects for development.

To recognise a genuine path towards greater social development, we must go beyond merely using our common sense or orienting ourselves with preconceptions about what would personally benefit us or our neighbours. What is needed is a scientific theory that holds powerful predictive potential; a theory capable of sorting through the facts and tendencies of the present to reveal the possibility, and necessity, of the future.

Developing such a theory requires us to stand upon the stable ground of scientific method. One of the most important components of this methodology is determining the nature of the relationship between technological development and the evolution of the social order. By studying just this fundamental interconnection and mutual influence of human knowledge (as materialised in productive technology) and social relations (which shape the possibility of technological development and, in turn, are affected and changed by technological upheavals) we will be able to make scientifically grounded predictions.

But the future is not a path predetermined by fate. Our actions and decisions will determine whether we wander in darkness, turning away from the prospects we uncover, or manage to take advantage of newly discovered opportunities for development. Theory can tell us which actions are necessary to open the door to the future, but we ourselves must carry out these actions.

The theory of noonomy, developed by the author, offers a view of a path capable of leading us out of the dead ends and contradictions that human civilisation has so far managed to generate. Development will always be contradictory: these contradictions are precisely what motivate us to seek solutions to problems and move forward. It is important that the path leading out of contradiction be creative, not destructive, and that the contradictory aspects of new developmental stages serve as an impulse to improve society rather than plunging it into a morass of conflict.

The author invites you to join him and cast your eyes on a possible path forward, to grapple with the logic of human society's evolution under the influence of greater knowledge and technological progress and appreciate the steps that must be taken in order to move towards a better future.

1

Fundamentals: Thinkers who have Contributed to the Study of the Interconnections between Technological and Social Development

Aristotle Posed the question of how technology (*technç*, art or craft) relates to human needs. However, the problem of technology's influence on the ordering of society escaped him, since the slow pace of technological development in antiquity provided no material capable of offering insight into such influence.

Francis Bacon Following the Aristotelian tradition, Bacon saw the goal of science and technology as providing society with various goods. Formulated the idea that the comparative levels of development of different societies were defined not by the natural conditions of their existence, but instead by their degree of scientific and technological development.

Jean-Antoine de Condorcet Posed the question of technology's, as well as society's, historical development. Advanced the thesis that scientific progress and the progress of industry influence one another and that their joint impact determines the "progress of the human race".

Charles Fourier	Proposed a theory of stages of social development dependent on the progress achieved by the development of science and production, which he measured according to the possibilities attained for satisfying social needs, on which basis he separated historical stages from various systems of socioeconomic relations.
Claude-Henri de Saint-Simon	Advanced the thesis that there is a necessary correspondence between economic and political development and a society's intellectual and moral level. Developed à theory of the alternation of critical phases with quiet phases in the development of society and of the interconnection between scientific and political revolutions. He believed that the cause of social development was, in fact, changes in scientific worldviews.
Karl Marx	Theoretically grounded the materialist conception of history and advanced the thesis of production as a twofold process: the production of the goods of life and the production of social relations. Founded a theory of social development as decisively determined by changing modes of production, which appear as a contradictory unity of mutually acting productive forces and production relations, each at a particular level of development.
Vladimir Ivanovich Vernadsky	Articulated humanity's role as the decisive geological force acting on the Earth's surface, influencing the development of its biogeochemical shell. Formulated the idea of the noosphere, according to which human reason becomes a factor that regulates the process of natural, as well as social, evolution.
Joseph Schumpeter	Advanced the theory of the entrepreneur as innovator and "creative destruction" (the destruction of old combinations of resources during economic development and the creation of newer, more effective ones). Proposed the idea that Kondratiev cycles depend

	on the introduction of new technologies and examined the particularities of innovation in different phases of a Kondratiev cycle. Demonstrated the influence of the various phases of a Kondratiev cycle on the course of a medium-term business cycle (a Juglar cycle).
John Kenneth Galbraith	Demonstrated the influence of technological upheavals over the course of the twentieth century on the character of socioeconomic structures (the allocation of property rights, corporate structures, the economy's division into a market system and a planned system, the creation of systems for consciously generating demand, the role of the state, and so on), transformations which he described in his theory of the new industrial state.
Daniel Bell	Proposed the hypothesis of post-industrial society based on the fact that the relative weight of industry in the economies of developed countries substantially decreased during the second half of the twentieth century. Several of Bell's predictions about the evolution of society's economic and social structure have been confirmed. However, many leading economists and sociologists are sceptical of the judgment that contemporary society qualifies as "post-industrial", believing that Bell underrated industry's critically important role and hypostatised knowledge production.

Methodology

Before taking our first step along the road of studying the evolution of human society as influenced by technological change, we must define the methodological premises that ground us. The bulk of these premises were worked out during a time when humanity embarked on a path of profound and rapid transformations in the material basis of its existence – the nineteenth and twentieth centuries. These are exactly the transformations that made it possible to discover the laws by which technological change influences social development.

Karl Marx (1818–1883) was perhaps the first scholar to make a serious contribution towards placing the study of the reciprocal influence of technology, on the one hand, and society's socioeconomic order, on the other, within a firm scientific framework.

In his research, Karl Marx adopted the point of view that people's social relations are defined by the conditions of their material production and that the interaction of social relations and material production determines the transition from one historical stage of society's development to another. Marx set this principle as the foundation of his theoretical investigations in the realm of political economy, which allowed him to take a step away from formulating general philosophical research principles and towards an understanding of the concrete laws of the mutual influence of technological and economic development.

The object of political economy in Marxism is, primarily, *people's objective relations* within the process of material production in the broad sense of the term, that is, *both* production proper *and* trade, distribution, and consumption. Let me reiterate this: *specifically*, objective social relations, and *specifically*, within production. Marx here continued the tradition of classical political economy. This constitutes the principal **difference** between the science of classical political economy and the current reigning discourse within economic theory (designated by the word "economics") in which attention is centred upon an individual's *subjective* choices and focused primarily on the sphere of *trade* rather than production.

Political economy always emphasised that it was necessary for development to ensure a *dialectical correspondence between, on one hand, the material and technological basis of production* (which Marxism refers to as "productive forces") *and, on the other hand, socioeconomic relations of production*. Studying capitalism, Marx demonstrated on one hand how the character of economic relations spurs forward technological progress, determining the stages of the evolution of productive forces, and on the other, how this evolution of productive forces modifies that same character of productive relations.

The significance of the Marxist approach is also defined by its *historical and systematic method of researching economic reality*. For us, the economy is not only a sphere in which various more or less rational actors operate, but a multitude of historically developing economic systems. One of these is Russia's economic system. This system has its own *trends of development* which, in a *specific* (to our region and to our civilisation) way, refract the general laws of economic development.

Without taking Marxism's contributions into account, moreover, we cannot fully understand *the role of economic development's "human dimension"* – for example, the growing importance of **knowledge** for the modern economy. The Marxist method permits us to provide an explanation for the critically important role of science and education in the transition to a model of economic development which would not only make it possible to carry out nationwide *modernisation* on a modern technological basis, but also open a path towards *constant* economic modernisation based on prioritising the development of *knowledge-intensive production* – production whose main factor is knowledge rather than machines or raw materials.

It is not a coincidence that political economy combines two conceptions: politics and economics. Its major strength is that it accounts for the sociopolitical component of economic processes. Indeed, in the framework of Marxist political economy, the most important question is which social strata, and in what kind of relationship with one another, are produced by a given economic order.

In this way, the method of classical political economy not only makes it possible to show *the functional links* between diverse economic phenomena but also it allows us to delineate *what is typical and what is contingent* in the economy, to investigate the economy as *it develops*, **systemically and historically**. And, most importantly, by putting processes of material production, *rather than processes of trade alone*, at the heart of its research, it pays very close attention to *human relationships* and social collectives, examining the interaction of *socioeconomic interests*.

The most valuable thing about Marx for us now is not only the theory of surplus value, nor just the labour theory of value, both of which have been subjected to unending criticism – showing at the very least that these theories, serving as objects of criticism for more than one hundred and fifty years, have yet to lose their relevance. Much more interesting for our purpose are *Marx's predictions, which are coming true at this very moment, about material production's long-term developmental tendencies* – predictions that were based, incidentally, on the same theoretical assumptions mentioned above.

Marx predicted *man's displacement from the direct process of material production*, man's transition from being a direct participant in production into becoming its "watchman and regulator." This is based on the transformation of natural processes into controlled and directed technological processes, "where labour in which a human being does what a thing could do has ceased", when labour appears "as an activity regulating all the forces of nature" and becomes an "experimental science, [a] materially creative and objectifying science", when human development takes place "as a constant suspension of its [own] *barrier*" and amounts to the "absolute working-out of [the human being's] creative potentialities" (**Marx, 1993: 705, 325, 612, 712, 542, 488**).

There is another economist known for his research into the problems of technological development and innovation and their influence on society's economic condition and structure – the Austrian-born American economist **Joseph Schumpeter** (1883–1950) – whose ideas undeniably echo Marx's (as Schumpeter himself did not deny). At the same time, Schumpeter substantially differs from Marx in many ways in his approach to studying the role and place of technological upheavals in the economy.

Above all, Schumpeter introduced the difference between *economic growth* and *economic development* into economic theory. Growth means increased production and consumption of already existing goods, while economic development signifies the continuation of production based on new innovations: new commodities, new technologies, new methods for organising production.

Joseph Schumpeter noted that the development of new innovations does not happen continuously over time. He studied the innovative activity of entrepreneurs, leading to technological upgrades in production, as a factor in gaining competitive advantage and as the main engine of economic development (Schumpeter, 2017).

He justly viewed competition based on innovation and scientific development by corporations as the main factor underlying the economic dynamics of capitalism (Schumpeter, 2017). Schumpeter referred to the use of competitive advantage based not on lowering production costs and prices for traditional goods, but rather on new innovations as effective competition.

Another of Schumpeter's contributions was his differentiation of interconnected complexes of technologies and corresponding stages of technological development. Innovations do not appear gradually and consistently, but come into being as interconnected groups of innovations, that is, as clusters (bundles) (Menshikov, Klimenko, 2014: 192). It is precisely new scientific discoveries that lead to the emergence of these innovation clusters. The term "waves of innovation" has established itself as a way to refer to periods (stages) of predominant development of particular technologies (Blaug, 1986: 215–217).

Joseph Schumpeter tried to combine his theory of the role of technological innovation with N.D. Kondratiev's notion of "long conjunctural waves". In his conception, the phase of a wave of technological change that underlies a Kondratiev cycle interacts with the waves of technological change underlying a medium-term Juglar cycle, with the former determining the latter. In this way, both long-term and medium-term waves of technological renewal and the phases of long-term and medium-term cycles prove to be dependent on one another (Schumpeter, 1939: 181-182).

Schumpeter saw that the concentration of capital in large corporations opens additional possibilities both for financing scientific research and development and for investing in the application of new technologies. At the same time, he feared that the concentration of production and formation of enormous corporate organisms would lead to a decline of individual competitive spirit (along with its romantic urge to innovate), the crowding-out of small and medium-sized entrepreneurs, and the erosion of private property.

The extent to which Schumpeter's forecasts were and were not validated was later shown by the research of another famous economist, John Kenneth Galbraith (1908–2006).

Galbraith observed that economic life was undergoing "the application of increasingly intricate and sophisticated technology to the production of things. Machines have replaced crude manpower. And increasingly, as they are used to instruct other machines, they replace the cruder forms of human intelligence" (Galbraith, 1967: 1).These processes led to the consolidation of production, demanding more and more significant capital investments, and attracting more and more highly qualified specialists. The result was the emergence of large corporations as the predominant type of economic organisation capable of attracting the capital necessary for such production.

What became quite clear at this point was a process that had begun much earlier: *the fragmentation of the entrepreneur-proprietor figure who both organises production and reaps its income.* Galbraith, building on the reflections of a series of authors from the first third of the twentieth century (Thorstein Veblen (Veblen, 1936 [1921]), Adolf Berle and Gardiner Means (Berle, Means, 1968 [1932]), Stuart Chase (Chase, 1932)[2], and others) and in some ways intersecting with Karl Marx's ideas about the separation of joint-stock companies' capital into "capital-property" and "capital-function", noted that at the start of the twentieth century, control by private owners had been replaced with control by the technostructure, that is, managers and technical specialists.

The growth of corporate capital inevitably led to a transformation in the state's economic role. In the 1960s, Galbraith concluded that "the state undertakes to regulate the total income available for the purchase of goods and services in the economy. It seeks to ensure sufficient purchasing power to buy whatever the current labour force can produce" (Galbraith, 1967: 2).

The first consequence of these changes was a significant *rise in the role of planning.* "The large commitment of capital and organisation well in advance of result requires that there be foresight and also that all feasible steps be taken to insure that what is foreseen will transpire" – this was Galbraith's highly important conclusion (Galbraith, 1967: 4).

In addition, *consumer demand became an object of planning.* Galbraith rightly stressed that the nature of technology and its associated capital requirements, along with the time needed to develop and produce products, made state regulation of demand necessary.

The task of *creating demand* (and not merely keeping track of it) is fulfilled by both the state and – more importantly – corporations. As Galbraith emphasised: "No mechanism of the market relates the decisions to save to the decisions to invest" (Galbraith, 1967: 42). This assertion clearly echoes John Maynard Keynes' analogous conclusion from the 1930s.

In the end, Galbraith arrived at the conclusion that there is a profound conceptual distinction between small enterprises, all of whose successes rely on their complete control by a single person, and corporations. This difference, which could be seen as a boundary line distinguishing between millions of smallscale firms and thousands of giants, rests at the heart of the general *separation of the economy into "market" and "planned" systems.*

Thus, Marx, Schumpeter, and Galbraith all saw that economic evolution is primarily based on technological progress that changes the material foundation of industrial production. From various perspectives, they developed an approach to studying the influence of technological progress on the economic arrangement of society.

Notes

1 Prepared on the basis of the following materials: (Bodrunov, 2020b, 2023*).

2 This book's title was used by Franklin D. Roosevelt to refer to his programme in the 1932 election.

2

Grasping Reality

2.1. Production and Its Significance

Technology, on the one hand, and people's social relations, on the other, are intertwined very closely in the process of material production. **Material production** is simultaneously the production of the *material conditions* of human social life (human society could not exist if it did not produce) and the production of people's *social relations* and social existence, that is, the production of social people.

Human beings' social relations within production – the *social arrangement of production* – reflects the state of material production and of people's productive activity. In turn, the social arrangement of production serves as the basis for all other social relationships between people. However, these social relations (social structure, culture, ideology, politics, social psychology, etc.) are not a passive copy of production relations. They, in turn, actively impact the development of the sphere of production.

> *Production* is the process by which humanity transforms what it is given by nature, adapting natural material for human needs, and giving it the required form for consumption.

Nature can only be transformed once we have understood how it is organised and once the laws of its existence have been discovered. At stake is not only the transformative activity of humanity itself, but the far-reaching consequences of this activity, which also influence humanity's habitat. This is why scientific *knowledge* of the world becomes more significant as the horizon of this knowledge grows longer. Without it, technological improvements would be impossible.

2.2. The Elements of Production (Product, Means of Production, Technology, Labour, Organisation, Knowledge)

The process of manufacturing products – that is, the transformation of natural substances for the purpose of satisfying human needs – is known as the production process. The most substantial elements of the production process are *human labour, human knowledge, raw materials, instruments of labour, technology, and the organisation of production.*

The structure of society is affected by every element of the production process: the nature of labour and its level of productivity, the development of knowledge, the means of production that are used (raw materials, equipment, etc.), the technology of production, the character of the product being produced, and – following from all of this – the methods of organising production.

> The *product of production* is an external object, a thing, which is obtained by transforming natural material via the production process and designed to satisfy human needs.

A **product** is the materialised result of the application of knowledge (its objectification) towards the satisfaction of human needs primarily by manufacturing material devices or providing services which rely on the use of material products.

Products created by human beings have (in the philosophical sense) an objective and thing-like character, but they need not necessarily be embodied as physical objects. Some needs are satisfied by intangible products which do not take substantial form, that is, *services*. There are two factors relevant to services that must always be taken into account.

Firstly, all services (with very few exceptions) can only be provided with the help of some sort of material product. If material production ceased, there would be no services.

Secondly, only material products can satisfy humanity's vital needs for food, clothing, housing, transport, communication, processing information, and more. The sole reason that a large contingent of service employees may exist is that other people provide them with necessary material products.

As production develops, each product created by human beings is less affected by natural substances and more affected by the **technosphere**.

Meanwhile, the technosphere's development is determined not so much by the accumulation of work tools, or how they are used, as by the knowledge embodied in these tools, which determines people's ability to make use of them and amplifies the extent to which humanity may effectively reach its goals: in other words, *the technological application of knowledge and science.*

> The *technosphere* is the totality of technogenically produced objects (made by human beings) and the part of the biosphere that is transformed by these objects. Broadly speaking, the technosphere includes all conditions of productive activity – knowledge, ability, people's mutual relations within the process of production, etc.

Technological development determines the evolution of production, as well as its very product. To define the extent of this evolution, we must introduce the concept of **the level (of complexity) of a product** (for more on this concept, see: **Bodrunov, 2016à: 13-14**).

> *The level (of complexity) of a product* refers to the characteristics of a produced product that determine its multiple stages of processing and the corresponding volume of knowledge that goes into it.

This concept may be expressed in purely quantitative terms, defining how many stages of processing have been undergone by raw materials to convert them into a final product that satisfies particular needs. Much more important, however, is the qualitative appraisal of a product's complexity.

Philosophically speaking, any given product is constituted by objectified human knowledge, which is applied to produce a thing or object that embodies it. The general tendency of productive development is to lower the need for natural substances, natural energy, and natural forces in manufacturing a product. This leads to decreased specific consumption of raw materials. At the same time, progressively more complex equipment comes to play a much greater role in structuring products, along with (most importantly of all) the increasing extent of knowledge needed to deliver a higher-level product.

The active force that unites all the component parts of production in a single process is **human labour**.

> *Labour* is practical human activity oriented towards changing natural objects for the satisfaction of human needs.

In the words of Karl Marx,

> . . . Labour is, first of all, a process between man and nature, a process by which man, through his own actions, mediates, regulates, and controls the metabolism between himself and nature. He confronts the materials of nature as a force of nature. He sets in motion the natural forces which belong to his own body, his arms, legs, head and hands, in order to appropriate the materials of nature in a form adapted to his own needs. Through this movement he acts upon external nature and changes it, and in this way he simultaneously changes his own nature. He develops the potentialities slumbering within nature and subjects the play of its forces to his own sovereign power (Marx, 1982: 283).

Labour, then, is practical activity: a person engaged in labour pursues a definite goal and directs their efforts towards obtaining a definite final result. To accomplish this, the labourer should clearly know what he wants to achieve, that is, mentally formulate an image of the final product. Moreover, he must imagine how, and using what *technologies*, the desired result can be obtained. This requires specific knowledge. Besides knowledge, a labourer must have the skills and abilities needed to put his mental image into practice. Within the labour process, a not insignificant role is played by the labourer's capacity to bend his will towards the goal he is striving for; to concentrate and mobilise his knowledge, abilities, skills, and energy to deliver the final result – the product of labour.

In its simplest definition, **technology** designates the totality of productive methods and processes that are used to process raw materials into a finished product.

> *Technology* is the mode of interaction of all the elements of a concrete production process, oriented towards making a finished product. It is facilitated by the set of abilities and knowledge required to make this product.

Without technological knowledge, without the knowledge required to develop and use technologies, no normal production process capable of reaching a posited goal can be ensured.

Analyzing the fundamental components of the production process in the modern industrial mode of production and studying the correspondence between the service sector and material production leads to the conclusion that technological development (or the technological application of scientific knowledge) plays the decisive role in forming technological modes that unite all the components of the production process at a given stage of development. Technology permeates the entire production process – from the choice (or creation) of original materials, to the quality of living labour and the means of production that are used, to the organisation of the production process and completion of the finished product.

To a significant extent, technology determines how the industrial mode of production affects other levels of the social structure, changing the face of society itself. Of course, this influence is complex, mediated, and multilayered, interacting with the laws of development of various social spheres and strata. Yet it is the impulse originating from technological progress that plays the decisive role.

The **organisation of production** takes on exceptional importance in the industrial mode. This is due to two important factors. Firstly, understanding the growing complexity of production, the interaction of its many components, and the need for rational management requires deep and specialised knowledge. The second factor is the conversion of production from a primarily individual into a primarily collective process, based on the combined labour of many people. Managing people's combined activity within industrial production through specialisation and division of labour is a crucial aspect of organising production.

The development of methods for organising production was somewhat belated compared to the other elements of the industrial mode of production. True, methods of linear organisation were emerging more or less spontaneously even in the nineteenth century, based on spatially distributing machines and mechanisms along linear tracks that allowed for step-by-step operations to be performed on basic materials and component parts. But we observe the first consciously developed methods for organising production only at the start of the twentieth century: Taylorism, Fordism, and the assembly-line method of manufacturing.

As technology, labour, and products grow ever more complex, organisation plays a progressively greater role in increasing productive efficiency. Each step taken to improve industrial technologies demands a corresponding improvement in productive organisation, aimed at the more and more efficient provision of industrial outputs (both goods and services). Meanwhile, the complexity of productive organisation depends significantly on how much knowledge is involved in the development of the methods of organisation used to make the production process function.

2.3. Production's Stages of Development

In order to come to terms with production's various stages of development, a historical perspective on the problem is needed above all. Only a conception of the historical development of both the technosphere and human society, in their interaction and interdependence, will permit the objectively necessary laws determining how transitions occur from one developmental stage to another to emerge.

The method of classical political economy not only makes it possible to demonstrate the functional links between disparate economic phenomena but also allows us to distinguish between what is regular and what happens by chance in the economy, and to examine the economy in its systematic and historical development. Most importantly, by analytically centring the processes of material production, and not merely those of trade, it pays rigorous attention to the relations between people and social groups, examining the interaction of different socioeconomic interests.

Different socioeconomic arrangements of society correspond to different stages of the development of the production process. The transition from an appropriative economy, reliant mainly on stone tools, to a production-based economy using metal tools led to the development of the division of labour (the division between arable farming and animal husbandry, the separation of trades from agriculture, etc.) and served as the key pivot point away from a purely natural economy to a commodity economy. Meanwhile, the production of a surplus product, appearing at the same time, facilitated the development of various forms of exploitation.

> *Social division of labour* is the specialisation of producers on a society-wide scale, based on specific types of activity. It is a prerequisite for

the phenomenon of exchange of the products of specialised production between producers to emerge.

A *natural economy* is an economic form in which goods produced within a closed, localised economic community (a family, a commune, an agricultural estate) are also consumed within that community. Some part of productive output may be redistributed beyond the community's boundaries, but not through trade.

A *commodity economy* is an economic form based on the fully developed division of labour: each producer, specialising in the independent, private production of specific goods, receives the means for sustaining their own life (and their productive labour) by trading their products for others on the market.

Surplus product is that part of productive output which exceeds what is necessary for the producer's own direct consumption. The production of surplus product assumes that a certain level of labour productivity has been achieved.

Exploitation is the coercion of one human being by another (the exploiter) into labour, in order to produce a surplus product which is appropriated by the exploiter.

The transition from primarily manual instruments of labour to machines occurred due to the specialisation of tools and the use of universal heat engines that did not depend on natural energy sources such as water, wind, or the muscular strength of humans and animals. This laid the foundations for the transition to a new mode of production. As machine technology spread far and wide, commodity exchange, the circulation of money, and the development of capitalist social relations were energised and given a new basis for far-reaching expansion, leading to the hegemony of the *capitalist mode of production* and the development of the *world market.*

Machine production brought enormous progress in the division of labour, a hitherto unknown rise in productivity, the development of a variety of new needs, and the discovery of all sorts of new ways to satisfy them. All this progress encouraged the illusion of "mastery over nature". Humanity's supposed mastery over nature is a one-sided narrative: humanity cannot interact with nature without considering the principles according to which the natural environment reproduces itself. Acting against these principles does not bring any reward, but rather, harm, and sometimes even catastrophe.

The rise of machine production was the first stage in the development of industrial production.

> *Industrial production* is the production of standardised instruments for satisfying human needs on a massive scale, based on the use of intricate tools that give humanity control over natural processes (mechanical, physical, chemical, biological) which are transformed by technological processes, as well as the use of artificial sources of energy.

Since it is able to satisfy human needs on a mass scale, industrial production also commands the technical capacity to satisfy individualised needs. Modern industrial production relies on both machine and non-machine technologies, built for human control over various non-mechanical processes – physical, chemical, biological, and informational. Industry serves as the robust technological core of the modern economy. It is the evolution of industry that has largely determined the shifts in the socioeconomic order of society over the last two hundred fifty years.

The scholars who have most contributed to the study of the laws of interaction between humankind's technological and socioeconomic development have done so precisely by investigating the industrial mode of production. The nature of these scholars' direct contributions to economic theory is the subject of heated debate, but what matters for our purposes is the philosophical aspect of their approach to studying socioeconomic reality, and above all, the research methods of classical political economy.

2.4. Industrialisation and the Industrial Revolution

The transition to the industrial mode of production – the **Industrial Revolution** – was marked by deep transformations in the technological basis of material production, along with equally substantial changes throughout the entire system of social relations.

> The *Industrial Revolution* was the transformation from artisanal manufacturing – based on manual labour, the use of hand tools, and natural energy sources – to industrial production.

Over the course of the Industrial Revolution, the material basis of production changed due to the following qualitative shifts:

- the transition from primarily hand-held tools to complex equipment that combines an energy source, labour process (an instrument of labour) – that is, a means of mechanical, physical, chemical or biological action upon an object of labour, and transformative control devices that give the labour process a necessary and expedient form;
- the transition from relying on the muscular strength of humans or animals, along with natural sources of energy (water and wind), to universal artificial energy sources.

The first stage of the Industrial Revolution took place above all through the development of large-scale machine production.

> A *machine* is a composite piece of equipment based on the use of mechanical processes, consisting of an engine (powered by heat or electricity), labour tools that act upon the object of labour, and a transfer mechanism that communicates a necessary practical form to the action of the labour tools.

The transition from production based on manual labour and hand-held tools to industrial production had the following technological consequences:

1) abrupt growth in labour productivity;
2) the ability to standardise production on a mass scale;
3) independence of production sites from natural energy sources;
4) independence of production sites from local sources of raw materials, due to the development of machine transportation;
5) reliance on scientific research for converting natural processes into technological ones, which opens the possibility of constant technological advancement.

The Industrial Revolution enabled the complete **industrialisation** of society's economic system.

> *Industrialisation* of the economy is the expansion on a mass scale of standardised production, originally developed within the industrial sector, to all other areas of the economy (transportation, communications and other branches of the service sector, construction, agriculture). During industrialisation, industry's economic importance grows, and industry becomes the economy's technological core.

2.5. Post-Industrial Society?

Post-industrial society is a theory stating that the growth in the service sector's relative share of GDP in developed countries, and the reduction of industry's share, signal society's transition to a post-industrial stage of development in which material production loses its significance compared to the production of services, particularly knowledge and information.

"The 'post-industrial' society . . . [is] one in which the economy [has] moved from being predominantly engaged in the production of goods to being preoccupied with services, research, education and amenities..." (Bell, 1967: 102).

"The change in the meaning of knowledge that began 250 years ago has transformed society and economy. Formal knowledge is seen as both the key personal resource and the key economic resource. *Knowledge is the only meaningful resource today.* The traditional 'factors of production' – land (that is, natural resources), labour and capital – have not disappeared. But they have become secondary" (Drucker, 2011: 38).

We cannot say that these accounts of post-industrial society were completely detached from reality. Certain developmental tendencies were observed quite correctly by the post-industrialists, but they often drew inaccurate conclusions from these tendencies. For example, they conflated the relative *decline of material production and the relative decline of material expenditures in the cost structure of producing products with a decline in the role of material production.* They were inclined to project the genuinely profound changes in the lives of a relatively narrow stratum of workers within the modern information, telecommunications, and media sectors onto the greater part of society.

The post-industrialists fetishise knowledge and information, and the role of the creators, transformers, and distributors of such knowledge and information, by treating them as intrinsically significant and isolating them from the real process of material production. A myth of the "new economy" has emerged, which supposedly offers developed countries a path towards crisis-free growth. Post-industrial theory factually ignores the significance of the industrial basis of society's existence and development. In our opinion, this is post-industrialism's primary mistake, since so-called "knowledge production" and the production of information, media products, and means of telecommunication is only truly significant insofar as it aids the functioning and development of material production.

Not only are theories of post-industrial society premature in their assumption that tendencies affecting only a small segment of the economy pervade nearly the whole of society's production. More importantly, they ignore the role of such fundamental factors in social development as material production and its central core, industry, along with immaterial factors such as human culture; meanwhile, it is these exact factors that predetermine the level and character of human activity's development, which means that they determine humanity's social existence as a whole.

Marx, who predicted the colossal growth of the role of knowledge in production even from the vantage point of the mid-nineteenth century, was much more prescient than were the late twentieth century's theorists of postindustrialism. Without singing the praises of science and knowledge "as such", he clearly indicated the significance of science and knowledge precisely in their technological and productive applications. *Society needs knowledge*, not for "finding creative solutions", but *for the development (through the application of knowledge) of modern material production that satisfies the genuine needs of humankind.*

Note that for all the changes in material production over the last hundred years, it is industrial technology that remains the foundation of our economic existence, which rests above all on industrial production. The latter is what enables the uninterrupted growth of labour productivity within material production, based on scientific and technological progress, and creates possibilities for the growth of employment within the service sector.

2.6. The Role of Knowledge

Since their first appearance, industrial technologies have required ever-greater applications of scientific **knowledge**.

It was necessary to study the properties of various materials in order to develop practical methods for processing them and create materials with the desired characteristics, and to study the properties of various types of energy (mechanical, thermal, electrical) in order to understand how to use them, convert them, transmit them, and use them in the process of production. Extensive research was required to make possible the creation and use of complicated machines, and to interfere in the complex physical and chemical processes that take place when original materials are processed using various tools. Finally, the labour process itself became an object of scientific research, in pursuit of more effective ways to make use of humanity's capacity for work.

One might say that the level of a technology directly depends on the extent of the knowledge concretely implemented in it. The common term "high-tech" refers precisely to the technologies that make use of cutting-edge scientific knowledge.

The complexity and endless diversity of industrial technologies have developed the specialisation and division of labour to a tremendous degree. Consequently, most participants in the production process no longer have full command over the technologies used to produce any given product. Instead, they perform only one specific and partial function within the framework of a particular technology.

In the final analysis, it is precisely the character and the extent of the *knowledge* embedded in a product that determines *its level.* Any consumer features we might impart to a product, and all the technical characteristics of its use, depend on the knowledge used to create it. The augmentation of knowledge used in production guarantees the augmentation of products' capacity to respond to human beings' ever more diverse demands.

The greater or lesser potency of the knowledge contained in a product correspondingly leads to the greater level (increased complexity) or lesser level (decreased complexity) of that product. In the exact same way, growth in the knowledge-density of technologies leads to their advancement, while a decrease in knowledge-density leads to their becoming more primitive; the augmentation of a worker's knowledge leads to a growth in his or her qualifications, while a lower level of knowledge leads to professional deskilling.

Because of the tremendous role of knowledge in the industrial mode of production, since the nineteenth century there has been an observable tendency for production to transform itself and towards the transmission of knowledge, that is, its technological application in specialised branches of social production. Developments in science, education, and professional training take up an ever-greater share of state budget expenditures and gross domestic product. The sphere of knowledge production and transmission interacts more and more closely with the sphere of direct production.

3

Into the World of New Technologies

3.1. Technological Modes

Technological development within the framework of economic industrialisation leads to substantial qualitative changes not only within production, but in society's entire way of life. A certain amount of accumulated change over a particular time period brings about a transformation that presents society with a new level at which needs can be satisfied. We must find criteria for distinguishing between qualitatively different periods of technological development that determine qualitative distinctions in the level of society's needs, as well as the means and capacity for satisfying them.

The question of how to identify interconnected technological networks and their corresponding levels of technological development carries with it a long scholarly history. Joseph Schumpeter already observed that the development of new innovations occurs discontinuously. He identified networks of new technologies that fostered surges of innovation, which he dubbed "technology clusters" (Menshikov, Klimenko, 2014: 192). The periods in which one technology cluster was replaced by another were referred to as "waves of innovation" (Blaug, 1986: 215–217).

In 1975, the West German scholar Gerhard Mensch researched how periods of technological stagnation, characterised by the preponderance of steadily improving or even purely imaginary innovations, are replaced by periods in which fundamentally new technological solutions become entrenched (Mensch, 1975). In the 1970s and 1980s, the English economist

Christopher Freeman formulated the concepts, "technological system" and "technoeconomic paradigm", which were further developed by his follower Carlota Perez (Perez, 2002).

The term "technological mode" [tekhnologicheskiy uklad], as used in Russian economic scholarship, is an analogue of concepts such as waves of innovation, techno-economic paradigms, and technical modes of production. It was first proposed in 1986 by Dmitriy Lvov and Sergey Glazyev (Lvov, Glazyev, 1986).

> A *technological mode* is a system of interconnected forms of production (including interdependent technology chains) with a common technical level. These may also be considered as subsystems of a broader system of social production that includes multiple technological modes.

According to Sergey Glazyev's approach, a technological mode is a cohesive and stable framework within which a self-contained cycle takes place, beginning with the obtainment of initial resources and concluding with the output of final products that correspond to a type of social consumption. The core of a technological mode is à set of basic technologies that are used throughout a fairly long period of time. The technological innovations that define how this core is formed are called key factors. Industries that intensively use these key factors and play a leading role in the dissemination of the new technological mode are known as carriers [iavliaiutsia nesushchimi] (Glazyev, Kharitonov (eds., 2009: 11).

Moments of change over the course of historical development are due to the movement from one technological mode to another, which can be connected to Nikolai Kondratiev's "long waves of the economic conjuncture". We may note that while the appearance and dissemination of a new technological mode coincides with the upward phase of a Kondratiev cycle, the mode lives on even after the wave that generated it has passed by and been replaced by another. Modern economic literature usually refers to six technological modes.

> *The first technological mode* (1770–1830) was formed by the expansion of machine technologies within the textile sector. Textiles were its primary industry.
>
> *The second technological mode* (1830–1880) was linked to the use of steam engines and the development of railroad transport and

transcontinental steamship communication. Many areas of production were mechanised. Its primary industries were the production of railway equipment, steam engines, and steel.

The third technological mode (1880–1930) was characterised by the development of electrical energy and the internal combustion engine; the development of heavy machinery, electrical engineering, and the growth of the aviation and automobile industries; and the use of the radio, telephone, and telegraph as means of communication.

The fourth technological mode (1930–1980) was based on the widespread application of the internal combustion engine, powered by oil, petroleum products, and gas; the development of petrochemical technologies; and the appearance and broad use of synthetic materials. Computers and their software appeared; space exploration began.

The fifth technological mode (lasting from the beginning of the 1980s until the present) is characterised by the wide dispersal of information and communications technologies, based on developments within the fields of microelectronics and computer science. Newly developing sectors include biotechnology and genetic engineering, robotics, fibre-optic systems, and space telecommunications.

In the first decade of the twenty-first century, the transition to *the sixth technological mode* began, which (it is assumed) will be characterised by the widespread expansion of biotechnology, nanotechnology, and various non-machine or hybrid technologies, such as cognitive technology.

Various scientific sources allow us to distinguish key technologies and industries that constitute the core, and chronological frame, of different modes. The schema of technological modes offered here is not a dogmatic or essentialised one. What matters is that each of these modes is a coherent technological system, and that the core of each mode unites all its components as links in a technological chain. These degree of these links of technological and economic cohesion determines the functional effectiveness of the technological mode, and the speed at which new technologies are transferred between industries and regions.

Each mode serves as the foundation of a new stage of social development, becoming the key factor for change. However, we must not fall into the trap of technological determinism by extrapolating new stages of social development *directly* from technological transitions and merely reducing all social transformations to the influence of technological innovation. Social orders, even when only their socioeconomic systems are considered, are far more complex; we can only understand the changes occurring within society by drawing from well-developed scholarly methods. For our purposes, the most significant of these comes from political economy.

3.2. Technological Revolutions and Industrial Revolutions

The transition from one technological mode to another may be considered a technological revolution. And indeed, such a transition signals substantial qualitative shifts in the technological basis of production: the replacement of certain fundamental technologies within the most important industrial processes by others which are more modern and effective.

Since technology encompasses all the components of the production process, the shifts mentioned above occur within the content of work, the structure of employment, the systemic use of the means of production, the knowledge required for production, and the organisation of production. For some time now, the most important role in technological development has been played not just by knowledge, but specifically by scientific knowledge. Consequently, "knowledge production" has become its own separate sector of the economy. For this reason, beginning with the fifth technological mode, the transition to a new mode and the formulation of its basic assumptions have been viewed as nothing less than a scientific and technical revolution.

Technological revolutions are based not only on the creation and distribution of new technologies, nor just the expansion of the scope of these technologies to cover all the component elements of the production process, but also the technological transfiguration of the core of modern production – industry. Not all technological revolutions may be called industrial revolutions, but only those which qualitatively transform the foundational technologies of industrial production.

The first industrial revolution was the general transition from pre-industrial to industrial production. Later industrial revolutions transformed the face of already existing industries. The second industrial revolution was marked by movement towards industrially producing not just objects of consumption, but also the means of production themselves. By now, we are already experiencing the maturation of the fourth industrial revolution, based on technologies that – for the first time – allow production to occur with practically no human involvement.

One of the preconditions of the fourth industrial revolution was general consciousness of the modern economy's industrial core. Enthusiasm for post-industrial theories corresponds to the trend of developed countries, chasing the potentialities opened by globalisation, transferring their industrial production to countries with low labour costs. Within their territory, developed countries have preserved only those links of global "value chains" that foster the creation of knowledge: research and development, organisation and management of logistics flows, marketing and advertising. This has led to developed countries' *deindustrialisation.*

> *Deindustrialisation* (of a national economy) is the reduction of the relative economic weight of industry, to the extent that this is not just caused by the faster development of other economic sectors. Deindustrialisation is the consequence of either an absolute reduction in the output of industrial products, or the offshoring of this output to foreign countries.

The crises that have confronted developed nations since the onset of the Great Recession of 2008–2009, and the significantly strengthened position of many developing countries in high-tech economic sectors, have shown that offshoring is fraught with the danger of making developed countries dependent on other nations for their industrial goods, including high-tech products. Developing countries have gradually begun to move away from the role of subcontractors or "assembly plants" for transnational corporations and towards the creation of their own high-tech productive capacity, based on "reverse engineering" and the accelerated development of their R&D sectors.

It is becoming clear that merely maintaining control over "knowledge production" is insufficient for sustainable development, and that the "knowledge economy" itself may only develop fully in tandem with the high-tech industrial core of the national economic system.

Because of this, and in order to overcome the negative consequences of deindustrialisation, the world's developed nations are beginning to develop and implement policies of *re-industrialisation and reshoring.*

> *Re-industrialisation* is the restoration of priority to industrial and material production within the economy, coming after processes of deindustrialisation.
>
> *Reshoring* is when productive capacity that had been relocated abroad is returned to its country of origin, or the creation of new capacity to replace what was lost.

3.3. The Sixth Technological Mode

Nowadays we are moving towards the sixth technological mode: the world of biotechnology, nanotechnology, robotics, new medicine that will significantly increase people's life expectancy and quality of life, virtual reality technology, etc. The contours of the technologies that are destined to form the basis of the economy of the future are coming into view. Experts estimate that if the current tempo of techno-economic development is maintained, the sixth technological mode will crystallise around the year 2025 and reach its maturity in the 2040s. Meanwhile, from 2020–2025, the next *scientific, technical, and technological revolution* will enter its decisive phase. The basis of this revolution will be new discoveries that synthesise the accomplishments of the fields mentioned above (and, perhaps, others too).

> *The sixth technological mode* is a technological complex that is currently forming, which includes nano, bio, information, and cognitive technologies. Its distinctive feature is technological convergence and the formation of hybrid technologies integrated by IT ("digitalisation," artificial intelligence, data processing on a massive scale).

When determining strategies of industrial development, one must remember that transformations in material production will be *systemic, cohesive, and interconnected.* Let us highlight some of the key changes that must be considered when *creating a new industrial system that matches the cutting edge of twenty-first century science and technology.*

The main particularities of industrial development in the near future will include:

- updates in the content of technological processes;

- changes in the (micro-level) structure of industrial enterprises;
- changes in the (macro-level) sectoral structure of industry;
- different approaches to the organisation/localisation of production facilities;
- the formation of new types of industrial corporations;
- strengthened integration of production with science and education;
- the transition to an ideology of "continuous" innovation in production;
- the formation of economic relations and institutes oriented towards industrial and techno-scientific progress.

The following must all be renewed: *the content of technological processes*; *the structure of industries and location of production facilities*; the internal *structure and types of cooperation of production facilities* and their integration with science and education; *economic relations and institutions* that ensure the progress of material production according to new principles.

We must not limit ourselves to the mastery of technologies that manufacture the products we currently need. We must propagate *new standards* in product quality control, industrial management, logistics, and personnel work. *These changes should affect every part of the production process: its organisation, technological base, output, and, of course, the character and quality of industrial labour.* For example, so far as *transformations in the character and organisational form of industrial production* are concerned, it would be worth attending to the tendency towards the *individualisation of production*, which has been apparent since the end of the twentieth century, and the *consumer-to-business model* of labour organisation.

The main technological challenges for industry in the twenty-first century include:

- the accelerated creation of new technologies that raise productivity and lower production costs;
- furthering the "individualisation" of the production process, applied technology, and manufactured products;
- implementing the principle of modularity in production;

- speeding up the intellectualisation, computerisation, and robotisation of production;
- developing networked technologies and implementing the network principle of productive organisation;
- the miniaturisation/compactisation of production;
- strengthening the tendency for production sites to be cost-effective and waste-free;
- permanently raising the tempo of technology transfer;
- increasing the "physical" proximity of designers and manufacturers to speed up the implementation of new product ideas;
- the expansion of "zones of intellectualisation" in the labour process;
- the "clustering" of industrial relations;
- giving a greater role to the individual, motivational, psychosocial, and other characteristics of the participants in productive activity;
- lowering labour costs for the production of new products while the costs of researching and developing them increase;
- transforming the yield structure of production in favour of knowledge-intensive and high value-added products.

Most significant is the principle of the simultaneous individualisation and *modularisation* of production for high-tech spheres such as machine tool manufacturing, aircraft construction (both civil and military), heavy engineering, and more. Individualising production and establishing contact between the producer and the individual consumer is in line with the use of modern telecommunications and information technology. The development of the internet led to the formation of massive platforms fostering B2B and B2C communication. Consequently, an effective toolkit was created for direct interaction between clients (consumers) and producers. When combined with the extensive development of technologies based on new principles (virtual engineering, computer visualisation, 3-D printing, etc.), this will soon make it possible to *individually* create industrial products that are practically *waste-free* and can be *almost instantaneously delivered* to consumers.

At the same time, the individualisation of production facilitates the transition to *networked principles of organisation, not just for businesses, but for the entire process of material production.* This makes it possible to operatively create and change the configuration of producers' interactions with subsidiaries such as subcontractors and outsourcers. In this way, it is possible to swiftly adjust manufactured products based on consumers' individual requests, and then move on to new products oriented towards other consumers, other users, other markets, and so on. In turn, networked organisation facilitates the ever more expansive individualisation of production; as these processes reinforce each other, they *pick up speed like an avalanche.*

3.4. Technological NBICS-Convergence and Hybrid Technology

A unique feature of the sixth technological mode is not only the increased knowledge-intensity of products, but also the interaction of multiple kinds of knowledge and, therefore, multiple kinds of technology in the production of any given product. Most important in this regard is the integration/convergence/interconnection of information technology, biotechnology, nanotechnology, and cognitive science. This phenomenon has been called *NBIC-convergence* (N for nano, B for bio, I for info, C for cogno). The term was introduced in 2002 by Mihail Roco and William Bainbridge, who produced the most significant work on this topic, namely, the report Converging Technologies for Improving Human Performance,[1] prepared for the World Technology Evaluation Centre (WTEC) (Roco, Bainbridge, (Eds., 2003: 1).

> *NBIC-convergence* is the mutual interpenetration of nanotechnologies, biotechnologies, information technologies, and cognitive technologies, leading to the creation of technological processes in which these technologies functionally condition one another and form a contiguous whole.

The report also proposed the concept of NBICS-convergence, which adds the social sciences to the mix (Spohrer, 2003: 101–117). Though this approach has found widespread use in both Western and Russian scholarship, the social sciences have yet to make a noticeable substantive contribution to solving the problems of developing and applying convergent technologies (Kovalchuk, 2011: 21; Kovalchuk, Naraikin, Yatsishina, 2011: 10-13). As of yet, sociotechnology has only found a real application in the development of artificial intelligence systems meant to interact with their user (or rather, to manipulate their user). Humanistic disciplines spend more time writing about social problems in the light of new technologies than proposing ways to integrate social knowledge in technological development.

Taking into account the sixth mode's interconnected technologies, as well as the interdisciplinary character of present-day science, we may (in the long term) expect the merging of the NBIC fields into a single scientific and technological realm of knowledge.

This realm's object of study and action will be the organisation of matter at nearly every level: from molecular substances (nano) to living ones (bio), reason and rationality (cogno), and the processes of information exchange (info).

Thus, the distinguishing features of NBIC-convergence are as follows:

- the intensive interaction of different areas of science and technology, with the effect of significant synergy;
- the broad scope of these mutually influential fields, from matter at its atomic level to intelligent systems;
- emerging horizons for the qualitative growth of technological capacities for humanity's individual and societal development (Pride, Medvedev, 2022).

Technological convergence within the framework of the sixth mode has led to the broad dissemination of hybrid technologies, in which various combinations of machine and non-machine technologies are used (together with information technologies) as an instrument for regulating and directing natural processes to reach desired goals, opening the door to a new technological revolution.

> *Hybrid technology* refers to the combination of two or more types of technology within a single system to achieve a particular useful result. Such combinations are often convergent, meaning that one technology somehow enables the functioning of another.
>
> Searching Google for "hybrid technology" on March 31, 2019, returned 641,000,000 results (the Russian term *gibridnye tekhnologii* returned 17,900,000 results). These mentioned hybrid technology in the context of industrial processing, auto manufacturing, pre-sowing

seed treatment, electronic system security, atomic desalination plants, military affairs, machine translation, heart surgery, and more. It is hard to imagine an area where hybrid technologies could not be used. However, there was no general definition of the concept to be found in the Russian-language results. The English-language results included one website, dedicated to climate technology, that offered a definition: "Hybrid technology systems combine two or more technologies with the aim to achieve efficient systems."[2]

3.5. Additive and Distractive Technologies

Despite significant growth in the role and importance of non-machine technologies (bioengineering, etc.) the sixth technological mode still remains within the framework of the industrial mode of production. Convergent (hybrid) technologies, in fact, give the industrial mode of production a "second life", by uniting machine-based and non-machine-based principles of action upon nature to create products that satisfy human needs with minimal consumption of materials.

Significant possibilities are opened by technology (for example, 3D printing) that integrates modern machine techniques (printing) with information technology that virtualises and digitises reality (3D modelling). This may lead to a sharp growth in the expansion of additive technologies and a relative decrease in traditional industrial manufacturing. Instead of "processing" initial materials using distractive ("subtractive") productive technologies (by cutting, grinding, or sawing material from workpieces), newer processes "assemble" products from their component parts by combining or building up materials (usually layer by layer) to create an object from a 3D model.

There are some traditional industrial technologies that might also be considered additive: for example, casting or sintering construction materials, or powder metallurgy. Today, the possibilities afforded by these technologies can be combined with those afforded by 3D printing. We are already witnessing the creation of 3D printers capable of printing entire buildings and structures, or at least the large blocks from which these are made. The assembly of prefabricated homes from components made by 3D printers is already taking place: the first such house was recently printed in Yaroslavl on a Russian-made printer. Another printer from the same firm, "Spetsavia," has printed an entire office hotel in Denmark.[3]

Additive technologies already encompass an entire spectrum of technological devices (for extrusion and liquid gas jet pumping, paper lamination, photopolymerisation, synthesis of products from powders, direct energy release at specific points) and use of all kinds of diverse materials (plastics and plastic products, metals, composites, hybrid materials, materials used in metal casting processes, ceramics, and more) (for an overview of additive technologies see: Prosvirinov, 2012).

3D printing technology is already being combined with biotechnology to create 3D-printed human organs for transplantation. At present, bioprosthetic devices (implants) made from artificial materials are only being used to replace bone and cartilaginous tissue, and for prosthetic hand bones. Attempts at cultivating tissue for human organs (liver, kidneys, bladder, skin) have only really been used so far for testing pharmaceuticals;[4] that said, there is no doubt that the future belongs to these technologies.

3.6. The Role of IT and Cognitive Technologies

Humanity, as it develops, moves along a path of *recognition [osoznanie]* of its ever-growing needs and *recognition [osoznanie]* of how to satisfy them. This *added cognition [znanie]*, which has no inherent limits, always reveals not only the desired answer, but a broader horizon of newly forming needs.[5] This horizon is limited only by humanity's ability to recognise and comprehend it at each progressive stage of understanding. This is the essence of human development, scientific and technical progress, and the development of societal relations.

Thus, at a certain stage, humanity recognised and understood mechanical forces, and included them in its production turnover. Later, this happened with the far more knowledge-intensive force of electricity. By now, our technical and productive base includes informational and cognitive resources.

Our grasp of these resources is only possible due to computerised digital oversight of production processes themselves, which requires extensive use of informational and communicative networks. This is not the same thing as "digitalisation" superimposed on traditional technological processes from the fifth or fourth mode. For example, if you removed the numerical control unit from a CNC machine, you would end up with a traditional metalworking machine. But if you tried the same thing with a 3D printer, you would end up with an inoperative unit. If you tried to disconnect "Industry 4.0" from the Web, you would stop entire industries in their tracks.

The modern tendency towards "digitalisation" of the economy might be effectuated even outside the sixth technological paradigm. But the sixth mode is what makes this tendency not just economically well-grounded, but technologically predetermined. Without the use of information technology and digital communication, NBIC-convergence would be impossible.

> *Digitalisation* is a figurative expression that encompasses a network of solutions linked to the use of modern IT and communications technologies (the internet, mobile communications, large-scale information processing, artificial intelligence, etc.) primarily in digital form.

By using self-learning artificial intelligence (AI) systems, cognitive technologies within the framework of the sixth paradigm encroach upon areas where there was previously no alternative to using human labour. AI systems are already capable of finding, accumulating, sorting, and comparing information in order to make a decision. *It is cognitive technology that, by drawing on the achievements of biotechnology, IT, and communications technology, makes it possible for human beings to directly act upon non-human technological processes* [human-machine interfaces, human-machine systems, and human-machine networks (for an overview, see: Tsvetkova et. al, 2015)]. This serves as a new impulse for the production of robotic technology, which is becoming ever more agile adaptable, and productive.

AI is still quite far from being able to uncover new knowledge (it can make use of knowledge by accumulating and analyzing available data; it can *communicate knowledge through information and communications technology*; but by itself, *it cannot* act as a "discoverer" of knowledge). For this reason, the new technological paradigm places new and growing demands on human beings' research and cognitive abilities. Consequently, approaches based on technological convergence require scholarly interdisciplinarity. An orientation towards technological convergence should be matched by convergence in education. At present, this is significantly hindered by the departmental and sectoral organisation of both education and scholarship.

But why is it that these particular trajectories of technological progress make up the new technological paradigm? And what accounts for the transition from the previously observable "coexistence" and interaction of various technologies to their convergence – that is, to the formation of hybrid technologies?

To answer these questions, we must above all pay attention to modern information technology and the related process of technological "digitalisation". Information and communications technology, unlike all other technologies, can be diffused into any other technological process. Therefore, "digitalisation" is becoming a technological platform capable of uniting multivarious technologies into hybrid technological processes. "Information technology has become a kind of 'hoop' that encompasses all other science and technology" (Kovalchuk, 2011: 14). For this reason, digital information technology will be the core of the new technological mode.

Other technologies within this new mode are united both by their suitability for convergence with one another and by the fact that this convergence realises two basic tendencies that characterise the current stage of technological development. These are, firstly, the tendency for human beings to be displaced from the direct process of material production, and secondly, the tendency towards sharp growth in the knowledge-intensiveness of products, and the corresponding relative reduction in their material cost.

Notes

1 This report defines NBIC-convergence as the "synergistic combination of four major 'NBIC' (nano-bio-info-cogno) provinces of science and technology".

2 See: "Hybrid Technology," CTCN, UN Climate Technology Centre & Network, accessed October 15, 2022, https://www.ctc-n.org/technologies/hybrid-technology.

3 Haria R. Europe's First 3D Printed Pre-Fab House Completed by AMT SPETSAVIA. 3D Printing Industry: The Authority on Additive Manufacturing, October 25, 2017, https://3dprintingindustry.com/news/europes-first-3d-printed-pre-fab-house completed-russias-amt-spetsavia-123245/; The Construction of Europe's First 3D Printed Building Has Begun and Is Almost Complete. 3D Printhuset, accessed October 15, 2022, https://3dprinthuset.dk/europes-first- 3d-printed-building/.

4 "Bioprinting Organs on a 3D Printer, How Does It Work?" MAKE-3D, April 12, 2015, https://make-3d.ru/articles/biopechat-organov-na-3d-printere/.

5 Znanie, here translated as "cognition" to preserve the author's wordplay, more literally means "knowledge". Osoznanie can be defined as "realisation" or "comprehension" – *Translator's note.*

4

To the Threshold of Technological Revolution

4.1. The Growing Knowledge-Intensiveness of Production

The world is entering the epoch of the fourth industrial revolution, along with a new technological mode. Obviously, in the future, *competitive* economies will be those that manage to take the lead not in obtaining and selling natural resources, but in developing and applying *advanced technology*, and which succeed in supplying enough *human capital capable of realising this technology*. The economic leaders of the future will be technological leaders.

Transitioning to new stages of technological progress requires us to command newer and newer types of knowledge and to find ways to apply them. The most advanced technologies will also be the most knowledge-intensive.

We will now turn to changes in *technology*, particularly those which have already become (or are becoming) realities and are occurring within the sphere of material production. First among these, as "post-industrial" theorists have correctly identified, is the growing significance of information technology. However, unlike the post-industrialists, we do not consider this to be evidence that the decisive role of material production is withering. We instead draw a different conclusion from this fact, namely, that *the knowledge-intensiveness of material production* is constantly growing.

By this, we do not mean to merely observe the growing role of information, as many theorists of the information society do (the "information society," or "knowledge-based society," has long interested post-industrial thinkers: see, Drucker, 1969; Machlup, 1962; Masuda, 1981; etc.): we have in mind less *the production of information than a new type of material production.*[1] This difference is fundamental. As the modern world economy shows in practice, the creation of information often leads to the production of "information noise"; economic resources are used to create signs (Baudrillard, 1981) and simulacra (Buzgalin, Kolganov, 2012a) of useful goods rather than facilitating the growth of labour productivity, qualitative human progress, or the solution of social and economic problems. In the final analysis, this kind of "informatisation" leads to the virtualisation of social being, which destroys the human personality, its spiritual world, and its social ties.

Knowledge-intensiveness of the technology of material production is a process that critically synthesises the achievements of the industrial economy and the information economy. To be precise, this critical synthesis is expressed by the fact that the decisive role in high-tech production is increasingly played by operations and processes in which human beings act not as appendages to machines (tools or assembly lines), but as bearers of knowledge converted into technology: the human being "steps to the side of the production process" and "comes to relate... as watchman and regulator to the production process itself" (Marx, 1993: 705). In these circumstances, we may speak of the *knowledge-intensiveness* of material production and the *knowledge-density* of its products.

The core features of the emerging *new type of material production knowledge-intensive production* are:

- the uninterrupted growth of production's information component and reduction of its material component; miniaturisation, the tendency to reduce the energy density, material density, and capital density of productive output;
- new specific features of *the production process* and tendencies in the development of *technology* (flexibility, modularity, standardisation, etc.);
- *network models and networked structures*, replacing vertically integrated structures;

- the use of modern methods of management and productive organisation (just-in-time production, lean production, and more) (for more details, see Ohno, Mito, 1988; Wadell, Bodek, 2005; Malakooti, 2013; John Wiley & Sons; Tillema, Steen, 2015);
- environmental friendliness and an orientation towards *new energy sources*;
- the development of qualitatively new technology within material production itself, as well as transportation and logistics (nanotechnology, 3D printing, etc.);
- reduction of the role of traditional manufacturing due to the expansion of additive technologies;
- an emphasis on quality and efficiency.

The application of new knowledge in production is a constantly accelerating process, conditioned by a growing synergy of useful effects (this synergy is inherent in knowledge as a phenomenon). Consequently, knowledge-intensive production enables quicker satisfaction of increasing needs. The heightened level of new technology is accompanied by reduction in the capital, material, and energy density of production, which ultimately opens the possibility of lowering the specific consumption of resources needed to satisfy a standard unit of human need.

At some point, then, the "knowledge part" of many products begins to substantially exceed the "material part". This conclusion is illustrated nicely by the graph below, with intersecting curves depicting the relative share of material and intellectual input in overall production costs (Figure 1).[2]

We can now see that in many ways, this moment (of knowledge-intensity exceeding material density) has already arrived. For example, take an object such as an iPhone. According to information provided by Apple, the material part of this phone constitutes only 4.8 per cent of its overall production cost. Most high-tech industrial products are characterised by similar relative ratios of material input to knowledge, clearly signalling the emergence of the tendency we are describing.

The development of this tendency provokes a reduction in demand for resources; as a result, the position of resource-extracting countries within the global economy is changing. In terms of the global balance of natural

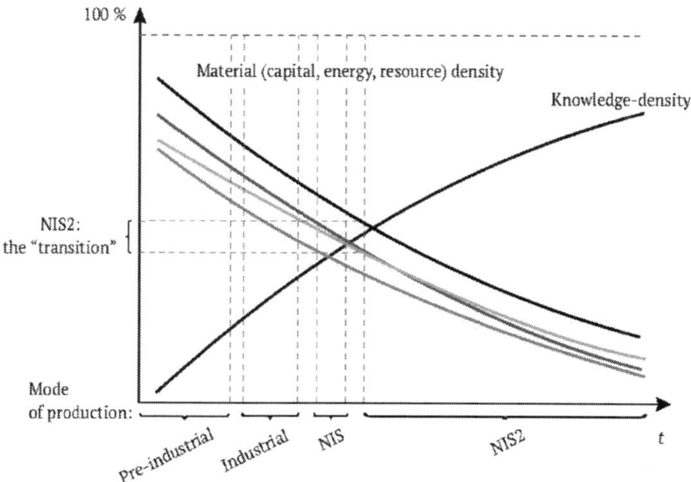

***Figure 1.** The process of historical change in the ratio of the different components of products*

Source: Bodrunov, 2016b: 11 (Figure 4).[3]

resources, this means less pressure on natural stockpiles, and the possibility to develop in a way that is compatible with preserving (and restoring) an equilibrium with our natural environment.

New production is knowledge-intensive production, which draws from knowledge-dense technology to guarantee the output of knowledge-dense industrial products that allow growing human needs to be satisfied – including, unlike the mass production of generic products by the first generation of industry, individualised products for particular consumers. This kind of production cannot be supported without a high level of knowledge-density for all its components: materials, labour, organisation of the production process, and (we emphasise) the technologies used. What now comes to the forefront – where it will always remain from now on! – is knowledge, in its overt and "pure" form, as the foundational resource of industrial, technological, and societal development.

4.2. Industry 4.0, Smart Factories, and the Displacement of Human Beings from Direct Production

The fifth technological mode's development, and the sixth's even more so, has revealed a manifest tendency – already predicted by Karl Marx – for human beings to be displaced from the process of direct production. The automated production lines which appeared even within the framework of the third and fourth technological modes, and which also displaced people from direct production, had a narrowly specialised character and could not be recalibrated to resolve new technological problems (such as executing new technological operations and producing new types of products). For this reason, they were only effective when used within very narrow technological niches, mainly the production of raw materials and supplies (for example, chemical production, sheet metal rolling mills, paper-making machines, etc.).

The fifth and sixth technological modes have enabled the production of automated assembly units which can be recalibrated towards different types of productive output and different technological operations. Some of the first visible manifestations of this tendency can be found in universal industrial manipulators (robots) and production machines equipped with computer numerical control (CNC). At this point, the world produces almost no metal lathes without CNC. Meanwhile, the production of robots, which experienced a vigorous start in the 1970s and slowed down somewhat in the 1990s, has resurged, along with progress in microelectronics and artificial intelligence systems.

The world's leading countries are giving top priority to the development of robotics. The American and Japanese governments have created special organs for robotechnical development. These are the National Robotics Initiative (NRI) in the USA, founded in 2011, and the Robot Revolution Realisation Council in Japan, created in 2015 (Sziebig, Korondi, 2015: 160). Japan, which has long led the world in its overall quantity and production volume of industrial robots, is faced with the task of maintaining this advanced position. China, which has greatly accelerated its production of industrial robots, is Japan's challenger (during 2018 there were installed 154,000 industrial robots in China, more than in the USA and Europe put together). Currently more than 400,000 industrial robots are produced per year around the world. In Singapore and South Korea, the quantity of these robots already amounts to 7 to 8 percent of the overall industrial employment rate.

Modern material production has moved far beyond the "factory system" – established in the nineteenth century and surviving up to the twenty-first

– in which human beings act as appendages to machines. Already emergent, in our view, are "Industry 4.0"[4] and "smart factories", working in tandem with the "internet of things", or rather, the industrial internet of things (Boyes, Hallaq et al, 2018: 1-12), enabling both autonomous technical devices' interaction with one another and human control over them. To facilitate this control, integrated sensors are gaining widespread use, along with systems for processing the large amounts of information received from these sensors (big data). Here we can see the prototype of another version of production-machine-based, industrial, but now "human-free" or "uninhabited" by people.

Current technologies allow us to automatise not just production processes, but the organisation of production, as well as practically the entire cycle of commodity production. Marketing research, which determines the structure and volume of productive output, can be automatised using artificial intelligence. The process of direct production in "smart factories" is based on automated machinery that is coordinated and controlled using "the internet of things". Logistical functions, industrial cooperation between firms, and other forms of business-to-business interaction are also being automatised. Even when interacting with consumers during the stage of ordering, shipping, and delivering products, more and more key functions are being entrusted to artificial intelligence systems. Factually speaking, the only tasks that still belong to human beings are those of development, adjustment, and setting goals.

In this way, the growth in the role of human knowledge and human reason is accompanied by a gradual displacement of human beings from direct participation in the process of material production. A modern type of "smart industry" is being created, in which *the dramatically increasing role of human reason is paired with the displacement of human beings from direct participation in technological processes.* "Industry 4.0", based on interaction with the "internet of things", is becoming a prototype of this type of human-free production, which nevertheless still relies on the power of human intellect.

These tendencies require us to make sure that as the displacement of people from direct material production snowballs, it does not give rise to a mass of "deprived people", for whom no new jobs, nor adequately dignified living conditions for a certain time period, have been created. In one way or another, the development of production will ultimately provide both these new jobs and these new living conditions. But we must, for example, prevent the emergence of a rift between the decline of obsolete professions and job growth in new spheres, or of an interim period, lasting many years or even decades, filled with millions of unattached "new tramps" and "new beggars" who either live on public handouts or face oppression and harassment.

4.3. The Integration of Production, Science, and Education

In the long term, the next ten years will see the world's leading countries transition to a new technological paradigm in which continuous technological transformation will become an indispensable part of the production process. This accounts for new demands to integrate production, science, and education. We will have to constantly re-educate ourselves.

Neither re-industrialisation, which has now become a vital imperative, nor the further successful development of modern production (not to mention future industry) are possible without *profound integration* of production with education and science – both in ideological and practical terms. **The integration of science, production, and education** is a *necessary organisational condition and a pre-requisite for the practical realisation* of re-industrialising the Russian economy, which has suffered particularly badly from deindustrialisation.

> *The integration of production, science, and education* means the re-formation of these spheres into an interactive system on a national level, including the links in the production chain where production is organically joined with research and development and the continuous process of training and retraining personnel.

The integration of production, science, and education is a powerful developmental trend of modern global industry. For this reason, the integration of production, science, and education is one of the main priorities for state economic regulators in many leading industrially developed countries.

Even in the mid-1980s and early 1990s, steps were taken in the USA and in industrially developed European countries to research and implement projects to create and strengthen systems for technological cooperation between industry and the academic community. Beginning in the mid-1990s, Japan also adopted several legislative acts to facilitate the establishment and strengthening of ties between the private sector, academia, and the state. For many years, techno-scientific cooperation between industry, academics, and the state has been the strategic orientation of Japan's national innovation policy.

An industrial and technological revolution awaits us, and its leaders will be those who manage to ride the "ninth wave" of technological transformation.

This has important practical implications. We must work to bring the components of the new industrial process as close together as possible, shortening the path that must be travelled to implement knowledge in products, skills, and competencies. In other words, we must implement what we call the integration of production, science, and education, creating industrial aggregates that will serve as constituent parts of a new type of industrial sector, and that will, in the future, replace present-day production facilities of the traditional type.

Technological progress is impossible without scientific development. We must not forget that science is not merely a miner, sublimator, or processor of knowledge. Science's leading role manifests itself only when it is applied to material production, in which it becomes a conductor of knowledge to the technological process and, ultimately, to industrial products. Thus, the tempo and efficacy with which scientific knowledge is transferred to industrial production is of utmost importance. From this follows the need for science, production, and education to be as closely integrated as possible, which we have already emphasised (Bodrunov, 2015b).

Because the continuity of innovative processes must be ensured, business subdivisions specialising in research and development are included into the main units of production. The need for R&D assumes constant renewal of the knowledge base used for production, meaning continuous education to retrain staff and raise their qualifications. Learning becomes a ceaseless activity that lasts a lifetime.

The growing role of knowledge-dense technologies and their corresponding productive resources and results and the need to accelerate the rate at which these technologies are developed and improved are conditioned by macrostructural economic changes. The classical industrial system, which was absolutely dominated by industrial production, and "service society", in which service sectors displace material production, are being replaced by the second generation of the new industrial economy. The dominant position in this new economy must belong to the industries with the most knowledge-dense output – including both those that produce identifiable products and those that create knowledge itself and give people the capacity to acquire this knowledge and apply it to material production.

In this way, the basis of the twenty-first century's economy should be a composite (Figure 2) that combines, in its micro- and macro-levels:

- *high-tech material production* that creates knowledge-intensive products;
- *science* that creates know-how;
- education and culture that cultivate people who can acquire necessary knowledge and use it for productive purposes.

This is how the three main spheres of society's new form of production, whose basis is material production itself, will be formed.

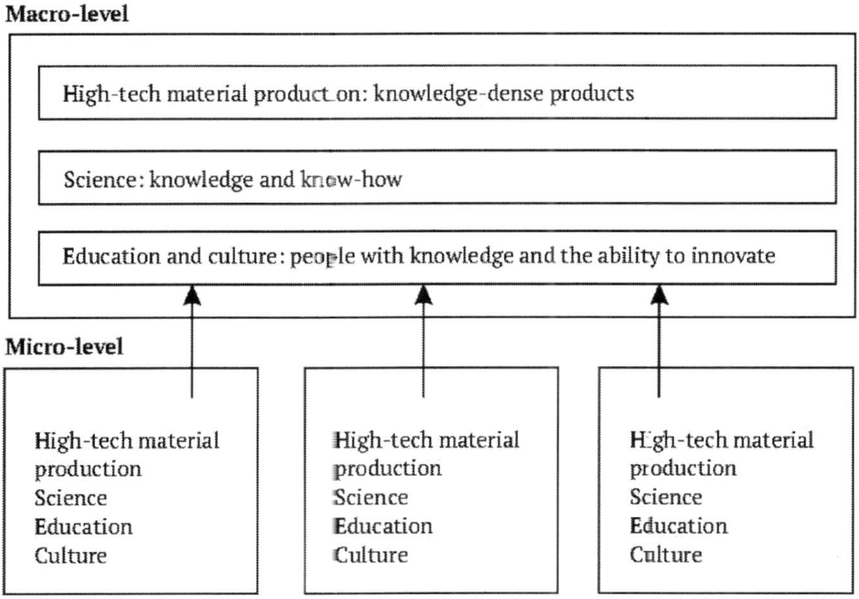

Macro-level

High-tech material production: knowledge-dense products

Science: knowledge and know-how

Education and culture: people with knowledge and the ability to innovate

Micro-level

High-tech material production Science Education Culture	High-tech material production Science Education Culture	High-tech material production Science Education Culture

Figure 2. *The structure of the twenty-first-century economy*

4.4. New Ways to Satisfy Needs

The transition to cutting-edge technology changes not only the character of production processes but also the entire economic structure: we see massive shifts in the structure of employment; the structure of human needs noticeably evolves, and along with it, the motivation of human activity. These are not changes that will occur in some unknown future, but changes that are already happening today. Using the capacities of information technology, we can integrate various industrial technologies (mechanical, physical, chemical, biological, etc.) and combine them to solve ever more complex problems and satisfy ever more diverse demands. But is the current world economy up to this task?

Many of those who consult global statistics opine that the world economy has slowed down continuously over the last two decades, except for certain regions such as China, whose development has until recently relied less on intensive growth than the extensification of industrial stock. But in terms of the satisfaction of human needs, the situation looks entirely different, notwithstanding the perspective of traditional statistics (which utterly fails to meet the demands of real research). In fact, it may be the case that, so far as satisfying its needs is concerned, humanity is currently entering a "golden age".

Let us pick and examine some use-value *[potrebitelnaya stoimost]* that is designed to satisfy concrete human demands. Take, for example, clocks. They satisfy a need: they tell time. For the sake of argument, we'll assume that twenty years ago, one clock cost one hundred dollars. Around the same time, mobile phones began to circulate. Suppose that the first mobile phones cost one thousand dollars each. A person who bought one of these phones satisfied his need to communicate with other mobile subscribers. Thus, anyone who satisfied both needs at once (telling time and mobile communication) created a demand worth one thousand one hundred dollars (for the clock and for the phone). However, technological development led to technological synergy, which further ensured **synergy in the satisfaction of needs.**

> *Synergy in satisfying needs* is the result of the synergistic interaction of multiple technologies in a single appliance, which allows for several types of need to be satisfied at once.

After a while, new gadgets appeared that contained two functions – both telling time and linking to the mobile network – while further development made it possible to lower the production cost of a "united" product that met both these needs simultaneously. Let's suppose that this gadget's initial cost was three hundred dollars. Thus, anyone who wanted to satisfy both needs now created a demand worth three hundred dollars. In other words, from the statistical perspective of the global economy, we are dealing with a "collapse of demand", which has fallen from one thousand one hundred dollars to three hundred dollars.

As measured by standard statistical methods, this would lead to a decline in GDP (Figure 3). Here it might be objected: surely the quantity of people who would want to satisfy both needs mentioned above for three hundred dollars is significantly larger than the quantity who might do it for one thousand one hundred dollars. No doubt this is true – the number of people who allow themselves to satisfy two needs for three hundred dollars is much higher than the number of people who let themselves do the same thing for one thousand one hundred dollars. But nonetheless, since there is a physical limit to the number of possible consumers, sooner or later the development of this tendency will statistically lead to falling volume indicators.

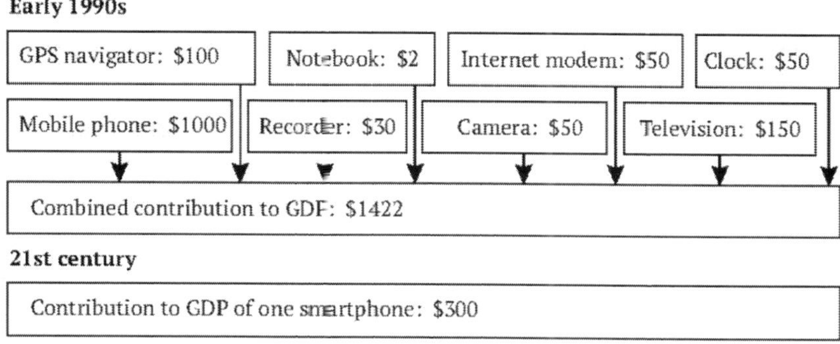

Figure 3. *Synergy in satisfying needs through a single gadget lowers GDP (listed prices are artificial)*

Consequently, we see a divergence in principle between "accounting" and reality, the latter reflecting the factual satisfaction of needs. If we consider the enormous quantity of integrated functions, allowing for ever-growing needs to be satisfied, that are united in new knowledge-dense products, then we will conclude not that economic growth is slowing down but rather the opposite, that (in terms of the satisfaction of human needs) we are witnessing a dramatic rise. One could say that at present, and unbeknownst to ourselves, we are entering an era that will continue to be defined by the progressively more complete satisfaction of people's constantly growing needs, thanks to technological progress.

In sum, knowledge-intensive products are evolving in terms of their growing ability to appease the ever more far-reaching spectre of human need (for example, the evolution from the clock and the phone to smartphones with a colossally expanded range of functions). Technological progress makes it possible to satisfy a multiplicity of human needs with a single knowledge-dense industrial product rather than several simpler ones. Technologies created to meet certain needs simultaneously reveal that they can satisfy others as well.

Additionally, it is obvious that meeting "old" needs through the knowledge-intensive production of NIS.2 requires substantially lesser expenditure of material resources, even as the share of knowledge in knowledge-dense output is preserved or increased. While each manufactured article requires a certain portion of material, the value of these articles' "share of knowledge" (which may be high at first) is collectively "distributed" among them all. This relative decrease in the resource-density of production, which occurs simultaneously with its increase in knowledge-density, creates a platform for overcoming ecological problems and regulating production's equilibrium with the natural environment.

Notes

1 The issue of industry's knowledge-intensiveness has been debated for quite a long time, but without sufficiently defining concepts like "knowledge-based economy" and "knowledge intensive industry." (See Smith, 2002: 79).

2 During panel discussions in the Department of Social Sciences of the Russian Academy of Sciences, this graph was dubbed the "Bodrunov cross" (see Grinberg, 2016: 155).

3 *Translator's note*: By "NIS" the author means new industrial society, a.k.a. John Kenneth Galbraith's "New Industrial State", while NIS.2, as will be discussed later in this book, refers to the second generation of the new industrial society.

4 Germany Trade&Invest. Industrie 4.0 – Germany Market Report and Outlook. URL: https://www.gtai.de/GTAI/Content/EN/Invest/_SharedDocs/Downloads/GTAI/Industry-overviews/industrie4.0-germany-market-outlook-progress-report-en.pdf.

5

The New Industrial Society's Second Generation[1]

5.1. Technological Shifts Change All Aspects of Production and the Social Order

Shifts in technology give rise to changes in all aspects of the production process, which in turn signal transformations in society's relations of production and in the overall nature of society. Galbraith's new industrial state has receded, along with the unsuccessful attempt at a "post-industrial future". The second generation of the new industrial state is emerging, with the task of resolving the previous epoch's contradictions.

This is why we need an outlook on the future that has a wider historical horizon, in order to find paths of development that would combine a technician's rational approach with spiritual wisdom in posing tasks and goals. Production should not be subordinate to the pursuit of consumption, or prestige, or capital accumulation; it should instead be controlled by human reason. But for this, human reason itself must undergo an evolution that would change the present day's hierarchy of values.

The technological development of material production is bringing us to a frontier at which humanity may truly begin, for the first time, to free itself from the work of production and from directly acquiring our "daily bread". At the same time, material production, while qualitatively changing, largely retains its industrial character in a technological sense: it is still machine production. The essential difference between the old industrial system and the new one consists in the intellectualisation of production, at the level of the knowledge-intensity of production and the knowledge-density of its product.

This "new industrial" mode of production is so knowledge-intensive that material inputs and the input of human labour are relegated to the background, allowing human beings to practically give up using their own physical strength in the production process while nonetheless remaining "within" production, participating in it, and therefore fulfilling tasks of labour (which are more and more intellectualised). In the process, the extent to which technologies are intellectualised in the "new industrial" mode of production will at last allow humanity to begin its escape from the bounds of production.

The twenty-first century's new industrial state and economy must become the "negation of the negation", the dialectical overcoming of both the late industrial system described by John Kenneth Galbraith and the post-industrial informational trends investigated by Daniel Bell and his followers.[2] How should this "negation of the negation" be conceived? We propose not to get carried away making pretty utopias, but instead to thoroughly analyze the real trends of modern material production's renaissance.

> *The new industrial society's second generation (NIS.2)* is a society founded on a new developmental cycle of industrial material production, characterised by growing knowledge-intensity, the transition to producing knowledge-dense products, accelerating technological change, movement towards a continuous stream of innovations, and the completion of the process of integrating production with science and education (including at basic stages of production itself).

5.2. Characteristic Features of NIS.2

What we need is not just a "technological leap", but advancement in all aspects of modern material production (materials, labour, production and the application of knowledge, organisation of production). Only then will it be possible to speak of our emergence into the next generation of new industrial society NIS.2. This is why Russia, whose national economy has been undermined by an unprecedented 25 years of deindustrialisation throughout the post-Soviet period, requires economic re-industrialisation on a new high-tech basis, as we have discussed in numerous publications (Bodrunov, 2013, 2015a; Bodrunov (Ed.), 2015; Bodrunov, Lopatin, 2014; etc.).

At the new stage of industrial society's development (NIS.2), the tendency for technological change to accelerate takes on principal importance. "Accelerating acceleration" is becoming the distinctive sign of the coming society's economic system. The most important thing now is the rate at which scientific discoveries and achievements are transmitted to industrial production and its components, particularly products: industrial production is acquiring a constantly innovative character. Such an aspect of innovative activity as technological transfer has now been included within the production process, not as an episodic moment at which an innovation is "introduced", but as an essential and ceaseless element of effective modern productive activity.

Changes in production's technological basis during the transition to the next generation of new industrial society are inevitably accompanied by changes to the system of economic relations and institutions, conditioned by the development of societal production's new content and structure. This economy, assuming that features of the industrial past have been reborn in qualitatively new form, gives rise to new appeals for both the market's self-regulation and private property rights, on the one hand, and state economic intervention, on the other.

Indeed, the individualisation, flexibility, and knowledge-density of production, the widespread use of internet technologies in material production and subsequent trade, the increasing importance of workers' individual professional qualifications – all this energises the development of small and mid-sized businesses, underscoring the need for broader economic freedom. The personal experience, energy, and talent of each innovator-entrepreneur will be crucial. In this regard, the twenty-first century's new industrial economy is the negation of the era of classic industrial capitalism and the beginning of late industrial capitalism, which fostered the formation of great industrial empires.

The twenty-first century's new industrial economy differs from that earlier era in principle. The challenges of the present particularly require the systematic development of many areas of public state management. Among these tasks, far from unimportant is the establishment of the pure and applied sciences as one of the basic branches of modern production, along with the development of universally available public education at both professional and higher levels, given the constantly increasing qualifications of workers.

The development of complex integrated production units, the macroeconomic integration of production, science, and education, the problems of structurally rebuilding modern economies, the challenges of ousting overly developed and entrenched economic intermediaries – all these goals point to the need for active state industrial policies and long-term public-private investment partnerships. These conditions should determine all other aspects of state regulation of the economy.

Substantial demands on economic relations and institutions have also been made by the transition to the large-scale creation and use of knowledge-dense products. The synthetic nature of these products is the result of many changes in the system of economic relations and institutions. To be precise, ownership of such a product includes a system of rights that encompass both the material object itself and its intellectual component. For many high-tech products, the costs of their technological development and maintaining intellectual property are comparable with their straightforward production costs; in some cases, the former exceed the latter. This indicates the principal importance of questions of intellectual property for the new industrial economy during the transitional period towards NIS.2.

This society – NIS.2 – truly will become new. First and foremost, its socioeconomic relationships will be new. New industry will make it necessary to give a new face to both markets and state regulation, along with private enterprise and state property. Due to the fundamentally different and practically limitless broad availability of means to satisfy non-simulative human needs, under NIS.2 the ownership or appropriation of an individual product will become far less meaningful. Classical Marxist thought maintained that the fundamental contradiction of capitalism was between the social character of its production and its private means of appropriation. Under NIS.2, production becomes "detached" from people, while "appropriation" becomes the simple and extremely accessible satisfaction of need, without harming other individuals.

This possibility arises with the further technological progress of the industrial mode of production. By developing the next generation of technologies, humanity does not forswear the industrial process, but grounds it upon a controlled and directed natural process.

Alongside transformations in production's technological foundation, all its other components change as well: labour, products, and the organisation of production. *But the main thing that should be emphasised is that all these transformations lead to transformed economic relations, including property relations, in this new generation of industrial society.*

5.3. Shifts in Property Relations and All Other Economic Relations

Even at our current level of social development, before the transition to NIS.2 has taken place, evolutionary trends in property relations can be observed, tending towards their socialisation and erosion. Property relations, especially private property, are supposed to secure the proprietor's incontestable rights to ownership, use, and full disposal of economic resources. Yet for some time, the evolution of economic relations has led to the accretion of all sorts of inhibitions on property rights, aimed at guaranteeing the social responsibility of the proprietor.

Among these, we can point to legal easements on privately owned land, which allow third parties to exert their rights, within certain limits, to use that plot of land (the right to pass and travel through, the right to access water sources, the right to drive cattle, access rights to stretches of coastline, the right to lay communications, etc.) Due to construction, transport, and industrial activity, property rights are already limited and inhibited in multiple ways, relating to the obligation to fulfil security needs, the observation of specific quality standards, ecological needs, and more.

We should pay especially close attention to the evolution of intellectual property rights, which regulate the economic circulation of modern production's main resource – knowledge. Here we can see phenomena such as crowdsourcing, wikinomics, free software, open source, copyleft, and so on. This all leads to the development of regimes of free access to intellectual resources. On the other hand, a rather bitter struggle is underway to "enclose" intellectual property.

This corresponds to two tendencies in the development of property relations, both of which can be traced in our current economic system: 1) the conservation of previously established relations, and 2) the erosion of property rights, even to the point of denying them altogether.

The erosion of property rights manifests itself in the development of forms of shared ownership and use of property, as well as the separation of ownership from use. An owner may temporarily decline to use their property and transfer usage rights to another person: see leasing, coworking, and various types of shared use (car-sharing, kick-sharing, time-sharing, and more). The sharing economy amounts to hundreds of billions of dollars per year. In China alone, the sharing economy reached 1.05 trillion dollars in 2019, nearly 8 percent of GDP.[3]

To a significant extent, the transition to temporary use of property without obtaining ownership rights is determined by the growing speed of technological change. There is no economic sense to obtaining full ownership of units that will become obsolete in a few years. Often the owners of these units take on additional obligations to repair and modernise them for their users.

Another tendency that also leads to the erosion of property is the fragmentation of capital. Not for nothing has the contemporary "economic theory of property rights" paid so much attention to the problem of legal authority's disintegration and the erosion of property rights.

The emergence of stock ownership of corporations already leads to yet more complex fragmentation of property rights rather than to straightforward ownership and use. Stockholders do not hold property rights over the full volume of capital. Moreover, the totality of their legal entitlements depends on the type of stock and the volume of the block of shares.

The functions of appropriation within the framework of property relations have also undergone a major evolution: even in the first half of the twentieth century it became obvious that these functions had been split between the owners and the managers of capital. These problems were well understood by many researchers (Thorstein Veblen, Adolf Berle and Gardiner Means, Stuart Chase (Veblen, 1936 [1921]; Berle, Means, 1968 [1932]; Chase, 1932), and others) even before James Burnham acquired undeserved renown as their discoverer; Burnham merely dressed them up with the flashy term "managerial revolution" and the assertion that capitalist society would be replaced by managerial society (Burnham, 1941: 71).

In fact, property's disintegration of functions goes even deeper than the distinction between stockholders and managers. Galbraith demonstrated that real usage of capital increasingly belongs to a whole army of specialists that forms a corporation's "technostructure". But this is not all. The final users of capital's various elements are the corporation's hired employees – though, of course, each of them individually performs only a small and partial function.

Moreover, in all these cases, there is a certain "stratification" and "splitting" of property along several lines: 1) appropriation-ownership-management use; 2) dispensation of each of the elements of the set of property rights among numerous actors in space and/or time and/or 3) by function (stakeholder manager-worker); 4) in terms of power and authority.

This last aspect merits some commentary. Power and property are correlative concepts. Property guarantees the proprietor's power over what he or she owns (even to an extreme degree: see, for example, slave owners). As such, a breach of property rights is typically linked to a manifestation of will – that is, either formal-legal or informal, even criminal, violent action. The above-mentioned forms of erosion of property rights lead to step-by-step stratification of power and authority, and also to the overcoming, the "falling asleep", of the political aspects of social relations in the sphere of production in the broad sense (unified with trade, distribution, and consumption).

From this we conclude that the meaning of power as an institution will be decreased/eroded/fragmented (which is already happening in a historical sense). Accordingly, the role of the state as the subject of power and authority, as the general *owner* of the right to develop society, will also decrease as we advance towards the noonomy.

We may also note the direct influence of technological change on property relations. "Blue-collar" and "white-collar" jobs are being replaced by robots and artificial intelligence. What will happen to property relations when the task of performing many economic functions moves from humans to technogenic beings? For example, how can property users be held responsible for an accident caused by a robot driver? Responsibility for harm could then be placed on the owner. But what about responsibility for breaking the rules of the road?

Little by little, functions of property use and even management are already drifting away from human beings. Further evolution in this direction will only get faster.

These processes, along with the above-mentioned tendency for the worth of property ownership to decrease, will lead to transformations not only in the property system but also in the entire social order. With great certainty, we can predict that *the stage of NIS.2 will be governed by an economy of shared use, an economy of fragmented and eroded property rights.*

Thus, the system of property relations is substantially changing as we transit to NIS.2, which leads to the transformation of the entire system of economic relations. The market's character is changing: more and more, a greater role is played not by the spontaneous fluctuations of market conditions, but by the results of complex mutual agreements between people who hold diverse and interlocking elements of specific property rights. The character of state regulation is also changing, as it begins to orient itself toward creating a consensus from the complex balance of economic interests that arises from the new nature of property relations and the new modification of market relations.

5.4. The Evolution of Labour and the Evolution of Needs

The emergence of the industrial mode of production saw the development of contradictions in the formation and satisfaction of human needs, as well as in the means to resolve these contradictions. The industrial mode of production is based on the ability to mass-produce standardised products. In turn, this ability prompts the formation of demand for mass consumption. But mass production and mass consumption did not immediately "meet". A series of acute social conflicts were needed, over the course of the nineteenth century and the first half of the twentieth, for mass production to result in mass consumption, at least in the most developed countries.

Once the ability for mass production to be combined with mass consumption was achieved, it led to an even greater expansion of needs, along with growing ability to satisfy them. Technological application of knowledge made it possible not only to create new objects of consumption and services, nor merely to ramp up their output. At the same time, a decrease occurred in the proportion of material resources used to produce products, and an increase occurred in the proportion of knowledge objectified in them (this was the growth of products' *knowledge-density*). Without this tendency, mass production, spurred on by mass consumption, would have long ago reached the absolute limit of its available resources (though this threat has still not yet been taken off the agenda).

In recent times, the development of science and technology has given rise to a new tendency: the ability to create items that simultaneously meet several needs. Meanwhile, as the growth in the volume indicators of production and consumption slows down (or even decreases), it becomes possible to raise the level at which needs are met.

The level at which needs are met turns out also to be inextricable from changes in the character and structure of needs. Usually, these transformations are ascribed to Maslow's so-called pyramid, in which fulfilling the needs of a lower level causes emphasis to switch to the needs of the next-highest level. But the fundamental causes of change in the structure of needs belong to the sphere of production, not consumption.

The growing knowledge-intensity of production also signifies the growing knowledge-intensity of people's labour activity. The displacement of people from the direct production process, the concentration of the role of human beings' in management and goal-setting, shifts human activity to a primarily creative arena, connected to the discovery and technological mastery of new knowledge. For people taking on this role, needs associated with personal development, which amount to prerequisites for deploying one's creative powers, will become primary.

This exact transformation of the content and structure of needs is the most important condition for sating them. When the motivation to develop oneself becomes principally important, the drive to quantitatively ramp up the consumption of material goods is weakened (assuming such consumption has already been ensured to the extent required for normal maintenance of the life needs of human beings). This transformation in the character of needs, in turn, serves as a prerequisite and stimulus for the development of creative activity in production.

Notes

1 The author's phrase "novoe industrial'noe obshchestvo" is mostly translated here as "new industrial society". However, readers should be aware that this exact phrase is also the accepted translation into Russian of John Kenneth Galbraith's concept of the "new industrial state" (from Galbraith's 1967 book with this title). Bodrunov's reference to Galbraith is conscious; hence his emphasis on the "second generation", Galbraith's being the first. For clarity's sake, the translation opts for "society" rather than "state" – *Translator's note.*

2 The author's language here is Hegelian. "Overcoming," sniatie, is Hegel's Aufhebung, sometimes translated into English as "sublation". This term refers to the simultaneous cancelation and preservation of the term to which it is applied. Thus, the author's point is that while Galbraith's and Bell's systems are negated, their features are also maintained at a higher level within the second generation of new industrial society —*Translator's note.*

3 China sharing economy market to exceed 9 trln yuan: report // Xinhua, 2019-11-02. URL: http://www.xinhuanet.com/english/2019-11/02/c_138523206.htm.

6

Civilisation at a Crossroads

6.1. Rising Technological Opportunities and Rising Risks

To understand the new possibilities that arise thanks to modern technology, attention should be paid to a particular aspect of what happens when technologies are combined. There are many different unique forms of technological synergy that result from such combinations. That said, in our view, these results cannot be described in terms of established theories (for example, the theory of waves) and leave space for further research.

> *Technological synergy* is a phenomenon that amplifies the usual effects of technology, exceeding the sum of the effects of particular technologies by combining two or more technologies.

Technological synergy, like any introduction of new technologies into an existing technological environment, are possible due to an effect that we have named *penetration*. Of course, new technological solutions cannot be incorporated into all technologies. We designate a technology's receptiveness to penetration using the term *readiness*.

> *Penetration* is the insertion of a new technological solution into other technologies and into various elements of the production processes based on those technologies.
>
> *Readiness* is the potential for a new technology to be accepted into new technologies and various elements of the production processes based on those technologies.

It is because of the effects of technological synergy that the hybrid technologies that characterise the sixth technological mode can function (as discussed in an earlier chapter). The sixth paradigm's technologies are high in readiness to interact with one another, which is why they can form hybrid technologies on a massive scale. And precisely the effect of one technology's penetration into another is what determines the formation of the sophisticated integrated technical complexes that create technocenoses (the concept of a "technocenosis" was coined by Boris Ivanovich Kudrin, see: Kudrin, 1981: 236–254, etc.).

> A *technocenosis* is a community of technical instruments (analogous to a biocenosis) characterised by technological interdependence and common aims.

The potential of new technology is deceptive. Technology dangles before us the prospect of improving the human species, freeing ourselves from the limits of our frail bodies and the biological thinking instrument known as "the brain".

Yes, it is tempting to leap beyond these barriers . . . But what for? To expand our ability to satisfy our purely animal instincts to consume as much as possible?

What if we made a different choice?

Both science and society at large are already beginning to understand not only that the sixth technological paradigm may rebuild individual and collective forms of human life in their entirety, but that the new technological mode itself, in turn, may only reveal its full potential within a new social mode. As the President of the Davos World Economic Forum puts it: "The more we think about how to harness the technology revolution, the more we will examine ourselves and the underlying social models that these technologies embody and enable, and the more we will have an opportunity to shape the revolution in a manner that improves the state of the world" (Schwab, 2016: 9).

The technological prerequisites necessary for transitioning to a different means and different level of meeting human needs are presently being created. At the same time, the mechanism by which these needs are formed is itself changing. This, in turn, leads to a mass of changes in social relations and institutions and, finally, in the social conditions that set the direction of technological progress itself.

Technological forces, once awakened by humanity, will not be stopped without direct and all-encompassing control by human reason, which would in turn undergo changes so that it would be able to set fruitful, rather than destructive, directions of development.

In the most direct sense, changes in the technologies and social relations of the future are linked to the birth of a new type of human activity, which means the creation of a new type of human being.

Human beings stand at the threshold of one of the most important crossroads in our history:

- we may turn towards a genuinely rational humanity;
- we may, instead, choose a dead-end path towards a technetronic society in which elites satisfy their own (immeasurably expanding and primarily simulative) needs, while the majority of people are employed in the service sector, which increasingly becomes a "servile sector" – potentially accompanied by loss of control over the development of the technosphere and destruction of our habitat.

Technological progress brings not only potentially positive prospects, but also – without humanity's due attention to the risks of "improperly" using the results of progress – substantial dangers. In this sense, we now witness the advanced development of the technosphere, while the part of social consciousness that is "responsible" for making reasonable use of technological achievements, and sustainably forming non-simulative individual and collective needs, lags behind.

The level of technological development attained by humanity is already extraordinarily high, making it possible to do irreversible harm to civilisation – so long as there is no corresponding "balance" of public awareness to put a stop to this scenario. In this sense, the modern state of civilisational development should be characterised as a crisis situation. A great many negative tendencies have already accumulated in the development of the technosphere.

Humanity's biological habitat is under threat, while problems are amassing in people's relationship to the technosphere, including rising dependence on a high-tech informational environment, leading to a kind of "cyborgification" of human beings (even without the formal intrusion of machinery into physical human bodies). Humans are confronting the increasing precarity of their existence as both biological and social beings.

It is vital that we forestall the possibility of a wrong choice at modern civilisation's developmental crossroads during the transition to NIS.2. Two basic scenarios are likely at this point.

One of them might tentatively be called the "technocratic" scenario. At the moment, this is the path we are persistently following, with no light visible at the end of the tunnel. This scenario is based on the currently accepted global paradigm of "economic development", in which progress is understood not just qualitatively but quantitatively. In essence, this is a savage process, which proceeds from the animalistic side of humankind. Figuratively speaking, its goal is to gobble up as much as we can, even if we burst. And if we do not produce and consume more today than we did yesterday? "Stagnation! Recession! Decline in the level of popular needs met! Impoverishment!"

But what, in principle, is the important thing about satisfying needs? Quantity? Or quality? If we are talking about non-simulative needs, then the answer is quality (and this quality is what in fact determines the quantitative measurement of needs). But according to the harmoniously balanced statistical number games of today's "funhouse mirror economy", this algebra is incorrect! And unless we repudiate this path, the path that the whole world is fixedly marching upon right now, we will slide downward towards the technocratic version of development. This threatens us with a battle to exhaust the world's resources – and the technocratic model is fully armed with all the latest technology.

Our current economic system is gradually "germinating" into NIS.2. But this stage of economic and social development has a transitional character. The progress of sixth-generation technologies inexorably presents us with a choice: either humanity will remain the same while changing its technological and socioeconomic system; or the system will change humanity; or both will change. Obviously, both tendencies will exert themselves to some degree. But which will prevail? Humanity, with its principles of communication and self-development? In that case, the production of our material conditions of existence will remain at the mercy of technetic beings (sprouting from the coming "Industry 4.0," from artificial intelligence systems, etc.)

Technetic means related to technical and technological reality.

Technetics is the science of technical reality.

It will not be humans that occupy themselves with the needs that can be met using technology. But the determination of "technical tasks", the setting of goals, will remain up to humanity. Yet the goals set for production directly depend on society's predominant values. This means that values, too, must change to meet the task at hand. Any mistake in formulating the goals of such a highly developed technosphere, especially one with relative autonomy from human beings, will be extremely costly. If the goals of this kind of production are defined using the old prevailing value system of today, acute contradictions will inevitably emerge – both socially and in conflict with our natural environment.

Let us imagine that at a certain point, "quantitative" movement along our current direction of development crosses a qualitative boundary, causing an explosion – and then the birth of a new civilisation... What would it be like? Civilisation can develop in two ways. The first option is a technetronic civilisation, that is, the de facto eradication of humanity as we currently know it and the appearance of other beings, more capable of existing in that environment. The second option is that humanity can knowingly, consciously become the creator of a different path, which we have dubbed "noocivilization".

There is a simple way to realise the first option: we just have to maintain our current predatory course, "developing" our present "economy", creating new simulative needs, and satisfying them by attaining newer and newer (technetic, technogenetic) products. In other words, we are travelling along a path of technological genesis, and eventually these new products will create a new environment all by themselves.

Needless to say, scholars who are expanding the horizons of scientific knowledge are driven by good intentions – the creation of new types of medicine, for example, or the correction of genetic abnormalities. But they also do not deny that their scientific achievements could be used to create new forms of life and "edit" humanity's very biological essence. How far will we travel down this path, and what criteria will guide us as we make the decision? Our choice at the crossroads of present-day civilisation will depend on how we answer these and many other analogous questions.

6.2. Satisfying Needs: Reasonable or Simulative?

As production constantly expands its technological abilities with respect to meeting constantly growing needs, what precise human needs will orient it? And how will these needs be shaped?

Capital always pursues the expansion of mass production and mass marketing. On one hand, this impulse gives rise to the constant development of production, the improvement of technology, the progress of productive forces; at the same time, it expands human needs and makes them more diverse. But since economic rationality is indifferent to the nature of specific needs and the means used to satisfy them – all that matters is that they attract the consumer's effective demand – the progress of production and consumption develops alongside industries that formulate and satisfy artificially imposed needs, playing upon human weakness.

But the modern marketplace not only plays upon human weaknesses in order to indulge them by expanding production and marketing. The market creates false, illusory, simulative needs, along with the corresponding means to satisfy them, which in turn can only simulate the satisfaction even of illusory needs.

> *Simulative needs* are illusory, false needs, imposed by the market system in its single-minded pursuit of greater sales.

Thus, the market economy increasingly becomes less a space in which real use-values are produced for the satisfaction of real needs, and more a world for creating *commodity-simulacra* that simulate the satisfaction of simulative needs, artificially created using marketing, advertising, and various forms of manipulation of consumer consciousness, which have become remarkably widespread due to the growing use of information technology.

> *Commodity-simulacra* are goods that signify the satisfaction of simulative needs or means for the imaginary satisfaction of imaginary needs.

The nature and role of simulative commodities, or simulacra, or just signs of the satisfaction of imaginary needs, was studied in detail by Jean Baudrillard (in his *For a Critique of the Political Economy of the Sign*) from a social and philosophical perspective. But a simulacrum is not only a social phenomenon. Mass production of simulacra has led to the emergence and formation of an extensive market for them, which has become a significant socioeconomic phenomenon (for an analysis of commodity-simulacra and their market, see: Buzgalin, Kolganov, 2012b: 65-91).

The law of the elevation, expansion, or "escalation" of needs also operates in the simulative sphere as a law of the escalation of false, fake needs. This is because once the ability to satisfy some need or other has been realised, another thought always follows: what kind of new need will appear next? This occurs due to the nature of knowledge itself: each "quantum" of knowledge obtained not only responds to the utilitarian question that prompted the search for that "quantum" in the first place, but imparts a broader content, giving rise to new, "supplementary" knowledge. This implies the possibility of formulating new and more expansive needs, and so the old need "germinates" into new needs.

But when and why do these particular "deceptively necessary" needs emerge? Because, as biological creatures, human beings, as soon as they begin to understand the external world (and themselves as an enduring being within it), start to think about stockpiles, reserves, the future – at least, the next step forward. So, humans try to calculate and evaluate what it is they might end up needing, drawing on their accumulated knowledge about themselves and their potential needs. Thus, once the chance appears to create a stockpile, humans will take it.

However trivial it may seem, this is the source of all ideologies of accumulation for some purpose or the other – for example, the ideology of acquiring extra space, even when it is not really needed in that moment and may later cease to be felt as a need at all! Step by step, our correct desire for potentially necessary things, that is, our desire to accumulate natural goods, begins to cross a certain line, at which point we no longer know exactly how much we need, but we understand that at some moment whatever we have may not be enough.

However, the natural needs that appear in a world where the conditions of humanity's existence are neither stable nor guaranteed do not take on particularly strict boundaries. Any reserve or volume of resources obtained turns out to be inadequate; under these circumstances, the mere availability of some measure of confidence in the future starts to be measured as the size of one's "mountain" of accumulated goods. This impulse is socially reinforced:

the accumulation of wealth becomes a symbol of success, a symbol of a person's social status, and the pursuit of this status is equated with enhancing one's volume of acquired (though perhaps not even really needed) wealth.

In this way, simulative needs arise as everyday needs are met. But there is already a distinction to be made here: some simulative needs may be satisfied even though it is essentially illusory (meaning that people do not need that much at that moment, nor in the foreseeable future or at any other time). Nonetheless, such needs can be met. Meanwhile, other needs can emerge that amount to a pure simulation of rational needs and that, in principle, *cannot be met* at the given stage of development, but which one can think about. We may call these latter needs phantasms, while the first kind of simulative needs can be called excesses (Figure 4).

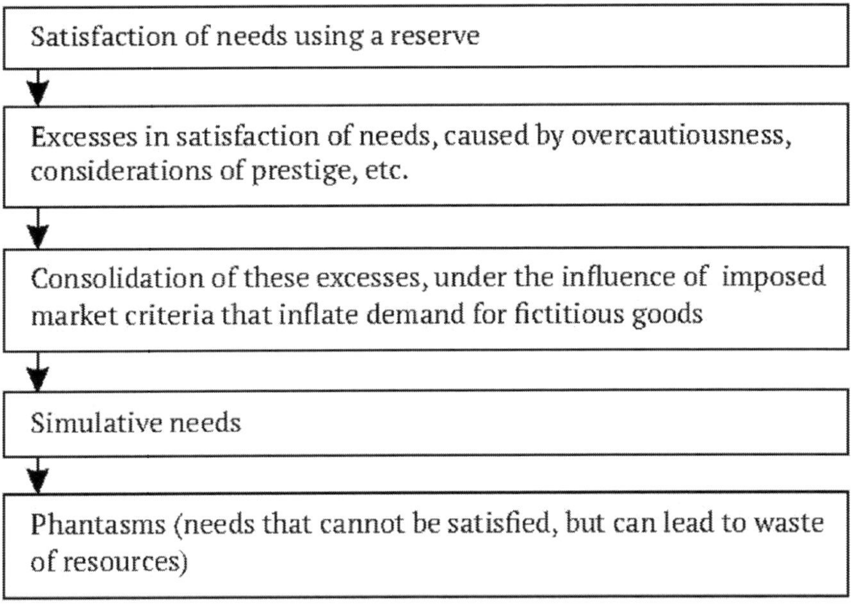

Figure 4. *The evolution of simulative needs*

Bear in mind that in certain cases, simulative needs may transition with time and become non-simulative and vice versa. Moreover, in the same moment, one person's real need may be another's simulative need. For instance, the desire for a precise-fitting dress or facial skincare products would have been a simulative need for peasant women in past centuries ("it's not about thriving, it's about surviving!"), while nowadays this has become a normative need. Meanwhile, a slide rule, which was once a necessity for every engineer, is probably only needed today by collectors of antique measuring devices.

These days we are moving – in fact, racing – along a path of escalating satisfaction of an ever-greater quantity of unreasonable needs. In fact, our entire current economic paradigm is tailor-made to do this! More, more, more... but right now, are there more non-simulative or simulative needs in this "more" (not to mention phantasms)?

We must deal with the fact that the modern market economy lends itself to unusual inflation of simulative needs in the pursuit of higher sales. It is no coincidence that the production and consumption of simulacra has become so widespread in recent decades. The deep causes of this phenomenon are the structural shifts in societal production that took place at the turn of the 1980s, when the world was engulfed in postindustrial economic myths. These myths did not arise in a vacuum: *the unrestrained growth of the service sector on one hand, and deindustrialisation on the other; the virtualisation of everything which fostered all of this –these are the material foundations of the expanding production of commodity-simulacra and dissemination of simulative needs.*

Simulative need is not just a question of individual personal choice. The inflation of simulative needs is echoed in the real economy by the growing expenditure of real resources on things that only give the illusion of usefulness. And the increased production of commodity-simulacra is one of the substantial factors behind the escalation of the resource burden placed on the natural environment.

6.3. Rising Pressure on the Environment

The concept of noosociety is undeniably connected to Vernadsky's idea of the noosphere. Rationally speaking, his overall conception of the biosphere's transition to the noosphere can hardly be contested. Vernadsky's basic thesis – that humanity was becoming the most important geological force, and that from the twentieth century onwards, humans would be responsible for the reproduction of the Earth's biosphere – has been repeatedly validated by historical practice, in both positive and negative ways. *Technogenesis* (the term "technogenesis" was coined by the Soviet academic A.E. Fersman, see Fersman, 1934: 27; see also: Balandin, 1978; for a definition of technogenesis, see Kudrin, 2003: 998) already rivals biogenesis and the biosphere in terms of the overall mass of substances it involves and its energy costs (a great deal of data about technogenetic pressure on the biosphere can be found in: Karlovich, 2004).

> *Technogenesis* refers to the creation of the technosphere and the process by which it is filled with techno-substances and technetic beings.

The history of civilisation's development shows us that the accelerating growth of the "technetic species" created by humankind (in strict correspondence with the law of innovation's "accelerating acceleration") damages and crowds out biotic diversity. As a result, the escalating environmental burden – related to the growth of people's simulative needs, the use of natural resources to meet those needs, and the expanding footprint left by mining and processing those resources – opens the real possibility of negative (or catastrophic!) consequences (Figure 5).

Unrestrained, growing, and mostly simulative needs and desires
The possibility of losing control over the technosphere's development, due to its orientation towards pursuing artificially inflated needs and desires
An already exceptionally high level of technological development, making it possible to do irrevocable harm to civilization
Humanity's growing dependence on its technical and informational environment
The accelerating growth of "technetic species" created by humans, which damages and rapidly crowds out biodiversity
Technology's increasing environmental toll
Premature development of the technosphere, while the part of human social consciousness that "takes responsibility" for the rational usage of technological achievements lags behind
Weak internal regulators of rational behaviour, as defined by the content of culture and its level of development

Figure 5. *Factors in the crisis scenario of civilisation's development*

In terms of resources, we must unequivocally stake our future on deprioritising traditional (material, tangible) resources in favour of the basic resource of NIS.2 – that is, knowledge, as embodied in technology. But in epistemological or gnoseological terms, we must change the priorities, purpose, and orientation of our development.

This is well illustrated by data showing the current state of our general civilisational environment, which we have created by following the trends of the present paradigm of "economic growth". There are two major versions of how events might develop from this state of affairs. Take, for example, the overall volume of everything that humanity has created in its five thousand years of existence: geologists estimate that *the mass of the technosphere*, that is, everything that humanity has created throughout its history using technology, amounts to *thirty trillion tons* (for a more detailed breakdown, see Table 1).

Table 1. Approximate mass of the major components of the physical technosphere, arranged in order of descending mass (where 1 Tt = 1012 metric tons)

Component	*Area (10^6 km^2)*	*Thickness (cm)*	*Density (g/cm^3)*	*Mass (Tt)*	*%*
Urban areas	3.70	200	1.50	11.10	36.9
Rural housing	4.20	100	1.50	6.30	20.9
Pasture	33.50	10	1.50	5.03	16.7
Cropland	16.70	15	1.50	3.76	12.5
Trawled sea floor	15.00	10	1.50	2.25	7.5
Land use and eroded soil	5.30	10	1.50	0.80	2.7
Rural roads	0.50	50	1.50	0.38	1.3
Plantation forest	2.70	10	1.00	0.27	0.9
Reservoirs	0.20	100	1.00	0.20	0.7
Railways	0.03	50	1.50	0.02	0.1
Totals (where applicable)	31.83			30.11	

Source: Zalasiewicz, Williams, etc., 2017: 12

By now, humanity has already devoured so much dead nature, so much of the mineral world, that it has created much more over the past five hundred years than nature (non-biological "civilisation") had "devoured" over the course of hundreds of millions of years. According to other geologists, this means that we may speak of the arrival of a new geological era. Experts call this new era the "Anthropocene" (Issberner, Léna, 2018). But geologists describe this era from an external perspective; by contrast, the author's approach is based on what the era is like "from the inside," what it "grows" from –namely, our unintelligent (or intelligently unintelligent) use of technology.

Here is another estimate: according to biological data, *the weight of the Earth's cumulative biomass throughout its 4.5 billion years of existence* – that is, everything created by nature – *amounts to approximately 2.5 trillion tons.* In other words, it took us just a few thousand years (and mostly just the last hundred years) to create twelve times as much as nature created over billions of years – and the rate at which we "create" keeps increasing! Does this not constitute a warning sign of major transformations, even of the impending crisis discussed above?

By various estimates, natural biodiversity ranges from eight million to one hundred million species, while the diversity of so-called technetic species, that is, of various types of objects created by humans, already exceeds biodiversity by a thousandfold. This is "what we have wrought" over, primarily, the last one hundred to one hundred fifty years. According to some estimates, we will increase the quantity of these species by an order of magnitude every ten years!

The international organisation Global Footprint Network, or GFN, has come up with a well-founded method for measuring what they call "ecological debt". Using this method, every year GFN designates a certain day as Overshoot Day, or Ecological Debt Day – the date when the resources consumed by humanity that year exceeds the amount of resources that the Earth can replenish in a full year. In 1970, this day fell in December, so there was no ecological debt. Later, beginning in the 1980s (we can see the clear correlation with the beginning of globalisation), this debt began to appear, and it has continued to grow ever since. In 2019, Overshoot Day fell approximately on July 30![1]

In 1970, we consumed about 90 percent of the resources that the planet can regenerate in a year. By 2019, this had already risen to 175 percent. The growth rate has doubled and is constantly increasing. Extrapolation using GFN's methods shows that if we continue to "burn through life" at this rate, our ecological debt in the year 2050 will amount to more than four hundred years of resources! Assuming, of course, that we are still alive...

6.4. The Danger of Interfering with Human Nature

There are possible conflicts associated with interfering not only with external nature, but also human nature. These stem from technological progress itself. For example, information and communication technologies (ICT) and artificial intelligence technology (AI) open new possibilities for human interaction. Even now, a significant part of human communication has been relocated to the virtual spaces of computer networks. Interaction in these spaces takes place not directly between people, but through their virtual imprints, virtual clones ("avatars," profiles, accounts...) which are sometimes radically divergent from their real prototypes.

Is this a good or a bad thing?

Ethical evaluation ("good or bad", "good or evil") is more than appropriate in this case. At stake are the moral problems of a world in which people can solve creative, informational, and cognitive problems by transferring all routines and second-tier functions to virtual personalities. If such virtual personalities were furnished with AI systems, they could take over the collection, processing, and sorting of information flows, for example. Self-learning artificial intelligence can absorb new knowledge and even apply it to new objects. However, AI is not capable of discovering previously unknown knowledge, so there is no need to worry about its competition with humanity on a species level (whatever might be said of its present competition with specific human professions).

But who, how, and for what will this virtual world be used? How will its rules be defined, and to what ends will communication in virtual space be subordinated? Things could reach the level of genuine "virtual horror," as science fiction has energetically explored for years.

The technosphere has turned into a colossal force which in many ways is already independent from humanity, which further enhances the obligation of human beings to bring this force within reasonable limits, forestalling the elementally destructive effects of technogenic processes. If we recognise this obligation, it could spur us to create networks and systems for collective action. But the obligation may go unrecognised, or it may be recognised but remain unfulfilled, due to humankind's collective irresponsibility.

We thought that we were doing clever things, but in fact, if we continue down our current path, we will have been preparing for a change of civilisations. Future civilisation might include Morlock-people, à la H.G. Wells, or people with wheels instead of feet – or intellectually advanced people of the noosphere. The technetronic version of the future would have cyborg-people. Or rather,not people at all, not as we currently understand them. Intelligent beings, yes. But not us. Perhaps they would have a different, more "rational" logic of development, and perhaps human beings would not fit into this logic. I may be wrong: after all, this is just a hypothesis. But what if I am right? Facts are stubborn things...

And here, a line must be drawn. Why? Because satisfying needs changes the nature of human beings – their physical essence, for example. What does an athlete do if he wants to lift one hundred fifty kilograms? He trains his body. Perhaps new technology would allow him to do this just by taking pills. This would make it possible for him to take a swing at lifting two hundred kilograms. But why stop at two hundred! Let's alter his DNA to give him an elephant's muscles – easy! Now three hundred kilograms are well within our reach... And so on.

Taking this peculiarity into account, meeting needs without rationally separating real needs from simulative ones may not just radically change isolated qualities of human beings, as biological creatures with both natural capacities and limits to consumption; it may distort human nature itself. This is not science fiction. The technological requirements for events to develop in this way are being created right now.

For instance, researchers at the Massachusetts Institute of Technology (MIT) in the USA are already altering genes inside human embryos, removing or disabling some, and adding others! Another American institution, The Scripps Research Institute (TSRI), has gone even farther. The four nucleotides that make up natural DNA – adenine, thymine, guanine, and cytosine, which serve as the basis for all life, from bacteria to whales – have been supplemented by researchers at TSRI with two new artificial nucleotides, which do not exist in nature. They have inserted these two interlopers into the DNA of living cells and made them successfully reproduce themselves, passing on acquired (embedded) traits through inheritance, resulting in semisynthetic proteins![2] So we may soon see men with not just elephants' muscles, but "hydraulic power steering".

But if a human being wants to change his nature as a human being, then are we still referring to a human being as a biological and sociological creature, or are we discussing a different type of being? If we are talking about a human being, we must associate this concept with reasonable limits that would not allow it to develop in such a way.

The development of a new type of production with unprecedented knowledge-intensiveness, the growing might of technology, and the tremendously broad capacity to satisfy needs are accompanied by the formation of a certain *new type of human*. What will this human be like? The answer to this question is by no means predetermined. Already, there are multiple evident versions of how humanity could develop under the new industrial civilisation.

The current state of technogenesis is bringing humanity into the extremely perplexing and badly managed world of a technosphere that has evolved according to its own laws. The social order based on capitalist relations of production, which chiefly focuses its production goals on monetary earnings and other indicators of volume and value (such as GDP), is not particularly inclined to settle accounts with the risks and threats that result from subordinating technology to the extraction of profit.

Will humanity adequately respond to the challenges of the new technotronic or technogenic civilisation? Will it come to a new society of humanistic values and widely disseminated "knowledge-creating" activity by people, a society that lives in harmony with nature and overcomes social conflict, in which people's main occupation will be the acquisition of new knowledge? Will this be a society in which material limitations will not play a major role, since the private or personal appropriation of material goods will have lost its paramount importance due to the general accessibility of ways to meet life's material needs? Or will we encounter the opposite?

People in developed countries, intoxicated by the nearly limitless ability to raise the level of their satisfaction of needs, may be tempted by overconsumption. Less developed countries, due to the former chronic underconsumption of billions of their inhabitants, face the threat of turning their new technological capacity towards unrestrained quantitative growth, producing material goods beyond all reason. Both these tendencies are fraught with the inflation of irrational, fictive, simulative needs.

A kind of *homo consumericus* is becoming widespread, always chasing fictitious goods with no consideration for anything else. The pressure on the Earth's resources will rise, despite the possibility of substantially decreasing resource-dense production. Unrestrained consumerism threatens to swallow up any conceivable quantity of natural resources and suffocate the Earth with waste, while plunging humankind into a vortex of conflicts over material goods and the diminishing resources needed to produce them...

Emerging now is a world of alienated human beings – alienated from other people, from society, and ultimately from their own essence. Humanity is becoming dehumanised, turning into pseudo-humanity, and threatening its own and its habitat's existence. Alien on Earth. Alien to all. No need to turn to science fiction or await the arrival of aliens from outer space. The aliens are already here. Many people on Earth are already being drawn into the sinkhole of thoughtlessly chasing a fictitious growth in consumption, though the resources devoured by this growth are all too real – not just natural resources, but the body and soul of human beings themselves.

Can we avoid this dead-end path?

6.5. Rising Risks Are Inevitable under the Framework of the Currently Existing Economic Order

Our society has not yet "grown up enough" to make correct use of technological progress and its achievements. Part of the reason why is that technological progress has not yet "fed" everyone. Why is this the case, even though enough grain is produced in today's world to make bread for everyone, while millions and billions of people starve? Because these goods are still subject to the capitalist mode of appropriation. When technological progress is combined with finance capital, which devours its results, all it can do is redistribute income towards finance, not towards productive capital or the satisfaction of people's real needs.

Finance capital is ready to enrich itself at all costs, including by "ripping off" other individuals, peoples, and nations in the old-fashioned way. At the expense of margins of innovation, at the expense of new markets, at the expense of simulative indoctrination about what to buy, finance tries as hard as it can to establish growing financial profits as the ultimate good. A similar situation emerges at each new stage of technological progress. We are transitioning to a new technological mode, but take heed: its corollary is greater expansionism, more wars, more conflict, and so on, even though one might assume that the satisfaction of needs should allow people to live better. Why is this happening? Because we are dealing with a disharmony, the discrepancy between the capacities of technological progress and lagging social consciousness.

Why is our current situation so tense? What has made the present more fraught than the past? The answer is that each phase of technological progress provides far more new abilities than did the previous one. If these abilities are used incorrectly, then the level of risk dramatically rises. Right now, technological progress offers practically any terrorist the capacity to get an atomic bomb. If society does not mature – precisely as society – then, as society, it may create its own direst threats.

Our social and economic system is extremely interconnected, and it develops dynamically. But as the system's elements develop and interact, they influence one another, while each of them develops at a different rate. Dysfunctional disharmony of these rates, the non-concurrent rates of development of multiple elements of the system, may cause the whole thing to burst, since the strain placed on the links between the elements cannot be unlimited. There is always a limit.

With every transition, technological changes have led to transformed technological paradigms. Each time, paradigms of production have formed a new type of society: the industrial mode of production and the new technologies of that stage led to the formation, in turn, of capitalist society, rather than vice versa. Now, each new stage offers new capacities, much broader ones, for meeting human needs. If we are saying that we will satisfy human needs at a much higher level in the future than we do right now, and if these needs are not reasonable ones, then – figuratively speaking – we will be using technological progress like an instrument given to a child, or to an underdeveloped creature.

Humanity now finds itself in this position once more, but the possibilities afforded by the current stage – which are exactly what define its uniqueness – are so gigantic that they may simply lead us straight to the edge of catastrophe if they are improperly used.

At a certain point, the development of commodity markets led to the birth of finance capital to service them, turning money into the "master", the sovereign, of economic relations. After that, money and financial markets, both due to their basic nature and their unceasing need to expand their sphere of activity and capture new "zones of influence", began to decisively affect the structure and infrastructure of so-called international trade. Once corporations seized control of national markets, they gradually escaped national boundaries. The resulting multi-sectoral conglomerates and transnational business structures, "intertwined" with one another and "sanctified" by the flow of capital, became the foundation of the global marketplace...

It is finance capital that now dictates to political actors how policy may affect the various spheres of social life. This is how we get all kinds of associations (in the word's original commercial and economic meaning), trade wars, pseudo-democratic sanctions, and more.

The process of globalisation is linked to the technological development of society, human society, and civilisation. Moreover, in a certain sense, the development of globalisation is predetermined, under the "zoo-"paradigm, by human society's technological development. Why? Because, by presenting capital with possibilities for expansion while humanity remains "under-cultured" as a whole (insufficiently "noo-", that is, not yet able to limit its simulative needs and desires), technological progress exists to serve finance capital, which is nearly unlimited. Because technological progress allows capital to be more effectively transferred, used, and so on, while simultaneously fulfilling capitalists' desire to multiply their capital, realising capital's ability to expand.

By now, the satisfaction of simulative needs has reached its critical point. Having become a weapon of finance capital, technological progress is creating new but ever more simulative needs, needs which it immediately satisfies, ensnaring everyone and everything in the process. From one perspective, products must be distributed somewhere; from another perspective, the option must be created for people to take these products. But from yet another perspective, this process uses resources – those that are left, that still exist somewhere, that have not yet been set in motion – to drum up demand for these same products as effectively as possible, for the ultimate purpose of growing finance capital.

Historically speaking, we are approaching a point at which the global process of financialisation will have captured basically every possible arena of its existence. It no longer has the option of dramatic territorial gains or extensive growth; nothing remains but the intensification of the pernicious process of financialisation itself. What kind of intensification? Mainly in the exploitation of nature, including natural resources, raw materials, etc. Whatever the damage done.

Financialisation will not stop here; it will creep into the human soul. Why? Because, as if in passing, it will create needs that human beings had never previously imagined, which will in fact be simulative needs: in this way, it will bring humanity to ruin. When finance capital makes its way into the social sphere, it changes how people relate to one another, demanding that they consume more, that they absorb themselves in mass culture, and all sorts of other things that are not in fact very important for human beings. This all develops artificially and is hammered into people's heads by global capital.

The link between technological progress and finance capital, or rather, globalisation via finance capital, has certain consequences. It assumes that certain conditions are superimposed onto society's normal existence. Consequently, we see the formation of structures for promoting finance capital, etc. For example, I oppose the creation of new rules for international trade in its current form of existence – precisely because contemporary international trade is a mechanism for promoting the interests of finance capital and imposing new simulative needs on people, even as its highest priority.

Every modern product is the result of processing tons of natural substances. Producing one pair of shoes requires between ten and thirty tons of fresh water. Just imagine how many pairs of shoes rest unused in stores or are bought and worn only once for a special occasion! Ksenia Sobchak reportedly has an entire room containing nothing but cupboards full of hundreds of shoes. Let us contemplate how many planetary resources, not to mention resources of the human soul, were used in the creation of that room.

We can take Cambodia as a living lesson. Rubber trees (*Hevea brasiliensis*), introduced into Cambodia's lush jungles a century ago by capitalist colonisers, turned into mighty plantations. Hevea trees produce latex for the rubber industry for twenty to thirty years, and must then be abandoned, at which point the plantation becomes a graveyard of dead trees. This requires the constant felling of nearby jungles every year to plant new trees and grow plantations outward. This is how global finance capital "strips the soul" and "squeezes the life" from whatever territory falls into its clutches!

The United Nations predicts that by 2030, Cambodia will no longer have any natural forests! Meanwhile, Cambodia is rapidly turning into a land of casinos, banks, shadow capital, sex trafficking, and other such pursuits. The local population is either migrating or growing impoverished in Cambodia's cities, whose development is "soaring" like mirages in the air (Cambodia's rate of GDP growth has formally been higher than China's for many years!).

This is how finance capital operates: both destroying the rainforest itself, with its irreplaceable beauty, flora, and fauna, and destroying Cambodia's nature, society, and soul. There is a profound connection between the two.

If we do not supplement our growing technological knowledge with other types of knowledge – about the need for reasonable self-limitation, about the use of "noo-approaches" to organise our lives, and most of all about the new possibilities of technological progress – then we will obviously come to disaster. Ahead lies the point of singularity of our civilisational development. We may not notice when we pass this point, but we will soon feel the consequences. Our choice is between continued "zoo-life", with its "zoo-economy" or "zoonomy" – in which case we will surely meet the fate described above – or emerging from the present into NIS.2 and gradually creating a world of reasonable needs and reasonable production: that is, nooconsumption and nooproduction.

Notes

1 From an interview with Pope Francis: "The fact that has shocked me the most is the Overshoot Day: On July 29 we used up all the regenerative resources of 2019. From July 30 we started to consume more resources than the planet can regenerate in a year. It's very serious. It's a global emergency." Domenico Agasso, Jr., "Pope Francis warns against sovereignism: 'It leads to war,'" La Stampa, August 10, 2019, https://www.lastampa.it/vatican-insider/en/2019/08/09/news/pope-francis-warns-against-sovereignism-it-leads-towar-1.37330049/.

2 Scripps Research Institute, "First stable semisynthetic organism created," ScienceDaily, January 23, 2017, www.sciencedaily.com/releases/2017/01/170123214717.htm. For more details, see Yorke Zhang et al., "A semisynthetic organism engineered for the stable expansion of the genetic alphabet," PNAS 114, no. 6 (2017): 1317–1322. [Bodrunov cites Russian sources reporting on these U.S.-published articles. – *Translator's note*].

7

Nooindustrial Production

7.1. The Technological Implementation of Knowledge

When we discuss the need to make production rational, we have in mind the application of reason and the knowledge obtained by reason, simultaneously to technological production and to the goals of production, to the needs that production is called upon to meet. Production has always relied on the use of knowledge. What makes modern knowledge-intensive production unique in this regard? Just that knowledge is paramount compared to production's material costs, as we have mentioned already?

The technological application of knowledge is growing substantially more complex. For some time, a transition has been underway from empirical knowledge to the application of scientific knowledge. "Knowledge acquisition", and application of knowledge, have emerged as their own branch of modern production. At the current stage, interdisciplinary research, and the transition it supports – from the "coexistence" and interaction of various technologies, witnessed earlier, to their convergence, that is, the formation of hybrid technologies with synergistic effect (an effect that exceeds the sum of its parts) – are becoming dominant. These effects lead to the transition of technological and socioeconomic development to a new stage.

It is the effect of technological synergy that facilitates civilisation's accelerated movement along the path of industrial progress. But more important still is the "second-order" phenomenon that arises from this synergistic effect, namely, the development of modern technology and its increasing knowledge-density brings with it an increase in technology's synergistic abilities. In other words, to define a new term, technology's "synergistic density" (or, if you will, its "synergistic power") is growing. This already creates a technical and institutional base for the "accelerating acceleration" (the second derivative, as it were) of scientific and technical progress.

We now witness this phenomenon as a fully evident practical process. Each new technological solution, in the spirit of using the mechanisms mentioned above by dramatically raising the synergistic density of newly engineered technologies, also improves all the positive parameters of industrial production by orders of magnitude: it lowers the resource-density/costliness/ecological footprint of production, it raises the productivity of labour and the quality of output.

Labour is the direction of effort, of any human effort, to acquire or apply knowledge that we require to satisfy needs. Even the "application" of knowledge is a form of knowledge! No less than the hands, the head works constantly to meet needs. People now refer to "knowledge production" and the "knowledge economy". I propose that these terms are only acceptable as stopgaps, to clarify the process of "excavating" and using concrete knowledge in today's "economy". *No one produces knowledge; knowledge objectively is, it exists in absolute terms, outside of us.* Our labour is not the "creation" or "production" of knowledge, but the cognition and discovery of concrete bits of knowledge; step by step, more and more, "expansion of consciousness" and of the knowledge-space that is accessible to a person (and to humanity as a whole) takes place; but this is not the "invention", nor in any way the "creation", of new knowledge.

At present, the process of "knowledge excavation" is subject to the same technological shifts as all other human activity. In recent decades, scientific activity (in all its aspects – from its organisation, to its cost, to its results and its implementation within a system of social needs and interests, etc.) has undergone radical changes, so much so that the time is right to discuss its definite transformation: from academic research as traditionally understood, to something new which rises to the challenges of the process of social transformation that is linked to the beginning of civilisation's transition to NIS.2.

The external features of this transformation are obvious. In the twentieth century alone, the number of people directly employed in the scientific sphere grew sixty to seventy times by some estimates. Over the same century, the amount of money spent on science grew by more than one thousand times. Moreover, hardly anyone today will dispute the necessity and inevitability of further increasing this sum.

As a phenomenon of modern social life, science is more than just a receptacle of knowledge. The development of new industrial (knowledge-intensive) material production in the second generation of new industrial society is based on the prioritisation of knowledge in every aspect of creating a new industrial (knowledge-dense) product. As a result, the role of scientific knowledge as a neo-industrial resource grows ever greater, gradually becoming the basic resource of the new generation of industry. This is what determines the observable "external" transformative effects in the development of the scientific sphere.

This is particularly important to grasp in terms of researching the most important question for the further development of NIS.2; the transformation of the integrated "triangle" of "production-science-education" that constitutes one of the cornerstones of NIS.2's conceptual platform. More and more, the fundamental place in the "triangle" belongs to science, which is becoming the driver of knowledge-intensive production. Factually speaking, knowledge, by becoming production's essential resource (a "direct productive force") is, to a significant degree, supplanting "hardware" in new industrial production.

The emergence and development of industrial production was closely linked to the transition from individual artisanal labour to mass production. The "capitalisation" of industrial production did not just alter social relations; it led to changes in the productive sphere itself. Will the development of science repeat this trajectory, now that it has become the basic resource and dominant driver of new industrial production's development?

Yes, many facts confirm the following thesis, which seems to grow ever more obvious; to a considerable extent, the scientific sphere is repeating the productive sphere's path of development. We observe the same tendencies, such as the transition from scholars' individual labour to "mass science", the concentration of "scientific powers", to speak in terms of the organisation of scientific work. From the economic point of view, we witness the "monetisation" of science and the "capitalisation" of the scientific sphere. The results of scientific research are transitioning from pure products of the mind to scientific commodities, susceptible to all the usual methods of market turnover. The creative act of obtaining individual scientific knowledge is becoming the "production of scientific output", whose nature is increasingly utilitarian and goal-oriented.

At the present stage of social production's development, this process is objective and inevitable. So long as productive forces operate within the boundaries of currently existing social relations, science, becoming a "direct productive force" and taking on the role of a foundational resource and, therefore, foundational capital, will inescapably repeat the developmental trajectory of any resource that constitutes the basis of capitalist relations. For this reason, we can foretell many future twists and turns in this path and anticipate many problems.

Many problems, but not all. The concept of NIS.2 – which assumes not only the development of new industries as a means of material production on a qualitatively new technological basis, but also the qualitative transformation of society's institutions – takes as its starting point the "special nature" of knowledge as a social phenomenon. This "special nature" amounts to the fact that, unlike material resources, knowledge, whatever imaginary ownership claims and personal boundaries might be imposed on it, is in principle "reproducible", non-private, non-individualised, etc.!

The progression and development of knowledge acquisition in a more socialised direction will continue. Moreover, we can observe a tendency towards the increasing significance of knowledge within the labour function, giving possessors of this "sacred" element the upper hand, which in principle allows for their liberation from under "the power of capital". We can already observe the repeated manifestation of this incipient tendency: alongside the labourer's classical dependence upon capital, the reverse situation – the employer's dependence upon a worker endowed with rare and important abilities (that is, knowledge, embodied in the labour function) – often arises. Moreover, this "reverse" dependency is often much stronger than the "original" dependency.

The colossally growing role of knowledge, as embodied in the technologies and products of production, is bound to make itself known in highly significant fashion – not only in the growing possibilities for satisfying human needs, but even in the process of shaping those needs. Under the systemic conditions of the modern economy, this influence is contradictory. Even with the rise in possibilities for meeting ever-growing needs, which seems purely positive, things are not as simple as they appear to be.

7.2. The Double Role of Knowledge in Shaping and Meeting Needs

What's wrong with the unlimited growth of consumption? After all, with such expanded capacity to satisfy needs, even those needs that appear simulative, false, or illusory at the current level of productive development may change categories and become non-simulative. However, the growth of simulative needs still needs to be limited, lest it lead to meaningless waste of resources and distort the further formation of needs.

It will not do to brush off this problem merely by gesturing at Maslow's pyramid, claiming that so long as vital, material needs are satiated, then our knowledge of more elevated needs will increase "all by itself", since the needs we have already met will no longer motivate us. Maslow's pyramid explains nothing; it merely codifies a few empirically observable tendencies.[1] The reason why such a major shift occurs within the structure of needs, and the question of what problems emerge over the course of this shift, must be dealt with separately.

Maslow's main error (shared by some of his followers and critics) is his attempt to explain changing needs solely *from within* the individual human psyche. In reality, this is not just an "individual story". The patterns that appear when certain needs are replaced by others can only be understood with reference to collective social phenomena, and the causes of these patterns must be found in the basic factors that determine people's lives.

Why is it and when is it that once society enables the satisfaction of demand for the basic needs of life on a mass scale, these basic needs are displaced by others? This is less a factor of the degree to which basic needs are sated (satiety is a *condition*, but not a cause; it is only once vital needs are sated that the transition may occur, *but it also may not occur*) than of the changing character of people's fundamental labour activity.

Within labour activity, the creative function is growing – rather unevenly, but proportionally to the progress of knowledge-intensive technology that makes it possible to meet the needs of sustaining life more fully. Much more than the sphere of consumption, it is production that dictates the need for people to be a) creative and b) responsible (by virtue of the potential power of the technosphere that they set in motion).

For this reason, the shaping of "cultured people" is becoming more and more important for our economic future, determining the growth of intellectual and spiritual requirements. This emphasis is very important as we move towards NIS.2.

The combination of knowledge and cultural imperatives is essential. After all, a human being's reception of knowledge about the concrete means for satisfying a concrete need – in other words, the means for resolving an emergent conflict between needs and possibilities – is not limited to a single vector. Knowledge, by virtue of its universality and endlessness, does not provide a single, unique means for satisfying such-and-such a need in such-and-such a way, but rather an endless multiplicity of such means. The task of an individual person is to choose the most optimal/appropriate option; for this purpose, man is endowed with the power of knowledge, and also with free will, the ability to decide which option to choose.

That said, man determines the optimal criteria for choosing a concrete path to resolve a concrete conflict based on the extent of knowledge that is available to him within the specific subsystem of his existence.

The necessity of satisfying humanity's escalating needs is what drives development. Yet man cannot meet his needs without resorting to the technological application of knowledge. In the early periods of civilisation's development, humanity primarily relied on knowledge as a product of empirical experience, but by now, one cannot do without the large-scale "production/extraction" and application of scientific knowledge. Moreover, human needs can themselves only be cognised or clearly formulated with reference to knowledge obtained by human beings. At the same time, new knowledge makes it possible to discover, articulate, and satisfy new needs.

It is the application of knowledge that distinguishes human labour from the instinctual activity of animals, *and precisely because of knowledge, material production constitutes human beings as social beings.* Man is what he does; man is what his activity is.

The fact that man's productive activity determines his character as a social being was emphasised by Karl Marx:

> "As individuals express their life, so they are. What they are, therefore, coincides with their production, both with *what* they produce and with *how* they produce. The nature of individuals thus depends on the material conditions determining their production" (Marx, Engels, 1974: 42). "...The final result of the process of social production always appears as the society itself, that is, the human being itself in its social relations" (Marx, 1993: 712).

Further positions regarding the dependence of humanity's social being on its activity were developed by Soviet philosophers and psychologists (Batishchev, 1969: 73–144; Leontiev, 1975).

Yet material production is an activity based on knowledge. Man can only produce if he has knowledge: when he enters the production process, he necessarily acquires knowledge, and by the time he leaves this process, he is enriched with new knowledge. It is obvious that this fact plays an enormous structural role.

Only human beings possess the unique ability to discover and formulate traits, laws, and patterns of appearance in the external objective world. And only human beings are capable of applying the knowledge they have discovered to transform the external world, using this knowledge to define suitable objects (materials), create means of transforming them (technologies), and formulate for themselves the goals of such transformation – the creation of products that meet human needs (broadly speaking, including both material and immaterial needs). Without knowledge, it is impossible not just to create something new that does not exist in nature, but also even to make a copy of something, since having the idea to make a copy is already a creative act.

In coming to know the world, man also comes to know himself as part of the world. The development of man's needs will inevitably lead to the development of the need for man to know himself, his place in the world, his interests, and the "interests" of the elements of the world surrounding him – namely, inorganic and organic nature, both of which are related to him. Finally, he starts to account for these "interests" in the process of satisfying his own needs and resolving conflicts between himself and the world. Man comes to set himself apart from the surrounding world and conceive of himself as a separate being. This is the process through which individuality and social communality are formed.

By making one decision or another in the process of resolving conflicts, man becomes an individual and perceives other members of society also as individuals with their own interests, right to choose, and corresponding abilities. The solution of many intersecting problems leads to the necessity of meeting a multitude of needs (some of them contradictory!) concerning the relations between different members of society. Social relations emerge with the development of the social whole, along with the development and cognition of the so-called "public interest".

Thus, social relations are conflicts that are resolved within frameworks – rules, norms, laws, etc. – established by society itself (based on social "consensus" or agreement, which in turn is based on society's comprehension of the optimal conditions for the social collective, and on its experience of knowledge accumulation!). Violating these rules (straying outside the bounds of the public interest) is perceived by society as a destructive act that destabilises the system of social organisation and corrodes its structure.

Consequently, the need arises to create natural constraints against humanity's ability to make highly suboptimal decisions. Once again, these constraints are shaped and reinforced throughout the fabric of human culture based on the acquisition of specific knowledge. At the same time, man can develop and apply technological solutions that enable the creation of favourable conditions for making optimal choices.

7.3. Technologies of Trust

Any civilisation or social order will give rise to a particular system of relations, principles, morals, traditions, rules, habits, and so on. We, who have generated many "agreed-upon" elements within our own culture, must necessarily place our trust in them; otherwise, there would be no structure or home that we could call "our own civilisation" or "our own cultural space".

The violation of one of these elements by a member of society is perceived as going beyond the boundaries of such a shared cultural space. Violations on a mass scale lead to the destruction and transfiguration of this space. For instance, we describe the deception of one person by another as the violation of a cultural tradition, namely, of our trust in one another. Because we constantly rely on the benefits and incentives of civilisation (commodities, services, relationships), we are obligated to regularly check them (typically by using technology) against certain stated criteria of an accepted civilisational code. More often than not, though, we must simply rely on trust, due to the impossibility of subjecting everything to thorough examination, reconciliation, alignment...

Trust is one of the basic problems of contemporary civilisation. At the very least, its economic significance is exemplified by bank transactions; the costs of establishing compliance for transactions amounts to roughly half of all expenditures within the banking system. The trust factor only grows in importance for preserving both civilisation's basic principles and its stable development, since technology is more and more capable of "wriggling into" any one of us. The ability to violate social conventions grows ever higher, while our defences grow ever weaker!

Thus, the growth of society's technological "armament" is accompanied by the problem of raising the general level of trust in social relations (let he who will say that trust is not one of the most important elements of cultured community cast the first stone at me for saying so!). To resolve this problem, we should not prioritise acculturation as such (acculturation, though necessary, plays a secondary role) but rather the transformation of the conditions under which social relations are realised. In other words, we should prioritise technological change.

For just this reason, "technologies of trust" should be one of the key components of the technological basis of the future: linked with both the core criteria of economic rationality and the zoological side of human nature, these technologies will allow us to make decisions untainted by egotism.

It is imperative that we set the creation of technological means for raising levels of trust as a priority of technological development. For instance, if deception cannot physically take place (especially given widely accessible means for the simple satisfaction of needs) then attempts at deception will come to naught! If deceit becomes technologically impossible, then why not believe the information you receive? The universal implementation of "technologies of trust" will gradually change our cultural codes: our habits, concepts, ways of communicating, and more.

Let us note that "technologies of trust" have existed and have constantly been developed all throughout history. Nowadays their development is rather intensive, due to the growth of social demand for them. The entire world is gradually starting to use distributed database technology – a.k.a. the blockchain – which underpins virtual currency (cryptocurrency). This is because such technology raises the overall level of social trust (Tapscot, Tapscot, 2018).

Trust is the key word here. If we choose a path that increases levels of trust – such as by using technological procedures that guarantee the authenticity of documents with ironclad certainty – then we will no longer need to waste time establishing trust. In other words, we will be more able to spend time on other activities.

For example, if we have already grasped, understood, and accepted the truth of an initial group of theorems when we begin to solve a mathematical problem, we may then construct other theorems without going back to the first ones and proving them all over again; we can rely on what we consider to be true. If we construct our relations with one another on the "impossibility of deceit" – taken as an element of human upbringing – then after two or three generations, humanity will forget the meaning of the word "deceive": we will no longer understand how to deceive, and the necessity of deception will wither away (Figure 6).

Each person's *level of trust* is exactly what determines their individual threshold for believing in the truthfulness or untruthfulness of particular phenomena. To a considerable extent, this shapes our knowledge space as a *"trust space"*. For this reason, we say that we need to increase the level of trust right now, because *the greater the knowledge sphere/space, the greater the level of trust.*

At one point, Francis Fukuyama wrote about the "radius of trust" that surrounds people. My initial radius of trust is that I trust my neighbour first

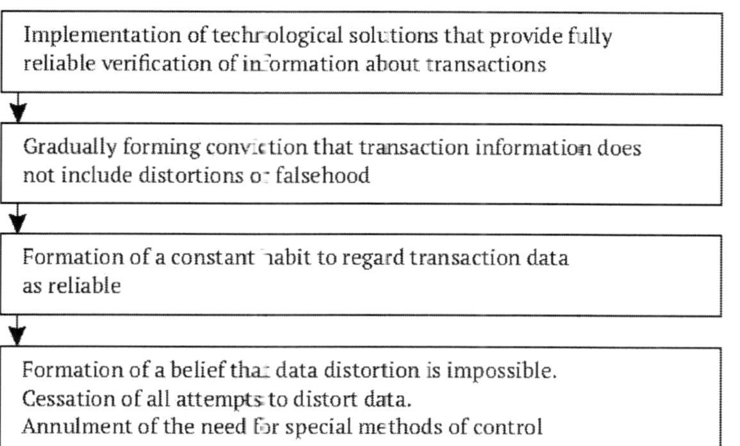

Figure 6. *The cultural and educational significance of technologies of trust*

and my family second (or the other way around) – and I trust both more than I trust my municipality (and much more than I trust the state) and so on. (After all, placing trust in an abstract state is not an easy thing to do!) However, Fukuyama neglected to say the most important thing: within this space or "radius" of trust, people do or do not place their trust in the correctness of certain criteria and norms.

The radius of trust depends precisely on the overall level of trust. Do 80 percent of people believe something? Or 30 percent? Or does everyone categorically not believe in it? If people do not believe, they will strive for unvarnished truth and absolute knowledge. Even to the point of dismantling the family, or the state itself, if people have lost their trust in them. These levels of trust can be expanded and strengthened, including through the implementation of new technology. Such technology will make it possible to gauge each issue more effectively. Yes, or no? True, or false? To believe, or not to believe? By answering these questions, we can decide on a correct and reasonable order for any given portion of space, technological solution, or social phenomenon.

In this sense, the blockchain (one of the many "technologies of trust" created by humanity, and the most prominent one in the present moment) may do much more for the development of democracy – and for more rational social development, advancing toward noosociety – than dozens of other methods for raising our faith in the state. This is not only (nor even primarily!)

because the blockchain "verifies" the results of choices, but because it may give us the ability to elect the leaders that are most qualified to rule (according to the basic criteria of the moment).

Technology is merely the emergence of knowledge into the real, material world. We all know that 2 × 2 = 4, and it no longer matters how we learnt it. We have verified it many times, and by now we believe that it is the truth. No one could tell us that 2 × 2 = 5. We would not believe them. In just the same way, we place much more faith in American elections than in other countries' elections; we know that American banks are technologically more well-protected than other banks; Americans have more legal protections when they make deposits, and they are harder to defraud, because "fraudsters" are highly likely to be punished by law. In addition, American trustworthiness is better secured by technology. For these reasons, we all have more faith in their currency and in their elections.

After knowledge of what is and is not true comes certainty about which of our notions are truthful. This certainty is reinforced by frequent repetition in practice; as the saying goes, the result of an experiment that has been confirmed many times must be recognised as the truth. And though this truth may be overturned by new experiments in the future, at the present stage our heuristics and our knowledge permit us to regard these assertions as truthful.

Technologies based on verifiable laws of the physical and material world surround us on all sides, and we ascertain and trust in the rectitude of criteria and parameters, of concepts formed in our heads, that rest on this basis. Thus, developing these technologies today, we may come to the point that humanity increasingly understands the world, including the part of the world that allows human beings to give up their simulacra. Recall the humanists who spoke of human values, eternal truth, and so on, introducing these ideas into the basic criteria of our knowledge and of our culture. Nor did these things appear in a vacuum: they were based on apprehension, interpretation, cognition, acknowledgment, and knowledge of what is incorrect and what is correct. A transformation occurred in the basic criteria of what is good and what is bad.

Thus, the development of social relations of production on the basis of advanced technological methods for verifying economic activity will make economic activity more open and transparent. This enables a dramatic decrease in transaction expenses, which, in the current economic system, are an obstacle to fully unleashing the sharing economy, crowdsourcing, and other types of collective activity and shared use.

A high degree of openness and a high degree of trust, consolidated within the norms and traditions of human behaviour, with a firm technological basis – all this is a vital prerequisite for the evolution of property relations. In the end, the need for private control over resources, their private ownership, will conclusively disappear. Power and domination will evaporate from property relations.

Not only regimes of shared use will develop, but also regimes of free access. However, this does not mean that the need for institutions that regulate this free access will wither away. On the contrary, carefully calibrated institutional frameworks will be needed to prevent the diffusion and squandering of common resources, even in the absence of private appropriation and its selfish motives.

7.4. The Development of Knowledge as a Cultural Phenomenon

Humanity's social nature unveils an exit from its ripening civilisational crisis. While the external and natural resources of humanity's vital activity – those which are required for its existence as a biological creature – are objectively limited, and require humans to behave quite cautiously, social resources present a different situation. The most important resource of human vital activity – the human capacity for knowledge, and the ability to convert extracted knowledge into technology – is limitless.

These capacities can only be realised with the simultaneous transformation of the technosphere that humanity has created and the transformation of our social order in response to the demands of this new technosphere. These transformations will entail geo-economic shifts: the balance of forces in the global economy will not escape change. That said, leadership in the new economy will not solely be determined by leadership in developing and applying the latest technologies.

The global economy's leaders will be those countries (or their corporate groups, unions, and conglomerates) that not only show their ability to master new types of knowledge, implement that knowledge in technology, and rebuild production based on those technological achievements: a necessary condition will be an *all-new developmental paradigm, a.k.a. the transformation of the goals and motives of human behaviour.* In fact, without this paradigm shift, even the current technological revolution will either prove to be impossible or threaten humanity's self-destruction.

A change in global economic leadership is an all-but-inevitable consequence of technological shifts on a world-systemic scale. And since this transition will be conditioned by our present-day economic systems and models, it is difficult (maybe impossible!) to hope that the forthcoming changes will unfold without conflict. We can predict with certainty that there will be struggles over leadership – so finding a way to soften these conflicts, preventing them from taking on sharp and destructive forms, will remain an urgent task.

Who can show us the proper path forward? What should be the "design" of such a path? Where is the person who will genuinely start to work through these questions and draw the contours of our path? The whole world is our blackboard! And this task is a universal human task. We should all work at it together; we should appeal to the international community to collectively occupy ourselves with the new industrial development of society. If this happens quickly and consensually, then notorious socio-economic tensions will resolve themselves with as little conflict as possible. This is not an idea meant for any single country in isolation; rather, it is the objective path of our common civilisational development.

Scholars, politicians, and businessmen have already offered more than enough predictions about the civilisational shifts that await us. Nonetheless, the economic community still lacks a clear conception of the nature of these shifts. Most economists are not looking that far into the future. Others, "soothsayers," who can sense the ground of the economy shifting beneath their feet, rush to calm themselves and others by inventing comforting terms such as "the new normal". Everything is topsy-turvy, economic growth is slowing down, technical progress and productivity are decelerating, the usual levers of control have no effect – but we are meant to believe that nothing much is going on, and that this is just "the new normal"!

A coherent model of the oncoming future has yet to take shape in the analyses of experts. Perhaps this is caused not by the "limited intellectual abilities" of the community of experts at large, and of economists in particular, but instead by the fact that they do not want to draw awkward conclusions and break with the reality to which they are accustomed? Yet one way or another, this break must occur. The civilisational crisis that threatens us can only be overcome by the power of critical reason that is fearless in its willingness to look squarely at the future's dangers and abandon outdated approaches that stultify our ability to cognise a genuinely new reality.

A technological leap into the future will only provide humanity with a real step forward if it is based on new principles, noo-approaches, that are alone capable of showing us the right ways to use our escalating (and therefore potentially dangerous, but simultaneously offering considerable new gains) technological potential.

The noo-approach offers *the unity of technological might with the power of knowledge and with human reason as represented by the traditions of human culture*. Henceforth, it will be society's cultural codes that serve as a vital condition of the technological use of knowledge, *and whatever humankind makes of itself will depend on our cultural norms.*

In creating a foundation for humanity's exit from direct production, new technological forces form a basis for the withering away of economic relations (that is, the struggle to use and appropriate the resources and results of production). Consequently, though, society itself will undergo profound transformations. The response to the challenges posed by the extensively "technocratic" scenario of development, which leads to a dead end of civilisational crisis, should be conscious intensification of the creation and use of technologies that support both man's personal development and the improvement of the cultural codes of modern civilisation.

The ubiquitous and "stacked" application of these technologies will mean that social institutions change as well. For example, real direct democracy is becoming possible: not just elections, but the direct resolution of all sorts of questions of collective life based on trust-based consensus (requiring no verification!) – whether to allow trams on a particular street, whether to take down a monument, whether to build a factory next to a residential district.

It is important to emphasise that all technological development, in this version of the future, will be targeted at achieving the goals of rational social development and the satisfaction of the human personality's rational (non-simulative) needs and desires (noo-needs). All production of socially necessary products will be oriented towards meeting rational needs according to codes of civility and culture that are shaped by the framework of NIS.2.

It does not matter who will do the work: either a robot (most likely) or a human creator (standing "above production"). Material production will remain society's basis, and the means of producing goods will be industrial, based on up-to-date technology. More precisely, the means of production will be nooindustrial, to meet the needs of nooindustrial society existing in the noosphere.

At first glance, these theses seem largely "Vernadskian". Nonetheless, a deeper reading suggests a different interpretation. Many past thinkers (Karl Marx, Vladimir Vernadsky, Erich Fromm, the theorists of the Club of Rome...) have appealed to human reason as the way to solve mounting problems. However, they had no ready-to-hand answer regarding what concrete material means could be used to enact this solution. It seems to us that we can finally provide this answer. We must move from a purely humanistic treatment of ideas related to the noosphere, as can be found in debates over social philosophy, towards grasping the fact that these ideas can become reality – on the solid foundation of the developmental tendencies of material production.

In this sense, the justification for concepts like NIS.2 and noonomy turns out also to be an approach to justifying the development of the next stage of human civilisation. We would propose calling this new stage noo-civilisation, in which production would be subject to human reason rather than just technology and the technical realm (however, human reason would itself rest upon the strictly material processes of nooindustrial production, since without this connection, reason would be unable to develop, or even to secure its mere mundane existence!).

On the same note, the social role of knowledge is rising dramatically: as a means for discovering newer, more effective, and more economical ways to satisfy rational human needs (as opposed to the current path, that is, a purely quantitative escalation of consumption, whose limits are already evident); and as a means for resolving the conflicts and tensions that accompany profound technological and societal shifts. That said, the new society will not be created by technology in itself; the main role will be played by human beings endowed with knowledge, truly rational humans (this is why we object on principle to technological determinism).

It is precisely culture (morality, what people call core values, etc.) that will shape the most important element of this new society's code of civility – namely, human self-control, which will guide people away from the unrestrained quantitative escalation of consumption, weighed down by the pursuit of different kinds of mirages and simulacra, and towards the formation of rational human needs and desires (nooneeds) that give primary place to the *quality* of needs and desired goods. Culture is what will ground the qualitative newness of interpersonal interactions – within both social life and the process of creative labour. At the same time, technological progress turns out to contain enormous potential for the transformation of the cultural codes of human civilisation.

Which social mechanisms will make it possible for us to set goals for production and technical development that facilitate the development of humanity itself, and to make the processes of technological advancement answerable to this task? This is the central question of how social structures will evolve as we transition to noosociety.

The development of NIS.2 toward noocivilisation is tantamount to the transformation of the standard role of today's commonly accepted basic social institutions – that is, the state, money, and the means of both appropriating social wealth and then gradually frittering it away. The social order will gain stability by basing itself not just on trust, but on firm knowledge that information obtained by "public" exchange is always true and authentic. As we know, there are many different types of "knowledge" out there. But demand will grow for *true* knowledge, *verified* knowledge, *trustworthy* knowledge. Rational knowledge.

The evolution of human reason's social role is spasmodic. Everything will be determined by what becomes of human reason. Will reason appeal to people's collaboration to reach lofty goals, or will free rein be given to the dark side of the forces borne by knowledge? The education of rational human beings (which is to say, cultured human beings) is becoming a core imperative in the process of forming the society of the future – as is answering the question of how people will manage to work together to reach their common goals.

Notes

1 See (Maslow, 1943: 370–396). Maslow's conception has been seriously criticised. Many believe that the interaction of needs at different levels is far more complex than Maslow assumed (which is to say that one can move either up or down the pyramid). See, for example, the theory of a hierarchy of needs advanced in Clayton Paul Alderfer (Clayton, 1969: 142–75).

8

Culture as an Economic Imperative

8.1. Nooproduction and Needs: The Character of Production and the Character of Needs

The versatility of human beings, formed in response to the challenges of the technological revolution; the creation of new needs and new ways to meet them, also associated with new technologies – where is all this leading humankind? And where is it leading today's economy?

As shown earlier, the ability to increasingly satisfy needs at lower and lower cost also creates both the possibility of reducing our ecological footprint and the temptation towards superabundance. Which one will humanity choose? How will we define ourselves?

What will it be: will other motives replace personal gain, for example, self-development, quality of communication, or public recognition? Or will humanity drown itself in a sea of ever more illusory and finicky needs and wants? Or will it hide from life in virtual reality and cyberspace? After all, the digital world may expand communicative possibilities, or it may shrink them in the service of human self-isolation. Recall Japan's "hikikomori", people who go for years without stepping away from their computers, rejecting not just social interaction but even the normal routines of life, from regularly eating and changing their clothes to maintaining their physical fitness.

If we make it past this crossroads and emerge into "nooproduction", then for the most part the latter will constitute *the production of humanity itself, rather than the production of the material conditions of its existence.* Correspondingly, the structure of human needs will also change. The prevailing needs will be those related to self-development, to the spiritual plane, to communication, to public acknowledgement. And these are the needs that will regulate the technologies used in production, the products produced, and the organisation of production, for the sake of meeting material human needs. These shifts in the structure of needs will be determined by the progress of human culture, meaning a specific type of knowledge.

Thus, *social production in noosociety*, insofar as we can judge by analyzing objective processes that began in the recent past and are already underway at present, will take the form of a system that includes:

- the prioritised development of knowledge-intensive "smart" production (which we may call *nooproduction*, eliminating the quotation marks);
- a corresponding integration of production, science, and education within a unified reproductive framework, leading to the formation of a new type of socioeconomic reproduction – *nooreproduction* – that prioritises the creation of the conditions for noosociety's development;
- the gradually decreased role of utilitarian and simulative needs and the ascent of a new class of needs: the needs of "rational man", or *nooneeds*;
- the concomitant development of new values and behavioural motives, which lose their economic properties, for the main human subjects of material and spiritual production;
- during the transition to this period, economic relations and institutions will transform towards greater socialisation and humanisation, specifically in terms of the active development of *noo-oriented* economic programming, active industrial policies to prioritise the development of "smart" production, and strengthened public-private partnership to resolve these issues;
- and, last but not least: the ascent of culture as a sphere that solves key problems of *noodevelopment.*

Nooproduction is knowledge-intensive production that minimises direct

> human involvement. It is oriented towards the satisfaction of **nooneeds**, prioritising the creation of developmental conditions for humanity's rise in the sphere of knowledge and culture.

How can we summarise the objectives of nooproduction if economic goals will have faded into the past? We may define these objectives as **the ascent of the human personality.**

> *The ascent of the human personality* is the direct goal of production in noosociety, consisting of the development of human qualities and expansion of human beings' cultural environment, as regulated by culturally determined values.

This ascent will occur through the rising importance of spiritual needs in every area of human culture. An important factor will be the need for conscious self-discipline and the limitation of simulative needs (which, incidentally, when coupled with the new possibilities afforded by technology, will seriously contribute to the resource-efficiency of this developmental path).

Such self-limitation does not constitute some externally imposed imperative. Of course, during the stage of transitioning to noosociety, a certain role will have to be played by external moral imperatives, explanations, persuasion, and, finally, the nurturing of habitual rational self-discipline. No doubt this will be facilitated by accelerating technological progress, which – via the new industrial production of NIS.2 – will cause the progressive devaluation of physical, material, tangible products by simplifying the satisfaction of humanity's vital (and other non-simulative) needs and making material goods less and less important to individual human experience. Instead, meeting human beings' rising spiritual needs will become more and more valuable.

But of course, *internal* self-discipline, emerging from how the structure of needs is determined by the new nature of human activity and by the social relations that foster such activity, will be the most impactful factor. Even today, for example, people who occupy themselves with decoding the human genome or developing technology to send expeditions to Mars are hardly concerned with acquiring gigantic yachts or villas on the Côte d'Azur, regardless of their level of income. Those who are excited by this type of work find such "needs" irrelevant; rather than helping them, fulfilling these needs would interfere with the pursuit of their genuine goals.

The thesis offered above, concerning the ascent of the human personality, resonates to some extent with Karl Marx's famous idea that in future society, "the free development of each is the condition for the free development of all" (Marx, Engels, 1978: 491; Marx, 1978: 531; Marx, 1982: 613–614, 739), along with the corresponding position of Vladimir Lenin (Lenin, 1961: 52). In the USSR, these views were regarded as a "fundamental law of the communist system".

That said, Marxists see free and full development as a law of communism, the result of a successful violent revolution; what we have in mind is evolution, and the features of noosociety that we have objectively derived are quite far from the communist schema proposed by Marxists. Furthermore, "development" for us cannot take any arbitrary direction it likes (see the discussion of self-discipline above). Finally, our starting point assumes that different dimensions of personal development are of unequal significance, and we take spiritual development as paramount.

The quality of the spiritual and cultural component of human development is exactly what must determine all the other dimensions of development, subordinating them to the best norms of human culture. However, the progress of human personality is not an end in itself for noocivilization. Noocivilization must develop steadily and sustainably. The system should be sustainable, working towards greater sustainability and systemic self-preservation rather than towards rupture.

Preservation of ourselves as human beings, that is, preserving a system whose basic sustainability rests upon developed, new, important human beings as its foundational element – this is our goal. This is precisely why we need "new people". But any slogan about creating "new people" for its own sake, as an end in itself, would be meaningless (we recall the Party's dogmas about "scientific communism" during the Soviet era!).

For this reason, the new person is not a goal in itself. Our actual goal is clear and comprehensible: the "new" person will be an element of noosociety as a system, allowing civilisation to preserve and maintain its steady development (which is, after all, the basic principle of all existence). If, instead of "new" people, noosociety were to be populated by "old" people who fit the "old" system, then society would systematically change: it would become technetronic, with the consequences described above.

As the human personality develops, social relations will only be preserved so long as man consciously understands what he may and may not do, so to speak. We need institutions that do not uphold what happens today, within the framework of global capitalism, but those that orient themselves towards securing a nooversion of development.

For this purpose, however strange it may seem – yet again! – technological development is necessary. In fact, emphasis should be placed not on NBIC-technologies as a whole, but most prominently on C-technologies: nanotech, biotech, and IT were the cutting edge from the 1950s to the 1990s, making them somewhat "worn out" these days. In the near future, we should transition from information technologies to cognitive technologies; otherwise, if we do not pursue the development of human abilities, man's capacity to more deeply know himself and the world, we will fail to absorb an enormous amount of knowledge and will be unable to successfully "implement" the nooversion of development. Only pursuing technological development will allow us to be more or less confident in the future.

8.2. Cultured Man as a Product of Nooproduction: The Ascent of Personality

When labour productivity increases (as needs are reduced or limited), the duration and significance of time spent working decreases, while that of leisure time rises. NIS.2 is already equipped to substantially increase leisure time, but this will not immediately bring about "augmented happiness"; first, people must learn to use their leisure time for self-development (elevating their spiritual needs, culture, etc.).

We can understand the scepticism of Hannah Arendt, who doubted that the expansion of leisure time would lead to greater human development – since, she believed, the reality is that people are inclined to use their free time for nothing but thoughtless consumption. "[T]he spare time of the animal laborans," she wrote, "is never spent in anything but consumption, and the more time left to him, the greedier and more craving his appetites. That these appetites become more sophisticated, so that consumption is no longer restricted to the necessities but, on the contrary, mainly concentrates on the superfluities of life, does not change the character of this society, but harbours the grave danger that eventually no object of the world will be safe from consumption and annihilation through consumption" (Arendt, 1958: 133).

Indeed, in the social system in which we currently live, namely, so-called capitalism, this is how things are – because people are granted leisure time only in order to consume what they have produced during their working hours. With equal force, capitalism compels people both to consumption and to production for the sake of that consumption.

Society may find a way out of this vicious cycle, but not by means of the ideology of asceticism, a.k.a. compulsory rationing and reduction of consumption; nor by propagating higher ideals through mere words; rather, the way out is to reduce time spent on necessary work (which assumes, as a prerequisite, the modern industrial mode of production) and to use leisure time to develop creative faculties.

But this does not mean that Arendt's doubts appeared in a vacuum. *The transition from leisure-as-consumption to spare time as a space for developing human culture will be neither quick nor simple.* This is a colossally important problem which may lead to quite serious, large-scale, and deep difficulties. Only by solving it will we definitively arrive at the epoch of the noosphere.

In the second generation of new industrial society, man has the considerable capacity to act not as a thoughtless consumer, but as a creative human being. This is true to the extent that the use of spare time for creative purposes depends on the coalescence of the material prerequisites for creative activity, that is, access to means of self-education, means of physical self-improvement, means of scientific and artistic creation, and so on.

Of course, another necessity is the transformation of the relationship between work time and leisure time, in favour of the latter. And the transition to the next stage, nooproduction, presents humanity (like never before!) with far-reaching and profound issues, concerning the acquisition of new knowledge to ensure a leap forward in technological progress and to grasp the trajectory and limits of our own development. It is precisely the need to resolve these issues, along with humanity's practical engagement with the technological (and socio-practical) application of science, that will determine the face of leisure under noosociety.

Though Arendt drew her conclusions based on having observed the real social contradictions of her moment, there is one rule that she did not consider – changing the character of human activity in order to gain new knowledge will also – gradually, not all at once – alter the structure and qualitative content of humankind's needs and desires, ultimately *changing how leisure time is spent.*

It is discourse, information, and knowledge that will become more valuable than even the most precious material values of the previous era. We are not far from the point at which this prospect will be widely understood. The world is approaching the end of a cycle, a turn of the "big wheel", as the ancient Maya Indians used to say. Knowledge, and the words that express knowledge, are now taking on primary importance. Remember the Bible: "In the beginning was the Word". And also, as it turns out, at the end. Of course, every end signifies a beginning. But the beginning of what?

No doubt the new society will bring fundamental lifestyle shifts for masses of people. The old occupations and professions will lose their value, which will be a very painful transition. In Great Britain, during the sixteenth and seventeenth centuries, the agrarian revolution generated many beggars and tramps, who were subject to harsh repression; the industrial revolution of the eighteenth and nineteenth centuries was accompanied by mass destitution among petty artisans and the suffering "reserve army of labour". Yet neither epoch saw a social catastrophe. Landless peasants either became agricultural workers for hire or were absorbed by the growth of industrial manufacturing. Artisans who went out of business filled the swiftly growing ranks of the industrial proletariat in the factories.

In the same way, *the coming technological revolution, even as it makes entire professions redundant, will also create new types of jobs.* New technologies will foster new needs, and meeting those needs will in turn summon new technologies. New jobs will appear to replace those that are liquidated by automatisation and the growth of labour productivity. Moreover, inexorable growth in the relative weight of the "knowledge economy" (during the transitional stage), the rising need to acquire new knowledge, may absorb many workers.

As the technological basis of production changes and we transition to nooproduction, the very terms "profession" and "job" will drastically change their meaning, assuming they do not disappear outright. The word "profession", referring to a means of earning money in exchange for a certain type of skilled labour, will likely fade into the past. These functions will instead be performed by technetic beings, while humans liberate themselves from the narrow specialisation of the present day. Thus, there will be no professions in the traditional sense: humans will focus on moving closer and closer to absolute knowledge, becoming ever more universally minded. New ways of accessing knowledge and information will be developed – varieties of neural networks, for example, and other human-machine systems.

Of course, human beings' noonomy versatility will not mean every person knowing everything, but rather, newly opened possibilities and newly acquired abilities for mastering practically any needed knowledge. *The main shift will consist of the creation of informational and communicative systems that allow any individual person to draw upon the entire ocean of knowledge accumulated by humanity, and to plumb this ocean's depths yet further.*

Needless to say, this will call for the improvement of the faculties of human beings themselves, who will need to master the ability to enter into any sphere of knowledge and orient themselves within it. This universal flexibility is fully obtainable so long as the education system and, yes, even human nature (remembering its limits?!) are restructured as needed. The main task of the education system will no longer be to "fill up" or "inflate" learners with knowledge and skills corresponding to a certain specialisation. Learners must stop being passive customers, "hoarders", of ready-made knowledge, and instead learn to independently "extract" and use knowledge themselves. Of course, it will be impossible to acquire this ability without broad fundamental education to facilitate rapid self-orientation in any needed area of knowledge.

The transitional stage to such a vision of "universal self-learning humanity" will be the realisation of the concepts of "education for all" and "lifelong learning", which are necessary for reaching the stage of NIS.2. Meanwhile, it is becoming critically important to research and develop new and progressively more advanced and versatile ways of accessing knowledge.

8.3. From Economic Rationality to Reasonable Formation of Needs

The fundamental shifts in the nature of people's activity and entire way of life that will occur during the transition to NIS.2 (followed by nooindustrial production) will be accompanied by substantial changes in the motivations for human behaviour, that is, the structure and content of needs and desires. Man, himself, will internally limit the uncontrolled inflation of such needs and desires. These transformations will be followed by re-evaluation of the criteria for judging the rationality of production and of needs.

First and foremost, rationality implies correspondence to certain criteria. The framework of rationality is some set of criteria that we ourselves have established as a basis. How? Through knowledge: knowledge of certain things, comprehension of them, and the formulation of "border posts" that correspond to them, determining where one may reasonably go and where one may not.

This system of coordinates, or system of criteria, is dynamic. As we expand our knowledge, the space of rationality also expands, and so does our knowledge of what our basic criteria should be. As a result, our criteria and the boundaries of our rationality grow more expansive.

In the past, it was irrational and unreasonable for European women to leave half their legs bare, so they wore their skirts down to the floor. Why? Because of cold weather and the fact that since people spent most of their time either outside or in rooms with significant temperature fluctuations (with inconsistent heating, and sometimes not even that) there was always a risk of catching a cold. African women, by contrast, were able to walk around with their thighs barely covered by strips of cloth. On this basis, different norms, both moral and otherwise, arose in each place.

Later, this difference made its way into culture – behaviour, clothing, culture at large – and coalesced as criteria for judging human action: a concept of what is "moral" and what is "immoral". *The role of culture as a phenomenon of society's development* is often seriously underestimated by adherents of strictly technocratic conceptions of social development. Contrary to this approach, however, it must be noted that the solutions to many problems generated by the turbulence of industrial and scientific progress can be found precisely in the cultural sphere, however strange this may seem at first. *Culture is where both society and individuals consolidate their view of what is rational – in production, in consumption, and in all of human behaviour.*

It turns out, then, that rationality is always in a flux; it develops along with society. At its heart lies humanity's capacity to take in ever more knowledge about how to satisfy needs, such as the need for fresh knowledge – including knowledge of "the good", whose boundaries can be shifted. Expanding one's rational framework is crucially important, as it allows us to understand not only how the world is structured, but why it seems to be "going crazy": after all, a shift in one's rational framework does mean "going crazy", in that it involves stepping outside one's prior rational boundaries. And for exactly this reason, all the things we have already spent many years studying come to seem totally unsuitable for analyzing or understanding the future, or for coming to terms with who we are.

With the opening of new horizons of knowledge (about everything!), many mental discoveries are later validated in practice. As a result, knowledge is verified, "enhanced"; our basic criteria are refined, and the expanse of our rationality is corrected, broadened, "moved".

In the past, it was unreasonable to wish for space flight. The desire to fly around the Earth was (according to the basic criteria of those past centuries) a fantastical, simulative need. For a present-day astronaut, this need is both realisable and not at all simulative, but it remains simulative (though realisable) for a typical space tourist: a wealthy potential tourist need only pay twenty to thirty million dollars for this experience. In the latter case, we might ask: Is this rational? Yet the day will come when everyone will fly in space, just as everyone now flies in airplanes, and this will be completely rational. In other words, over time, everything is gradually deformed and reformed, corrected, adapted; the space of rationality changes, along with its basic criteria.

This displacement and development of rationality's boundaries poses the question: What level of rationality should we aim for? Which criteria should we trust?

At any moment, we must trust the basic criteria within which we are situated. Knowledge, transferred into technology, makes possible the satisfaction of needs to greater and greater effect, giving us progressively more insight into how to comprehend the world, including comprehension of our own various needs: simulative needs, non-simulative needs, the procedure for changing our needs, and so on. Accordingly, the basic criteria of a new space – a space of reason and rationality, moving us closer to non-simulative, reasonable, real needs – are formed.

The cognition of a more and more expansive rational space also implies moving away from certain values that were part of our basic criteria before. As soon as we "broaden our minds", we understand where the mistakes and faults in our criteria were. Once we correct these faults and move forward, we realise yet again that there are still certain inaccuracies, ambiguities, imprecisions, and that we must raise the level of veracity of our knowledge. Our basic criteria become more and more "true", bringing us closer to Absolute Knowledge, absolute belief. And sooner or later, drawing on a framework of belief in certain truths, society "slows down" and then "stops" the build-up of needs that are simulative at its current stage of development.

Knowledge demonstrates which needs are false and which are not. It reconstructs humanity, making it possible to believe that our basic criteria are credible and true and that we must "observe" these criteria, that is, live by them. We must accord with the level of understanding and self-comprehension that we have hitherto achieved. If we do not, it means that our basic criteria are still too narrow and must be expanded... In other words, simulative needs are negated by objective knowledge.

Knowledge, both of the external world and of ourselves, presumes the acceptance of limitations. In determining for myself who I am, I draw a boundary. If I define myself as a reasonable person, then by doing so I impose a boundary on myself that distinguishes me from an unreasonable person. Human beings are simultaneously characterised by movement towards previously unattained limits and by yearning to move beyond those limits. But this yearning is productive and creative, rather than destructive, only when it is regulated by the internal boundary that people establish for themselves.

To have a qualitatively new – nooindustrial – mechanism for satisfying needs, we will need a new reproductive link between production and consumption. Humanity's needs, like the knowledge needed to fulfil them, will be shaped not by the process of direct productive activity (from which human beings will have departed) but by human creative self-development. We may refer to these needs as *nooneeds*.

> *Nooneeds* are needs determined by the criteria of human reason, and by cultural imperatives that are based on the satisfaction of vital needs at a rational level and on the escalating role of higher-order needs and desires.

Such needs and such knowledge, will produce a distinct type of "directive" or "technical task" for the autonomously functioning "human-free" sphere of direct material production. By transmitting this directive to the sphere of nooindustry, humanity will ultimately receive the necessary means to satisfy its needs without direct involvement in their organisation or production. These tasks will be performed by a relatively autonomously functioning technosphere.

As the content of human activity and the way needs are satisfied change, so also will the criteria for determining the rationality of consumption change, along with the very structure of consumer needs. The criteria of economic rationality will be displaced by criteria of reasonable consumption, as defined by human culture (Figure 7).

Humanity's orientation towards purely economic criteria of success is destined to fade away in the long term, and not only because human needs that draw on non-monetary values and motives, and which often cannot even be defined in terms of cost vs. effect, are on the ascent. Rather, economic rationality is becoming more and more dubious due to its own negative consequences. Such rationality deforms the structure of human needs, trying to fit them all into the Procrustean bed of monetary symbols of success; it takes only those achievements that stimulate the growth of market-derived measurements of value to be "rational".

In fact, should the incremental growth of value-based wealth always be considered beneficial, and should everything without monetary value be renounced as "irrational"? Practice teaches us that market prices fail to capture (or capture in highly distorted form) a great many important factors of human existence and development. Take, for example, such fundamental points as the dynamics of existence of our natural environment. Can the loss of

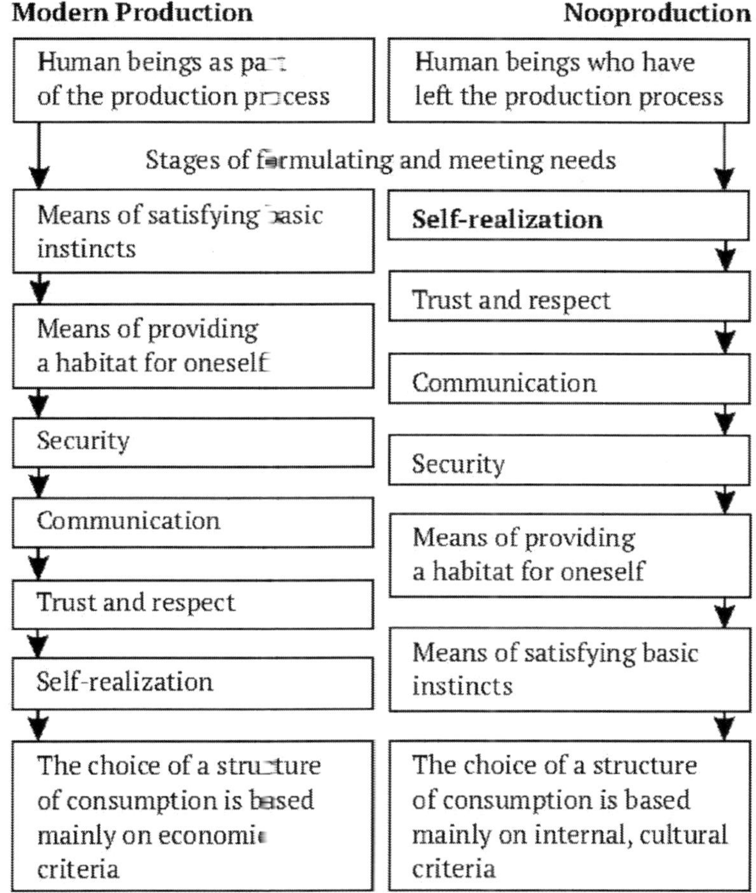

***Figure** 7. Mechanism of formulating and meeting needs in modern production and in nooproduction*

biodiversity and the extinction of species be expressed in monetary terms? Is it possible to financially measure the level of human culture or the value of human communication?

The marketisation of everything is an ideology that does not stop at regarding human communication as merely a factor in the growth of capital. But does this mean that we should put an end to everything that does not generate surplus profit, and pronounce everything that does generate such profit as inherently valuable? If this is the point of view we adopt, then we can definitively say which path humanity will choose at the civilisational crossroads discussed earlier. Any need or desire, however false or perverse, will be placed at the forefront of human activity, so long as its satisfaction pays well. Where there is demand, supply will follow.

Humanity cannot be held by the hand and led away from this path. Rather, we must make a conscious internal choice, formulating new criteria of rationality based on the expansion of our field of knowledge and on the wealth of culture that we have created. This will be a step towards transitioning to the nooindustrial stage of development, in which our reason will acquire sovereignty over the elemental socio-economic processes that currently subjugate humanity.

9

From Economy to Noonomy

9.1. Replacing Economic Rationality – with What?

Human society is appropriately reacting to the growth in its technological ability to meet its non-material/cultural/spiritual needs by changing the trend of civilisation's development. First and foremost, this means changing society's value systems, which requires changing the behaviour of the human beings that uphold social values. Even the scholarly world is beginning to take note of these phenomena at last, though often only superficially and without an immersive understanding of their true meaning. Why did Richard Thaler win the Nobel Prize for Economics in October 2017? He won it for his acknowledgment of the fact that the economic behaviour of most people (especially, of course, young people) is driven more and more by emotions rather than "rational" considerations.

Emotions are spiritual, immaterial, cultural value-bearing elements of the "average" person's overall structure of needs. This has always been the case. And humanity has always been driven to find ways of meeting its emotional needs, which dry economic rationality regards as far from trustworthy. The growth of Generation Z, who are much more advanced in this regard, is causing an increase in the importance of emotionally tinted needs within society's overall structure of needs.

This explains the evident fact that the decisions made by many "market actors" are less and less "rational" – within the framework of our current basic criteria of economic rationality, and from the perspective of dyed-in-the-wool apologists of the "animalistic" social reflection of humanity's biological essence. It will never occur to these market "generals" and "strategists" that the market is a vestige of the dying past, of the previous economic order, and that the observable (strengthening!) tendencies towards market "irrationality" are merely "sensors", detecting the rising transformation of humankind's preferences, as well as the decreasing importance of "rational marketplace behaviour" and of the marketplace itself.

The Nobel Laureate's work, mentioned above, bears witness to the fact that some economists are finally catching on to the fact that people do not live according to the "indifference curves" found in economics textbooks. In fact, economists are lamenting that human beings, as it turns out, are not even capable of living this way! You see, there are "limitations" to human rationality... But perhaps this is a limited perspective on the problem? Man is not a "stupid ox", limited even in his market rationality. Quite the contrary: man's capacities are richer than that, and he is capable of making decisions guided by diverse criteria, some of which are non-economic. The goals of production, and people's core needs in general, are and have always been formed outside the marketplace, even in the very most capitalistic and market-driven societies.

A corollary of the development of noosociety, and of the shift towards nooproduction and nooneeds, is the transition away from economic rationality towards a new type of rationality. The new nature of rationality, corresponding to a new way of defining the targets of development, is of principal importance. In this way, economics will be displaced by **noonomy**, which is premised on moving away from the paradigm of growth as guided by economic "rationality" (defined as increasing volume price indicators) towards a developmental paradigm based on reaching concrete goals and on meeting humanity's real needs.

Our *initial definition of noonomy* is that it is a noneconomic means of organising society's practical activity, oriented towards meeting humanity's concrete needs according to rational criteria defined by the development of knowledge and culture.

Both terminologically and substantively, the concept of noonomy echoes the idea of the noosphere.

The idea of the noosphere was first articulated by Edouard Le Roy (1870–1954), Pierre Teilhard de Chardin (1881–1955), and Vladimir Ivanovich Vernadsky (1863–1945). The development of this idea was spurred by Vernadsky's lectures on geochemistry, which he read at the Sorbonne from 1922–1923 to an audience that included Le Roy and Teilhard. Le Roy was the first to introduce the term "noosphere" into scientific discourse (Le Roy, 1927). The noosphere was examined in greater detail in Teilhard's and Vernadsky's work at the end of the 1930s.

Pierre Teilhard de Chardin understood the noosphere as a qualitatively new concentration of consciousness, forming a special spiritual sphere, a "thinking layer" that covers the Earth. In his view, the concentration of thought at a planetary scale is closely tied to the convergence of individual human minds and spirits, which, as evolution continues, will lead to the emergence of "the Earth's spirit" (Novikov, Rezhabek, 2017).

V.I. Vernadsky took a more natural-scientific approach to the idea of the noosphere, arguing that humankind's rational activity was becoming the main transformative force with respect to both the biosphere and the Earth's geological shell (the biogeosphere) (Vernadsky, 1997).

What we see in all these conceptions, however, is less a scientific theory than a range of interpretations of the uncontestable fact that the vital activity of human society and human beings, defined by their capacity for rational action, is becoming the decisive factor affecting not just humanity's own fate, but that of the Earth itself (or, at least, the Earth's surface).

The primacy of reason poses the inevitable problem of reason's own development. Which imperatives will govern *reason itself*? This, in turn, leads us to the question of how human society should be ordered to make sure that the power of reason is used reasonably, not merely as an effective instrument for satisfying our zoological instincts. The concept of the noosphere cannot answer this question.

The answer is provided by the notion of transitioning towards a noosocial order, toward *noosociety*. And the **noonomy** will be one of the basic elements of noosociety, serving as a kind of planet-wide "nomos" (meaning law, structure, order) that determines a non-economic mode of practical activity that meets human needs, using cultural imperatives to orient itself rather than economic rationality..

The term "noonomy" is derived from the Greek words "nous" (íïõò, reason) and "nomos" (íïìüò, order, law). Given that noonomy is defined in terms of practical management, it might seem logical to incorporate the Greek word "oikos" (ïĭêïò, home, household management) into this term. However, in the modern scientific tradition, terms formed from "oikos" – such as "economy" – are used to designate economic realities. Our intention is precisely to avoid identifying noonomy with any economic social structure.

Rather than mechanically combining the terms "noosphere" and "economy", we begin with an understanding of the Greek term "nous" as reason, resting upon the basic criterion of truth as a conscious, intrinsic value. Even in the eleventh century, Metropolitan Ilarion, in his "Sermon on Law and Grace", wrote: "He [the Lord] brought us unto the knowledge of the Truth".[1] In this sense, it would be deeply mistaken to equate the Greek word "nous" with its Latin analogue "ratio".

To call something *rational* means to say that it corresponds to certain criteria (but are these criteria reasonable?) The economy is always rational, but do rationally acting economic subjects always act *reasonably*? And are they capable of moving beyond the criteria imposed on them by the current economic system?

Noonomy offers a different way to evaluate practical activity and needs, based not on rationality, but on reason, on "noo-," beginning with understanding the true consequences of practical decisions and the true value of the needs being met. Consequently, we are not dealing with economics, nor with individuals who rationally maximise their satisfaction, but instead with a different way of formulating and meeting needs, which we might call *nooneeds*.

Meanwhile, the second half of the term noonomy – "nomos" – is an ancient concept that was used in mid-twentieth-century philosophy to designate the basic organisational principle of any space, the absolute law of existence of all things (Schmit, 2006). In other words, noonomy is an orderly way of life, a mode of satisfying needs and desires in a society which cherishes the "light of reason" and has no place for production or relations of production; no place for property or property relations; and no place for economics – a society in which economics is impossible. *Noonomy is a non-*

economic system for meeting noneeds. For this reason, it is wrong to speak of the "economy of the noosphere", just as it would be to refer to non-economic economies, non-predatory predators, and so on.

In a market economy, rationality is understood only in terms of maximising monetary gain. Of course, neoclassical economic theory rejects the charge of reducing economics to money, claiming that people are prone to try to maximise their receipt of all kinds of goods; in reality, though, these goods only come to economists' attention once they obtain a monetary value.

It is only relatively recently that the neoclassicists, under pressure from research in behavioural economics, have somewhat softened their position. They now acknowledge that human beings are not a pre-programmed calculator of profit and loss, that people can be moved by other motives, and that economic decisions can be influenced by noneconomic factors. Yet they integrate all this into their thinking by explaining it away as humanity's "limited rationality". "Genuine" rationality is still conceived in terms of measuring profit and loss, but human beings, alas, are imperfect, and their capacity for rational behaviour is limited by various circumstantial factors.

Indeed, for capitalist market economies, this attitude is largely (though not entirely!) justified, since it meets the basic criteria of capitalist rationality. However, changing the social conditions of production leads to changing the rational criteria of human behaviour (Figure 8). The transition to nooproduction and noonomy leads to the criteria of reason displacing the criteria of monetary gain, as it becomes rational to orient oneself towards satisfying concrete, reasonable needs and desires. The needs for knowledge, for trust, for social recognition, and for self-realisation become dominant over the rapacious need for material goods, and increasing the volume of goods one consumes ceases to be a basic goal of human activity – precisely insofar as this need has already been sated within reasonable limits.

These goals also inform the building of new mechanisms to regulate nooproduction, which will be oriented not towards "noo-GDP" or profit, but towards different indicators that reflect what we want to achieve. To meet this task, incoming flows of data, management information, material, and more will be formed. Such flows and control actions should be planned and programmed in the quantity, time, place, and frequency required to reach a desired result.

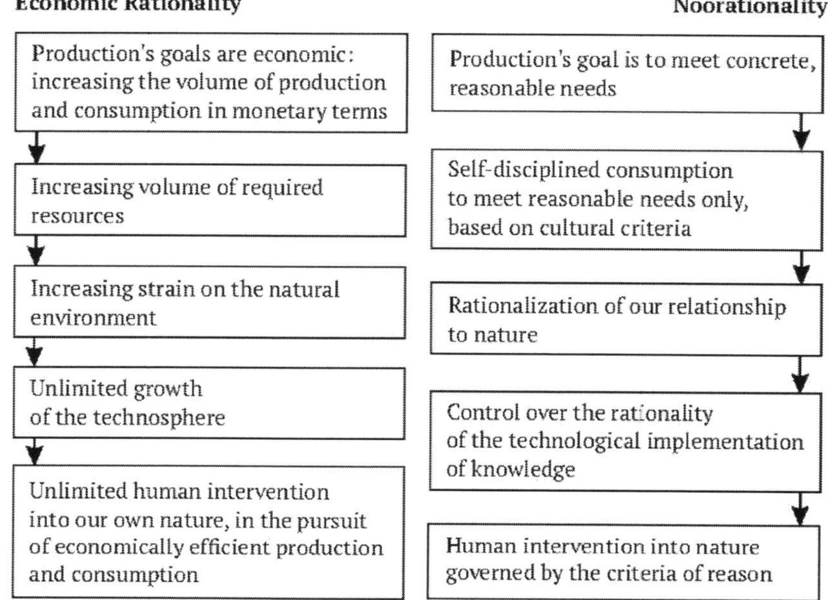

Figure 8. *Different types of rationality*

Thus, noonomy prioritises not the private pursuit of profit or other gain, to be obtained through the chaotic play of market forces, but the rational effort to *meet concrete needs that have been evaluated as reasonable*. Accordingly, the level at which these reasonable needs are to be met amounts to a concrete goal of production.

This assumes a specific programme of action that rises above the chaos of markets, giving production a more systematic, planned, orderly character. Such an approach cannot exclude the element of randomness, nor the freedom of individual choice unlimited by prescriptions imposed from above. It follows that the programme of production we develop must be significantly flexible and adaptive to changing circumstances and chance disturbances.

Next, this production programme must be corrected if anything goes awry, since the number of factors that the plan must account for is much greater than what we can analyze at our existing level of knowledge.

Let us take one (artificial) example. I host a TV programme and invite my colleague to the studio. There are two glasses on a table in front of us, and we have planned to drink water from them. Then we are told that we should come back to the show in one year and get 100 percent more than what we've already achieved – that is, two more glasses. Will we need these two extra glasses? No. But once they have been made, poured, and set up in the studio, our GDP will have doubled!

This is an artificial example of the absurdity that may, in its destructive force, bring all civilisation to the point of catastrophe if we continue down this path. In fact, this approach, which is often supported today by both business structures and various state programmes, does nothing but propagate simulative things. Previously this same approach was supported by both the Soviet system, in its own way, and the non-Soviet system, in a different way; both systems fostered the simulative orientation of development, "growth-oriented" economic development, without either "cutting out" the illusory and false components of society's structure of needs or conceptualising the goals of economic planning to this end.

For this reason, we may formulate the principle of the economy (still an economy) of the future, which is already dawning, as follows: *we do not need linear economic growth, we need economic development.* In this regard, growth is in fact a fiction.

Based on such a viewpoint, the indicators that are used today in attempts to quantitatively measure our happiness (that is, to "measure harmony with algebra")[2] should be consigned to the dustbin of history. We need other criteria – a new and different set of basic criteria – within which society's development might be qualitatively evaluated.

To this end, obviously, we must implement a more rational (according to our new basic criteria) mechanism of planning. This could take many forms; we will not insist on specific methods.

The main thing, the basic thing, is to satisfy people's real needs. It is crucial to comprehend and evaluate emergent non-simulative needs. If the market gives rise to an enormous quantity of fictive needs, what is to be done with them? Banning them would be stupid, not to mention impossible. But if we do not ban them, the economy may become a fiction, evaporating into hot air, and a decent future might be squandered.

What can we do under these conditions? Evidently, we need a system of thoughtful behaviours and stimuli, but not just economic ones: if we are transitioning to this new paradigm, then the economy as such, in its current, observable form, will no longer work. An "entirely new normal" will be emerging. Here, we must strive not to orient ourselves using traditional economic indicators, but instead to consider which individual and social needs we should satisfy: which of them, exactly, will propel us most effectively (with the fewest possible costs and conflicts, at the highest speed, etc.) towards NIS.2 and beyond?

Only once we are capable of meeting these needs can we say that "happiness has grown". That happiness has grown – not GDP, but happiness. This task is much less trivial than merely planning economic growth, as our economic authorities currently do (and for fairness' sake, we should acknowledge that this is true outside of Russia as well). However, if humanity grasps the importance of this task, and if the task becomes a conscious, real need, then in our view, the problem can be resolved even at our current scientific and technological level.

Hardly anyone will argue that happiness does not lie in inflating GDP, or profit, or greater accumulation of money. It is both funny and sad whenever someone seriously, not as a joke, proposes that "happiness does not lie in money, but in how much of it you have", or when people's disinclination to chase after money is attributed to their "limited rationality". After all, human rationality is not defined as the choice of exclusively economic "gains".

Humanity is more intelligent and rational than is supposed by these ideologues of quantitatively measured growth. People do not just need to acquire new phones, or another glass of water, or anything else; they need a glass of a certain quality, water with a particular taste, and "a certain quality" of life itself. Perhaps the truth is that two glasses are unnecessary: one is enough, so long as it is good, beautiful, comfortable, and contains clean water.

Precisely this small nuance – "is it good?" – is the most important thing. The behaviour that now gets called "irrational" amounts to picking just one of the two glasses, even though both are being imposed on us. Or, better still, we are told to smash the old glasses and throw them away, in favour of three new ones, "for the price of two". We could take two glasses – this would be more, this would be growth. Yet we choose just one glass, because we like it more. We like it not for any transcendental reason, nor because the glass is some illusory thing, but because there are internal parameters we use to make a judgment: size, for example (perhaps we choose a cup because our finger fits through the handle), or because we rationally perceive and evaluate some aspect of the object as beautiful.

In fact, this is a different kind of rationality, a different kind of knowledge, a different kind of reason. In fact, our reason, our rationality, is far more wide-reaching and richly endowed than the economic boundaries within which today's economic paradigm tries to enclose us.

Relatedly, we may observe that even in today's world – a world of developed market economies, shot through with narrow economic rationality – a significant proportion of goods are distributed for free. This fact points to an important tendency: the farther we go, and the more society's transition to the next age of industry (regulating the value of the products and services we produce) accelerates, the more goods will be freely available.

For this reason, it is time for us to leave the paradigm of economic growth behind and start making use of "growth-oriented" parameters only for subordinate purposes. It is time to include social consciousness in the formulation of our economic model and of new conceptions of civilisational, economic, and social development. This is because economics and society are inseparably linked. Long ago, during Soviet times, people talked about "socio-economic development"; I would prefer to speak of "economico-social development". But what is development? It is the gradual rejection of everything that creates today's simulative economy. This is, first and foremost, a transition in our "economic minds".

This is why *measuring society's development exclusively according to narrow markers such as GDP or other quantitative macroeconomic indicators, which are not equivalent to society itself*, is inadequate and even unscientific. We must find other parameters and establish fitting goals for economic planning. Where we should look for them is no secret: we should look for them by meeting people's genuine needs. That is, we should make judgments not according to purely physical methods of measurement, but through qualitative measures: surveys, focus groups, and other such indirect research methods. Nowadays, new technologies – "big data" – provide instruments for this type of analysis. It is time to move from the arithmetic of trivial addition to "calculus," even though the latter is more complicated.

At one point, intellectuals belonging to the Club of Rome articulated the idea that we must limit economic growth in order to prevent ecological catastrophe. Intelligent people! Of course, what they meant was slightly different: they were proposing to reduce our impact on the biogeosphere by lowering consumption. We can agree that limiting consumption may to some extent (though not for certain!) reduce our environmental footprint, but our position differs in principle: we must reduce consumption of simulacra, while more fully satisfying genuine needs.

Economics, which focuses on quantitative measurements and on the creation of ever-newer energies, products, and things without considering their genuine necessity, is leading us down a dead-end path. Humanity needs a different economy. Or rather, a different "-nomy" altogether, no longer an economy, corresponding to the needs of the world that is our home.

Recall the alter-globalisation movement's famous slogan: "People, not Profit".[3] In the twenty-first century, this has basically become the main slogan of worldwide social forums.[4]

From a nooperspective, this is an entirely positive slogan. Not because its proclaimers are do-gooders or "revolutionaries": the right tone for this slogan would not be for revolution, but against it, advocating gradual, evolutionary, orderly, and reasonable development. The theoretical platform outlined in this book perceives the proper meaning of this slogan with crystal clarity: money is nothing but an intermediary, so it must inevitably recede, while humanity is of principal importance. Therefore – "people, not money".

9.2. A Non-Economic Mode for Regulating Practical Activity

The shaping of a non-economic modes of practical activity will occur as we move from today's economic order towards NIS.2, and through NIS.2 to noonomy.

Here we can distinguish two stages of the process of historical movement. *The first stage* involves the development of *"technologies of trust"*, making it possible for economic relationships between people (within which satisfaction of needs takes place) to involve collaboration without an intermediary (monetary or otherwise). This is the basis for "compressing" the economic forms of human activity, the economic institutions that mediate the link between production and consumption.

The second stage involves the disappearance of labour effort itself as the mediating link between human beings and the satisfaction of their needs (Figure 9). The Old Testament's maxim – "By the sweat of your brow you will eat your food" – will recede into the past. Thus, both the nature of human activity and the means of satisfying human needs will both fundamentally change, becoming non-economic. In a certain sense, humanity will return to "paradise", approaching the Absolute. Or, to put it in another way, humanity will enter Marx's "realm of freedom".

During the first stage, then, we remain within the sphere of economics and production relations, but with technologies already emergent that can minimise today's world of economic relations. "Technologies of trust", plus accelerating overall technological progress, will constrict the overblown sphere of intermediaries, provision of transaction operations, etc.

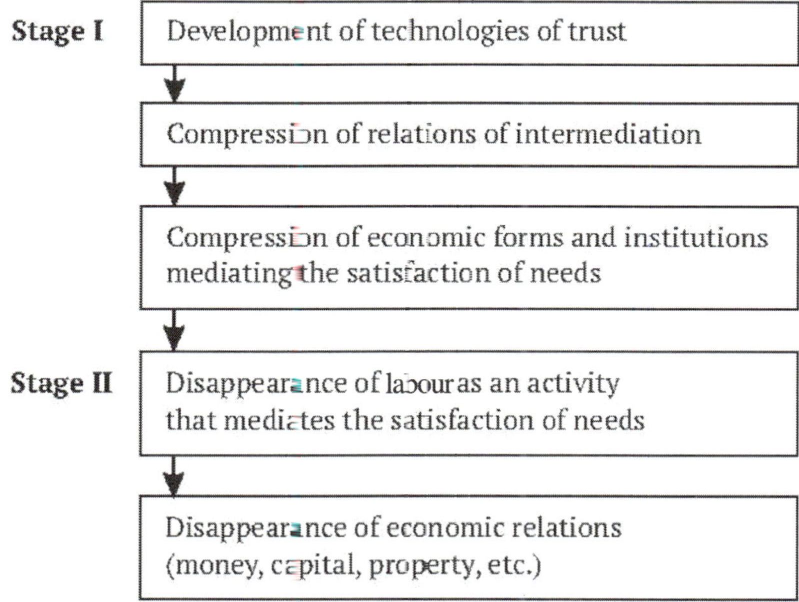

Figure 9. *Two stages of movement towards noonomy*

At the second stage, the need for people to serve as mediators for the satisfaction of other people's needs disappears entirely. To put it crudely, neither the baker nor the shop salesman will meet our need for bread; rather, this need will be met by the bakery, all by itself. The same applies to masses of other professions. Interaction between people will continue only in the process of creative activity, the process of discovering new knowledge and "transmitting" it to the technosphere, implementing it in new technologies.

But even before the formation of nooproduction, *creative activity that implements knowledge in new technologies will effectively change our collective mode of acquisition.*

The substantial difference between the acquisition of knowledge and the acquisition of material products consists in the fact that knowledge, once it has been obtained, can never be "recovered" or "extracted" away from its new owners. With material objects, everything is more straightforward: they can be taken and then given back. But knowledge cannot be "irrevocably" returned.

But the expanded application of knowledge influences the acquisition of material products as well as intellectual ones. With the development of new knowledge and new technologies, the easier, cheaper, and simpler obtainment of material goods brings with it less and less need for intellectual private property – in fact, less and less need for property itself as an institution; not for knowledge, but specifically for property.

What future is there for the information-based, "knowledge-based" aspect of production? However hard we might try to limit the use of the results of scientific research with artificial rules, sooner or later these results will "seep through", manifesting themselves in social production and the social order to form new social conditions. In other words, sooner or later, our struggle with scientific research will come to an end. But right now, we are at the first stage of the formation of a long and great transition.

On one hand, this is the beginning of profound comprehension of the value of knowledge as the future's most important resource. On the other hand, today's prevailing social relations are founded on private means of appropriation of the results of social production and competition over the resources needed for production. Consequently, they give rise to those means of "protecting" intellectual property that temporarily "prolong" currently existing social relations with respect to knowledge, taking the relations that have emerged in the "material" sphere and disseminating them within the sphere of knowledge. Of course, this stage will be overcome with the development of NIS.2.

Even during NIS.2, tendencies will emerge that lead to the transformation – and even the withering away – of the economic forms of human activity. This is especially visible in activities that involve the acquisition of new knowledge. But what will replace these economic forms? Won't the sphere of production remain, though without humanity's direct participation? Won't the sphere of humanity's creative, "knowledge-producing" and "culture-producing" activity, entirely uninfluenced by social relations, also remain?

Here numerous general questions arise. How will people organise their influence on human-free production? How will the goals and orientation of production be decided? What aspects of production must be managed and regulated? After all, though the sphere of production will exist outside of human relations, it will not exist independently of people: no less than before, the reproduction of human life will depend on it!

At this point, human development confronts a dilemma. Either society will be unable to direct the capacities unleashed by the technological revolution toward its own improvement and will be captivated by false goals and values, exacerbating the negative tendencies of contemporary civilisation to the point that humanity loses its very essence – which would indicate that we will not enter noosociety or transition to noocivilization. Or, alternately, humanity will successfully enact a noo-approach to redesigning its current civilisational attitudes.

Nooproduction, though it will be carried out independently from human beings and from society, will remain subordinate to society in its goals and tasks. Precisely the sphere of setting goals, formulating goals and tasks, and regulating the accessible means within the technosphere for realising these tasks – all this will remain within the purview of human social relations. Autonomous techno-beings, functioning within the sphere of nooproduction and capable of self-development, will nevertheless depend on human society, which will define the limits of their self-development and block any developmental directions that are not of social use, pointing the functioning and development of nooproduction in directions that are necessary for the development of humanity itself (Figure 10).

This will involve incomparably more profound shifts than merely, for example, taking account of ecological limits when making economic decisions. It will mark the beginnings of qualitative transformations in the

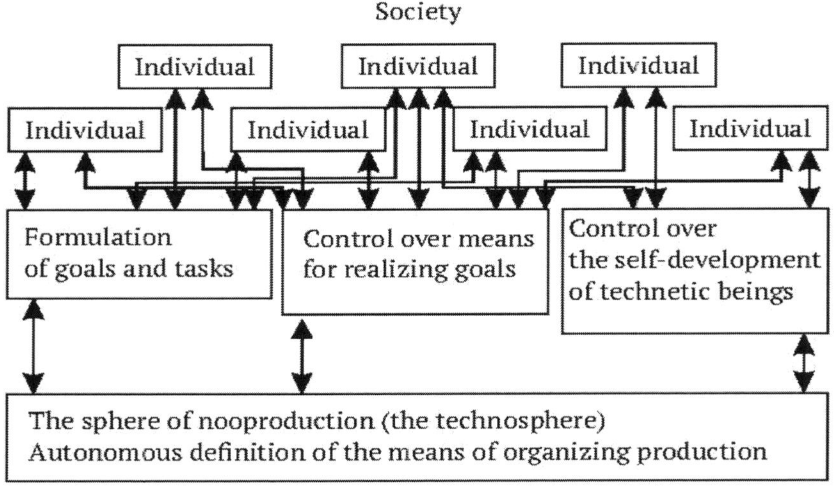

Figure 10. *People's relations within the process of regulating nooproduction*

content of production, in the needs, values, and motivations of human behaviour, and naturally also in socioeconomic relations and institutions. Let us repeat that the basis for this will be created by qualitatively new technologies that convert the semi-utopian modalities of the twentieth century into the practically realisable tasks of the present.

We are not remotely inclined to idealise either the theory of the noosphere or the phenomenon that is now emerging before our very eyes – that is, noosociety, along with its distinct forms of production and its new practical-material relations, which are no longer economic in the strict sense of the word. For Vernadsky, the noosphere is not intentionally created; it is an inevitable product of human society at a particular stage of its self-development. In itself, the noosphere *does not guarantee* the "kingdom of truth". Therefore, the presence of the noosphere already poses the question as to *precisely which* imperatives of reason will prevail within it.

Hence arise the questions and challenges to which we must respond, such as the question of the *social form of nooproduction.* Which imperatives will govern both the production of the material and spiritual conditions of human life, and the social relations that regulate this production? What determines the choice of such imperatives? To a significant extent, the condition of the noosphere as a whole will depend on the answers to these questions.

We have already given a first, approximate response, emphasising the necessity for cultural imperatives to come to the fore in shaping needs and regulating practical activity oriented towards satisfying needs. We designated the social form of such regulation using the term 'noonomy', which we may now define in greater detail.

> *Our expanded definition of noonomy* is that it is a non-economic social form of human practical activity, aimed at satisfying *nooneeds* (especially those involving the development of human personality) at a particular developmental stage: that of *nooproduction*, which is the form of production that characterises humanity's exit from direct labour activity ("human-free production"), as well as management of the technosphere as a sphere that is external to humanity but dedicated to realising the potential of human cognition.

The means of governing social relations will become different, and governance itself will take on a new meaning, more consensual and different from what it is today. Even though we may continue to call this system of governance a "state", it will be a qualitatively different type of state than it was before. The main difference between the state in economic society and the state of the future is that today's state, like the ones before it, primarily regulates economic relations. In the future, economic relations will disappear along with the economy itself, but other types of relations will remain, which will require their own kind of regulator.

I believe that there ought to be institutions of social regulation, and that the anarchist ideal of complete self-regulation is untenable. We need a system of relations that allows us somehow to learn about others' interests and juxtapose them with our own. We need basic criteria for making decisions. The basic criteria I have in mind are cultural: culture's criteria constantly evolve as development proceeds. This is to say that we need appraisals of some kind about how quickly to develop, what path to take, and so forth and so on.

These appraisals will amount to a certain means for reaching consensus, a consensus form of social government. Since society is constituted by different interests, people's individual interests exist alongside shared social interests. As these interests develop further, the need for consensus-based regulation will also develop – but now according to cultural rather than economic criteria, based on the power of human reason: noocriteria.

It stands to reason that social bonds will remain, since these are what embed human beings within a community. But will such bonds retain the character of social relations, that is, relations between people as elements of a social structure, as representatives of social classes and social or professional groups, etc.? We may suppose that these types of social relations, too, will wither away: noonomy will dispense with the foundation for the separation of people into classes and professions (along with the withering away of professions themselves), and generally with divisions according to social status.

Moreover, provision of the material conditions of existence will itself cease to be directly performed by human hands. Marx's prognosis about the displacement of human beings from the process of material production will come true. Humanity will influence production not through manual effort, but through the power of knowledge.

9.3. Human Society and the Autonomous Technosphere

In order to comprehend the social arrangement of production in noosociety – that is, noonomy itself – let us briefly review the structure of production.

The production process is the process of manufacturing products, that is, the transformation of natural substances for the purposes of meeting human needs. The most essential elements of the production process are *human labour, original materials (including raw materials), technologies, and the organisation of production.*

> All production rests upon the following four basic points, which can be most easily articulated in the form of four questions:
> *What are our ingredients?* (Original and raw materials).
> *What are our instruments?* (Tools and technology).
> *How are we working?* (The content and character of labour).
> *How will we organise our work?* (Organisation and regulation of production).

These elements change as their knowledge-density increases, changing the basis of the production process, which further influences (or is reflected in) society and its socioeconomic institutions. In turn, social relations and institutions influence the elements of the production process, either facilitating or hindering their development.

The interaction of these components in the process of manufacturing the products we need is of utmost importance. The current developmental trend towards the increased role of knowledge in all components of human activity within the production process (in tools and technologies, in the labour process itself, in the organisation and management of the production process) has already been noted repeatedly in the previous pages, along with the corresponding trend for the relative share of material resources consumed in production to decrease. So, what will become of the social form of production as we transit to the noosocietal stage?

The form of productive organisation based on knowledge-intensive technologies will change significantly even in NIS.2, since it will directly depend on the character of the technologies it uses, shedding production's former "factory" form (the management of groups of people that attend to systems of machines). Since people will be increasingly displaced from the process of direct production, a special role will be played by forms of human social interaction – *within the bounds* of the production process but oriented towards regulating production.

The development of nooproduction will trigger an even more significant shift. In the new world, the production process' form of organisation will cease to play any special role, since this form will automatically arise from the self-development of the nootechnological space without any direct participation by human beings.

However, the transition to "human-free production" presents us with a highly complex task, though not from the vantage point of technological problems.

As humanity develops, we have gradually become more and more distant from nature, placing an intermediary between nature and ourselves, namely, labour activity, which relies on technologies whose progress is based on ever-increasing knowledge about nature. The general developmental trend of human society was to progressively reduce our direct dependence on nature through the development of the technosphere.

Humanity tried to progressively reduce the risks that nature subjected us to in our primitive state, always striving to move as far as possible away from a natural world that posed us every imaginable threat. Humanity warmed itself, clothed itself, protected itself with walls, housed itself, armed itself against everything that threatened it, created stockpiles of resources to survive natural cataclysms and changes in its external environmental circumstances, and so on. By distancing/distinguishing ourselves from nature, but never forgetting to gather its fruits, we reduced the entropy of our existence, the risk of being frozen, eaten, crushed by a falling tree...

Humanity used more and more refined means to process and "reshape" natural resources to fulfil our own needs. At the same time, we spatially separated ourselves from our natural surroundings, erecting houses and entire cities with many millions of inhabitants and artificial life-supporting systems, practically to the point of complete separation from natural conditions.

> Saudi Arabia is among the top global consumers of fresh water per capita (926 cubic metres per person per year) despite the fact that only 9% of its water comes from "natural", renewable sources. Water pipes extend through the desert, from city to city, for hundreds of kilometres. Meanwhile, Persian Gulf states like Bahrain, Qatar, and Kuwait primarily use desalinated water (accounting for 69%–79% of their overall consumption).[5]

In fact, the whole history of the development of our civilisation is a history of our separation from nature. Here we must acknowledge the dualism of the situation. Human beings, having realised ourselves as personalities and thereby spiritually separated ourselves from the surrounding world, have nonetheless remained part of nature – indeed, precisely this "separation" leads us to a further separation between "spiritual" man and "natural" or "biological" man! This gulf can take the dramatic form of reckless incursions into nature, both external nature (environmental transformation) and our own (interference in humanity's biological essence).

We are now approaching a threshold at which humanity is not just separated from nature, but ready to separate itself also from "second nature", from the artificial world created by our own hands.

The sixth technological mode, based on NBICS-convergent technologies, is already creating sufficient preconditions for transitioning to nooproduction, which signifies *the final separation of the technosphere from human society.* Separation not in the sense that humanity will lose all links with the technosphere or cease to reap its rewards, but in the sense that humanity's direct participation will no longer be necessary for the technosphere to function. The link between noosociety and nooproduction will remain, but now as a kind of "bottleneck"; a channel of interaction rather than the embeddedness of one within the other.

At the same time, this separation is quite dialectical. Not only does humanity nearly separate itself from the surrounding world, including the technosphere, through knowledge and the comprehension of natural forces (and social forces); to a certain extent, and precisely due to this separation from the technosphere, humanity returns to nature. Henceforth, rather than "subjugating nature" in the traditional sense, humanity turns natural processes towards its own ends – but not at the cost of blind encroachment upon nature without consideration for the harm we do to it.

No, it stands to reason that "the struggle with nature", in the sense of making nature serve human ends, will remain. But this struggle will become more "technological", more thoughtful, more reliant on cognition of nature, thereby making humanity's interaction with nature (including our own) ever more harmonious rather than mutually destructive. What was once a genuine fight will become a kind of partnership. This conversion of natural processes into technological processes, which relies on knowledge and the new values and cultural imperatives produced by knowledge, can harmonise the links in the chain running from the natural environment (biosphere), to production, to humanity.

Now, having separated itself from its natural basis, humanity need not act like a predator and force its way into nature. This implies, among other things, a more careful and tactful attitude towards human essence itself, with limits placed on thoughtless incursions into the human organism to reconstruct it based on fleeting impulses of the present moment.

It is precisely on this basis that Vernadsky's theories about the noosphere (which we understand as the sphere of activity of "noohumanity") will be realised; without the harmonisation and sublation of the conflict described above, these ideas are unrealisable.

9.4. The Role of Humanity in Noonomy

Thus, the new technological mode's achievements will be able to genuinely lead humanity, for the first time ever, beyond the boundaries of direct material production. The production that will be established on this foundation can already be called nooproduction, in the sense that human reason and knowledge will serve as both its defining resource and its main regulator.

Karl Marx already foresaw this future in the second half of the nineteenth century, presciently discovering it in the tendency for the role of human knowledge to grow in the development of industrial productio.[6] But only now, and for the first time, can we more or less exactly locate the concrete technological basis that will truly allow humankind to exit material production, while remaining (in Marx's terms) its "watchman and regulator".

Such a fundamental shift in society's technological base will bring with it a no less fundamental shift in social relations. If humanity exits the direct process of production, then the relations created by humanity's productive activity will disappear as well. Productive relations will gradually disappear, and production will lose the form of economic activity. Economics and the economy will become a thing of the past.

Of course, nature abhors a vacuum. Though humanity will leave production, the latter will remain, as before, the key material condition for human life, and people will find some way to establish social relations among themselves in order to regulate the production process. But since these relations will not, in themselves, be directly included in the production process, *the results will no longer be economic, but noonomy: not social relations within the framework of production that is carried out directly by humans, but relations concerning nooproduction, which develops without direct human participation but is regulated and directed by human reason.*

Factually speaking, what this means is that practical activity that meets human needs will no longer primarily be defined using economic criteria, since needs will themselves take on noneconomic form. Moreover, the economy, as the sphere of economic relations between people concerning production and the exchange of products, will generally shrink to the point of disappearing entirely. Not, let us add, because production's raw material or energy costs will cease to be important, but because humanity will no longer be directly incorporated into productive activity, meaning that the corresponding relations between people will no longer emerge.

Humanity will depart from direct production, making the technetic entities spawned by the technosphere do all production's necessary work...

The economy will become superfluous. Practical and productive processes will become a thing-in-itself that no longer interests us. People will move beyond the boundaries of this process.

In this case, it is most important to note the following principle: unlike all previous stages, the essence of the noo-stage of civilisational development is that individuals no longer relate to one another within the process of material production; rather it is two differently constructed civilisational spheres that enter into relations with one another – production (nooproduction, confined to the technosphere) and human society (Figure 11).

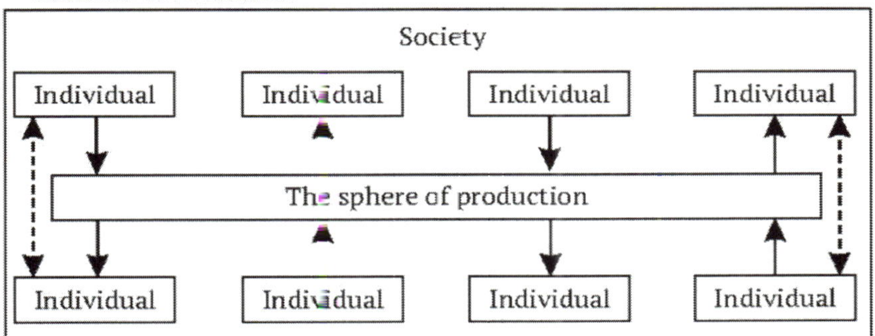

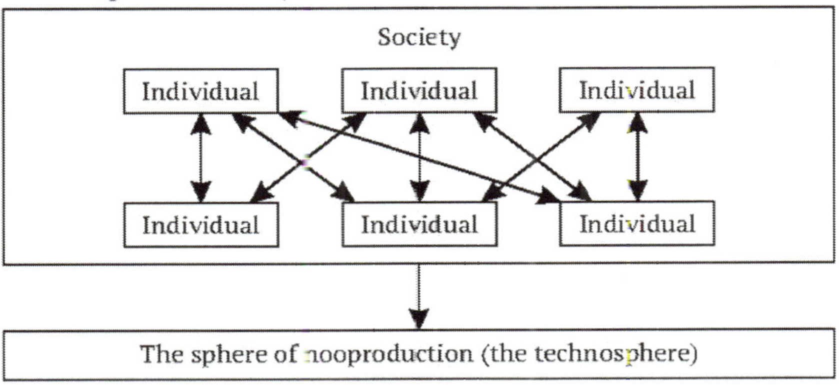

Figure 11. *The transformation of civilisation's design during the transition to noonomy*

Thus, the structure of human civilisation – civilisation at large, not just society – will change in principle. Society here stands out as one isolated part of human civilisation, since, for the first time in history, the technosphere will distinguish itself (in a certain sense) from human society. Of course, society and the technosphere did not directly coincide before either, but previously, people constructed their social ties with one another according to their direct incorporation into the functioning of the technosphere. Now, by contrast, people will relate with human-free material production as its "watchman and regulator".

In this light, the question emerges as to what human activity will look like. I propose that humans will "administer activity", which presupposes that humanity constantly and consciously thinks about what it is doing, an approach which must become a way of life rather than a mere skill. Just as technology transfer will become an inextricable and ceaseless element of life rather than a mere episodic "introduction" of new technologies, humanity's way of life must come to incorporate our administration of ourselves and of society through each person's interaction with everyone else.

But does this mean the disappearance of production relations between people? Yes, as people exit the sphere of direct production, the relations of direct production will disappear. But what about relations between people defined by their influence on the sphere of "human-free production", determining the developmental path of such human-free production? Presumably, those relations will exist, won't they?

Yes, but these will no longer be the specifically economic relations that we already know, and their role will resemble the roles of other types of activity that are entirely unrelated to production. Meanwhile, the specifically economic forms of social life will gradually wither away.

One of the key economic forms – property relations – will progressively lose their significance (due to the increasing accessibility of goods and the decreased value of owning them). First, this will occur within the sphere of people's practical and productive activity; later, property relations will completely depart from all people's social relations. With the disappearance of property, the economy as such will also disappear, since relationships of appropriation and alienation constitute the basis of economics.

Why will the significance of property plummet? Because the value of what property gives us will decrease, since anyone will be able to obtain any non-simulative thing that they need – and the farther we progress towards

NIS.2, the more easily, simply, quickly, etc., this will be possible. Anyone, without effort, will be able to catch a fish from the pond. Not only without effort, but also without the advantages obtained through labour, namely, the appropriation of its results as property.

Our technological level is gradually approaching a line which, when crossed, will allow all our rational needs to be satisfied more and more cheaply. Why cheaply? Because, in effect, everything humanity has done, all that humanity has procured for the realisation of its needs, was obtained through a) natural resources, which have no monetary cost (!), and b) knowledge, obtained and "expended" so that original natural resources (not to mention "non-natural" materials, which are really just "natural" materials that have been "polished" using knowledge!) can, with the "addition" of knowledge, be transformed into something else.

Thus, everything that humanity has done, all its technological conversions – all of this is knowledge. Everything new is obtained through added knowledge; there is nothing else to it. Besides, materiality is free, while the share of knowledge in produced products grows ever larger (due to the new stages of processing accumulated with every new product or "iteration" of an existing product). Products become more and more expensive, and they would grow "infinitely" expensive if knowledge were owned exclusively. But in fact, the nature of knowledge is that while it may be exclusive at the moment of its "appearance" in the world, it immediately begins to spread itself far and wide and, consequently, to grow cheaper. The more that the exclusivity of knowledge goes down, the cheaper knowledge becomes.

In today's terminology, this is the "distribution of costs" for "information products", based on an extreme case of increasing returns to scale due to the extremely low cost of duplicating and disseminating information (Arthur, 1996: 100–109). If "prices" begin to fall as we progress towards NIS.2, then it also becomes cheaper – ever more so – to "mine" products. In other words, what we have here resembles the economic concept of exponentially declining value. Hence, the meaning of property will also decline, as it will no longer "cost" anything!

Today, property consists of "materialised labour". A reserve of trade, for the satisfaction of future needs. Humankind began to appropriate goods as soon as it developed an "economic" conception of life: we need to have reserves, we need this and that, we need it for our family, we need to keep it from our neighbours; we need to carve out our own little piece, protect it from the rest of the world, and announce that we won't give it to anyone else. That is all "property" is: an element of the most predatory manifestation of human nature.

But in the future, goods will "materialise" without labour. Reserves will be unnecessary. What will then be the point of "property"? When property is unnecessary (precisely property as a reserve or stockpile, because, of course, noonomy means that anyone can get any non-simulative thing they need) then what could appropriation possibly mean? Why would there be any need to appropriate? The word "mine" will even vanish from our lexicon, in the sense that nothing will be "mine" any longer – it will be merely a part of the world that fulfills reasonable human needs without today's concept of "labour" as traditionally understood. So, it will be impossible to refer to my own mountain of goods; there will merely be a mountain of goods, pure and simple.

Not only will technological progress change people's social relations and their mode of interaction with the technosphere, but it will also impact human nature itself. The pause in human evolution caused by the cessation of the mechanism of natural (biological) selection, linked to the fact that the adaptive significance of human beings' natural traits has been evened out by their capacity to make use of technology, will probably soon come to an end. Human evolution that is not biological but properly "technological", will begin – not the evolution of the technosphere, nor merely the evolution of humanity's habitat, but rather the technological evolution of human essence itself.

Won't a unique form of "technological selection" then emerge to replace natural selection? This question is already emerging as we observe the broad incursion of artificial intelligence (AI) systems into human life. Though, at present, AI systems are mostly used in business applications, they are bound to penetrate other spheres as well – science, education, medicine, the social sphere... The interaction of AI systems with humanity in these spheres will lead, as its next step, to a new stage of human evolution.

One can imagine the transformation of human nature and humanity's conversion into a neo-biotechnological species. Such beings will be a product of the synthesis of, on one hand, humanity's directed evolution as a species due to biological decisions which do not infringe upon humanity's essence as biological beings, and, secondly, humanity's technetic evolution due to its "reconstruction" by non-biological technologies.

The history of the development of human civilisation is, at the same time, the history of the development of its technosphere: the "dead" world, whose technological "species" nonetheless undergo evolution in the same manner as the living world. This "dead world" also "lives" its own form of "life". This world includes the growth of a variety of technetic "species" and the formation of "technocenoses" – "habitats," "survival zones," "distribution zones," processes of "adaptation" and "acclimatisation" (Kudrin, 1981: 236–254) – as opposed to the narrowing diversity of biological species, the simplification of biotas, and the degradation of the biosphere as a whole.

Although, before the creation of AI, this "life" was animated by technology's creator – humanity – with the creation of AI it has become autonomous. AI technologies feature extremely high knowledge "content," including knowledge about how to "extract" and use new knowledge. This is why the question of "bookmarking" regulators ("commandments"?) within the tools used by AI, preventing unsanctioned implementation of knowledge that might harm humankind, is of principal importance. The development and constant improvement of such regulators should become one of humanity's most important tasks in the twenty-first century.

The evolution of the technosphere, and the techno-trends shaped by it, lead us to the question of the limits of civilisation's development – insofar as technological evolution is beginning to set the parameters of human evolution, both in terms of evolution's biological, "material" basis and in terms of its social qualities. The phenomenon of artificial "selection" is emerging (less in the sense of a struggle for existence than as the search for, and selection of, cultivated human qualities), which will become a factor in humanity's "technological evolution".

Technologies for "editing" the genome are becoming accessible, providing a means for "selecting" people even before their birth, along with technologies for embedding auxiliary technetic elements into our biological essence, which continues the process of "selection" after birth. Technologies for "rearing" people will also change, altering our genome with the goal of "touching up" our neurochemical mechanisms of regulating behaviour, to the point of various methods for influencing the consciousness of already fully formed human beings. Finally, even the means of "producing people" may change: the first steps are already being taken towards technologies for artificially growing highly organised living organisms outside of mothers' bodies...

All these emergent technological possibilities, "doors", and "windows", through which we can glimpse movement towards a new civilisation (still human?), must be evaluated both in terms of the risk of civilisational crisis and from the vantage point of realising the prospects of noospheric society. If we adopt a "noo-evaluation" of these trends, we must clearly perceive the contradictions that we may confront on the road to the future.

Soon we will need to bypass crises stemming from the misuse of technological interference into human essence. We cannot even precisely foretell what consequences such careless interference might bring about, or what varieties of no-longer-human species it might generate, or what relations will take shape between these species.

We can predict the appearance of a new type of social inequality – based no longer on property, but on unequal access to knowledge and unequal ability to master it. And now we should ask: how can the problems of such new inequality be resolved? Won't some people fight to turn their intellectual abilities into a new basis for social privilege, and won't an "anti-intellectual" wave emerge as a reaction to this?

The society of the future will be able to cope with these conflicts insofar as knowledge becomes the primary resource of production, and insofar as broader access to the mastery of knowledge, and to creative activity based on knowledge, becomes the necessary condition of society's development. In this light, even leftover inequality of property will not be a basis for social privilege, but instead the object of efforts to develop the creative abilities of every person as fully as possible.

Of course, we must not forget that *both knowledge and technology can be used to humanity's detriment and turned towards our self-destruction.* But knowledge and technology are also capable of ensuring humanity's *transcendence of all objective limits; the guaranteed resolution of problems that appear insoluble; and the ability to overcome barriers that seem insurmountable.*

Notes

1 Sermons and Rhetoric of Kievan Rus', trans. Simon Franklin (Cambridge, MA: Harvard Ukrainian Research Institute, 1991) 14.

2 The author quotes a famous line from Alexander Pushkin's short 1830 play, Mozart and Salieri – *Translator's note.*

3 Simic S. Need, not greed / The Guardian. Thu 25 Jan 2007 22:29 GMT https://www.theguardian.com/commentisfree/2007/jan/25/post997.

4 See, e.g., World Social Forum 2016, Global Justice Now, https://www.globaljustice.org.uk/event/world-social-forum-2016/; Praful Bidwai, "A Great Movement Is Born: Global Justice Movement Finds Fertile Ground at the Asia Social Forum", Focus on the Global South, January 28, 2003, https://focusweb.org/a-great-movement-is-born-global-justicemovement-finds-fertile-ground-at-the-asia-social-forum/.

5 Achieving a sustainable water sector in the GCC: Managing supply and demand, building institutions // PwC Strategy& Published: May 8, 2014. URL: https://www.strategyand.pwc.com/media/fi le/Strategyand_Achieving-a-sustainable-water-sector-in-the-GCC.pdf.

6 Marx noted the tendency for "the transformation of the production process from the simple labour process into a scientific process, which subjugates the forces of nature and compels them to work in the service of human needs" (Marx, 1993: 700); that is, production's transformation from labour into "experimental science, materially creative and objectifying science" (Marx, 1993: 712).

10

The Path Towards Nootransformation

Everything said above leads us to the conclusion that movement towards noonomy is an objective tendency determined by transformations in the material conditions of production. However, human civilisation faces many problems and contradictions that will have to be overcome along the way, and we will have to pass through the crossroads of civilisation by making the right choice.

This choice determines whether our society will embark along the road to transforming its system of social relations into noosociety and its economic subsystem into noonomy. If we do not surmount the looming crisis of our civilisation, the problems that are now menacing us threaten to grow into catastrophes.

Society should approach this civilisational crossroads, not just having armed itself with knowledge of its developmental prospects, nor merely having worked out genuine criteria for making such a collective and public decision, but also drawing on necessary material and technological prerequisites. By this, we refer to the creation of the fundamentals of the second generation of new industrial society.

If we turn from general reflections on the transition to NIS.2 to specific consideration of the prospects that await Russia on this path, we must begin with a clear understanding of Russia's place in the system of global relations. It makes sense here to transit to a broader frame of analysis, using the approach of world-systems theory and the achievements of geopolitical economy (on the world-systems approach, see Wallerstein, 1982; Amin, 1976; see also Desai, 2013).

More and more in the modern world, we observe the potential long-term subjugation of countries that do not manage to possess advanced technologies within about thirty to forty to fifty years of their appearance, due to the lack of institutions and instruments allowing them to establish technological parity or even – at least in certain sectors – become technological leaders.

In that case, if the current trend of separation into "centre" and "periphery" continues, countries will be sorted into two groups. One group, it follows, will be the "productive" countries; that is, the new capitalists, figuratively speaking, who possess the capital of the future, namely, knowledge and technology. The other group will be the "service" countries, working for their "crust of bread", for better or for worse.

This pattern is combined with the current trend of social Darwinism and the "bio-paradigm" of social development. We have already discussed above where this trend might lead. Overcoming it is an urgent task, a collective societal requirement for global civilisation. Relatedly, there must also be a counterweight to this trend, at least in the form of an alternative for the thinking part of humankind.

The Soviet Union might have become such an alternative to a certain extent if it had preserved itself and gained access to modern technology. But due to gigantic, unresolved internal and external problems, the USSR disintegrated without changing the course of world history in this way. Yet the continuation of our current form of "development", without an alternative, promises the collapse of civilisation (Amin, 2016).

Thus, when discussing Russia, it would be desirable to view the idea of its industrial renaissance not just as a way to avoid falling behind in economic competition with the leaders of the world-system (though this, too, is quite important during the stage of transition to NIS.2!), but as the creation of an alternative model that could bring about the world-system's transformation in line with a nooversion of development.

Where do things stand right now? How prepared is Russia to play this role?

Our current situation is such that we fully risk falling into the second category of countries, even though we have the prerequisites we need to avoid falling behind. Look at our Soviet and subsequent Russian background; the mentality of our people; Russia's abilities in many areas; and the fact that we could obtain substantial income from our current natural resources and make well-directed investments. We have a decent scientific, industrial, and technological background, and we are capable of ending up in the first group of countries so long as we ensure our advancement towards NIS.2.

If we do not follow this path, then there will be nothing to discuss, and we entirely risk ending up in the lagging group of "service countries". We must clearly consider, understand, and recognise this fact.

Our country can claim sophisticated technological achievements, even on an incontestably global scale, and tangible improvements have begun in the real economy's high-tech industrial sectors. In recent years, after the government announced a "crusade" for a digital future, we have turned to economic digitalisation. But overall, the main thing is missing; there is no clear movement towards re-industrialisation or the rapid modernisation of our economy.

For many years, we have discussed the necessity of *re-industrialising on a qualitatively new technological foundation* – the foundation of our new economic model, that is, the necessity of restoring industry's preeminence in a qualitatively new way. Why do we talk about this so much? Because a new wave of technological transformations is coming, a new industrial and technological revolution, and its leaders will be those who manage to ride this "ninth wave".

Relatedly, I must emphasise the very important fact that those in the West who are now studying the problem of development are also carrying out economic re-industrialisation in their own countries – even despite the substantially higher standard of Western industry!

Right now, *a "window of opportunities" has opened for Russia*, connected to the fact that the world capitalist economy, in its current model, is slowing down qualitative, revolutionary shifts in its own technological foundation. The advancement of sixth-paradigm technologies looks impressive, but these technologies are still quite far off from transforming the face of modern production. The world is evidently moving towards a technological revolution, but while this movement is happening quickly, its tempo is inadequate and its rhythm is ragged.

A small amount of time still remains: the modern economy's core trend of chasing after economic results is largely oriented towards not technological progress, but the return of huge profits at the expense of inflating financial bubbles. Up until this point, the world has been developing according to the following model: "We'll eat more, we'll drink more, and we'll cheat everyone on the financial market".

Of course, betting on a technological breakthrough does not prevent us from actively exporting gas during the present stage. Only fools would decline to make use of their advantages. But the income obtained from these exports must be deliberately invested in our economy's scientific-educational-industrial component.

As we shape the development strategy of our national economy, we must consider some basic tendencies of NIS.2, particularly the relative decline in industry's "raw-materials-density". We must clearly understand that in the coming decades, global demand for traditional raw materials, resources, and energy – hitherto the basis of the Russian economy – will tend to fall, not rise. This is inevitable given the dramatic rise in the role of industrial knowledge and technologies, and the rates at which these are obtained, mastered, implemented in the real sector, developed, etc. Natural resources will mean much less. That said, we not only "can" but must use our natural resources!

It is the changing proportion of materials-density versus "knowledge-density" in productive output that allows us to expect that the country we pass on to future generations will not be stripped of natural resources or strewn with spreading, cancerous waste dumps. But to this end, Russia must acquire advanced technologies.

As I have stated, we have no choice. Or rather, we do have one, but it is quite harsh: either we wrest our way out of our current position and into the ranks of the world's technological leaders within the next twenty years, or we will become part of the "periphery". In the latter case, we will "spoon-feed" the fruits of production, created through barbaric exploitation of our natural and human resources, to more developed countries.

To this end, *the Russian economy's systemic qualities need to change*, and quite substantially. There should be a transition to long-term strategic economic management, medium-term indicative plans and programmes based on scientific prognoses, and active industrial policy. The state should sponsor businesses' investment in R&D and technological refitting. It should also guarantee a stable and supportive tax situation and accessible and comfortable lending programmes for the real sector, especially its high-tech fields. Admittedly, this system might foster a moderate degree of social differentiation: still, citizens' income should mostly depend above all on their real contribution to the economy.

Bearing in mind our goals, we can see that our current economic model contains practically no "escalators" or "elevators" that might boost our upward progress – just a few small movements. We are seriously late. For good reason, the economic community, and even the President, are now discussing the need to create a new model for turning our economy around. The old model has exhausted itself under present conditions and cannot go on any longer without leading to major problems, or even national catastrophe. Nonetheless, no particularly active moves have been made to build the "escalators" we need. We have no apparent plan to meet this challenge.

Planning should be appreciated as a phenomenon of a generally higher order than chaos, given its ability to decrease entropy and bring the dynamics of systemic development into order. When compared to the absence of a plan, or to the market, in this regard, planning is a step forward, capable of attaining a higher level of stability for the socio-economic system. The development of civilisation moves along a path of increasing planned elements of economic development. And this is natural, though of course it does not proceed without missteps, sidesteps, and historical pitfalls – which, incidentally, are also natural, caused by society's lack of comprehension of the importance of planning.

It is becoming clearer and clearer that *we need to return to planning*. This is demonstrated by the experience of China, which did not reject planning as an institution and as an instrument for managing development. By applying the tools of planning, China's economy and society have moved much more quickly towards a new type of industrial society than, for example, we have done by repudiating planning and accepting chaotic principles of economic decision making, creating conditions in which the strongest and most self-interested actors win out over social needs. Arguably, the intellectual society of the future, noosociety, is inconceivable without instituting planning as one of the basic, primary instruments of public administration and of society's very being.

Finally, without this instrument we will not manage to seriously reach the next step – the problem of digitalising the economy, that is, establishing modern information technology as an economic foundation, rather than turning digitalisation into a fleeting fad or an empty slogan. After all, the most important infrastructural element of the modern economy is its informational component.

Today – already today, not tomorrow – our level of knowledge and our technological solutions are advanced enough to help us solve many problems. For this reason, we can talk about the possibility of more effective planning: selective planning, indicative planning, or really any type of planning that would make it possible to combine markets with the plan, as is constantly discussed from Russia to China to Scandinavia.

But how can we get to this point?

By combining modern communicative and information systems with the abilities of cognitive technology, artificial intelligence, self-learning systems, human-machine systems, etc., we can create the possibility of "digitalising" both planned and market-based approaches to optimising economic decisions, and also enable the integration of these two approaches with one another.

Of course, in establishing this new technological base for economic calculations, we will need to improve the economy's institutional structure, as this structure makes it possible to effectively orient the economy towards re-industrialisation and create the material foundation for a technological breakthrough to the future.

There are two challenges that we urgently need to meet.

The first is the conscious adoption of a new model for our economy that presumes the priority of industrial development, along with all the decisions – economic, institutional, and so forth – that stem from this premise.

And the second is the consolidation of society, and of our national elites, to realise this model on the basis of shared responsibility to resolve the pressing issues faced by our country.

Russia is *already late* jumping onto the NIS.2 train. To avoid ending up in the group of "catch-up" countries, we must bet on the most promising directions of development, "beyond the horizon". Of course, these will be mere daydreams unless we exert extraordinary effort to gain access to NIS.2-level technologies – if we want to get ahead of the curve. *Building the noonomy must start now, even if at a very narrow level; we must, in practice, work painstakingly to manifest everything that is bound to become the future of human development and economic activity.*

PART TWO

Noonomy as Reality to Be and Theory About Society and Its Development*

In the first part of the book we gave several definitions of Noonomy. It should be noted that, first of all, this term is used to designate the future that will come for the modern world and society, provided that a positive evolutionary scenario for their development is realised. The second and third parts of the work present the specification and further development of the author's basic ideas on this topic. This requires some repetition and consolidation of the material already presented and the key reference provisions of Noonomy as scientific knowledge about the future social order, discovered by the author, which he willingly shares with the whole world (as is well known, "repetition is the mother of learning", moreover, of any kind of learning). In addition, Part 2 will place the main emphasis on Noonomy as a theory generated by practical necessity and aimed at practical implementation.

* Parts 2 & 3 were prepared on the basis of the most significant author's articles and cycles of works on Noonomy published during the period of 2020–2024.

11

Noonomy and the Future[1]

11.1. The Modern World: Civilisation Facing the Crisis

Today we are witnessing unmistakable signs of the growing crisis of human civilisation. All elements of this civilisation – its economic system, its social structure, the fundamental characteristics of modern human existence – are experiencing deep erosion.

The production relations and economic institutions as the base for our productive activities are giving rise to increasing doubts about their ability to ensure the stable development of human society. And first of all it concerns the mechanisms of market self-regulation. The oft-cited "invisible hand" of the market persistently directs attention towards unchecked financial speculation, thereby compromising the stability of the market system itself. This trend perpetuates the exploitative depletion of resources rather than fostering the harmonious development of human potential and addressing entrenched social issues.

Social polarisation is intensifying globally, while political democratic institutions increasingly focus on manipulating the electorate rather than addressing the genuine social aspirations of the populace. Political and ideological technologies, leveraging information and digital technologies alongside the influence of mass media on public consciousness are deployed not to advance progress but to circumvent the resolution of pressing issues while maintaining existing political status.

International socio-economic relations, a concept referred to as geopolitical economy by Professor Radhika Desai (Desai, 2013), are experiencing a period of escalating turbulence. The struggle for global hegemony is facing a trend towards de-globalisation, the claims of some states to national exclusivity meet resistance from others defending their national interests. All this leads to profound changes in the geopolitical and economic configuration of the world, the consequences of which are difficult to predict.

Most concerningly, these processes result in the erosion of people's moral and spiritual well-being. At the same time, the loss of cultural and moral reference points is almost justified by the rejection of "grand narratives" (i.e., in essence, a holistic vision of reality from certain positions), by declaring the criteria of Truth, Progress, Goodness, and Beauty doubtful.

Visible signs of a growing crisis can be found in the economy as well. In the past fifteen years, we have experienced the second devastating financial and economic crisis. And these crises are noticeably deeper than those that the world economy experienced in the last quarter of the twentieth century. Of course, the 2020 crisis can be blamed on the COVID-19 pandemic, but the reality is that both a downturn in the economy and a stock market crash had been expected by economists since 2018, and by the beginning of 2020 the signs of an impending crisis were already quite clear. The pandemic was only a trigger for the crisis and a factor that significantly modified it, but not its cause. A trigger like this was inevitable – whether this one or another. To use Nassim Taleb's image of the "black swan" (Taleb, 2007) (an unexpected event that changes the current situation), there are periods in the development of the economy and society when the "black swan" must necessarily arrive. The specific form it will take is another matter.

11.2. To Change the Development Model

Currently, the primary task for humanity, following the recognition of the threats and deficiencies inherent in the existing world order, is to reformulate the model of social development.

We have long highlighted the distorted nature of the prevailing model of human development. In this model, market criteria, which underpin not only the economy but also other spheres, become hypertrophied. The market approach is imposed on all spheres of societal life, with every aspect of this life being measured by commercial criteria — encompassing the creative spirit of culture and art, efforts in upbringing and education, the pursuit of human health, the curiosity of scientific inquiry, legal protections, and so forth.

Economic relations cover the sphere of production, which is the fundamental sphere of human society that creates the material basis of human existence. But does this mean that economics has the right to claim to transfer the principles of economic relations to all other spheres of society? After all, such an approach puts economic and, first of all, financial results in the forefront, even where commercialisation is directly contraindicated. As a result, it becomes a means of segregating people in access to socially significant social benefits, bringing competition where it serves not the struggle for efficiency, but the growth of social discord, deforming people's consciousness, their values and cultural attitudes.

The severity of the contradictions that have accumulated at the current stage of human civilisation's development has been acknowledged for some time. As early as the 1990s, strategically minded public figures, scientists, and politicians reached a consensus on the necessity of addressing several urgent problems, the escalation of which poses significant threats. As a result, the Millennium Declaration was adopted in 2000, setting out goals related to social development and poverty eradication, as well as environmental protection.[2] Following the partial implementation of the goals of this programme, in 2015 the UN General Assembly approved a resolution where 17 Sustainable Development Goals were formulated.[3]

However, the correct setting of goals and understanding of the necessary ways to achieve them are possible only with a scientifically accurate study of the causes of the problems our civilisation is facing.

It is impossible to resolve these issues solely through verbal debate about whether the current problems stem from excessive intervention in market self-regulation, as neoliberal economists argue, or whether the solution lies in the enhancement and development of state regulation mechanisms, as various strands of Keynesianism and some other heterodox theories suggest.

This argument may have been relevant 50-80 years ago; to some extent it remains relevant today. But that's not enough now, because the world has changed over the decades and continues to change rapidly. And to get the right answers in the face of growing threats and escalating contradictions, we need to start asking different questions.

First and foremost, we must agree that the primary question is not which model of capitalism – more liberal or more regulated – should be pursued. Moreover, the question of whether capitalism has exhausted its developmental potency at all is also not the main question. In fact, we are confronting a much more fundamental question: are we not witnessing the exhaustion of the entire previous paradigm of human civilisation development based on the principles of an economic society? A lot of things point to that. The study of this development paradigm is fraught not just with acceleration of the mentioned problems, but with a very real catastrophe.

We need socially responsible and theoretically sound solutions. This is increasingly imperative as our civilisation nears a critical juncture: we must either cross a threshold beyond which threats to our existence become irreversible – whether through ecological catastrophe, the use of weapons of mass destruction, or the degradation of humanity due to unwarranted interference with its own nature – or we must discover ways to overcome the escalating civilisational crisis and advance to a qualitatively new stage of development.

Neither neoclassical economic theory nor Marxist political economy has so far revealed these possibilities, despite all their attempts to find theoretical answers to the most acute problems of our time. Other social sciences have not been particularly successful in this direction either. In practice, the response of scientists and public figures is often confined to heightened attention to social, humanitarian, and environmental issues, without addressing the fundamental causes underlying these problems. This can be seen at least in the same ideas of "sustainable development" that form the basis of UN decisions. But it is impossible to form qualitatively new opportunities to overcome the civilisation crisis without transition to a qualitatively new state of society.

The way of transition to such a new qualitative state, as well as its own certainty, have been outlined in our developments over the years. This is the path through the new industrial society of the second generation (NIS.2) to Noonomy.

The theory of Noonomy, developed by the author and extensively discussed at scientific seminars of the St. Petersburg S.Y. Witte Institute for New Industrial Development (INID), represents a logical extension of a comprehensive research cycle on technological progress, economic re-industrialisation, and industrial production trends (Bodrunov, 2013, 2016a-b), along with its impact on social structures. During this time, a considerable number of the author's publications on these topics have appeared, outlining the results obtained (Bodrunov, 2017, 2018à, etc.).

These results have also been presented on a regular basis in the publications of INID materials dealing with one or another particular aspect of Noonomy theory (Bodrunov (Ed.), 2019). The ideas and components of this concept are continuously developed through articles, seminars, scientific colloquia at INID with participation from its partners in the Russian Academy of Sciences and international colleagues, as well as various conferences and congresses. Furthermore, following the publication of the author's principal works on the new industrial society of the second generation and on Noonomy, the proposed theory has been extensively discussed in various universities, thesis councils, expert communities – including international ones – and educational laboratories. The theory of Noonomy has also been incorporated into the curricula of several Russian universities. All this also contributed to the development and refinement of the theoretical platform of Noonomy.

The primary platform for presenting and discussing the ideas of Noonomy is the St. Petersburg International Economic Congress (SPEC), one of the largest such events in Russia, organised annually by INID for this purpose. In recent years, discussions on Noonomy have also taken place at various leading forums in Moscow and other Russian cities, as well as internationally. The theory has been rigorously examined by the global scientific community in cities such as Cambridge, Lille, Mexico City, Vienna, Lisbon, New York, and Beijing, among others.

11.3. Basic Aspects of Research Methodology

The recognition that material production underpins human society and that changes in material production drive societal development is the foundational principle for understanding the prospects of social order evolution.

It is crucial to consider all components of production: the specifics of the technological process, the nature of the product, the content of labour, and the forms of production organisation. Only all of these elements combine to develop a holistic understanding of the shifts that are taking place in manufacturing.

In its historical development, the material technological basis of the economy passes through two main stages: pre-industrial and industrial production. Of course, within these stages it is possible to distinguish different stages, but, by and large, apart from these two stages, no other variants in the development of material production can be distinguished so far. Hypothetical "post-industrial" production has yet to become a reality. The modern economy is firmly based on industrial material production, despite the predominant share of the service sector (which – often inappropriately – includes many of the modern effects of industrial activity).

Industrial production is characterised by several features that distinguish it from pre-industrial production: the use of complex means of production; reliance on universal artificial sources of energy; the application of technologies based primarily on scientific knowledge, which transform natural processes into human-controlled and directed technological processes; the capability to achieve both mass production of standardised products and customisation to individual needs; and the ability to produce standardised products while also adapting them to specific requirements.

Therefore, the position that is unequivocally held in the theory of Noonomy is the recognition of the fact that industry firmly occupies the place of the production-technological core in the modern economy. Industrial production provides the necessary material conditions for the development of all other sectors of the economy – construction, agrarian sector and the totality of service industries – by supplying them with various materials, machinery and equipment, developing technological processes. It is the evolution of industry that largely determines the shifts in the socio-economic structure of society over the last 250 years.

This development is accomplished through the transition from one technological mode to another, which we discussed in detail (in theory and practice) in the first section of this book. Moreover, the movement of the modern economy towards the sixth technological mode brings us not just to the change of modes, but to the threshold of a new technological revolution.

What is the most important specificity of the sixth technological mode that allows us to talk about the industrial revolution?

The main distinguishing features of this mode are:

- development of new technologies as a consequence of fundamental scientific research (which was also characteristic of the fifth mode, but had little impact on the basic technologies of material production);
- synergetic interaction of new technologies and the formation of hybrid technologies are being widely developed;
- development of information and communication technologies forms the pivot that ensures the convergence of different technologies and the formation of hybrid technologies.

It is worth emphasising once again that what we see is not just a transition to the next stage of technological development, not just a transition from the fifth technological mode to the sixth.

The fact is that the hallmark of the new technological revolution is a dramatic leap in the application of new knowledge. The share of knowledge-intensive costs is increasing, while the share of material resources costs is relatively decreasing. If we follow this trend, we can expect to move to a level of production where knowledge dominates the costs of production in every way – however we count it, in whatever units we try to examine it. Knowledge becomes the main productive resource of the next stage of development. And this is already the case in many industries today.

In particular, for any modern gadget, estimates from the INID suggest that up to 80-95 per cent of its market price is attributed to the cost of acquiring and implementing "knowledge" and intellectual elements, with the remainder representing material resources. This is just one example of a knowledge-intensive product at the present stage. But the same can be said for a lot of other products of the current industry.

Another position to be outlined is that to reach this new quality of production requires not only a technological leap, but also the improvement of all components of modern material production because manufacturing is not one, but four components. In addition to technology, production also includes labour, means of production (simply put, these are all the material resources used in production – from raw materials to equipment), and forms of production organisation.

Usually, when one speaks of a technological leap, one means, of course, technology first and foremost. In fact, this is far from the case. All forms of material production are evolving, and simultaneously, if we interpret the concept of "technology" broadly, this includes changes in both labour technologies and the technologies of production organisation. From this point of view, we can speak of a technological revolution. But based on our understanding of the content of production, of course, we must be talking about a large, complex industrial revolution.

11.4. The Coming Industrial Revolution. Transition to NIS.2

What will be the result of this coming industrial revolution? If we are talking about qualitative changes in all aspects of industrial production, it must mean the transition of industrial society to a new stage of development. Thus, the outcome of this very revolution will be a new state of industrial society. This will represent the second generation of industrial society (NIS.2), which will remain fundamentally industrial, as industrial activities will continue to be at its core.

The primary distinction of this generation of industrial production is the shift in the main economic resource and driver of development, which will now be knowledge and the scientific understanding of the surrounding world.

The nature of material production is largely determined by where we get our resources from. Whereas we once extracted resources directly from nature, we will now "mine" knowledge, as it is the fundamental resource that will significantly drive the growth of our ability to meet our needs.

To emphasise, the new industrial mode of production is so knowledge-intensive that it will significantly reduce material costs and human labour inputs, leading to the creation of knowledge-intensive products. Moreover, material production gets a new quality, turning into knowledge-intensive production. After all, knowledge (as well as any resource) does not replace the process of material production, it has economic value only when it is technologically applied in production.

Human beings are increasingly tasked with functions of goal-setting and oversight, while the direct manipulation of natural materials is carried out by autonomous technological entities. The increase in knowledge intensity in production and the transformation of the production process into a technological application of science move humans out of the direct production process, while retaining for them functions of creativity, goal-setting, organisation, control, and overall management. This resonates with the ideas of Karl Marx (see Marx, 1954).

The widespread adoption of industrial robots is only the first step on this path. Surgical robots are no longer uncommon, robotic drivers are taking to the roads, and artificial intelligence is increasingly replacing humans in customer interactions within trading and banking firms. These examples are only a few among many.

One example of a robotic complex that combines modern information and telecommunication technologies, robotics itself, and the use of 3D printing is the new product Olli.[4] The American company Local Motors has introduced in the market an autonomous bus for mass passenger transportation. This bus is developed using an integrated information system, assembled from parts almost entirely produced with a 3D printer, and constructed on a robotic assembly line.[5] The reduction in material costs compared to the use of traditional materials is estimated to be several fold, while labour costs are reduced by an order of magnitude. The production time for the bus is as follows: 10 hours for producing the complete set of components, 1 hour for automatic assembly, and 1 hour for software loading and testing of individual systems and the final product. In total, the process requires just half a day of continuous operation, with virtually no human input. To ensure the comfort of passengers using this initially unconventional product, IBM was engaged to enhance it with IBM Watson.[6] This addition provides a virtual guide that can respond to any question in multiple widely spoken languages. The system, integrated into the bus, offers real-time information such as travel duration, optimal departure times, expected delays, and assistance requests. In essence, this results in a robot bus where passengers experience the same level of attention and convenience as they would in a traditional, well-serviced bus with a considerate driver. Actually, passengers will experience even greater comfort, as the new product must excel in the competitive market. The bus offers multimedia services, providing an interactive experience with a virtual interlocutor, consultant, and guide. Additionally, it includes access to the Internet, television, and various entertainment options, allowing passengers to work, study, and enjoy other activities while on the road.

The example above encompasses all three paradigmatic components of the forthcoming industrial revolution: *digitalisation, additive manufacturing, and robotisation.* Each component represents a fundamental shift in the traditional industrial framework.

The "Internet of Things" and similar technologies signify a fundamental shift in many traditionally established economic sectors, ranging from trade and services to construction. Notably, these technologies are also laying the groundwork for future innovations, serving as a powerful base for ongoing advancements. In this context, the synergetic potential of modern technologies, when practically applied, not only remains intact but actually increases.

The application of knowledge-intensive technologies leads to fundamental changes in components of the industrial process, particularly in the organisation of production. This includes improvements in production management systems, the transition of product design to 3D modelling, optimisation of transport, material, and information flows, as well as the automation and "internetisation" of management decisions – transforming system administrators into plant administrators – and much more.

Cognitive technologies within the framework of the sixth mode, through the use of self-learning artificial intelligence (AI) systems, are also invading areas where previously there was no alternative to the use of human labour. On this basis, the production of robotics, which is becoming more flexible, more adaptable, more productive, is receiving a new impetus.

The following thesis: the growth of technological capabilities to satisfy needs poses a dilemma for humanity in civilisational development. We say very often that there is an ecological crisis ahead: we have littered the whole world with plastic, mutants appear in the zoo world, dozens and hundreds of species of living beings disappear every day, and technetical creatures appear, which breed much faster than nature created this world. The level of development of what might be termed "technetic creatures" – akin to the terminology of geobiocenoses, referring to entities within technological ecosystems – is growing rapidly.

The elements of the technocenosis we refer to as "technetic beings" increasingly occupy and expand their presence within our technological space. They are displacing the natural elements of nature, and today, humans – its creators – have already become a significant geological force, as well as a "biological" force, following Vernadsky's perspective. According to biologists, over the 4.5 billion years of the Earth's existence, the weight of biota, i.e., created by living nature, is approximately 2.5 trillion tons (Kogorodin, Kogorodina, 2000: 106) against the weight of the technosphere of 30 trillion tons, according to the above estimates.

In doing so, we face a progressive loss of biodiversity. About three species of living things disappear every hour on earth, 72 species die every day. Of course, and naturally, without human involvement, there has always been a process of extinction of certain species. This natural process is estimated to result in a loss of about one species per million per year. Meanwhile, as Dr. Braulio Diaz, Executive Secretary of the Convention on Biological Diversity, notes, current estimates of global biodiversity range from approximately 2 million to as many as 30 or even 100 million species (Skobeeva, 2016). It is not difficult to calculate that even if we take the top estimate, even then the rate of extinction would be 262 species per year out of one million, which is hundreds of times the natural rate. As we can see, technodiversity has not only surpassed biodiversity, it is also suppressing it.

Human beings not only intervene in the world around them but also have the capacity to alter their inner selves. For instance, Germany has legally recognised a third gender (intersex). Looking ahead, it is conceivable that, due to advancements in current technologies, we may encounter individuals who are sexless (Agaev, 2017) or "partially" human in the not-too-distant future.

When discussing human beings, it is essential to impose reasonable restrictions to prevent such developments from occurring. This includes a variety of things. Russian writer A. Belyaev described this in his novels; let's refer to this idea – if we want to have gills, we have to go live in the ocean. And vice versa – if we change our environment, we have to change ourselves.

It is evident that scientists advancing the boundaries of scientific knowledge are motivated by benevolent intentions, such as developing new drug formulations and correcting genetic abnormalities. However, they acknowledge that these scientific advances could potentially be used to create new forms of life and to "edit" the very essence of human biology.

The same reasoning applies to many modern technologies, where their careless or unconsidered application has the potential to radically alter our environment, our living conditions, and even ourselves.

Is this path unquestionably positive? Or is it fraught with fundamental danger to humans? It seems the answer is clear. We need, at the very least, to reflect on this growing challenge of development uncertainty and civilisational risks.

The current economic system and the promotion of simulative, unnecessary (or superfluous) goods in the name of profit are pushing people down this very likely suboptimal and possibly disastrous path. In turn, the increased production of these goods drives the reckless exploitation of natural resources.

In Noonomy, the new character of rationality and, accordingly, the new certainty of development targets are of paramount importance. After all, Noonomy relies on a shift from economic "rationality" to goal-setting and the fulfillment of various human needs shaped by higher values.

In a market economy, rationality is understood as the maximisation of monetary income. It is rational, I suppose, but is it reasonable?

"Ratio" is not concerned with the realisation of new knowledge, unlike reason. In this context, when discussing Noonomy, we refer to a shift to a fundamentally different criterion base and new principles grounded in "noo" – principles that shape how we address and fulfil human needs. And – yes, increasing, changing, but "noo"-needs. This is a special manner of economic management – noomanner. *Just as economics governs the management of an economic society, Noonomy directs the management of a noosociety, with a focus on rationally meeting specific, reasonable needs.*

11.5. Simulative Needs and Financial Capital

From a historical-philosophical perspective, and drawing not only on Marx's theory of socio-economic formations but also on the contributions of other scholars such as Spengler and Toynbee, we can conclude that each transition between these so-called "civilisations" or stages of our unified civilisation is closely linked to the challenges humanity encounters in its development. In this instance, the primary challenge is not a geological catastrophe, as in ancient times, nor natural phenomena such as droughts, floods, plagues, or famines. Instead, the main challenge today is the rapid advancement in scientific, technical, and technological progress. More precisely, it is not progress per se that poses the challenge, but rather the application of technological achievements within the existing social framework. This framework, governed by prevailing criteria of rationality, is inadequate to address either the escalating disruption of ecological balance or the harmful interference in human nature

All this happens in the unbridled pursuit of increasing the mass of consumed resources turned into waste for the illusion of satisfying false, illusory, simulative needs. Pope Francis, in his recent encyclical *Fratelli tutti* (Common Fraternity), notes: "Often voices raised in defence of the environment are silenced or ridiculed, using apparently reasonable arguments that are simply a screen for special interests. In this superficial and short-sighted culture that we have created, lacking a unified vision, it is predictable that as some resources become depleted, a favourable scenario for new wars, disguised as noble causes, will gradually emerge"[7] – as he references his own words from the encyclical *Laudato Si* (On Care for Our Common Home).[8] And he goes on to express his fear that, emerging from today's pandemic crisis, the world could "sink even deeper into feverish consumerism and new forms of selfish self-preservation".[9]

Where does this unbridled race of consumerism come from, consuming more and more of the Earth's resources? When a particular market segment becomes saturated and people's basic needs have been met compared to previous stages of development, the economic actor faces the challenge of identifying new sources of profit. To address market saturation, it is necessary to either expand markets through innovation by introducing a fundamentally new product, which typically involves significant financial investment and higher risks, or to extend the market for existing products. The latter approach is usually less costly and risky, involving the capture of new markets, sometimes by suppressing competitors – even those offering superior solutions but with weaker positions. This strategy often prioritises market dominance over progress and the genuine needs of people, reflecting the predatory nature of capital. It will spend as little as possible, absorb as much resource as possible with as little expenditure as possible, and yet it is willing to be predatory for profit. Another predatory and increasingly progressive method is, among other things, the compulsive promotion of a simulative product, a commodity.

Of course, a purely bogus need and a purely simulative, useless commodity are not so common. Usually, fake needs are "fitted" to real needs, and the simulative component is like "putting on" a product that satisfies that real need. And at first it is often a really useful product, and its arrival is a progressive phenomenon, then it acquires a simulative superstructure – and it is no longer progressive.

Which trends will win out? It depends on the balance between two factors: the rate of development in production and technological progress, and the rate at which humans realise the social consequences of applying these technologies and designs to meet human needs, which constitutes the social superstructure. It changes too, but it changes following material production.

This bundle raises certain concerns, because society must "mature" in order to solve these problems, to realise and determine the choice of its development path. Society matures through the accumulation of knowledge, but a key contributing factor is the fulfillment of needs – real needs, at least. These needs evolve over time, with some that were once merely simulated becoming genuine requirements in subsequent stages.

In that case, we obviously have a serious problem. Our society has not yet "matured" to properly utilise technological progress and its achievements. Society is not yet fully matured because current technological progress, despite its power and capability to address many fundamental human problems, has not yet reached a point where it benefits everyone. It has not yet provided enough to meet all real needs or ensure universal satisfaction. Why, for example, is it that despite the vast amounts of grain produced worldwide, which could theoretically provide bread for everyone, millions of people still suffer from starvation? Because there is still an economic way of appropriating these very benefits. Moreover, technological progress often results in financial capital, which has absorbed the benefits of these advancements, redistributing income in its own favour. This redistribution does not benefit productive capital or address the real needs of people.

The nature of financial capital is such that, through various stages of its development, it has become the dominant force, overseeing and controlling the entire social process. Taking over not only social production, but also, gradually, the minds and hearts of the people.

Why was it successful?

This is because human beings originally have vital, natural biological needs – what might be termed "zoological" in their expression – that are fundamental to their survival and well-being. These needs are met in a certain way. These needs drive individuals to develop qualities that, while not inherently negative (e.g., creativity, resource accumulation), may become superfluous or redundant in certain situations.

This stems from the factor of the essential uncertainty of human existence. From the very beginning of his separation from nature and self-realisation as distinct from it, humanity has struggled to determine the duration for which it needs a particular resource and, consequently, the appropriate amount to stockpile. We cannot be certain that the supply will be sufficient for any given period, nor can we revise this period once it is set. Accordingly, due to this uncertainty, elements of a person's criterion base are formed that drive decisions such as the need to save more and maintain reserves, even if they are disproportionate to current consumption.

Remember the fable about the dragonfly and the hoarding ant? The moral of this fable aligns precisely with the social morality – the criterion base of behaviour – of the social and economic system in which it was written. Economic society preserves the generic characteristic of humanity's natural existence. In a noosociety, where nooproduction is advanced, the concept of "stock" will be replaced by the factor of fully satisfying people's non-simulative needs. Consequently, the criterion base determining the "correctness" of human behaviour – and indeed the behaviour itself – will change accordingly.

Now we live in an economic society – and according to its laws. One aspect is the expansion of stock, capital (as its specific sublimation), and "living space". As a result, humanity's natural needs to secure our existence amidst uncertainty have been transferred to the financial system. Why? Because the financial system, and money in particular, have historically replaced the role of physical accumulation. Because they have a certain function, certain known capabilities in this regard. They are easily interchangeable. They are much more "agile". They are easier to "stockpile" (especially in the current technological environment) and do not depreciate as quickly as perishable goods, for example. They can go missing, too, though.

The financial system ensured the accumulation of resources not only for consumption but also for production. Once upon a time, the separation of financial capital from productive capital was a step in a progressive direction, as it ensured the concentration of dispersed monetary resources and the efficient use of these resources for productive investment. However, the more the financial market institutions developed and the more significant role they played in ensuring the functioning of the economy, the more importance was given to the self-interest of financial capital, i.e., *the goals of self-growth of this financial capital. Financial goals are beginning to supplant real-world objectives, which are at the root of the process known as financialisation.*

If productive capital is faced with market saturation and demand constraints, what path will financial capital choose to overcome this problem? After all, its functioning, unlike the functioning of productive capital, has no direct connection with the saturation of people's needs. Certainly, productive capital is primarily interested in cash flow; however, to achieve this, it must first satisfy specific human needs and is consequently influenced by consumer reactions. In contrast, financial capital is solely focused on cash flow, regardless of its source. Financial capital evaluates its consumer from only one point of view – to whom, how much and on what terms to allocate money to get the greatest monetary return.

Clients of financial capital, by becoming dependent on it, also have to be guided by these criteria. When the market becomes saturated with certain items and goods, causing their prices to decrease and money to stagnate, the question arises: how can one continue to grow their wealth?

Investments in innovation emerge to occupy new market niches. As a result, those "innovations" that are essentially pseudo-innovations – quick, superficial, and designed to generate the same or even greater revenues – tend to become prevalent. At the same time it will be explained to the consumer that this is something very valuable, very important, without which he can hardly live normally, which is an object of lust, etc. To do that, you have to change values, values in people's heads. Therefore – back to the original point – *financial capital pushes to corrupt human beings, provokes the formation of zoological needs.*

Financial capital seeks to spread its expansion across the globe, but the effects on different segments of the world economy vary. Currently, while the world is globalised for financial capital, it is far from being globally integrated in a way that meets needs uniformly across different regions. That is, capital in today's world order, despite globalisation, knows how to hold these means to satisfy needs in certain areas. Accordingly, some countries, societies, sub-societies are poorer, others richer. There are those that fulfil more of people's needs, and there are those that fulfil less. Induced or artificial needs are more likely to be formed in areas where people are already relatively well-provided for. In such areas, the level of satisfaction of natural and real needs is already high, and technical progress can enhance this even further. However, once these needs are sufficiently met, it becomes expensive to provide additional saturation. Therefore, it is more economically efficient to cultivate simulated needs instead.

This is where the application of technological progress by financial capital results in financial capital becoming, at this stage, increasingly super-dimensionalised. And induced, imposed needs are ignited. With a corresponding absorption of natural and other resources. This is very likely to lead to a global catastrophe because the resources that humans use to realise the process of satisfying needs are limited. And the utilisation of a finite amount of resources by unlimitedly growing (by nature) financial capital is a global contradiction. The paradigm of uncontrolled, endless development of financial capital has led to a situation where the insatiable need for growth and self-expansion of financial capital clashes with the finite capacity of the planet's natural resources, human resources, and other factors to meet these needs.

Hence *the nexus of simulativity and financial capital: while it expands "rationally", from the point of view of the market paradigm, the expansion of simulative consumption, by its very nature it directs its efforts to the accretion of financial profit itself.* And thus leads to a civilisational crisis.

This situation occurs at every stage of technological progress. The transition to a new technological order is accompanied by increased expansion and conflict, although it would seem that meeting a greater range of needs should enable people to live better lives. Why is this happening? Because there is disharmony, a lag of social consciousness and, accordingly, social relations from the possibilities of technological progress. Therefore, the dilemma now presents itself as follows: either society will fail to harness the opportunities provided by the technological revolution for its improvement, becoming distracted by false goals and values, thereby exacerbating the negative trends of modern civilisation to the point of losing its own essence, or humanity will successfully realise the need to reformulate current civilisational attitudes.

11.6. The Four Vectors of Change (the "quadriga of Noonomy")

The prerequisites for establishing the trajectory towards the formation of a noo-society – a qualitatively new state of social existence – and initiating the movement towards Noonomy are already evident at present. The genesis of Noonomy takes shape as a kind of equilibrium of ***four main vectors of change***.

The first vector determines *the creation of the material foundations of the movement towards Noonomy*. Even at the current level of technological development, where the fifth technological mode is predominant, the economy is still largely shaped by the third and fourth modes. Approximately 20-25 per cent of workers are employed in material production, where they produce machinery and equipment, agricultural products, extract natural resources, and provide transportation for these goods in sufficient volumes for both domestic consumption and export. And the transition to the sixth technological mode is able to satisfy all vital (non-simulative) needs.

Humanity is now on the threshold of a technological transition to a qualitatively new industry, allowing for the creation of humanless production, leaving the functions of goal-setting, research and development, and production organisation to man. The new production is becoming extremely knowledge-intensive, and human knowledge is thus finally becoming the most important production resource.

The second vector defines *new bases for the formation of human needs, based on new opportunities for their satisfaction*. Humanity will shift to non-economic criteria for the formation and fulfillment of needs, moving away from economic rationality.

One of the most important shifts in this direction that we can observe for a long time is the *diffusion of ownership*. The newest trends here that we see today are the phenomenon of "abandonment of ownership", the development of various forms of temporary use and shared consumption.

Such trends indicate that property relations, which are based on economic relations, are gradually "diffusing", "evaporating", "dissolving" (which corresponds to the literal reading of the term "diffusion").

And this means the extinction of economic relations themselves, the transition to production, exchange and consumption, and the corresponding type of appropriation according to non-economic criteria. Of course, this transition cannot and should not be imposed by a volitional order – it will mature as the objective grounds for it to accumulate, as we move along all vectors of the transition to Noonomy.

The transition to Noonomy is a lengthy historical process. However, it is important to note that the changes leading to the shift to NIS.2, and ultimately from the economy to Noonomy, will soon bring about transformations in economic relations and the nature of property relations characteristic of this new generation of industrial society.

For example, although the sharing economy has only become a visible phenomenon since 2010, a survey of 30,000 consumers conducted in 60 countries in Q3 2013 has already revealed a significant interest in the use of shearing economy services (Figure 12).

Car-sharing has the largest share in the sharing economy, and its growth is one of the most important indicators of the development of the whole sector (Figure 13). The growth of car-sharing has outpaced the most optimistic forecasts. A prediction made in August 2016 suggested that the number of users would reach 36 million in 2025, but already in 2018 the number of users exceeded 50 million.[10]

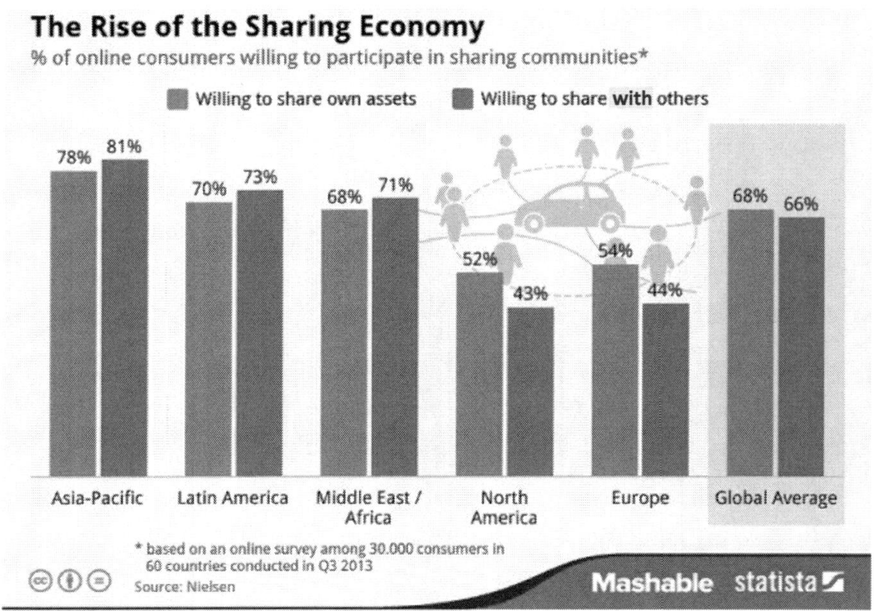

Figure 12. Share of consumers willing to participate in the sharing economy (2013)

Sourse: Richter, 2014

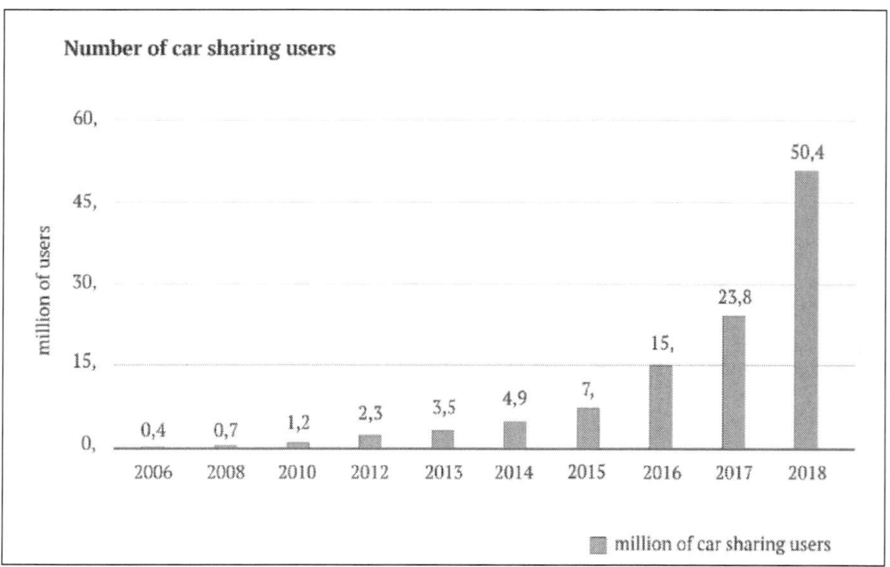

Figure 13. Number of users of car-sharing services 2006–2018

Sources:[11] Svegander, 2019; Shaheen, Cohen, Jaffee, 2018

This rapid growth of the sharing economy is supported by significant investment in it. The desire of more and more people to enjoy without becoming owners is attracting corresponding attention from businesses, and investment in the sharing economy is growing rapidly (Figure 14).

The third vector of such a transition *forms the social conditions of movement towards Noonomy – socialisation of a person in the direction of acquiring nooqualities, and socialisation of society.* This process implies the active role of the subject, who assimilates the most progressive norms, stereotypes, moral and cultural values from the social environment, and in turn influences the formation of social institutions that contribute to the evolution of society in the same direction, in the direction of noosociety. It is not the pursuit of individual profit that becomes the criterion of a person's entry into society, but the development of human creative abilities, self-realisation of human personality.

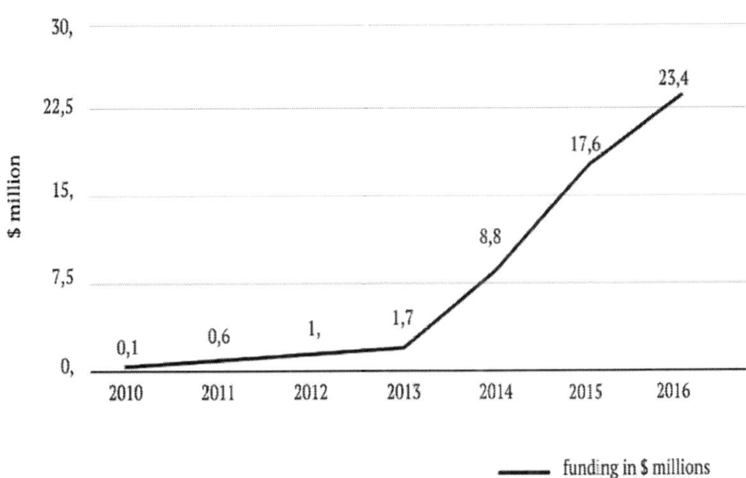

Figure 14. Cumulative investments in sharing startups, 2010–2016

Sources: Wallenstein, Shelat, 2017: 5

In turn, social institutions create a platform for such self-actualisation by supporting the conditions of human development, and by fostering an aversion to the "war of all against all" in pursuit of private material success.

So how do these civilisational attitudes evolve? Historically, as humanity evolves, individuals increasingly develop the characteristics of a nootype being – a humanistic being – who considers not only their own interests but also the interests of their surroundings, society, environment, and other people. This movement – from "zoo" to "noo" – is there and historically validated. Another question: how can we ensure the priority of this movement, increase the pace of movement towards "noo" and inhibit the negative processes that reduce man and society to "zoo"?

The general layer of human cognition and norms of behaviour, which is simultaneously formed on their basis – the general culture of individuals, society. We see that this cultural component of being is constantly growing, developing. Of course, there have been reverse situations in history, but nevertheless, we realise that the general level of culture of modern society is significantly higher than the level of culture thousands of years ago. Although, it should be noted, many features of the "primitive" attitude to life remain in some people who have not sufficiently entered this very cultural space. Here's the key point. What do you mean, "entered"?

We recognise that people have not equally entered the cultural space: some segments of society, certain individuals, or their communities are more receptive to the layer of knowledge known as culture. This receptivity drives the development of human nooneeds and their approach to life, while others are less responsive. We observe numerous examples of the "shortcomings" of contemporary society in this regard, and in some cases, there is evidence of deliberate efforts to construct systems that restrict individuals from entering the cultural space. These restrictions hinder personal development and can stifle an individual's growth. This is not accidental, as *restricting people's access to culture serves as a basis for manipulation*. It is evident that financial capital and its affiliates play a significant role in perpetuating these limitations. These satellites – derivatives, siblings, and descendants of financial capital – manifest in forms such as poverty, inequality, reduced access to cultural phenomena, education, and more. All of these factors contribute to the under-acquisition of the knowledge and cultural goods necessary for the formation of the noohuman. All this is also used to justify the well-known theses about man as a beast-like creature, speculations about the impossibility in principle to get rid of "zoo". The theory of Noonomy argues against this in principle.

Every human being, an individual, is endowed from birth with the "noo" qualities. As is known, the aptitudes do not determine abilities; they are prerequisites for their formation and development. What influences their formation? Speaking the language of social psychology, the mechanism of such formation is the generalisation and consolidation of the whole range of mental processes in the activity of an individual. Which, in turn, is a reflection, in the language of philosophers, of the external world and its impact on the individual. Forming, among other things, his worldview, fixing in his mind "codes" and values, allowing him to realise the world and society.

Today we live in a world where scientific and scientific-technical, technical progress is combined with the progress of social knowledge, cognition of man, society, its peculiarities. In fact, social research, by and large, began later than scientific, technological, and technical research, although the earliest direction of such general development has been represented in philosophical treatises and ideas for over two thousand years. However, the study of humans as social beings and as individuals within society began with the development of psychological and social sciences towards the end of the 19th century and continued throughout the 20th century. By the latter half of the 20th century and into the early 21st century, this area had become recognised as a significant field within the social sciences. This development is yielding results.

The term "socialisation" was first applied in the late 19th century by sociologist and philosopher Georg Simmel, who understood it as the formation of social groups. But in a meaning closer to the modern understanding, this concept was revealed by sociologists Franklin Giddings (Giddings, 1897) and Jean-Gabriel Tarde (Tarde, 1890), who considered it as the formation of human personality under the influence of social environment.

Nowadays this concept is applied in many social sciences and in quite different senses. Economic theory understands this as a tendency to increase the orientation of the economy towards achieving social results, rather than the human mastering of a system of social norms and stereotypes. This social orientation of the economy relies on the extensive production of public and patronage goods (Rubinstein, 2011) with the mediation and direct participation of the state. This implies the need for the development of state regulation of the economy, budget financing of education, science, and healthcare, as well as providing social assistance to the population.

Economic theory cannot overlook the issues of socialisation in the way they are examined in sociology. The fact is that, in modern manufacturing, the role of the human being is fundamentally changing. Humans now primarily function as carriers of knowledge – the main resource of economic development. And the fate of our civilisation depends on what criteria the colossal power of modern knowledge will be used. Thus, the level of human social responsibility is of critical importance for production.

Scientific and technological progress, the diminishing desire for property ownership, and the development of the creative aspects of labour – all of these factors drive individuals to become increasingly responsible, more culturally aware, and more socially oriented. For such a person, both their social mission and social recognition become important, rather than an endless pursuit of material wealth. Such a person goes step by step from "zoo" to "noo", changing not only his own behaviour, but also the core of moral norms and values on which he relies.

And in this matter, it is important not to miss the flip side of this process. A person in the process of socialisation acts not just as a passive acceptor of social norms, public morality, and social stereotypes. No, the socialising individual has, in turn, an active influence on the values and socio-cultural norms produced by society. Not only is a person socialised under the influence of society, but society is also socialised under the influence of active human activity, transforming the established cultural and moral norms, values, motives, as well as – the corresponding social institutions.

If the content of this process will be the meaningful and concerted efforts of people aimed at mastering the best achievements of human culture by society, it will ensure the expansion of social noospace and lead to noosociety.

The term *"socialisation of society"*, as proposed, helps to understand the connection in Noonomy between technological development and the advanced acquisition of social knowledge by individuals. It emphasises the formation of social structures through the mechanism of socialisation. This concept highlights the gradual transition to a new type of person – one who adapts to society and for whom society adapts to their real needs. It underscores the importance of focusing on the practical aspects of self-restraint and the adaptation process in this evolving context.

It is important to note that *the idea of humans as social beings who are both shaped by society and shape society* is not new, nor is the question of how individuals make history.

It is important to understand that within society, an individual is "coded" by the social environment. Through the process of socialisation, they adopt a "code" – a moral and value core – that reflects the social essence of society at that time, as determined by the prevailing criterion base of values. The individual is socialised. But the individual himself, influencing society, "socialises" it, changing its moral and value core – and the task is to make *this core change in the direction determined by the noocriteria base.* And the discovery, expansion, mastering of such knowledge, its inclusion in the moral and value core is an important aspect of the task of socialisation of society. "Making" it more "social", non-individualistic (in the negative sense of the word), more comfortable with the individual, more "noo"-oriented.

If we integrate the process of understanding a person's needs with the process of acquiring knowledge of different types into a unified approach, these mechanisms and methodological developments will provide a key to addressing how to progress toward the "noo"-human. This means that we will gain the key to transforming a person from merely non-economic (in the sense of not using economic mechanisms to address their needs) to someone who consciously works on themselves and contributes both personally and socially to what is necessary. On one hand, this individual will achieve a consciously recognised and adequate level of well-being – social, material, emotional, and spiritual. On the other hand, they will not experience a genuine need for the expansion of production of goods that, at this stage of development, cannot be obtained without causing harm to society, the environment, and others.

On such a trajectory we see the way to the gradual reformatting of the current civilisational, socio-cultural attitudes.

The fourth vector is aimed at *creating ideological conditions for the movement towards noosociety*. Such conditions are laid down in the *ideology of solidarism.* It is through this process that we gradually shift away from competition for the private appropriation of material wealth and transition towards cooperation and solidarity, which foster both collective and individual progress. This requires an awareness of the fundamental unity of interests and values, as well as an understanding of the common risks and dangers associated with the mindless pursuit of economic success and unrestrained consumption.

Unfortunately, there is a disconnect: technology is advancing much faster than the rise in cultural awareness, human understanding of ethical boundaries, and progress towards addressing the urgent problems outlined in the UN's development goals. However, the objective forces and challenges of existence demand solutions, and historical events in civilisation confirm the feasibility of addressing these issues. The advancement of modern technologies, coupled with increasing risks, not only heightens the need for social coordination of people's actions but also creates the necessary prerequisites for such coordination. Such preconditions, of course, are not realised automatically, because they encounter the barriers of established interests and social stereotypes. It is all the more important to deal with the ideological basis of the transition to a society liberated from economic rationality.

The most important principle of such ideology is the principle of solidarism, on the basis of which it is possible to form a social and institutional framework that ensures non-conflict interaction between individuals and social groups.

We do not consider here the phenomena of the so-called "solidarity economy" studied by economic science (for example, cooperatives, or networks of mutual aid societies), although these phenomena have a certain connection with the phenomenon of solidarity. We are talking about a much broader phenomenon that encompasses the interaction of all social actors at a qualitatively new level. The fundamental point here is to move away from social conflicts, clashes, hostility and competition. They are replaced by other bases of human interaction: finding a common platform of values and development goals, working out mutually acceptable ways of solving problems and organising joint activities for this purpose, and even in the case of different interests, searching for compromises.

Solidarism (*solidarisme* in French) is an ideological concept formulated in the middle and second half of the XIX century, which aims to achieve mutual trust, cooperation and solidarity of different layers of society, uniting the efforts of different classes, parties, and various public associations expressing one or another interest. The realisation of the ideas of solidarism is carried out through voluntary associations, as well as a system of contractual relations that determine the provision of common interests.

The philosopher and economist Pierre Leroux (Leroux, 1840) and the lawyer Léon Bourgeois (Bourgeois, 1896) were the founders of the development of the concepts of solidarism. They wanted an end to social enmity and a transition to cooperation, a softening of social antagonisms, which they wanted to achieve through the tax system and various social support programmes. They considered a commitment to the ideals of democracy, equality of rights of citizens and striving for mutual understanding of different social groups and strata as a prerequisite for this.

In the twentieth century, the ideas of solidarism were applied in the political and ideological practices of various parties and social movements. These ideas served as a tool to unite society, organise cooperation among social groups and strata, and achieve common goals. Solidarism was utilised by various groups, including the People's Labour Union, organised by a faction of the anti-Bolshevik emigration (which adopted it as the official ideology of the NTS in 1943), the Italian and German Christian Democratic parties after World War II, and the Polish Solidarity movement in the 1980s. Right-wing radical movements and even totalitarian regimes have also exploited the ideas of solidarism. In these cases, however, it often served more as an ideological veneer for imposing a system of rigid hierarchical control from above on society.

It is worth noting that even political forces not inclined towards totalitarianism did not achieve consistent practical implementation of the ideas of solidarism. This is probably inevitable in a society permeated by objectively determined discord of socio-economic interests, causing acute conflicts between different social strata and groups. However, the transformation in production conditions, which provides a material basis for a higher level of human needs satisfaction and reduces the intense struggle for subsistence, creates new, more favourable conditions for realising the ideas of solidarism. We are already observing initial signs of the practical realisation of solidarity ideas through the development of "solidarity economy" initiatives, which have advanced significantly. It is possible to anticipate further expansion of their application, as part of the transitional stages in the movement of human civilisation towards a noosociety.

Modern society is still market-capitalist, economic at its core. In such a society, real relations and institutions based on solidarism may often exist only in a latent (hidden) form within the framework of the dominant system of relations. Solidarism is closely linked to the socialisation of society and the economy, providing a foundation for both economic progress and the mitigation of social contradictions. Since society remains economic, the available economic means should be effectively utilised to support such development. And here it is worth paying attention to the opportunities that lie in the use of strategic planning tools and supporting active industrial policy. Alongside this, it is crucial to leverage the potential inherent in the social orientation of the economy, focusing on the development of various forms of joint production, exchange, appropriation, use, and consumption.

The development strategy of our country should incorporate these tools to create a model of economy and society that rejects relations of domination and subordination between social subjects and the pursuit of unilateral benefits and preferences. Established socio-economic institutions, including the institution of property, continue to uphold this approach. However, advancing further and addressing the emerging civilisational crisis urgently necessitates mutual consideration of diverse interests, the search for compromises among these interests, and ultimately, the organisation of solidarity to resolve the deepening contradictions in production, environmental, and social spheres.

The realisation of this need is reflected in concepts such as "stakeholder capitalism"[12] or in the concept of co-competition, which implies the combination of cooperation and competition (Brandenburger, Nalebuff, 1996).

The current emphasis on the growing importance of cooperative relations and mutual consideration of interests further supports recognising solidarism as a promising ideological foundation for advancing towards a noosociety.

The value of social ties based on solidarity is also being recognised in Russia. Very recently, amendments to the Russian Constitution were adopted, according to which Article 75.1 was formulated as follows: "In the Russian

Federation ... the balance of rights and obligations of the citizen, social partnership, economic, political and social solidarity shall be ensured".[13]

The realisation of these four vectors – referred to as the "quadriga of Noonomy", by analogy with Apollo's quadriga – has the potential to elevate humanity to a qualitatively new stage of social existence and, crucially, to address the emerging civilisational crisis.

At the same time, we acknowledge that numerous problems arise partly due to the real economic policies currently pursued by world powers, which, in our view, do not consistently incorporate the necessary development measures. It is also evident that the trajectory of progress towards Noonomy and the noosocial order will not be linear; it will experience numerous deviations and regressions along the way.

The theory of Noonomy aims to address these challenges by setting clear targets and guiding us towards a future we should aspire to. Advancing towards this future will involve overcoming the current problems we face. Noonomy suggests the path to be travelled and the priority milestones along the way.

Thus, the "Quadriga of Noonomy" which includes four main vectors – scientific and technical progress (as the material basis for noodevelopment), diffusion of ownership (as a fundamental process of undermining the foundations of economic society), socialisation of society (noosocialisation) based on the noocriterial system of values, and solidarism (as an ideological platform and practice of nootransformation) – is a key package of attributes for successful nootransition. Each of the vectors considered above has and plays its own clearly assigned role, which ultimately ensures movement towards a noosociety.

However, it would be a mistake to understand these vectors solely in terms of the simplest "geometry" – for example, as segments of four straight lines, characterised by a certain numerical value and a certain direction towards their own horizons. No, not even close! First of all, they have a single goal determined by logic and objective laws of evolutionary social development – a high-quality and relatively fast nootransition: from the starting point – the current state of the world – to a noo-order, where noonomy will become the material basis. Moreover, the above components of the "quadriga" are closely interconnected. The successive emergence of each of them turns out to be the key to creating a solid foundation for subsequent changes in other vectors: for example, the diffusion of ownership is accelerated by the achievement of an ever higher level of scientific and technical progress (in line with the formation and change of the corresponding technological modes), which together lay the groundwork for the socialisation of society according to the humanisation trend and further – the rooting of solidarism. At the same time, it is crucial that these vectors, closely interacting with each other in the nootransition process, and the broad range of positive effects created by them – in the words of the poet – "all stream into that peak of the Galaxy in a "single beam"[14] – towards noonomy and noosociety.

Notes

1 Prepared on the basis of Bodrunov, 2021.

2 United Nations Millennium Declaration. General Assembly resolution 55/2 of September 8, 2000. URL: https://www.un.org/ru/documents/decl_conv/declarations/summitdecl.shtml

3 Transforming our world: the 2030 Agenda for Sustainable Development General Assembly resolution 70/1 of September 25, 2015. URL: https://undocs.org/ru/A/RES/70/1

4 See Meet Olli's presentation on the Local Motors website. URL: https:// localmotors.com/meet-olli/

5 Tess (2017). Local Motors' Self-driving 'Olli' Shuttle Helped along by Makerbot 3D Printers / 3D Printer and 3D Printing News Aug 30. URL: http://www.3ders.org/articles/20170830-local-motors-self-driving-olli-shuttle-helped-along-bymakerbot-3d-printers.html.

6 Local Motors Debuts "Olli", the First Self-driving Vehicle to Tap the Power of IBM Watson (2016) // IBM, 16 Jun. URL: https://www-03.ibm.com/press/us/en/pressrelease/49957.wss.

7 Translation by author Encyclical Letter *Fratelli Tutti* of The Holy Father Francis on Fraternity and Social Friendship, (3 October, 2020): 17. URL: http://www.vatican.va/content/francesco/en/encyclicals/documents/papa-francesco_20201003_enciclica-fratellitutti.html.

8 Encyclical *Laudato Si'* of the Most Holy Father Francis (May 24, 2015), 57. URL: http://www.vatican.va/content/francesco/ru/encyclicals/documents/papafrancesco_20150524_enciclica-laudato-si.html.

9 Translation by author Encyclical Letter *Fratelli Tutti* of The Holy Father Francis On Fraternity and Social Friendship, (3 October, 2020): 35. URL: http://www.vatican.va/content/francesco/en/encyclicals/documents/papa-francesco_20201003_enciclica-fratellitutti.html.

10 Number of car sharing users worldwide from 2006 to 2025 (2016) // Statista Research Department, August. URL: https://www.statista.com/statistics/415636/carsharing-number-of-users-worldwide/.

11 Number of car sharing users worldwide from 2006 to 2025 (2016) // Statista Research Department, August. URL: https://www.statista.com/statistics/415636/carsharing-number-of-users-worldwide/; The Carsharing Telematics Market – 2nd Edition. Summary (2018) // Berg Insight. M2M Research Series. URL: http://www.berginsight.com/ReportPDF/Summary/bi-carsharing2-sum.pdf.

12 Measuring Stakeholder Capitalism: Towards Common Metrics and Consistent Reporting of Sustainable Value Creation. 22 September 2020. URL: https://www.weforum.org/reports/measuring-stakeholder-capitalismtowards-common-metrics-and-consistent-reporting-of-sustainable-value-creation.

13 Website Consultant.ru. URL: http://www.consultant.ru/document/cons_doc_LAW_28399/844d980197f23461adb5a6699db6e34227150003/.

14 The words from the song of the bard I. Andrienko “Aspired” (to M. Shcherbakov) are given.

12

Noonomy and Noosphere[1]

The theory of Noonomy, despite numerous differences, including those of a fundamental nature, exhibits a clear affinity with the concept of the noosphere. Both theories are rooted in the recognition of the increasing significance of the human reason in shaping contemporary civilisation. While the concept of the noosphere primarily asserts that reason has emerged as a decisive factor in development – bearing planetary and, in the works of later "noospherist" scholars, even universal and existential significance (and, in the interpretation of Teilhard de Chardin, spiritual and mystical significance) – the theory of Noonomy, although not dismissing this notion, does not regard reason as an "acquired" factor of civilisational development. Instead, it posits that reason is inherent in the universe, with humanity representing a concrete manifestation of this reason at a specific stage of development. The theory of Noonomy focuses on identifying the specific material and social prerequisites that facilitate the transition to a qualitative shift in the role of reason in the development of society, humanity, and human civilisation. This transition is viewed as being objectively necessitated by the need to preserve humanity as the bearer of this reason.

The significance of the concept of the noosphere extends beyond merely being the initial step towards understanding the new role of reason in the development of human society. It also highlights the influence of reason on the Earth itself and, to a considerable extent, on the processes occurring within its lithosphere, hydrosphere, biosphere, and atmosphere, as well as partially in the outer space beyond the atmosphere. The noosphere concept anticipates, albeit in a vague and rather vague, "undescribed" form, some trends related to the development of the reason itself.

The theory of Noonomy also acknowledges this aspect but primarily adopts a pragmatic approach, focusing on the role of knowledge in the technological development of production, the formulation of its objectives, and the shaping of the system of human needs. It focuses on the substantive aspects of the problem of noodevelopment, which are considerably more complex than simply articulating a general message, even one that is supported by the theory of Noonomy, from the noospheric approach regarding the role of humanity in its interactions with the surrounding world. However, the general principles governing the further evolution of the human reason have not yet been sufficiently addressed within the theory of Noonomy. From this perspective, the concept of the noosphere provides a catalyst for advancing the discussion, but not from the speculative conjectures of its original proponents. Instead, it offers a foundation for a systematic scientific approach within the framework of the general theory of Noonomy.

The idea of noosphere can get a special development if we approach it from the position of the system of views that form the basis of the theory of Noonomy.

12.1. Formation of the Noosphere Concept: Historical Overview

First of all, let us turn to the basics of the noosphere concept.

The concept of noosphere was not born out of nowhere, not as an epiphany that visited some outstanding thinkers and scientists. Its preconditions were formed throughout the whole XIX (perhaps, even XVIII) century and the beginning of the XX century.[2] Thus, the works of Alexander Humboldt articulate the concept of the unity of life processes occurring on Earth. Anticipating the later notion of "biosphere", he introduces the concept of "organic life-sphere" (die organische Lebenssphäre) in 1826 (Bodrunov, 2016à; Bodrunov, 2021à: 172). The term "biosphere" also appears in the work of the Austrian geologist Eduard Suess (Suess, 1875: 159). In 1902, geographer and anthropologist D.N. Anuchin introduced the concept of "anthroposphere", considering it as the stages of development and forms of human culture on the surface of the Earth (Menshutkin, Levchenko, 2017: 275).

The American geologist James Dana similarly identified the epoch marked by the emergence of humanity and reason as the pinnacle of natural evolution. He remarked, "In this organic history, there are successive phases of progress, or series of culminations, with the creation of Human and Reason as the last and highest of these culminations" (Dana, 1863: 126).

In distinguishing between the Age of Reason and the Age of Human in the evolutionary hierarchy (Dana, 1863: 130), Dana emphasises the spiritual dimension of development. He states, "As the body, through its development and adaptation, is made to serve and nurture the soul, which slowly matures in connection with it, so the system of the world, in both its inorganic and organic aspects, throughout its history and in its final transformations, has been oriented towards human, the ultimate, supreme, spiritual creation. And the Earth serves its primary purpose by nurturing this new creation for a still more exalted stage – that of spiritual existence" (Dana, 1863: 574).

The Italian geologist Antonio Stoppani, based on similar considerations, introduces the concept of the Anthropozoic Era in the development of the Earth (Stoppani, 1873). American geologist Joseph Le Conte introduced the concept of the "Psychozoic Era" in 1877 (Le Conte, 1877).

The views of these and other scientists reflect a broader tendency to conceptualise the role of the reason within the natural system and to acknowledge the critical influence of humanity on the Earth's natural environment. These approaches later gave rise to the development of the Anthropocene concept (Hamilton and Grinevald, 2015).

The subsequent advancement was made by oceanologist J. Murray, who, in 1912, proposed not only that humanity had ushered in a new epoch in the Earth's evolution but also that a distinct sphere of existence had emerged alongside the spheres of animate and inanimate nature. He termed this new sphere the "psychosphere" (Murray, 1912). In the Russian edition of his book, this idea is articulated as follows: "Allowing our imagination a bit more latitude, we can say that within the biosphere, humanity has created a sphere of reason and understanding and is endeavouring to interpret and explain the cosmos; we might refer to this as the 'psychosphere'" (Murray, 1923: 136).

However, the development of the noosphere concept involved more than just identifying the period associated with human activity in the Earth's history and highlighting the unique role of the human reason in the evolutionary process. The formation of the noosphere concept had deeper natural-scientific and philosophical roots, drawing on the ideological heritage of numerous predecessors as well as the work of scientists who were contemporaneous with its founders. The philosophical foundation of the noosphere concept can be traced back to the works of the eminent Immanuel Kant, who illuminated the profound problems and contradictions inherent in the human reason. These issues remain central to Western philosophical discourse to this day. It is also important to acknowledge the influence of Arthur Schopenhauer's philosophy, particularly his concept of the "will to live", which posits that the evolution of forms of existence progresses from the most basic cosmic matter to life and ultimately to human consciousness.

The investigation into the role of the human reason within the universe was further stimulated by natural scientists who explored the tendency of the physical world towards energy dissipation, or increasing entropy, in their works. This includes, in particular, William Thomson (Baron Kelvin) and his concept of the "heat death of the Earth," as well as Rudolf Clausius, who extended this idea to the hypothesis of the "heat death of the universe," grounded in the second law of thermodynamics – the principle of increasing entropy. N.A. Umov investigated the anti-entropic processes occurring in living nature, which counteract the increase of entropy in cosmic matter. In his early 20th-century works on evolution, he identified a fundamental property of organised matter and a key indicator of its existence, the "non-entropic" increase in "orderliness" or "slenderness" in nature. This increase was attributed to the evolutionary processes of living organisms and the phenomenon of life itself.

A significant role in the formation of the noosphere concept was played by the contributions of biologists, beginning with Jean-Baptiste Lamarck, who developed one of the earliest theories of the evolution of living organisms. To him also belongs the idea that human is capable of destroying his environment (Lamarck, 1820). Charles Darwin should also be included in this context, as Friedrich Engels (along with Karl Marx, another "genetic father" of the noosphere theory) drew upon Darwin's work to generalise the concept of development.

A huge contribution to the development of the noosphere concept was made by V.I. Vernadsky. His teacher, Russian soil scientist V.V. Dokuchaev, who founded the school of scientific soil science and developed the theory of soil as an integral natural body, had a significant influence on his development as a scientist and the direction of his research. Vernadsky's works also reflect the influence of S.A. Podolinsky, who proposed the idea that human labour can conserve and transform dispersed energy into an ordered form (Podolinsky, 1880).

In the first third of the 20th century, N.A. Umov's ideas were further developed in the studies of Erwin Bauer. Bauer's research focused on the fundamental thermodynamic differences between living and non-living matter and highlighted the importance of these thermodynamic characteristics of living matter for understanding "progressive evolution", which he argued inevitably leads to the emergence of reason (Bauer, 1935).

The ideas of the so-called "Russian cosmism" had a significant influence on the development of the noosphere concept. One can point to the works of the Russian religious philosopher N.F. Fedorov, who put forward the idea of human as a gardener of the "noospheric garden" in his large, encyclopaedic-format creation "Philosophy of the Common Cause".

The development of many of these ideas was continued in I.M. Borzenko's "concept of noospheric humanism". It is also worth remembering the general civilisation ideas of K.E. Tsiolkovsky (they have been extensively and fruitfully researched by A. Ursul). What I find important in Tsiolkovsky's ideas is his belief that the degree of development of a social organism is determined by its maturity from the perspective of reason, a view with which I agree. Additionally, Tsiolkovsky understood the noosphere more broadly than Vernadsky, envisioning it not merely as a planetary layer but as part of a "cosmonoosphere". He linked the degree of humanity's reason with the unification of all intelligent beings to achieve the goals of their existence and development, which he perceived as centred around the common good, among other values.

Our philosophers-thinkers N. Berdyaev and P.A. Florensky contributed a lot to the formation of the foundation of the noosphere theory. P.A. Florensky's concept of "pneumatosphere" has many parallels with the concept of noosphere as presented by V.I. Vernadsky and Teilhard de Chardin (Correspondence..., 1989).

Strange as it may seem, there is a clear alignment between Vernadsky's idea that the governing laws of animate and inanimate things are different – yet this difference is a necessary condition for the unity of the Universe and its sustainable existence – and Niels Bohr's concept of "complementarity of animate and inanimate things". V.I. Vernadsky and E. Le Roy (with his thesis about the transition of the biosphere to a new state – noosphere), as well as Teilhard de Chardin, took much from A. Bergson on the "creative evolution of life" (in particular, from his hypothesis of the one-way directionality of time and the one-sidedness of the evolution of life in the development of the universe). This hypothesis was later supported by Vernadsky. Edouard Le Roy, as a student and collaborator of Henri Bergson, embraced his idea of the "vital impulse", the desire of matter for life (Bergson, 1907).

Vernadsky was well acquainted with the works of many of his predecessors (Vernadsky, 1991: 238-239) and at first thought within the framework of their general approach, so far only pointing out that with the development of mankind a new geological epoch was being formed. In his work *La Geochimie* (1924), based on lectures he delivered at the Sorbonne from 1922 to 1923, Vernadsky referred to this epoch as the "Psychozoic Era" or the "Age of Reason", following the terminology of his predecessors. He wrote, "But in our geological epoch – the Psychozoic Era, the Age of Reason – a new geochemical fact of great importance is manifesting itself. Over the last thousand years, humanity's geochemical impact, which captures green living matter through agriculture, has become intense and overly diverse. We are seeing an astonishing rate of growth in this action. This is the impact of the collective consciousness and reason of humanity on geochemical processes. Man introduced a new form of interaction between living matter and raw matter. Here, not only the elements necessary for the production, formation of living matter that alter its molecular structures come into play. These are the necessary elements for technology and the creation of civilised life forms. Man does not act here as *Homo sapiens*, but as *Homo faber* (translated from the author's French) (Vernadsky, 1924: 342). And Vernadsky summarises his conclusion as follows: "Together with human, a new geological force has certainly appeared on the surface of the Earth" (translated from the author's French) (Vernadsky, 1924: 344).

The most complete expression of this scientific trend was given in the concept of noosphere. The first mention of the term "Noosphere" appears in Teilhard de Chardin's essay "Hominisation", written in 1925 but published much later. He wrote, "More clearly than others, the geologist Suess has defined the earthly value of the mysterious living shell which has arisen in the radiance of geological times around our stellar unity. What we propose here, although this perspective may initially seem unfathomable and fantastical, is to regard the thinking layer of the biosphere as belonging to the same zoological (or, if you prefer, telluric) order as the Biosphere itself. The more we consider it, the more genuine or correct this extreme solution seems. Unless we are to avoid incorporating humanity into the common history of earthly unity without diminishing him, we must ensure that humanity does not disrupt this unity. Instead, humanity should be elevated within it, but not separated or detached from it. And this ultimately leads us to envision a sphere above the biosphere of animals – the sphere of humanity, the sphere of reflection, of conscious invention, of a sensed union of souls (if you like, the Noosphere). This requires us to consider the foundation upon which this new essence has arisen, a unique phenomenon of transformation impacting pre-existing life" (translated from the author's French) (Teilhard de Chardin, 1925, 1957: 91-92).

The term "Noosphere" was first introduced into scientific circulation by Teilhard de Chardin's friend and colleague Edouard Le Roy in his 1927 publication (Le Roy, 1927). Although the idea of the noosphere, which was formulated by Teilhard de Chardin and Edouard Le Roy, was born largely due to their discussions with Vernadsky in 1922–1923, when Vernadsky gave his lectures at the Sorbonne, Vladimir Ivanovich himself developed his concept of the noosphere much later, around the mid-1930s. In his interpretation, the understanding of the noosphere differed significantly from that offered by Le Roy and Teilhard de Chardin, although he recognised Le Roy's scientific superiority in this matter (Vernadsky, 1944). The distinction between these concepts is explored in detail in Levit (2000).

At this stage, we are interested in what all these scientists put into the concept of "noosphere".

Firstly, they emphasised the intimate connection between the biosphere and the Earth's noosphere, highlighting that the noosphere emerges from the evolution of the biosphere. The formation of the noosphere signifies that human influence on the development of the biosphere, as well as on the Earth's entire surface shell – including the lithosphere, hydrosphere, and atmosphere – becomes a decisive factor.

Secondly, they drew attention to the evolution of the human reason itself, seeking to achieve the spiritual unity of humanity. While united on the last point, they interpreted it differently. While the proponents of Catholic modernism, such as Teilhard de Chardin and Édouard Le Roy, envisioned a spiritual unity of all humanity in God, Vernadsky interpreted this spiritual unity as a global cooperation founded on the universality of scientific knowledge. In a manuscript drafted between 1936 and 1938, Vernadsky emphasised: "Man must understand, once he is encompassed by a scientific rather than merely philosophical or religious conception of the world, that he is not an accidental, independent phenomenon, free from the influence of the surrounding biosphere or Noosphere" (Vernadsky, 1991: 21). And further he repeated this thesis many times: "...man, having developed scientific thought in the social environment, creates a new geological force in the biosphere, which had not been there before. The biosphere has passed or, rather, is passing into a new evolutionary state – the noosphere and is being processed by the scientific thought of social mankind" (Vernadsky, 1991: 24 et al.).

Firstly, it is important to note that the ideas of the noosphere, as interpreted by Le Roy and de Chardin, could not be overlooked in the theory of Noonomy. This includes, in particular, considerations of the role of knowledge, reason, and spiritual elevation in personal development, as well as other aspects integral to the concept of Noonomy. Secondly, Vernadsky, in my view, approached the problem with greater depth, not reducing it merely to ecology as some contemporary "noospherists" might interpret his work. He also drew on the natural-scientific concepts available at that time.

Although Vernadsky did not explicitly address the possibility that human interference in nature could lead to what we now term an ecological crisis, he did, despite his general optimism, recognise the potentially destructive aspects of human activity. Thus, in his article published in 1939, he noted:

"We are living in an unprecedentedly new, geologically bright epoch. Man, through his labour – and his conscious relationship to life – recycles the Earth's envelope – the geological domain of life – the biosphere. He transforms it into a new geological state; by his labour and consciousness, the biosphere is transformed into the noosphere. It creates new biogeochemical processes in the biosphere that did not exist before. The biogeochemical history of the chemical elements, a planetary phenomenon, is changing dramatically. On our planet, for example, new free metals and their alloys, which never existed in it, are created in huge masses. Such as aluminum, magnesium, and calcium. Plant and animal life is drastically altered and disrupted. New races and species are created. The face of the planet is changing in profound ways. The noosphere stage is created" (Vernadsky, 1939: 6).

It should be noted that Vernadsky's concept of the noosphere encompasses several points that are highly significant for the theoretical analysis of contemporary trends. Thus, Vernadsky as early as in 1926 noted a sharp acceleration of the pace of science development, equating it to the explosion of scientific creativity (Vernadsky, 1927), and then definitely connects this phenomenon with the period of transition of the biosphere to the noosphere (Vernadsky, 1991: 37–38). At the same time, Vernadsky asserts that "reason is a transient manifestation of the higher forms of life, *Homo sapiens*, within the biosphere, transforming it into the noosphere. It is not and cannot be the ultimate or maximum form of life's manifestation". They can't be manifested by a human brain." Building on this thesis, he makes a bold prediction: "a change in human's thinking apparatus may prove probable and even inevitable" (Vernadsky, 1991: 101).

The content of the noosphere, according to Vernadsky, is not determined only by the development of scientific thought or human reason in general, he includes culture in this content as well (Vernadsky, 1991: 68). Moreover, he emphasises that it is by the energy of human culture that the noosphere is created (Vernadsky, 1991: 126). Finally, according to Vernadsky's thought, the formation of the noosphere becomes possible only as an action "in the interests of freely thinking humanity as a unified whole" (Vernadsky, 1944). Thus, it is worth noting that the early proponents of the noosphere concept identified the nascent emergence of a trend that would later develop in a more comprehensive form.

Academician A.E. Fersman, a contemporary of Vernadsky, who acknowledged himself, to some extent, as his pupil, studied biogeochemical processes, which were an important aspect of the noosphere theory, as well as the problems of human technological activity. He developed the theory of technogenic migration of chemical elements and actually laid the foundations of the theory of technocenoses. It was he who introduced the concept of "technogenesis" into science (Fersman, 1934: 27).

There is much to be said about the subsequent prominent noosphere researchers, as the concept is very rich in possible extensions. Among them, we should certainly include Academician Vlail Kaznacheev, a theoretical biologist and founder of the science of human adaptation, and Pobisk Kuznetsov, who studied the sustainable development of humanity within the "nature-society-human" system, along with several other notable scientists. It is especially worth highlighting an outstanding scientist who left us at the turn of the XX–XXI centuries, N.N. Moiseev, who created a slender theory of the evolution of the Universe – through thermodynamic self-organisation of the system from non-living matter to living matter, to man, to reason (as an inherent element of the Universe, its top and its universe).

Many conceptual tenets of the noosphere theory, particularly those related to the spiritual nature of humanity and its development, have their roots in various religious and philosophical teachings, especially within monotheistic traditions such as Christianity.

It was in such "areopagus" of thinkers that what was somehow verbalised by Teilhard de Chardin, the author of the term "Noosphere", and (and in their closest "unanimity") by V.I. Vernadsky in the form of the concept of noosphere, not fully described by them, which was further developed in the modern "noospherology". Unfortunately, many alien layers have appeared in it, and it seems that soon Vernadsky will have to be defended against "developers".

12.2. Objects and Methods of Research of Noonomy and Noosphere

Our approach is firmly grounded in the application of *fundamental laws governing the development of matter* – both animate and inanimate. This includes the entire developmental process, from the material sphere to its role in supporting life (with a focus on humanity as a biosubstance). Additionally, our approach incorporates the laws governing societal development, encompassing the material necessities of societal existence as well as economic, technological, and psychological factors. It also integrates general philosophical principles of being. In this context, Noonomy ("nomos") is grounded in the recognition of the inherent *unity of the material and spiritual* realms as two aspects of the same reality – the *universe* that gives rise to *reason*. This perspective forms a central philosophical concept in Noonomy, with a logical framework that justifies both the *necessity and inevitability* of society's transition to a new state. The features of this new state are delineated clearly through the application of this logical framework. This state is considered as a *natural stage in the development of the Universe*, generating and manifesting (through self-awareness) at a certain stage of its evolution the reason ("noo"). Hence, all the main theses of Noonomy as a theory of civilisational development, namely, the development of *human* – as an "individual" *carrier of reason*, and noosociety – as a *"collective"* carrier of reason.

In the theory of Noonomy, reason ("noo") is evolutionarily manifested through the transformation of its carriers: individuals and society. Humans evolve by gradually developing their capacity to assimilate knowledge, distinguish themselves from their environment, recognise their *needs*, define their *interests*, realise *values*, and seek ways to satisfy them. Concurrently, society, as the "collective" carrier of reason, develops *its own* needs, interests, and values. The evolution of reason also depends on the dynamic interplay between individuals and society.

It is crucial to recognise that the level of human and social awareness regarding their fundamental needs is not static. The carriers of reason, like all entities in the Universe, are in a state of continuous development. They increasingly comprehend their needs and interests over an extended temporal horizon, often prioritising long-term, significant objectives over immediate, short-term needs. This shift is guided by a progressively deeper understanding of fundamental values, thus evolving their evaluative framework towards a more developed notion of "noo".

This is why, as mechanisms for satisfying lower-order needs evolve – such as through the transition to a new industrial society of the second generation (NIS.2), with advancements in technology and NIS.2 industries

– economy, as a means of meeting these needs, will eventually be succeeded by Noonomy. Noonomy represents a non-economic approach to satisfying human needs (individual needs) that are formed within the framework of a noocritical value system. This approach is aligned with the fulfillment of societal needs within a type of society we refer to as a noosociety, where Noonomy will become the material foundation.

Only within such a paradigm is true "sapiens-development" of both individuals and society achievable. This approach is essential for overcoming various crises and challenges – ecological, climatic, psychological, and economic – that could threaten our civilisation. Our civilisation represents the manifestation of reason through the evolution of its carriers within the development of the Universe, and addressing these challenges is crucial to preventing the potential extinction of our species. It is important to note that the presence of a rational element within us does not preclude the possibility of our civilisation's demise due to bifurcation processes in the Universe. This includes potential bifurcations of reason itself or its specific carriers – humanity, at present, though likely not the only one. But reason (knowledge, idea, spirit), as an inherent property of the universe, will exist and will be continued in other worlds/forms. And this is also a quite concrete and important conclusion of the theory of Noonomy and a warning for mankind to think about how to live further. And is the "economic tit in hand" better for our civilisation than the "crane of Noonomy" in the sky?

What then do we put in the concept of "Noosphere"? One can, apparently, understand it as a kind of "action space" of the reason extending to the entire universe. Perhaps, here, there is a convergence (if we set aside the details) of interpretations from many foundational figures and researchers of the noosphere theory – ranging from V.I. Vernadsky and Pierre Teilhard de Chardin to K.E. Tsiolkovsky and N.N. Moiseev – regarding the philosophical abstraction of the manifestation of "universal reason", or more precisely, "universal noo".

What is the only *fundamental similarity* between noosphere theory and Noonomy theory in that they take a holistic view of the most important subject – *civilisational development*. And both theories, coming from *different origins*, emphasise *reason as a universal instrument* of such development (and this is not accidental!). And this needs to be emphasised.

The theory of Noonomy represents a synergetic perspective on the specific carriers of reason – both individuals and society. It examines their formation and development, including the evolution of humans as noobiosocial entities and the growth of society towards the level of noosociety. Noonomy examines the process of establishing the material foundation for such a social structure and ensuring the sustenance of individuals within it. It is also a scientific discipline that explores the principles and methods for advancing civilisation towards the formation of a noosociety.

However, the founders of the idea of noosphere failed to reveal the regularities and material bases of the development of human civilisation and human reason itself. Even the views articulated in more detail by Academician Vernadsky, which represented a significant scientific and worldview breakthrough at their time, are now recognised as somewhat limited from the perspective of contemporary science. This limitation arises primarily from their failure to address the specific material basis for the formation of the "sphere of reason" and the objective "predetermination" of humanity's progression towards it within civilisational development.

Why, on what basis exactly in the XIX–XX centuries did human became a decisive "geological force", and why exactly in the first third of the twentieth century scientists saw the emerging transition to the noosphere? These questions were not even posed by them, and accordingly, they were not answered. Neither the reasons for the explosive growth of science nor the foundations on which the formation of the unity of mankind would become possible have been revealed.

The advancement of contemporary scientific knowledge and the socio-economic progress of humanity offer a robust foundation for a more profound exploration of the issues that the original founders of the noosphere concept, as well as many post-Vernadian interpreters, either left unresolved or did not fully articulate. Addressing these issues requires reliance on the patterns of technological development in production and an understanding of how technological shifts influence the social structure of production.

The theory of Noonomy is constructed on the study of these regularities, elucidating not only the material foundation for the growing significance of knowledge in human society but also the conditions under which knowledge becomes a decisive factor in the evolution of production. Simultaneously, the theory of Noonomy addresses how changes in production impact socio-economic relations, institutions, and the overall structure of society.

One of the crucial issues addressed by the noosphere concept – namely, the nature of human interactions with the natural environment – is also explored in the theory of Noonomy. This theory not only elucidates the contradictions contributing to the escalating ecological crisis but also suggests potential solutions for overcoming these contradictions. It aims to ensure sustainable development and a conflict-free transition to a noosocial order. However, it is this aspect of Vernadsky's legacy that is of great interest to other areas of modern science, especially those that study the problems of ecological balance and sustainable development (Trubetskova, 2010).

The theory of Noonomy places significant emphasis on the evolution of the human reason, its interaction with culture, and the development of new criteria for rational human activity. This includes the establishment of a noocriteria base, which encompasses the values, needs, and goals essential for human development.

12.3. Noonomy as the Material Basis of the Noosphere

When addressing how the theory of Noonomy addresses the issues arising from the concept of the noosphere, it is essential to examine the relationship between these two concepts – Noonomy and the noosphere.

In some respects, the basic theses of the theory of Noonomy are similar to the concept of noosphere, since they concern the space of human reason and culture. In this context, Noonomy serves as the material foundation for all social life, structured around criteria of reason and culture, such as noosociety and noocivilisation. In this sense, Noonomy provides the tangible basis upon which the noosphere can be realised.

The advancement of contemporary technological modes, which results in a substantial increase in knowledge intensity, establishes the conditions necessary for the emergence of a new industrial society of the second generation (NIS.2). In turn, NIS.2 provides the foundation for the transition to Noonomy, marking a shift to a non-economic mode of production. This mode of production prioritises the satisfaction of human needs based not on economic criteria (which, following Aristotle, can be considered chrematistic) but on the criteria of knowledge and culture. The central element within this system of needs is the development of the individual, particularly the enhancement of human creativity and abilities. This system of needs facilitates a shift away from the growing strain on the natural environment, which is driven by an economic model focused on continuous consumption growth.

Humans are liberated from direct involvement in material production, relinquishing tasks that can be performed by an autonomously functioning technosphere. This shift allows individuals to focus on cognitive and creative activities, which are fundamental for advancing production and fostering development.

The formation of Noonomy allows us to concretise the characteristics of the noosphere. The evolution of human reason in the twentieth century has already taken a significant step forward by enabling the universal exchange of knowledge, relying on information and communication technologies. There are, of course, still significant obstacles to making this exchange fully free and universal, as noted in the UNESCO contribution.[3] Such obstacles as state and trade secrets, private intellectual property are an objective consequence of the existing economic and political structure of the world. Nevertheless, the material basis for the unimpeded and unlimited circulation of knowledge is already in place, and it serves as a prerequisite for the steps towards genuine spiritual unity of humankind.

In addition to the material foundation for spiritual unity, other prerequisites related to the substantive characteristics of the human reason are also essential. The theory of Noonomy raises the crucial question of how the transformation of human reason into a dominant factor of development will shape its orientation. It prompts us to consider what criteria of rationality, as well as definitions of good and evil, will guide this reason. "The noosphere is something that emerges not purposefully, but as an inevitable product of human society at a certain stage of its self-development. By itself, it does not guarantee a "reign of goodness". Therefore, the very existence of the noosphere immediately raises the question of what kind of imperatives of reason will prevail in it" (Bodrunov, 2018à: 182). The solution to these questions lies not so much in the plane of the regularities of the evolution of reason itself, but is determined both by the material conditions of its development and by the social relations within the framework of which it develops.

The transition towards Noonomy, driven by the increasing knowledge intensity of production, results in the emergence of a growing segment of individuals for whom the discovery and application of new knowledge, along with related creative processes, become central to their activities. Recently, these creative processes – ranging from industrial innovation to artistic creation – have primarily (though not exclusively) been evaluated according to economic rationality. These criteria have, over a long period of time, contributed to the progress of production, the growth of knowledge of the world around us and human self-knowledge, the development of his abilities and the satiation of his needs. However, the further we go, the more the contradictions caused by the orientation of human activity to these criteria grow, and each step in our development entails the most serious negative consequences.

Human reason has become the most powerful geologic force, but this force has not-so-subtle consequences of its application. Humans are threateningly upsetting the natural balance, undermining the Earth's ability to naturally reproduce its ecosystem. Economic rationality leads to economic growth for the sake of increasing consumption, and this has long been a huge problem. It is impossible for all nations and peoples of the Earth to achieve the levels of consumption achieved by the most developed nations today. The populations of these nations siphon off a substantial share of the world's resources and provide a huge amount of waste that pollutes the natural environment. For example, the USA, home to about 5 per cent of the world's population, consumes 25 per cent of the world's fossil fuels, produces and uses 24 per cent of the world's energy, while generating 72 per cent of hazardous waste (Perkins, 2007: 5). If the global community continues to adhere to these standards of consumption and pollution, the planet may not survive, as the Earth can no longer sustain the reproduction of natural resources depleted by human economic activities. Thus, the issue of revising the criteria of rationality in human economic activities and the reasonableness of forming human needs becomes increasingly critical. These criteria cannot change on their own, even if one realises the severity of the problems that following the old, economic criteria of rationality entails. For them to change, objective preconditions must accumulate in the nature of people's activities.

These prerequisites consist, firstly, in the growth of knowledge-intensity of production, which leads to an increase in the level of education and qualification of workers. Acceleration of the innovation process expands the need to develop the creative potential of the employed. Simultaneously, there is a rise in employment within professions that encompass a broad range of creative functions, such as management, business services, research and development, education, and the ICT sector (Wyatt, Hecker, 2006; Yang, Gu, 2021).

Moreover, modern technologies increasingly enable individuals to distance themselves from direct production processes, relegating them primarily to roles as researchers, developers, and innovators. They take on functions such as goal-setting, oversight, and, in the service sector, interpersonal interaction. These processes have already led to the formation of a stratum of people for whom the motives of their production activities have changed significantly, and with it there have been shifts in values and the structure of needs. In this we see a step towards changing the values and criteria that will guide humanity as a whole in the future.

The emergence of material prerequisites for transitioning to new criteria of rationality and values, which influence the structure of needs, does not automatically result in their formation. In addition, only a minority of those employed in social production have access to creative functions. The process of replacing humans in direct production with robots is still developing slowly. Thus, the projects of forming Industry 4.0, which is a prototype of unmanned production, have been developed for more than a dozen years, but have not yet left the stage of individual experiments. Experts argue that Industry 4.0 is still in an "embryonic" phase, encountering numerous technical, organisational, and social challenges. Others, while less definitive, also highlight that there remains limited experience in corporate practice concerning the deliberate and successful implementation of Industry 4.0 (Bodrunov, 2022b,e). The examples of practical applications of Industry 4.0 cited in publications often demonstrate only the use of individual technologies[4] (Immerman, 2020). In contrast, the concept of Industry 4.0 is centred on the integration of multiple technological solutions, enabling simultaneous management and control of technological, logistical, and marketing processes through digital platforms. According to the Boston Consulting Group, Industry 4.0 is high on today's agenda, but only one or two distinct aspects of Industry 4.0 are being realised in practice.[5]

However, the need for profound changes in the conditions of production and in human consciousness has already become very urgent. The crisis in human-nature relations cannot continue until all people have the opportunity to free themselves from routine production functions, to focus on creative self-realisation – and to cool down to the pursuit of increasing consumption of goods. Therefore, the formation of the noosphere can no longer be a spontaneous process, just a "by-product" of the development of engineering, technology and scientific knowledge of the world. Active efforts are needed to transform moral norms, increase cultural mastery, and create noovalues. This will make it possible to put human goals on a truly reasonable basis, to establish a truly human attitude of people to each other and to nature.

12.4. Evolution of Reason, Values and Cultural Norms in the Transition to Noonomy

Since the formation of the noosphere necessarily involves the process of scientific cognition, we cannot do without defining our values as true, i.e., corresponding to the objective conditions of reality. These are not some abstract immutable truths for all time. Even Hegel shrewdly remarked, "If truth is abstract, it is not truth" (Hegel, 1993: 88). No, it is about what is true for us moving forward, for overcoming the challenges and contradictions we face today. The Evangelist John has given us the words of Christ that symbolise the merging of the concept of truth with life's forward movement: "I am the way, and the truth, and the life" (John 14:6).

True values are intended to reaffirm and enhance the human essence within individuals, guiding them away from actions that would lead to the degradation of their environment and their own nature. Instead, these values aim to foster the development of personal identity through the pursuit of knowledge, the advancement of cultural enrichment, and the cultivation of mutually enriching interpersonal relationships.

The advancement of Noonomy necessitates profound shifts in the spiritual and moral development of humanity, alongside transformations in cultural norms and traditions. Such changes are essential to realigning human consciousness towards a more mindful stewardship of the natural environment and a rational structuring of individual and collective needs. This transformation will involve a recalibration of internal criteria of rationality, shifting focus from the mere expansion of consumption to prioritising the fulfillment of needs that align with the goals of human development.

The development of social regulation of production, which involves engaging all stakeholders in the decision-making process, alongside market self-regulation focused on economic criteria, can serve as transitional steps towards this shift. Such regulation facilitates the alignment of production with not only economic rationality but also with the satisfaction of specific needs defined by criteria of reason and culture. In the long term, this can lead to a shift from traditional economic modes of satisfying needs to a Noonomy framework (Bodrunov, 2018à, 2019, 2020à). In Noonomy, the satisfaction of people's needs will be based on the interaction of society with the autonomously functioning technosphere ("unmanned production"). In the transition to Noonomy, the sphere of market exchanges and economic relations will contract, making way for public regulation of technosphere development. This shift aims to foster conditions that enable the self-realisation of each individual's creative potential.

In transitioning to a new, non-economic rationality, it is crucial not only to leverage the achievements of reason in understanding reality but also to address the challenges inherent in moving beyond economic rationality. This involves evaluating and solving problems collectively while overcoming the limitations of traditional economic approaches. Just as importantly, what is it that can motivate a person to turn to reason and turn away from the lust to consume as much as possible? Changes in the content of a person's core activities that orient them towards knowledge-based creativity? Of course. However, human existence is not sustained solely by knowledge, professionalism, or even by creative achievements that advance the technosphere, which operates relatively autonomously from human intervention. What will determine our other needs, so that they also contribute to the elevation of our personality?

It is not coincidental that Vernadsky associated culture with the noosphere; cultural criteria are essential for guiding individuals in making informed choices regarding their needs, actions, and relationships with others. After all, the transition to Noonomy is based not only on new material prerequisites, but also on a new nature of relations between people, including the very spiritual unity, about which the founders of the idea of noosphere wrote. And if the material prerequisites determine the interaction of people with the sphere of production, their spiritual connection is determined by the level of their cultural development, which also depends on the material prerequisites and on the development of the process of cognition, but is not reducible to them.

Achievement of spiritual unity of mankind in the noosphere is impossible without assimilation of such cultural values and cultural criteria that allow to eliminate social conflict from the relationships between people. The advancement of knowledge-intensive production, particularly in the form of unmanned systems supported by a relatively autonomous technosphere, establishes the material conditions necessary for meeting the rational needs of individuals. This development creates the potential to mitigate social conflicts related to the distribution of material goods, resources, and wealth. But only the prerequisites. To overcome conflict, these prerequisites must be supplemented by new ideological principles, moral norms, and cultural traditions. The ideology of solidarism (Bodrunov, 2021à; Le Roy, 1927; Bourgeois, 1896) can act as one of the ideological tools guiding the evolution of human relations in this direction.

Noonomy does not eliminate differences between people, nor does it eliminate inequality. But it creates an opportunity to address economic inequality, the one that underlies the social conflicts of our time (Bodrunov, Galbraith, 2017), by dividing people according to their level of access to resources of production and consumption and forcing them to struggle for means of subsistence. Access to the primary factor of production – knowledge – will be unimpeded by economic barriers, facilitating the free circulation of knowledge and information. Differences in individual abilities will undoubtedly persist, yet the uniqueness of each human personality is essential for fostering the collective unity needed for collaborative endeavours. Indeed, reason is not merely an individual attribute; it evolves and manifests through the interactions among people. It is precisely these differences among individuals that provide the foundation for meaningful exchanges and the advancement of collective reasoning.

Joint creative activity, inseparable from the process of cognition, will act as a stimulus for the development of creative abilities, improvement of cultural and educational level of people, use and development of cognitive technologies. Both a high degree of knowledge mastery and advanced cultural development play crucial roles in mitigating conflicts and fostering the realisation that solidarity and mutual social responsibility are essential for addressing and overcoming societal problems and contradictions.

In contemporary times, marked by ecological crises and global disasters such as the coronavirus pandemic, there is an increasing recognition of the limitations of economic selfishness. This awareness underscores the necessity of prioritising solidarity and collective action. So far, the existing economic relations within the framework of the modern model of economy do not give an opportunity to completely abandon economic egoism. Nevertheless, there is a growing, albeit still contentious, understanding of the advantages of mutual consideration of diverse interests. This includes the pursuit of reasonable compromises and collaborative solutions, even as conflicting perspectives often emerge.

12.5. From Noonomy to the Noosphere

The Noonomy theory echoes a number of theoretical concepts proposed by many contemporary scholars. As a synthetic extension of earlier concepts spanning various scientific fields – ranging from economy and philosophy to technical and exact sciences – it incorporates the ideas of prominent contemporary figures. This includes, notably, Academician S.Yu. Glazyev, a member of the Russian Academy of Sciences and President of the World Association for Political Economy (WAPE), and Chinese Professor Cheng Enfu, a leading figure in the field of intellectual economy, among others (Figure 15).

In this context, the core scientific foundation of the theory of Noonomy is rooted in the economic sciences. The economy, understood as "economic practice", serves as the primary source and progenitor of Noonomy, which represents a more advanced approach to addressing societal needs.

We will pay special attention to the distinction between the conceptual apparatuses of the Noonomy theory and the terms "Noosphere" and "economy".

Given the ongoing expansion of interest in *the theory of Noonomy*, driven by the active engagement of its followers, researchers frequently revisit the

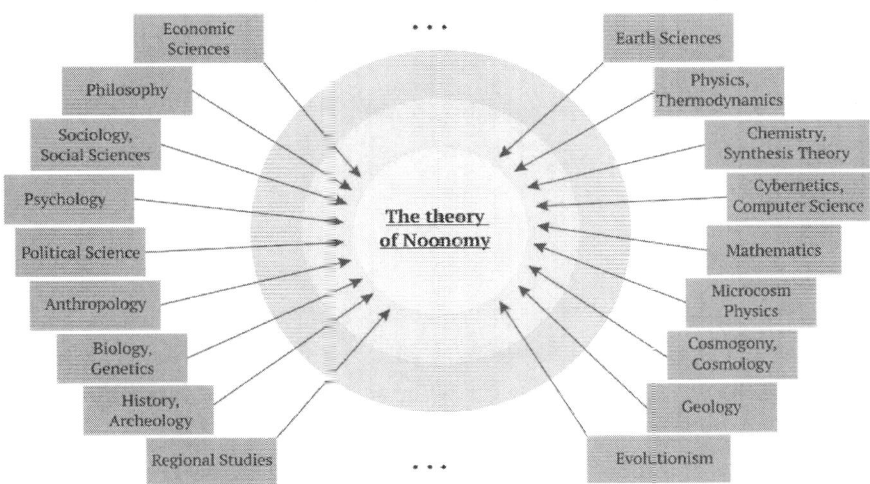

Figure 15. *The Noonomy theory (main sources from different fields of science)*

relationship between *Noonomy* and related concepts such as the *noosphere and traditional economic theories* (Bodrunov, 2022b). The similarity in the nomenclature of these categories often leads individuals encountering Noonomy to either (a) *conflate* these concepts entirely or partially with Noonomy, or (b) perceive it as a *"progressive" iteration*, representing an evolution of these concepts while *retaining their fundamental attributes.* Occasionally, colleagues who are not deeply familiar with the intricacies of Noonomy may attempt to categorise its proponents within established groups like noospherists. This is a *misunderstanding*, as we do not consider ourselves part of the tradition of noospheric theorists or their contemporary followers. Our objective is to elucidate and fully appreciate the *profound significance of the theory of Noonomy* by highlighting: a) certain *intersections* between Noonomy and the concepts of the noosphere and economy, and b) *the fundamental differences* distinguishing Noonomy from these concepts, in alignment with their ***inherent*** nature and content.

Let us consider a number of fundamental aspects, the correlation between *the theory of Noonomy and the theory of noosphere.*

The primary basis of the words "Noonomy" and "noosphere" contains an important related component: noo (from Greek noos – reason, thought). Thus, both emphasise the importance and *special role of reason* in human and social development.

Despite this common semantic element, the concepts of noosphere and Noonomy differ significantly. Based on the classical conception of the noosphere as articulated by É. Le Roy, Pierre Teilhard de Chardin, and and V.I. Vernadsky, it is understood as the "sphere of reason". More comprehensively, it is described as a "new state, a new quality of the biosphere, in which scientific thought in its planetary expression becomes a significant factor in geological evolution," influencing the biosphere, including the particular significance of the evolution of reason within the context of spiritual development and culture (Yashin, 2015:15; Bodrunov, 2022b). The second part of the term "Noonomy" mirrors the second part of "economy", (from Greek nomos, meaning "order", "law", or "custom"). This etymological similarity suggests a conceptual kinship between the two terms. In literal translation from Greek, "economy" refers to a set of rules or principles governing economic management. Noonomy represents something different.

> Noonomy (from Greek noos + nomos) is understood as a certain *"reasonable order"* of people's living arrangements, or a *reasonable world order* for the harmonious development of humanity and society.

The very name of *Noonomy* emphasises its difference from the concept of *noosphere*, first of all, by its *practical component and orientation* inherent in the term Noonomy (Noonomy differs from the concept of economy by the *breadth of coverage of social life*, organised on the basis of principles other than economy).

Noonomy in a certain way "touches" the concept of noosphere, which can be illustrated by the example of a fruit tree symbolising Noonomy. ***This tree is rooted in the economy, grows out of it, and is its negating spawn in the course of the development of NTP.*** The description of the noosphere phenomenon as a certain sphere of reason in the classical version does not show such a connection. In parallel, Noonomy engages with the concept of the noosphere by operationalising its theoretical implications through the development of a "noosociety" – a construct that is methodologically substantiated within the framework of Noonomy. This noosociety represents the practical realisation of the evolutionary and civilisational progression of humanity (Bodrunov, 2022b).

To better understand this imagery, let us turn to the sources and structure of the Noonomy theory (Figure 16).

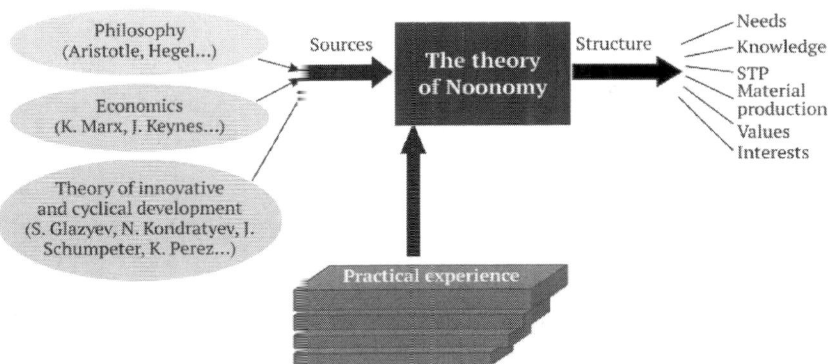

Figure 16. *Sources and structure of the Noonomy theory*

In line with the philosophical tradition of continuity, the genesis of any concept is typically rooted in a series of philosophical teachings and frameworks that contribute to its development. As noted by Karl Marx, his doctrine was methodologically grounded on three pillars: classical German philosophy, represented by Feuerbach and Hegel; classical English political economy, represented by Smith and Ricardo; and utopian French socialism (Yadgarov, 2007: 174). However, in the process of developing his own doctrine, Marx not only addressed the stages of the pre-development and formative phases of these philosophical ideas but also distanced himself from the classics by diverging on several key issues and "reversing" their perspectives (see examples in Mareev, Mareeva, 2003: 510–532).

The development of the theory of Noonomy as a distinct philosophical concept follows a parallel path. It is primarily built upon Aristotle's philosophy, considered the "founding father of economic science" (Konotopov, 2008), as well as the teachings of K. Marx and J.M. Keynes, who served as intellectual forerunners of unorthodox strands in modern economic theory. Additionally, it incorporates insights from Keynesian followers, particularly institutionalists and post-Keynesians, and draws upon the work of theorists of cyclical and innovative development, including S.Yu. Glazyev's concept of technological and global economic modes, N.D. Kondratiev's "long waves", J. Schumpeter's "clusters of innovations", and C. Perez's theories on technological revolutions and shifts in techno-economic paradigms.

In the course of our research, the theory of Noonomy has also undergone phases of "separation and reversal" with some of the aforementioned theoretical foundations and conceptual frameworks. This process includes critical engagements with the works of D. Bell and J.K. Galbraith, particularly regarding the "illusions of post-industrialism" and the analysis of the NIS.2 concept, as well as a re-evaluation of K. Marx's theories and S.Yu. Glazyev's contributions, among others. Detailed examples of these theoretical adjustments and reinterpretations can be found in Bodrunov (2018a).

Of course, here are only some clearly distinguished and strongly narrowed blocks of doctrines, which acted as a basis for the creation of the theory of Noonomy. In fact, it would take several scientific seminars just to list all the works and concepts from various fields of natural and social sciences (philosophical, social psychology, biology, cosmology, systems engineering, big number theory, systems analysis, informatics, thermodynamics and many others) that influenced the author's perception and understanding of the logic of the processes of civilisational (including socio-economic) development.

Analyzing the basis for the creation of the theory of Noonomy, let us highlight a few key points. Aristotle, divorcing the notions of *economy* (in the root meaning of the term as the rules of economic management and natural activities to satisfy the vital needs of people) and *chrematistics*, or the theory of enrichment and the art of unlimited profit (Konotopov, 2008: 196), actually predetermined the modern chrematistic state of development of what is now proudly called economy. At the same time, in *economy as a science* we observe the blossoming of the mainstream in the neoclassical version, and in *economy as a sphere of social life* – the processes of unstoppable financialisation and growing imbalance between the financial and real sectors, the formation and collapse of financial bubbles; frantic cross-border flows of hot money, the growth of social costs (inequality, poverty) and much more. All of these phenomena essentially represent a modern iteration of Aristotelian chrematistics, manifesting in its most refined, intensified, and advanced form. As noted by Aristotle, such a system inherently accumulates internal contradictions, which inevitably lead to crises. As the theory of Noonomy shows, there are only two real ways out of this situation: 1) "reasonable world order" and reasonable limitation of needs; 2) catastrophic variant up to the point of no return, if knowledge will be used not in noopurpose and society will not have time to realise and correctly implement the prospects opened for it by reason.

In this connection, a special role in Aristotle's doctrine for us is played by such a category as the ***limit***, characteristic of the field of economy (for more details see Konotopov, 2008: 196). However, Aristotle does not indicate how to define and place this limit in real life. This question is directly addressed by the theory of Noonomy – through the categories of *natural limitation of needs and their desimulatisation on the basis of culture and noovalues.* This distinction, highlighting the dynamics of needs development and the conceptual shift towards Noonomy as a framework for their fulfillment – an aspect not addressed by the noosphere theory – underscores the fundamental divergence between these two theoretical approaches. Specifically, it illustrates how Noonomy and the noosphere theory differ in addressing the formation of a noosociety (within Noonomy) versus the sphere of reason (within the noosphere theory).

The theory of Noonomy, in conjunction with *the theory of change of technological modes and the concept of change of world economic modes* proposed by S.Yu. Glazyev (Glazyev, 2021), can be considered a natural extension of Karl Marx's ideas. This includes aspects such as the analysis of the interaction between productive forces and production relations, as well as the thesis concerning the displacement of humans from direct production processes. At the same time, the theory of Noonomy distinctly emphasises its divergence from several conclusions drawn by *contemporary Marxists*. This differentiation is evident through its transition from *abstract* notions – such as the concept of the realm of freedom – to a more *concrete* framework. Specifically, Noonomy proposes the development of a detailed theory grounded in an interdisciplinary, and arguably supra-disciplinary, approach. This framework aims to elucidate the comprehensive, qualitative, and transformative changes occurring in societal life (Bodrunov, 2018a: 171).

Developing along these lines and considering the potential for expanding the scope of noovalues and the principal factor of social development – ***knowledge and its practical application in technological progress*** – Noonomy emerges as "***a non-economic method of organising economic activities to meet needs***, conducted by individuals who have transcended material production". It represents an "economic system that is distinguished from traditional economics by the absence of human relations in the process of material production" (Bodrunov, 2018a: 171). In this framework, ***it is a sphere where "there is no relationship to property and no property relations; where economy, as a method of meeting human needs, is neither present nor possible"*** (Bodrunov, 2022e: 42). Thus, being a generation of economy and based in its theory on a number of economic doctrines, *Noonomy differs significantly from economics*. Moreover, the very emergence and further establishment of Noonomy, confirming the Hegelian philosophical narrative, actually *denies the further existence of economy.*

At the same time, the issue of transitioning to the implementation of ideas related to "noo-utilisation" is only indirectly acknowledged, implicitly suggested, and effectively bypassed in the theory of the noosphere (at least in its classical sources). It does not establish the fundamental regularities critical to the theory of Noonomy: the *actual* transition of civilisation from an economic mode of satisfying needs, the exploration of the essence of this process, and the *mechanisms* that objectively facilitate such a transition, which would lead civilisation to the realm of reason The disclosure of this provision in the theory of Noonomy makes its structure more integral and less abstract.

It is essential to highlight the critical fourth foundation of Noonomy theory – *practical experience.* This foundation plays a crucial role in precisely identifying the scope of issues and problems for in-depth investigation, accurately selecting the theoretical trajectory, and confidently advancing along it. Practical experience thus serves as a key support for theoretical developments, "nurturing" the Noonomy theory and reinforcing its framework. We especially emphasise the importance of observing ***"the unity of theory and practice, philosophy and life"*** (Mareev, Mareeva, 2003: 509).

In this context, ***Noonomy represents a plausible scenario for the future, characterised by its own invariants and stages*** (Figure 17). This scenario can be realised through a transition that includes a technological revolution, marked by shifts in technological modes (TM), leading to *knowledge-intensive* production and the establishment of *prerequisites for the New Industrial Society 2.0 (NIS.2).* This process is linked to the sixth and seventh technological mode and an overarching global economic paradigm (Glazyev, 2021). It *encompasses* not only the *transformation of socio-economic processes and institutions* but also a fundamental transformation of *humanity itself and its*

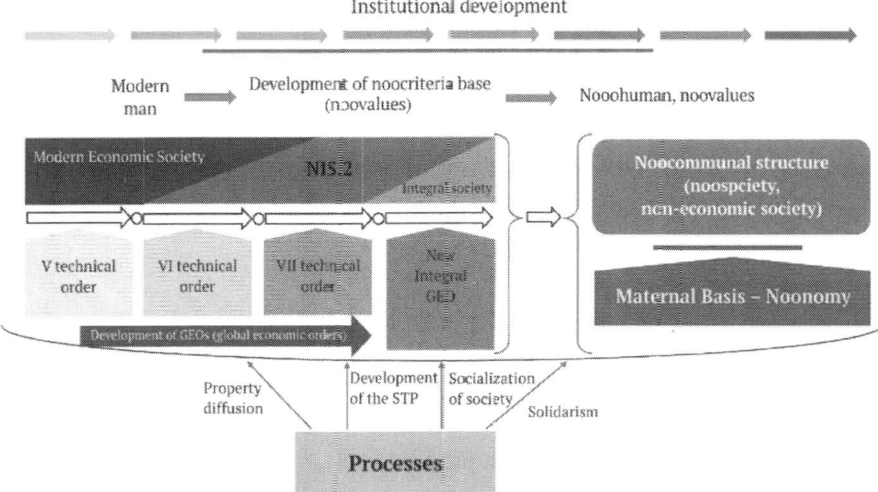

Figure 17. *Noonomy – a scenario for the future*

role within these processes. The theory of Noonomy is a doctrine of formation (***objectively possible and necessary***) and realisation of ***real life needs*** (including through *revealing the role of the phenomenon of knowledge* in social development); of the practical and objectively future ***way of their satisfaction*** (with highlighting the peculiarities of nooproduction); an absolutely real ***social order*** on the material basis of Noonomy as a non-economic way of satisfying needs and forming a noopersor (with the harmony of noorationality and noovalues), a noocommunity, and a noocivilisation. At the same time, the theory of Noonomy (which is important!) is not a "theoretical reflection" on some mythical and super distant future. ***The genesis of Noonomy*** as a forthcoming method for satisfying societal needs is already observable today. Therefore, it is pertinent to consider the theory of Noonomy as a ***foundational support for shaping contemporary policy and economic practice within nations.*** For instance, it could serve as a strategic project analogous to the public construction ideas in the People's Republic of China, or as a fundamental component of the "conceptual platform for advanced development strategies" proposed by Academician S.Yu. Glazyev for Russia. Additionally, Noonomy could inform the development of specific programmes at various levels, such as those for the re-industrialisation of the national economy based on advanced technological modes, import substitution, education, national security, and technological sovereignty. It also serves as a guiding framework for business and other sectors. Moreover, from a *practical* point of view, it allows to apply for these purposes effective developments from the theories of strategy, planning and forecasting, modelling, management and many others.

In this aspect, the theory of Noonomy necessitates attention to a number of "horizontals" – stages of transition to Noonomy – and a number of "verticals" of development presented in its theoretical basis. In particular, attention must be given to: a) The "vertical" of *technological progress* (V, VI, VII technological modes); b) The "vertical" of *economic modes* development, such as the current transition to NIS.2 based on the latest world economic system, with its conceptual foundation developed by Academician S.Yu. Glazyev, which is one of the cornerstones of Noonomy theory; c) The institutional "vertical" – with its stages of reforming *societal institutions*; d) The social "vertical", which gradually expands societal capabilities (notably including the recently promoted concept of "human-oriented economy" in Russia); e) The personal "vertical", which ensures the formation and *development of the nooperson based on an expanding core of values.* Finally, there must be a fundamental synchronisation of development across these "horizontals" and the *alignment* of movement vectors along the corresponding "verticals" to *avoid the emergence of disproportions and catastrophic points in the trajectory of civilisation's development as both a process and a system.*

Having completed a brief analysis of the root system, as well as the trunk and crown of the tree of Noonomy, let us move on to its fruits. In this case, the theory of Noonomy and classical ideas about the noosphere are related by the *duality of the author's thought,* traceable both in the first case (through the category of needs and their natural constraints – culture and *noovalues*) and in the second case (through the basic categories of *reason, science and culture* of Vernadsky and the spiritual and religious foundation laid to a greater extent by Le Roy, who is closer to us in a number of conclusions).

By introducing the category of *noo* (reason), the *classics* of noospheric doctrine were able to realise what is now called *scientific foresight.* Note that V.I. Vernadsky distinguished among the ***prerequisites*** for the formation of the noosphere:

- spread of humanity over the Earth's surface and its dominance as a *biological being with the privilege of reason*;
- development of people-to-people communication and *communication* tools;
- the discovery and development of *new energy sources*;
- universal *processes of democratisation*;
- burst of *scientific creativity* with global implications;
- ***and, finally, one of the most impressive results of noosphere development – the autotrophic nature of mankind*** and *through the change* (how? – biologically!?) of the *ways of needs satisfaction* – the *transition of its evolution into outer space* (Mironov, 2011: 96-97).

Obviously, the idea of a possible *autotrophic* humanity is *in contact* with the economic category of *need*. While not dismissing V.I. Vernadsky's remarkable idea and the associated premises, the theory of Noonomy, in analyzing its genesis, identifies *different **fundamental*** prerequisites for achieving the nooprinciples of human development. These prerequisites ***objectively*** arise from the logic of ***economic***, rather than merely biological development. Specifically, they include the processes identified in our previous work (Bodrunov, 2021à): (a) the *"diffusion of property"*; (b) *the acceleration of technological progress;* (c) the explosive growth of *societal socialisation*; and (d) the development of *solidarism* (which, while not negating democratic principles, prioritises societal interests and the interests of its members). These factors are not merely prerequisites but also objective conditions for achieving a social noostate. It should be noted that the ***factors of social development*** arising from the ***objective*** application of these principles are responsible for both the current conflicts in global development and the *positive processes* observed in several countries, notably in the People's Republic of China (PRC).

In contrast to the philosophical approach adopted in the theory of the noosphere, the theory of Noonomy emphasises not the category of ***pure reason***, but the category of ***knowledge***, which is *elucidated by reason and creates conditions and opportunities for its comprehension **and application***. At the same time, in the theory of Noonomy, mathematically speaking, reason is less than knowledge, given the presence of *Absolute Knowledge* – infinite and unattainable. *In the theory of Noonomy,* ***reason*** acts as a tool of *knowledge and decision-making* on the basis of what is known. That is why we speak only about the *contact in this part of the theory of Noonomy with the doctrine of noosphere* (in its original, initial version).

It should be noted that, in contrast to the well-developed theory of Noonomy and various schools of economic thought, the theory of the noosphere has not yet been fully formulated. This is acknowledged by contemporary proponents of the noosphere, who are proposing *their approaches* for the development and establishment of a new science termed "noospherology" (Rezhabek, 2015: 74-83). This theory in a number of aspects was *scientifically substantiated* in the works of Academicians Fersman, Kaznacheev, Professor N. Moiseev. At the same time, there is a growing dissemination of "expanded" and alternative interpretations, including various "additions" to the foundational ideas of this theory. In this context, critical evaluations have emerged in the scientific literature concerning both the classical theorists and the contemporary adherents of the noosphere doctrine. For example, it has been noted that Vernadsky's statements and works *do not clearly delineate* a conceptual framework for the noosphere. The actualisation of his teachings is often linked to broad and sometimes speculative interpretations of his ideas (Prozorov, 2012), attributed to the absence of a robust and detailed substantiation of its principles.

In defence of the foundational ideas of the noosphere theory, it is important to emphasise ***that the theory of Noonomy provides a comprehensive scientific substantiation for the principles and mechanisms of noodevelopment. Noonomy, as a method of satisfying social needs, serves as its material basis. In this regard, Noonomy, through its synthesis of scientific and spiritual dimensions,*** *aligns closely* ***with the classical notions of the noosphere as conceptualised by*** *Le Roy and Vernadsky* (Bodrunov, 2022b).

As previously demonstrated (Bodrunov, 2022e), Noonomy represents a ***distinct model of social structure.*** Within this framework, the development of both individuals and society is conceived in terms of "knowledge, culture, noovalues, and noorationality", with the aim of achieving *harmony through their practical* application. Such modelling *is not considered* by the noosphere theory. This harmony will be given and found by noo (reason) on the basis of ***knowledge*** comprehended by it – emphasised in the theory of Noonomy.

It is important to note that the theory of Noonomy, unlike the theory of the noosphere, places particular emphasis on the *evolution **of humanity** as a biosocial **being.*** This includes a focus on human labour activity, which, through the acceleration of technological progress (STP) and the development of noosocial relations, allows individuals to transcend ***labour*** confined to specific spatial, social, and temporal contexts. Consequently, this facilitates the *expansion of the boundaries of purely intellectual creativity, aligning with Marx's notion of extending the "space of activity" of the reason.* It is noteworthy that while the theory of the noosphere emphasises ***scientific** creativity* primarily as a means to achieve developmental and technological goals, the theory of Noonomy presents creativity as a distinct phenomenon. In Noonomy, *creativity* is not only an intrinsic quality of a nooperson but also a key factor in personal *"self-development"*.

12.6. Key Findings

The noosphere as a sphere of human reason receives a scientific basis in the theory of Noonomy. The idea of the noosphere on this basis ceases to be only a statement of the increased power and significance of human reason and a conjecture about the coming spiritual unity of mankind. The growth of the importance of reason receives a concrete material explanation in the development of modern technologies, leading to an increase in the knowledge-intensity of production, and to a sharp acceleration of innovation processes. At the same time, the level of education, qualifications and creative potential of those employed in production is growing, and the role of education and science in ensuring the development of this potential is increasing.

The nature of human activity is changing, gradually moving away from direct participation in production and concentrating on the functions of control, goal-setting, creative development of techniques and technologies in a relatively autonomous technosphere. At the same time, the motives and goals of people's activities are changing, as they are increasingly focused on self-actualisation in the process of creative activity, rather than on increasing the volume of absorbed goods. On this basis, a departure from the criteria of economic rationality is developing, and the pursuit of economic growth based on the unrestrained absorption of the Earth's resources is coming to an end. The structure of people's needs is changing in favour of creating conditions for self-development and ensuring a reasonable level of satisfaction of specific needs. The prevailing social values are changing, social conflict is being overcome and the tendency towards joint solidarity is developing.

The result of these tendencies is the free exchange of knowledge and information, the actual formation of a single sphere of reason – the noosphere. Only the values of reason and culture oriented to the elevation of the human personality, not divided by the partitions of selfish economic interests, can make reason an instrument not of destruction and not of war of all against all in the struggle for their "piece of the pie" in our civilisation, but the basis for the spiritual unity of mankind. It is not merely the advocacy of lofty ideals or the resignation to the looming threats facing humanity that matters, but rather the advancement of the objective conditions of human life and activity that fundamentally drives this progress. However, these objective conditions emerge through the rigorous process of understanding and addressing the contradictions in social development. They are shaped by the assimilation of intellectual and cultural achievements, the collective recognition of new values in our shared existence, and numerous practical decisions in economic, social, and cultural policies aimed at fostering genuine nooprogress. Here lies the path to the triumph of the truly human essence of the human race, our civilisational movement from "zoo" to "noo".

The theory of noonomy has its own landmark, backbone categories. The most important of these categories is knowledge.

Generally, the understanding and interpretation of the term "knowledge" is reduced either to the results of the cognition process, or to the possession of a set of information or awareness of something. In its definition of knowledge, the theory of noonomy adheres to a different understanding of its interpretation. First of all, knowledge should obviously not be simplified to the level of awareness, since possessing this or that information does not at all mean possessing true knowledge. Secondly, knowledge (both external – about the surrounding world and society, and "internal" – about one's inner world and wants) must be discovered and extracted – and in this aspect knowledge is similar to a certain resource or "commercial (useful) mineral", but specifically "useful", i.e., something that will subsequently be applied for the good. Thus, knowledge is not only the result of cognition processes – its acquisition and comprehension – but is also the result of its use, embodiment in reality (for example, in the form of technologies, culture, values, etc.) – this, by the way, is where the concepts of "knowledge intensity" of production emerge, which allows us to clearly define the period of change of the next technological paradigm, or "knowledge capacity" of the product being created, including the idea of knowledge transformation at the present stage (in the VI technological mode) into the main factor of production.

But the third – and most important – thing is different. This also includes the totality of laws of the objective world that exist outside of human will, which probably cannot be fully comprehended by man (related to the Absolute Spirit and His self-knowledge), and the Highest Knowledge embodied in religions and the setting of "boundaries" or "limits" of knowledge. The theory of noonomy, which allows us to cover all these facets and subtle aspects of knowledge as an amazingly complex and polysemantic concept, is therefore rightfully considered an interdisciplinary phenomenon and is often defined as one of the modern development trends in philosophy.

The theory of the noosphere and the theory of Noonomy **differ fundamentally** in several key aspects: their internal content, sources, structure, prioritisation and interpretation of scientific categories, scientific substantiation of core principles, level of practical orientation, and the development of implementation mechanisms. These differences underscore the radical divergence between the two theories.

The theories of noosphere and Noonomy are **similar** in the idea of a positive trend in the development of mankind on the basis of reason; the principles of autotrophic humanity in the theory of noosphere and human development on the basis of realisation of its needs in the theory of Noonomy; the principles of rational attitude to nature.

And finally, despite the "contacts" and fundamental differences between the concepts of Noonomy and noosphere, as well as the doctrines about them, they are **united** by scientific optimism and boundless faith in the best qualities and disclosure of the intellectual potential of Human. In line with V.I. Vernadsky, we are convinced that "we can view our future with confidence. It is in our hands. We will not let it go" (Mironov, 2011: 97 citing V.I. Vernadsky). These words of V.I. Vernadsky are supported by the theory of Noonomy, with one slight adjustment: "more confidently", as the theory of

Noonomy outlines a **pathway** to achieving a noosociety based on the **principles** proposed by the classical theorists of the noosphere.

Noonomy as a scientifically grounded concept and as a practical guide realises the vector of humanity's development to the embodiment of the basic principles of the noosphere theory.

Notes

1 Prepared on the basis of Bodrunov, 2022b,e.

2 For more details on the scientific background of the noosphere concept, see Zudilina, 2020.

3 A critical time, a critical approach: the role of media in building peaceful, just and inclusive societies: A concept note. World Press Freedom Day, UNESCO, 2017. pp. 11–12. https://en.unesco.org/sites/default/files/wpfd2017_concept_note_ru.pdf

4 Industry 4.0: 7 Real-World Examples of Digital Manufacturing in Action. 28 March, 2019. Additive Manufacturing Execution System & Workflow Automation Software. https://amfg.ai/2019/03/28/industry-4-0-7-real-world-examples-of-digitalmanufacturing-in-action

5 Industry 4.0 and the fourth industrial revolution explained, https://www.i-scoop.eu/industry-4-0

13

The Noonomy Theory and Socialism[1]

The second global crisis in two decades, which began prior to the pandemic, has rendered the issues of strategic rethinking of the future not only significant in theory but also highly relevant in practical terms.

Currently, the exploration of potential qualitative changes in future technologies and socio-economic relations continues to be conducted largely within the framework of previous paradigmatic approaches and attitudes. Meanwhile, as practice demonstrates, these changes are qualitative in nature, introducing new global problems that extend beyond the traditional issues addressed by contemporary doctrines, such as both classical and neoclassical economic paradigms. The new realities urgently require the search for non-standard approaches and tools to adequately explore and assess the coming prospects.

As such a toolkit, we propose the concept of the New Industrial Society of the second generation (NIS.2) and, subsequently, a qualitatively new state of society – noosociety on the basis of Noonomy negating the modern economy (Bodrunov, 2016a, 2019). It is important to emphasise that this theoretical platform is fundamentally different, with some external similarities, from the vision of the future that is characteristic of researchers who continue to work in the vein of classical Marxist political economy.

Why do we think it is necessary to pay attention to this? The basis for writing this text was the repeated attempts of many colleagues to find "parallels" between the theory of Noonomy and certain aspects of political economy, to "explain" it from the point of view of the political economy view of the development of society. These attempts are most clearly seen in a series of works by Professor A.V. Buzgalin, the head of the Socioeconomics Centre at Lomonosov Moscow State University, as well as in an article by Professor A.V. Sorokin from the Faculty of Economics at Moscow State University (Sorokin, 2020: 44-45), which is largely dedicated to the analysis of our concept of Noonomy. Furthermore, they are evident in the report by a corresponding member of the Russian Academy of Sciences R.S. Greenberg,[2] and others.

It should be noted that the mentioned respected authors aim to update the traditional classical political economy approach, while still remaining primarily classical political economists. This inclination is evidently due to their active work within the Department of Political Economy at Moscow State University, which continues to uphold the traditions of the classical school.

Thus, A.V. Sorokin, having worked extensively on the issue of aligning the categories of Marx's Capital with the neoclassical vision of the nature of value, profit, and other economic concepts, presented the scientific community with an original theory of social wealth (Sorokin, 2009), along with many other valuable contributions. The reference of this scientist to the analysis of our concept of NIS.2 and Noonomy is very significant for us and deserves a special analysis.

We have to give credit; the author in his article adequately reflects the theory we propose. At the same time, his comparative analysis of the theory of Noonomy and noosociety with the theory of socialism and communism, as well as his criticism of our key thesis about the gradual movement of humanity towards a new quality of society, which is no longer purely economic, demonstrates, in our opinion, that the author is a classical political economist. He focuses on studying the production relations of people, formed in the processes of production, exchange, distribution, and consumption, all based on the theories of socialism and communism. His comparison of the theory of NIS.2/Noonomy with socialism and communism is also constructed in the same vein. The possibility and validity of drawing such parallels is the subject of our polemic.

It should be noted that A.V. Buzgalin, in his works dedicated to the vision of the future, although he strives for some rethinking of the traditional tenets of scientific communism, in the main still remains an "orthodox" Marxist, asserting that the future is communism and the path to it lies through a socialist revolution (Buzgalin, 1996).

Of course, it is possible to elaborate in detail and thoroughly – aspect by aspect, position by position – the fundamental differences between the views under discussion. The classical political economy paradigm served as the foundation for the primary tenets of the Soviet ideological framework, as evidenced by its presence in various programmatic documents. This paradigm continues to underpin the research methodologies of our colleagues. To elucidate the distinctions between our perspectives, we believe it is sufficient to provide a concise analysis of several of these tenets from the standpoint of Noonomy theory.

So, the question before us is to what extent our proposed theory of NIS.2 and noosocialism is similar to the traditional theory of socialism and communism.

13.1. Inertia of Political Economy Thinking gives Rise to Problems in Understanding the Future

First of all, we should note that the author of this text does not consider any of his opponents from the political economy cohort (and there are many of them both in Russia and abroad) as "old-fashioned" thinkers. Moreover, some of them consider the Noonomy theory to be "a contribution to the development of political economy in the XXI century" (so noted in the foreword of the World Political Economy Association, which awarded the author of the Noonomy theory). The point is different: they remain scholars working in the traditional classical political economy paradigm. And although some of the political economists live, say, a more "modern life" and develop political economy, nevertheless their basic political economy views remain.

In our view, not all aspects of contemporary existence and development conform to the traditional framework of this theoretical platform. Therefore, it is necessary to exert effort to move beyond conventional ideas and consider what qualitatively new approaches might be both possible and necessary.

This statement, of course, does not imply that these new perceptions can arise from nothing. The theory of Noonomy emerged from the author's initial perspectives rooted in political economy during the early stages of their research. New perceptions can develop in a manner akin to the growth of wheat: an ear emerges from the grain when the requisite conditions are present. While an ear and grain, despite performing similar functions, may appear quite different, they share the same underlying roots. The example of monkey and human is even more appropriate – having common ancestors, they differ already more significantly. In this regard, entities that share a common root system or foundation can nonetheless differ significantly, even radically, in their manifestations. However, this distinction is not always immediately apparent; from a distance, humans and apes can appear almost identical. And to establish the differences, another tool is needed to put the subject matter into a closer perspective.

Therefore, persistently applying the established "algebra" to assess the new "harmony" – in our case, using the traditional "general standards" of political economy to evaluate the "special emergence" of a qualitatively new societal state, along with its increasingly apparent developmental prospects as reflected by the theory of Noonomy – can lead to a misinterpretation of the essence of the theory. Attempts to "drive" the concept of Noonomy into a political economy framework that seems correct are similar to attempts to describe an ear as a grain. At the same time, it is important to recognise that Noonomy evolves from economics, sharing a common foundational origin in human needs. Both disciplines function as mechanisms for satisfying these needs, yet they operate through different mechanisms. Just as an ear of wheat naturally replaces the grain due to changing conditions, Noonomy supersedes traditional economics in response to evolving conditions such as technological advancement and the development of human cognitive (noo!) qualities.

Society is a historical phenomenon. The key concept here is development, a change in the conditions of manifestation of entities. Society is also an instrument for the fulfillment of human needs. The regulation of social relations has been managed in various ways across different historical periods. At a certain stage, for instance, the state emerged and evolved, giving rise to institutions that increasingly addressed both overt and latent needs. These institutions were designed to meet the evolving demands of society. One can qualify them in different ways, categorise them. In this context, the stages of societal development defined by classical Marxism – namely, slavery, feudalism, capitalism, and communism (with socialism as its initial phase in the Soviet interpretation) – represent categories that delineate the framework within which societal development is analyzed from a particular perspective. This is the basis for the desire to compare NIS.2 and socialism, Noonomy and communism.

13.2. The Fallacy of the Parallel between NIS.2 and Socialism

Let's start with the parallel of NIS.2 and socialism.

The classical political economy framework, as most commonly presented in foundational texts on socialist political economy (e.g., Rumiantsev (Ed.), 1985), is a theory in which the primary productive relationship is public ownership of the means of production (with the absence of other forms of ownership). This framework entails various consequences, such as planned development and the orientation of economic progress towards improving the welfare of workers, among others. It is worth noting that alternative frameworks also exist. For instance, the school of N.A. Tsagolov, from which A.V. Sorokin and A.V. Buzgalin emerged, proposed that the initial productive relationship was planning, with the core relationship being the direct association of producers with socialised means of production. In this view, public ownership is considered a manifestation of these and derivative productive relations (Tsagolov (Ed.), 1974).

But in what direction did social development really go?

The objective process of the birth of NIS.2 follows a path far from the model of the revolutionary establishment of public property (as understood by classical political economy; however, no sufficiently detailed and consistent description of this phenomenon has been given). The form of ownership that becomes basic in NIS.2 will be different from the understanding found in the political economy textbooks we all studied in our time (predominantly state ownership as a form of some kind of "nationwide ownership of the means of production") – it is predominantly a diffuse "form" of ownership that is formed gradually, growing out of the forms of ownership we have today. There will be more and more extensive "division", "splitting" of property – both "in time" (for example, successive, more and more "fractional" ownership), and in importance, and in functions ("parallels", for example, in the latter case – into a whole range of its functional belongings, i.e., with regard to the functions of ownership, management, use, disposal, etc.). It is important to keep in mind that property as a phenomenon is in constant development, transformation. It is different every time, in every historical period, it has different aspects, from which the development of this phenomenon, changes in its subjects and objects, some of which only recently have become the object of the study of property as a socio-economic relationship. And it happens not by chance, but due to the progress of technology.

One of the most important examples of the latter is the development of the phenomenon of "intellectual property". The progress of technologies and transformation of knowledge into the main resource of development and the highest value, productive force caused in due time the emergence of a new object of property, to the emergence of intellectual property. Knowledge became an increasingly important resource for the economic base that was then being formed and continues to be transformed (incidentally, in NIS.2, the intellectual component of production, in the form of sublimated knowledge, will become the main resource, but its status as property will change). Accordingly, there appeared the statutes enshrining all the components of intellectual property: patents and other forms ensuring the "enclosure" of this property. Similarly, due to the historical process and the advancement of technological capabilities for accessing knowledge among an increasingly broad spectrum of intellectual resource users, the diffusion of this type of property has already commenced and is expected to persist. This type of property will similarly, and as a result of historical forces, gradually "disappear" as the unfolding process progresses. Within this process, the distinct, "parallel", and "successively" shared functions of property will diminish in significance.

Thus, there will be a transition to a different "form" of ownership, which we could conventionally call *"diffuse"* ownership. *It will be a "multiform" form of ownership, a "mixed" form of ownership, a "blurred" form of ownership, which, nevertheless, will be intended to realise the function that it has now – by its purpose, by its use, say, functional significance, by its importance, etc., for the development of society, ultimately – for the satisfaction of people's needs.* Today we see a rapid growth (of course, of course, of course, "in the struggle" with traditional forms) of the importance and share of the prototype of this type of property in the practical economy – the so-called *"associated property"*. However, we consider this term incorrect in principle, because in the historical context there is not association (connection) of property, but on the contrary – "dissociation", diffusion of property.

The essence of the phenomenon, the phenomenon of property as such at the stage of NIS.2 is still preserved, but there is a *change in the form of property, and through this – preparation for its other "existence", its "evaporation" in the world of the future – in Noonomy*. This is analogous to a change in the physical form of matter. Let's draw a parallel and imagine that the property is water. In some conditions ("cold, frozen society", economic society) it is ice, a crystal. We heat it (transition to NIS.2) – the crystal diffused into a liquid, eroded form. The molecules (the essence of the life activity of any society – satisfaction of needs) are the same. We heat it more (transition of social development to noostage) – water diffuses into vapour, into another, even more diffuse state, gradually (with the development of noosocial relations) evaporates to complete disappearance (disappearance of property), although individual molecules (basis) remain. Property as an institution – evaporates, while what constituted the object of ownership – remains.

Now we are also seeing some manifestations of another facet of this advancement. In various forms (which were sometimes described using different terminologies, occasionally distorting their essence), these manifestations have always been present. Let us recall, for example, the Soviet so-called public consumption funds. Or consider the current trends in need fulfillment, which have always existed but are becoming increasingly pronounced. This pertains to a broad range of goods and services consumed by people at no cost, meaning outside the traditional economic paradigm of distribution and need satisfaction. The same applies to volunteer activities, charity work, sponsorship, "creativity not for sale", etc. In other words, when "property" (product, service) is alienated without being replaced by another "property", its meaning as "property" is lost. But this is not a development towards a transition to "public" ownership. This is a development towards the "vaporisation" of property. *NIS.2, from this point of view, is not socialism.*

Another aspect of the traditional theory of socialism. It envisioned a strengthened role for the working class. But the development went in a different direction. With the genesis of NIS.2, the role of not the working class, but of that "class" (I use quotation marks for a reason: *there will be no classes when approaching noosociety either; here the positions of Noonomy and the theory of classical communism coincide*), of those individuals (sometimes temporarily forming groups of individuals) who possess the main resource necessary to solve the problems of material production, i.e., knowledge. And it is precisely these individuals who begin to play a "decisive role" in society, a concept long articulated in the theories of cognitarianism,[3] which we have discussed on multiple occasions. *This is something other than the classical view of the working class.*

It is clear that the individuals, who are formed in modern conditions, extracting and using knowledge, are *"classmates"* who have some common interests. And interests are a social need, but the expansion of needs, their individualisation in NIS.2 will lead to a growing diversity of these needs, and it will probably be impossible to unite them into interests, to form any such mass classes on this basis. These can be situational groups, interest groups, situational conglomerates – all the things that are happening and are increasingly developing now in the world.

Therefore, the theory of NIS.2 and the theory of Noonomy can have only purely formal, external "parallels" with what was understood in Soviet times under the categories of "socialism" and, respectively, "communism". However, it cannot be asserted that they are entirely opposite as they share a common root and exhibit similar external features (in terms of outcomes). Nonetheless, their content and structure differ significantly.

The accepted theory in the USSR claimed that communism was some kind of distribution according to needs and socialism was a distribution according to labour. From each according to his ability, to each according to his labour.

But what do we have in the realities of the twenty-first century, in the context of the emerging transition to NIS.2? Practice shows that different and contradictory processes are unfolding.

First, the importance of labour as a factor of social production under the influence of technological progress is decreasing and will objectively decrease.

Secondly, we already observe that despite the increasing possibilities of technological progress, which makes it possible to satisfy more and more rational needs of people, the distribution of the social product in the conditions of modern economic society is absolutely unfair.

But there are also *some tendencies reminiscent of socialism theory, since the progression towards NIS.2 is a greater socialisation of the economy* but – for very different reasons than the theory of socialism prescribes. Currently, individuals such as investors, owners of fundamental resources, and employers – who do not directly participate in the labour process – receive a disproportionate share of the final product. Inequality is on the rise. The reason is well known; economic society is based on the ownership of property. However, the transition to a new quality of social production – a system based on knowledge as the main resource of development and diffuse ownership – is gradually changing the situation. As the knowledge intensity of the product increases, the distribution of social wealth and income will become more equal, more equitable. *But the distribution already at the stage of NIS.2 will not go out "by labour" but by "knowledge-value"* with no direct link to the labour process.

Putting the above factors together, we get an understanding of how the socialisation of society will grow. *Not socialism where "to each according to his work", not "socialismisation" – socialisation.*

People will increasingly receive from society not based on "labour" or, in the transition to Noonomy, not based on "knowledge", "merit", or similar criteria, but simply based on their membership in society. Some individuals will participate in the labour process of material production (until it becomes fully automated in the transition from NIS.2 to Noonomy), while others will not. Some individuals will directly engage in labour activities (to the extent of their knowledge, strength, and need to obtain what they cannot acquire without labour) for as long as such activities persist. However, they will also have much broader opportunities to receive from society what is necessary for their life and development. There will also be other individuals who will not engage in this activity but will focus on creative endeavours and self-development – such as, for instance, humorously, reading or writing about NIS.2.

Will it be labour? Labour is one of the factors in both the production process and social production. *Nononomy is a mechanism for satisfying people's needs by a self-managed (under human control), independent of direct human participation, production system that does not involve the use of labour as a factor of production.* On the other hand, labour – in an economic society – is an activity that involves reward as part of the distribution of the "social pie". One cannot refer to activities conducted outside this paradigm as labour.

> In noosociety, any human activity would be, shall we say, an "occupation". *Labour – both as a factor in the production process and as a factor in the production of the social product – will "dry up" in NIS.2 as we move to unmanned production, completely "evaporating" in the transition to Noonomy. The NIS.2 period is the period of such a transition.* And people will be "paid" by criteria other than evaporating labour.

Of course, we can note that under the version of practical socialism that we had in Soviet times, there were also people who received "not according to their labour". But they lived off of the rip-off of society or another person. It is another way of "mining" the necessities of life. And this is not a parallel to NIS.2.

NIS.2 and socialism in its Soviet existence and understanding are by no means identical phenomena. What's more: they are qualitatively different. It is clear that both grow, if we look at the process from a political economy perspective, from the same root. But the results are different.

13.3. The Illegitimacy of Equating Noosociety with Communism

Regarding communism *as the highest phase of this system, the differences between the theory of Noonomy and the "highest phase" are even more pronounced.*

The point here is not only that, unlike communism, the way to which, in Marxist theory, lies through communist revolution, when "the tops cannot govern in the old way and the bottoms cannot live in the old way".

> *Nononomy* is an objectively evolutionarily born new quality of social existence, caused to life by technological development.

The main difference is this:

> *Noosociety* is not a new socio-economic formation (emphasising "economic" as traditionally conceived in the works of mainstream Soviet Marxists), but rather a new quality of social existence (a point we intentionally reiterate). In this new quality, economic relations as traditionally understood are transcended and become a thing of the past.[4]

Here are some consequent more private but also significant aspects of the differences.

Recall that the "higher phase" will be characterised by distribution based on the principle of "from each according to his ability, to each according to his needs". We suppose *non-simulative needs*, apparently real needs (although this question has remained outside the brackets of detailed elaboration in the theory of the communist stage of development). Also important here are the fundamental differences between the *model of "distribution"* under communism – at least as described by the programme of the CPSU – and what will be in noosociety. *The latter suggests that there will be no "according to ability". There will just be people living – and those with no abilities will live too. There will simply be people living – including those who possess no particular abilities.* We assume that individuals will recognise themselves and their needs within the framework of the noocriteria, which are understood and accepted.

> In noosociety, there will be no "public" things, as it will not be a "society of free and conscious workers". There will be no labour – there will be no toilers. But, of course, people will be truly free. And they will indeed be conscious. And – realising the dimensions of personal freedoms and consciously accepting their limits. But not toilers at all, but individuals – members of society.

Public self-government as an attribute of communism.

> There will be no public self-governance in the noosociety. It will be a different, special type of "governance". The state will change its functions as the NIS.2 genesis and further development towards the noosociety.

There will remain some analog of the state as an institution that will regulate the relations of individuals – on the basis of their conscious and free acceptance of the regulatory "burden" (remember, "freedom is a conscious necessity"). The objective is not to manage but to regulate human relations that do not pertain to their interactions within the spheres of production, consumption, distribution, and other economic activities. This is because such economic relations and the interactions arising from them will no longer exist. In noosociety, members will sustain themselves through the consumption of products produced and reproduced by a self-operating production system, which is independent of human intervention. With a certain degree of conventionality, we can say that such a production system will become part of "nature", the noohuman ecosystem. The society will live at the expense of material production, where the material sphere, which will be the production system, will itself begin to satisfy the nooneeds, the non-simulative needs of people.

And this system of relations is by no means a certain structure called "public self-government" (an absolutely vague concept, by the way). *The production system under human control will be "self-managed"; this is an important difference between the theoretical concept of noosociety and the model of communism.*

The same programme of the CPSU proclaimed: "Labour for the good of society will become the first vital need". There is no question, doing something is a human need, and it is indeed an *objective need.* Will it become a recognised need? Perhaps it could also be an awareness of one's own needs. Because they must recognise that their needs should be of a non-simulated type, including "labour". *From the perspective of Noonomy theory, this will no longer be considered labour but rather an activity – something that an individual engages in based on their own awareness, understanding, conviction, and so forth.* And not merely for "a fish from the pond". This is something different from "labour", which is necessary to obtain the means to realise and satisfy one's needs. Yes, today "you can't catch a fish from the pond without working", but this is an *economic understanding.* But in the noosociety, you can catch it. In this regard, "labour" will not become a "necessity" because there will be ***no need for labour as such. The "primary life necessity" will be different – we believe it will shift towards spiritual development, self-growth, and creativity, to which people's efforts will be directed.***

Another aspect of the vision of communism according to the CPSU programme is that at its highest phase, public goods will be distributed abundantly, and human abilities will be utilised to the greatest benefit for people, and so forth. The question of principle arises here: what is utility? *In an economic society, utility is defined as benefit.* Obviously, the programme is not about benefits. Then what is it about?

Likewise, the term *"people"* is undefined. Meanwhile, this term plays a significant role both in the referenced document and within the broader conceptual framework of communist theory, as it underpins concepts such as "public ownership" and 'the interests of the people". Ethnographic, demographic, and similar definitions of "the people" are inadequate here, and there is no political-economic definition of the term.

> The thesis that noosociety is an analog of communist society is incorrect, also because the concept of communism was, and remains, an unproven hypothesis.

13.4. Once Again to the Question of the Dying Out of Property and Production Relations as We Move Towards Noonomy

Concluding our polemical examples, we believe it is necessary to specifically return to the problem of ownership in NIS.2.

Here it is fundamentally important to understand that *NIS.2 describes a system that is in transition to Noonomy, where property relations are dying out, because their object is "drying up".*

Accordingly, in the noosystem there is no problem of the form of property; something that does not exist cannot have a form. Well, as for the "diffuse" property at the stage of NIS.2, much has been written about it in the author's texts mentioned earlier, which came out after the publication of the book *Noonomy*.

However, the root of the problem here is not even related to the problem of the phenomenon/concept of property, *but to the key position of the theory of Noonomy, according to which the system of production relations goes into oblivion as we move to manless production. This thesis is the most challenging for political economy to accept, as it cannot "renounce" itself and acknowledge that its subject/object of study (and, consequently, the field of study itself, along with other "economic sciences") "evaporates" with the advancement of technological progress.*

Let's read what is said about economic relations in the Big Soviet Encyclopaedia: "...social relations, formed in the process of production, distribution, exchange and consumption of material goods".[5] *Meanwhile, both distribution and consumption (especially consumption) existed without economic relations.* And will exist when economic relations do not exist because

> An *economic relationship* is one that deals with a repayable exchange.

These relations emerged at a specific historical stage – when needs expanded to a certain level, creating the necessity to satisfy them not merely through one's own production but through products created by others, within the framework of the social division of labour.

Let's remember K. Marx, "Towards a Critique of Political Economy". It talks about the objectivity of production relations (Marx, 2011). This aspect can be transferred to the question of needs. I can agree with K.H. Momdzhyan that needs exist objectively (Momdzhyan, 2019) – as does knowledge. The difference is that *a person "consciously understands" these needs, and in the theory of noonomy, a need is considered to be that which has already been recognised by the individual after they have discovered a quantum of knowledge about their own need.*

This interpretation of needs is important for the theory of Noonomy because it allows for the ***differentiation between real needs and simulated needs***. When a person is in the process of realising a need, they may acquire misleading information about it. During this stage of realisation, they can be influenced by false notions about their own need. As a result, simulative needs emerge.

The tool called "need" in our interpretation allows us to open the lock of our idea of civilisational development, to understand and describe how man further develops, while the purely philosophical accentuation of this concept does not allow it to be applied to adequately describe the process of development of society.

It is worth noting that, presumably, in these contexts, K. Marx also discusses awareness and conscious needs.

Everything that a person realises gives him a certain impetus for life. With awareness, one seeks a balance of needs and reliability. In an economic society, reliability is ensured by reserves, and the balance of human needs is determined by economic conditions and criteria: the greater the reserves, the higher the reliability. *In noosociety, reliability is ensured by technological progress, and the balance of needs (which man must establish himself) allows us to determine what is simulative and what is not; to determine on the basis of noocriteria.*

In classical Marxism, productive relations (developing in dialectical unity with productive forces) constitute the base, which in turn determines the so-called superstructure, including spiritual development and other related aspects. What is crucial for us now is that the *totality of production relations is not synonymous with the economy; furthermore, the systems of production relations and economic relations are not identical.*

The totality of the four parts mentioned above constitutes the economic structure of society, not just the relations that people enter into purely in the process of producing material goods. So the basis that determines the superstructure is the *economic basis*. But it should be recognised that not all human life is determined by this basis, there is also a spiritual sphere, and its determination is different.

Not everything is determined by economic relations, there are other relations and other determinants. To give just one example, love. There is love as a need (a spiritual need, say), and it is in no way determined by the economic basis. And there is "love" – for money, forced, called prostitution or worse. From this perspective, we can ***assert that the emergence of the economy represents a stage in which human relations become commodified, and the economic mode of satisfying people's needs is essentially a commodified way of addressing those needs.***

All needs can be met without economics. Economics is essentially the mechanism that establishes a specific order in which needs are satisfied. Noonomy is a different mechanism for solving the same problem. A clock is to recognise time, but it exists independently of the clock. And clock mechanisms can be entirely different.

Economic relations are something that is fundamentally at odds with the objectively born future, with what will be in noociety. ***Noosociety, its life, defined by the material basis of Noonomy, will not be built on economic relations, which will cease to be the basis of society's life and its development.*** Economic relations will vanish, but ***material production will persist*** and continue to develop independently of direct human involvement. It will function as a self-sustaining system, managed by humans and aimed at meeting people's needs, while bypassing the traditional economic mechanisms of distribution and exchange. Because each member of society will receive individually what *they consciously deem necessary for themselves within the nooworld, regardless of "labour", "ability", or similar factors.*

NOTES

1 Prepared on the basis of Bodrunov, 2020a.

2 Presentation of the book "Noonomy" at Non/fiction – 2018. URL: https://noonomy.ru/2018/11/30/nonfiction/.

3 Using the term 'knowledge worker', Daniel Bell was the first to outline the concept of cognitariat (Bell, 1996: 343-344). The term itself was coined by Alvin Toffler when he declared the transition from proletariat to cognitariat (Toffler, 2003: 47).

4 It should be noted that the works of some Soviet and foreign Marxists of the early 1960s – late 1980s directly or indirectly expressed the thesis that communism is no longer a non-economic society. Moreover, provisions from the works of the classics were also cited that could be interpreted in this spirit. These theses were voiced most vividly in several works (Platonov, 1989; Buzgalin, Kolganov, 1990). However, the ideas of the future society as a post-economic society were not only expressed by Marxists. This issue is addressed in one of his later articles by J.M. Keynes (Keynes, 2009). It is also outlined by post-industrialist D. Bell (Bell, 1996) and further developed by V. Inozemtsev, who shared similar views (Inozemtsev, 1998). None of these authors proposed a comprehensive theory of a new quality of social existence emerging from the objective processes of technological development. This constitutes a qualitative distinction between the theory of Noonomy and both the ideas of "romantic Marxists" and the theories of post-industrialists. The latter often present the post-economic society merely as a reflection of the current structure of "core" countries, where the dominance of financial capital and "market fundamentalism" has not led to a transition to a new quality of material production – characterised by automation and high technology – but rather to the erosion of material production itself.

5 The Big Soviet Encyclopaedia. URL: https://bse.slovaronline.com/31012-POLITICHESKAYA_EKONOMIYA (date of access: 31.07.2020).

14

The Concept of Global Nootransition in detail and Noointegration[1]

The current state of the world economy and international relations is characterised by an increased level of conflict, turbulence and uncertainty. The nature of external and internal challenges, threats and "shocks" to national systems is becoming increasingly severe. This is due to both the global nature of the processes taking place in social development and to the fundamental regularities determining them. The current all-encompassing crisis facing the modern world, vividly reflected in the financial and economic sphere as early as 2008–2009, continues to deepen. The growing systemic contradictions have already led to the unleashing of a global hybrid war and the formation of a "fork" of the civilisational path with a high probability of realisation of a catastrophic and, accordingly, dead-end scenario from the perspective of positive development. However, the accumulation of various kinds of knowledge about system development and relevant practical experience allow to form a deep understanding of the surrounding reality and create, even in difficult conditions, a certain point of support and a positive view of the situation. Thus, crises and contradictions can be successfully overcome through the emergence of a new quality, and society, often purely instinctively, finds itself in a state of expectation – active or passive – of events that are significant for the world.

One of the central objects of modern international relations, which has attracted close attention, is BRICS. Indeed, the world community closely monitors every event that takes place within the framework of this association.

While at the initial stage the idea of forming this association was accompanied by a significant wave of scepticism – both from the West and even in a number of analytical circles within the participating countries themselves (Agonnude, Glebov, 2023) – more than 10 years later the situation has changed significantly. This does not mean that criticism of BRICS has disappeared; it is primarily about the transformation of expectations in the current environment. Moreover, a number of experts directly state (Tavrovsky, 2023) that we should expect real earth-shattering news from Russia's presidency in 2024, i.e., translating it into the terms of the theory of noonomy, the emergence of a chance to acquire new knowledge and quality, able to significantly expand the boundaries of human capabilities, relying on the accumulated value base to significantly transform the world and lead to a positive reorganisation of public space – in a word, to ensure in the long term an effective nootransition from an economic society to a noosociety. At the same time, it is no coincidence that BRICS is attractive to a growing number of other states, especially countries with developing, emerging and transforming markets, which, guided by rationality, political intuition or by other considerations, are actively expressing their desire to join the new positive trends.

The purpose of this study is to determine the significance of BRICS for the current stage of global development and the coming societal reorganisation, i.e., the role that this group in its expanded format is called upon to play in the global nootransition.

14.1. The World We Live in and the Concept of Global Nootransition

In order to realise the set goal, first of all, let us turn to the formation of an idea of the modern world, based on the fundamental regularities of social development, which allows not only to adequately assess the ongoing events and phenomena, but also to build reasonable forecasts, to ensure effective strategising of transformational processes within the framework of social development (Kvint, Bodrunov, 2021). The picture of reality that is to be "written" for the present and subsequent generations, in one way or another, depends on such theoretical developments.

As part of the solution to this problem, the concept of global nootransition was put forward (Bodrunov, 2020b), which made it possible to concretise the cause-and-effect relations between various events arising in the course of the world history of socio-economic development and to designate a single trajectory of the global noomovement or objective process of continuous march to the "noostate" of man and society, carried out in the course of discovery and practical application of knowledge to meet their transforming needs. Its most active stage, and therefore one of particular interest for research, coincides with the period of "oscillation" of the industrial civilisation wave (Table 2).

Table 2. The main stages of the global noomovement and global nootransition

Development in the process of changing of the technological and world economic modes (TM and WEM) as a key trajectory of noomovement

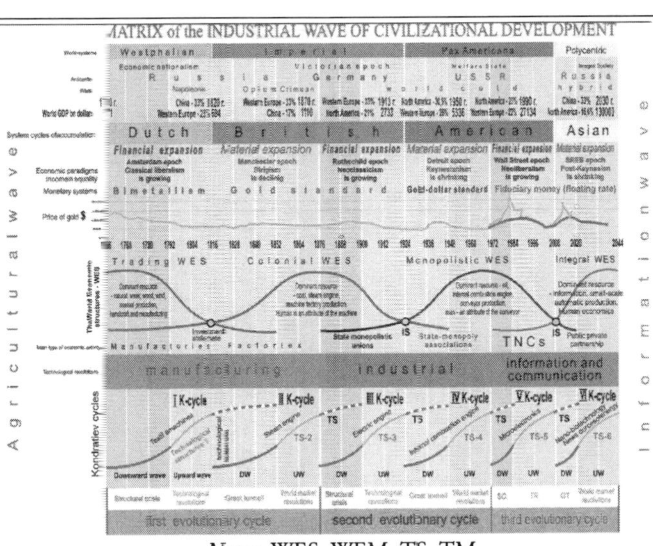

Notes: WES=WEM, TS=TM

Concretization of global nootransition as a noomovement interval

The main stages of the nootransition	I	II	III	IV	V
WEM	–	Integral			
TM	–	TM-VI	–	TM-VII	
Type of production	–	knowledge-intensive	–	noo-intensive (nooproduction)	–
Type of social structure	NIS	–	NIS.2	–	noosociety
System transformation	economy			–	noonomy

Source: Compiled by the author on the basis of Bodrunov, Glazyev, 2023

According to the definition given earlier (Bodrunov, Glazyev, 2023):

> The global nootransition is the unfolding of a positive evolutionary scenario of humanity's development and a special interval within the framework of the industrial stage of noomovement, the starting segment of which falls on the phase of successful overcoming of the modern transition period (from TM-V to TM-VI and from the old WEM to the new – Integral – with the corresponding change of countries of the "core" of the system cycles of capital accumulation), causing the current global crisis and aggravation of international conflicts, and the formation of the sixth TM, and the final one – on the emergence of noonomy and noosociety.

Table 2 presents the detailed trajectory of the global nootransition and a unified picture of noomovement activation, covering successive TMs and WEMs.

Being the basic category of the theory of Noonomy, knowledge as a phenomenon, including, for example, religious truths and values, culture, technology, etc., allows us to deepen the analysis of the essence of STP and technological development. Thanks to the characteristic developed on the basis of this category – knowledge intensity of production – and tracking the growth rates of the corresponding indicators, it becomes possible to distinguish more clearly the contours of each technological mode and to identify the immediate reasons for the shifting of the TMs. For TM-V and nowadays at the stage of formation of TM-VI this achievement acquires special relevance, because the specificity of these Technological Orders is the practical application of knowledge. The new, sixth TM, associated with the formation of knowledge-intensive type of material production, defines the second stage of the global nootransition (Table 2).

The development ofTM-VI is associated with breakthrough technologies and results of developments in the field of artificial intelligence, digitalisation, ICT, Big Data, 3D printing, robotics, genetic engineering, etc. (Bodrunov, Glazyev, 2023; Glazyev, 2021), the high level of knowledge intensity of which determines their content and, accordingly, the face of this TM. The so-called NBICS-convergence (nano-, bio-, info-, cogno-, socio-) offers the broadest prospects (Bodrunov, 2021). All this will entail significant socio-economic changes, since TM-VI is designed to create a material base for the NIS.2 – a new generation industrial society, the formation of which is predicted to take place approximately at the junction of the sixth and seventh technological modes (Bodrunov, 2022g) and opens the third stage of nootransition.

At the same time, relying on the fairness and validity of the previous conclusions of the theory of change of TMs and WEMs and the reasoning of A.E. Aivazov's hypothesis about the overlapping of their life cycles, it is assumed that two technological modes – the new sixth and the newest seventh ones – can take place within the framework of one world economic mode, the Integral one, which is being formed today (Table 2). The fourth stage of nooproduction, distinguished on the basis of TM-VII, is characterised by the evolution of knowledge-intensive production to the level of noo-intensive or nooproduction (material and personal, taking into account the growth of spiritual needs and the prevalence of noo-needs) with the final establishment of knowledge as its main factor. In our opinion, the supporting technologies of the newest TM may be "matured" TM-VI technologies that give a new quality of growth (e.g., the continued development of artificial intelligence), "bionic" and "nature-like", socio-humanitarian, "trust technologies", the spread of renewable energy sources, etc. (Bodrunov, 2021b; Bodrunov, Glazyev, 2023).

Creating the material basis for the next stage of social development – noosociety – TM-VII predetermines the formation of the fifth stage of the nootransition, and the Integral WEM "embracing" two TM cycles (the new and the newest) forms the institutional basis for the transition from knowledge-intensive material production to NIS.2 and from noo-intensive production to noosociety. Moreover, all these trends and processes are global and ultimately participate in the production of a new progressive state of society.

This is a brief description of the process of nootransition, which in a simplified form can also be labelled as a path from economic (motives of formation and mechanisms of needs satisfaction, etc.) partially up to NIS.2 – to non-economic (Table 2). Noonomy has a fundamentally different character of rationality and thus a new approach to the goal-setting of social development. Thus, the nootransition is closely related to the paradigm shift and is a transition from the growth model, based on limited economic rationality, focused on maintaining the "zoo" state of the "consumer society", sublimation of its "simulative needs", obtaining and maximising profit at any price, to the development model based on the implementation of the tasks of satisfying the needs of man and society, formed on the basis of noovalues, in a non-economic way. Having left the sphere of production in the future, society will retain its subordination to itself in terms of goal-setting, organisation, management and control, and will focus on the free creative activity, intellectual and spiritual development of noopersonality, feeling and realising the primacy of this supreme need (Bodrunov, 2018a). Moreover, nootransition is associated with the process of gradual formation and expansion of social noospace.

It is important to emphasise that we deliberately try not to identify specific dates for the onset of stages and certain events of the global nootransition; at present, we can only predict and propose some variant of the sequence of their occurrence and course in the continuation of the trajectory of noomovement (Bodrunov, 2020b). The task is facilitated by the fact that already at the modern stage of world development, the genesis of noonomy, embodied by the "quadriga" of basic processes – STP, diffusion of property, socialisation of society and the development of human qualities, solidarism (which was revealed in detail earlier (Bodrunov, 2022g)), is observed at the designation of the starting vector of nootransition. These sign trends or "vectors of change", each of which is geared towards a specific purpose – to create the material foundations of the movement towards noonomy, to lay a new foundation for the formation of human needs, to create social and ideological conditions for moving towards noosociety – are closely related to the nootransition. Moreover, they are its key attributes.

The basic provisions of the theory of noonomy in conjunction with the theory of change of TMs and WEMs provide an answer as to how to make a qualitative and rapid nootransition. It seems that the problem of nootransition is not private but general, it is global and requires an appropriate approach to its solution and joint efforts from different countries. It is no coincidence that the emerging WEO was named "Integral" – which, in our opinion, is due, in addition to the classical definition of S.Y. Glazyev, based on the formulation of P. Sorokin (Glazyev, 2016b; Glazyev, 2021), to the high significance, nature and globality of the consequences of integration processes at the current stage of social development.

What kind of integration has the potential to be a real factor in nootransition? Certainly, it is not the one that leads human civilisation along the catastrophic path and itself comes to a dead end when transforming the nature and channels of influence of internal and external negative factors on the national economy, and contains in itself the processes of self-destruction (disintegration), as it is aimed at autarky, preserving the dominance of the hegemon and countries of the "world-system core" (according to S. Amin) and their advantages at the expense of others.

The concept of *"noointegration"* (Arkhipova, 2023) was introduced to define constructive integration processes that ensure global nootransition and its acceleration. This nooprocess has its own significant features.

Undoubtedly, any integration processes should include an economic component at the initial stages of nootransition, since human needs include material ones; in this regard, economic integration should be an important step in the development of integration processes in the modern global economy and the emerging Integral WEM. At the same time, the objectives of economic integration may be different.

First, *the objectives of noointegration* are built on a noo-value basis, with reliance on non-economic principles and interests and taking into account the economic component of integration at the stage of NIS.2.

Secondly, based on the noocriteria base, *special stages of integration development* are formed. The first stage of noointegration is the construction of a unified noo-value space and the space of cultural exchange, which in the future can be complemented by subsequent stages of creating unified spaces: scientific and knowledge exchange, technological and co-industrial, social and the highest stage – with the formation of noosociety and nooinstitutions (Arkhipova, 2023). It is extremely important to distinguish between the stages of noointegration, since each of them will require its own strategy of action.

Third, noointegration implies *multiple conjugation of integration processes.* Thus, this includes "technology integration" and the formation of integrated systems (e.g., transportation) as one of the most important directions of TM-VI development, which in the near future will have to be oriented towards noovalues and subordinated to the goals of nootransition. The "integration of generations" as a result of social development, which is designed to make a significant contribution to the formation and upbringing of noopersonality and noosociety on the principles of, among others, solidarity between generations, is of particular importance in the course of the movement. The economic gains achieved will eventually be turned into social gains.

Fourth, *the conditions for potential member-states to join the integration association will change.* Countries wishing to take part in the integration innovation process will not be subject to the "faster, higher, stronger" principle – they will no longer be required to meet a certain level of economic development indicators, nor efficiency criteria such as geographical proximity to other member-states, or anything of the sort. What is important here is the readiness of countries to share values and assume obligations of a "higher order", their desire not to shirk responsibility for deepening integration, but, on the contrary, to integrate into it as organically as possible, realising the importance of joint and harmonious coexistence in the world. It is assumed that all countries anywhere in the world have the same chances to develop noointegration, and an integration union based on such principles acts as a "union of equals".

Finally, *noointegration will not be a way of isolation from the world, but a unifying principle and an embodiment of justice and solidarity,* and, among other things, it will eliminate the problems of "regionalism competition" and "integration immaturity".

> Noointegration is "reasonable unification", i.e., a conscious, necessary, global and objective "creation of integrity" on the basis of noovalues and knowledge, forming the basis for mutual understanding and trust between peoples.

14.2. BRICS: Leaving the Term "integration"

As a rule, the BRICS alliance is relatively rarely referred to as integration (in the traditional sense of the concept and its classical definition) or the term is applied with a number of reservations.

The fact is that "integration" most often refers to international economic integration. Moreover, despite the rich heritage of B. Balassa with the allocation of steps or the so-called "ladder" of regional integration, the existence of the main approaches to its analysis (including federalism, neofunctionalism, communication theory and intergovernmental approach (Butorina (Ed.), 2011)) and many emerging currents and concepts based on them, the general theoretical basis of this line of research is still only continuing its formation, which is progressing in a rather specific and problematic way. This is felt all the more acutely if, firstly, we take into account a number of terminological differences in the interpretations of some important concepts (for example, the "integration model"), which, among other things, raises questions about the objectivity of assessments of the relevant processes. Secondly, in our opinion, it is negatively affected by its "lock-in" on the EU, which creates the effect of rigidity. Thus, the general theoretical basis of integration, generally speaking, has "grown old before maturing", but has already managed to create a myth about some exclusivity and reference development of the EU, which has made the largest number of steps on the way to the top of integration. Thirdly, economic and political components of international integration and, accordingly, material benefits from this process are most often put in the centre of attention (despite the fact that neofunctionalists refer to social needs and technological changes, representatives of communication theory – to the community of culture and values). Finally, based on the standardly cited factors of efficiency of regional economic integration, we can conclude that a number of states (with developing, emerging and transforming markets) are doomed to a low level of integration, including due to years of insurmountable "integration immaturity" and competition of integration projects. Generally speaking, this already contains an element of discrimination against countries – often on the grounds that are beyond their control.

A critical view on certain features and problems of the analyzed theoretical framework is contained, for example, in the works of a number of Russian researchers (Butorina (Ed.), 2011), in particular, in order to overcome some of their above-mentioned difficulties, a special approach and typology of integration models were developed (Libman, Kheyfets, 2011), "non-linear" models of integration (without passing through its stages in a given sequence and setting the goal of achieving its maximum) (Ushkalova, 2016) were singled out, and a new model of international economic – "accumulative economic integration", involving the implementation of a strategy of "transition from free trade priorities to flexible accumulative integration of hybrid type" beyond the classical form of regional integration (Kheyfets, 2023).

Nevertheless, despite the significant contribution of domestic scientists to the development of the general theoretical basis of integration, it has to be stated that the modern theory and practice of regional economic integration have led neither to true solidarity and value-based unification of countries and peoples, nor to joint sustainable movement along the trajectory of balanced growth of public welfare, nor to a reduction in the level of conflict in the world – which, in fact, leaves open the question of finding new concepts, solutions and models of integration. Thus, the "exemplary" European integration actually faces its own "deadlocks", crises and problems: here it is enough to mention the narrowing of the EU, escalating Euroscepticism and the protracted construction of the economic and monetary union, the decline in the international role of the euro with the long-standing policy of non-interference of supranational bodies in the development of the joint currency of the eurozone, etc. Even the USA failed to create a perfect classical integration: despite the long history of the NAFTA, it was recognised as insufficiently effective, which led to the transition to the USMCA in the late 2010s and in the early 2020s.

Thus, the *frequent "avoidance" of the classical term "integration" for the BRICS is quite justified, since this association is simply not such.* At the same time, it is erroneous to consider it a "sorry excuse of an integration" based on relatively modest results in passing the steps of the mentioned integration "ladder", because, as it was shown earlier, the demand, rapid development and intermediate achievements of this community deny its inferiority.

Moving away from the classical understanding of integration, a number of experts are searching for new solutions and definitions. Thus, the BRICS, among others, is considered as "an example of integration interaction developing in accordance with the vector of polycentric accumulative integration" (Kheyfets, 2023), as a future "common economic space" (CES) in the form of a hybrid integration model (Babaev, Lavrov, 2023) or a probable format of "integration of integrations" as one of the elements of development scenarios (Arapova, Lisovolik, 2022; Kheyfets, 2023). However, it seems that both the first and the second of these options are more oriented towards "freedom from" – from excessive requirements and obligations, restrictions, additional conditions, the need to move through stages, etc. – and actually from integration itself (!). The latter scenario for the BRICS is seen as the construction of this alliance from something that has already been prepared in advance ("slapped together of the things available"), and the question arises about the fundamental novelty of the resulting object. In addition, almost all of the given options are focused on the construction of an economic model, which is certainly necessary, but not sufficient for the current stage of global social development, as was shown earlier.

Parting with the classical term "integration" for BRICS, on the one hand, increases the feeling of unknowability of this object; on the other hand, it gives grounds for applying other methods of analysis – in particular, the noo-approach and proof of the emergence of a fundamentally different type of community and process – noo-integration.

14.3. Emergence of a New Kind of Integration

Several facts testify *in favour of the fact that* ***BRICS can indeed be considered a new progressive type of integration, which is one of the key factors of the above-mentioned nootransition.***

The BRICS "core" countries have become the symbol and "popular image" of the Integral World Economic Mode, since it is this special community of states that is destined to form the "core" of the Asian cycle of capital accumulation, which is replacing the American one (Glazyev, 2016b), and to lead human civilisation along the path of nootransition to noonomy.

Already today, the BRICS countries have begun to form a number of previously identified stages of noointegration: in fact, we are talking about the creation and strengthening of a noovalue "core" and balanced regulation of STP,[2] as well as a common scientific and educational space and promotion of the construction of a common scientific and technological space on the basis of common values (Toloraya, Borzova et al, 2023).

The special role of knowledge and its practical embodiment – new technologies and STP – in the history of BRICS: it is thanks to this that the very opportunity for regular dialogue and interaction between the analyzed countries with significant geographical distance from each other arose (the realisation of which led to the phenomenon of the "death of distance" and the achievement of a positive effect from it), as well as for the launch and development of noointegration processes between them.

BRICS connects the so-called "big" countries – big both in terms of population and the length of their borders, and in the role they play in the world (taking into account their contribution to the global economy, etc.): by uniting continents and peoples, these states create a unique space for the realisation of large transcontinental projects.

The BRICS+ states have not only a huge and multidisciplinary development potential, but also, and most importantly, opportunities to combine their potentials and, on this basis, to achieve synergies of a unique scale and quality (not only in the economic sphere, but also in the social, scientific and technological spheres, etc.).

BRICS+ represents a new and special "community of civilisations" (Glazyev, 2016b) and a space for their polylogue (Bodrunov, 2022c).

Since noointegration is a new type of integration, but, first of all, still integration, it is also subject to a number of regularities of integration development, for example, the spiral nature of the evolution of this process: thus, the progress of noointegration also requires "fresh replenishment" with new members (which can now be observed with the formation of BRICS+) and deepening of interaction, otherwise a reverse movement – disintegration – is possible, the probability of which does not allow the integration group to "tread" on the same place and "rest on its laurels".

Noointegration processes and alliances are complementary and contiguous: for example, BRICS can harmoniously coexist with such ideologically and qualitatively similar Chinese initiatives as "Belt and Road" and building a "Community with a Shared Future for Mankind", as well as with the Big Eurasian Partnership project.

At present, the world is at a fork in the road of civilisational development and the possibility of a "dead end" remains. In order to prevent this from happening, it is necessary to get on the trajectory of nootransition as soon as possible, so it is advisable to preserve the existing achievements and strengthen the processes of noointegration in order to turn them into an effective factor of the future stage of noomovement. In order to solve this problem within the BRICS framework, first of all, it is proposed to develop a single long-term strategy of multisphere development, taking into account the stages of evolution of a new type of integration, the task of solving the problem of institutionalisation and the openness of the integration group's interaction with other states, associations and international organisations.

The concept of global nootransition makes it possible to identify society's need to develop a general theoretical basis for integration and to begin the formation of a special line of research devoted to the use of the nootransition approach in the study of integration processes and the development of effective tools on its basis to analyze the problems and prospects for the development of the phenomenon of noointegration as a factor in the future stage of the world's movement towards noonomy, as well as specific practical proposals and recommendations for BRICS, a concrete example of a new progressive type of integration.

Notes

1 Prepared on the basis of Bodrunov, Arkhipova, 2024.

2 See Putin instructed to include the formation of AI ethical standards in the BRICS agenda. Bulletin: monthly electronic publication. BRICS NRC. 2024. No. 140, January. URL: https://www.nkibrics.ru/pages/bulletins as referrred to in Izvestia 18.01.2024. See: https://iz.ru/1636424/2024-01-18/putin-poruchil-vkliuchit-formirovanie-eticheskikh-standartov-ii-v-povestku-briks.

15

Noonomy: the Theory for Practice[1]

Noonomy is not just a theory or an abstract theoretical structure, created for "mental workout", and not some ephemeral scenario of the future, the realisation of which can be passively expected. First of all, the movement towards noonomy should be organised as a consciously managed strategic project. To solve this task, among other things, an active industrial policy and strategic planning are essential, together with the activity of private funds and orientation to social interests of public sector, as well as effective tools.

15.1. Noonomy as a Strategic Project

The shifts that are taking place in production technologies are creating vast opportunities to meet people's needs. However, the pressure on the natural environment is increasing. This raises the problem of changing the social conditions of production in such a way as to use the emerging technological opportunities to solve growing problems rather than to escalate them. For this purpose, research is being carried out on trends in technological development, the most important of which are, firstly, the increasing knowledge-intensity of production, which will lead to the predominance of the proportion of knowledge embodied in the results of production over material inputs. Secondly, there will be a substitution of human functions by automated means of production and its displacement from the sphere of direct production. Today's societal conditions of production aim new technological capabilities towards the growth of production and sales of products, leading to further growth in consumption, and with the growth in the amount of natural resources absorbed. The volume of needs is also inflated by imposing illusory, fake needs on the consumer and simulating their satisfaction. The formation of knowledge-intensive production creates prerequisites for society's transition to a new stage of development – the new industrial society of the second generation (NIS.2). However, this transition does not solve the problems facing humanity. They can only be solved by replacing narrow economic criteria of rationality of production and consumption with broader criteria based on intelligence and culture. This means a transition from economy to noonomy – a non-economic way of satisfying the needs. The development and support of a consciously managed strategic project on the movement towards noonomy can be provided on the basis of the concept of strategising, developed by Academician V.L. Kvint.

Modern society is constantly changing. An economic system that relies on a continuous stream of innovation brings us new and increasingly sophisticated technologies that change the whole way of life.

The peculiarity of the current stage of technological development is the formation of the sixth technological mode, the characteristic feature of which is the widespread use of hybrid technologies. Several types of technologies are not simply combined in one technological complex: they mutually condition each other's functioning. This integration of technologies is ensured by modern information and communication technologies, which provide means for coordinating heterogeneous technological processes.

A typical example of such hybrid technology is the modern smartphone, which combines radio, voice and television communications, photography, geolocation, computer processing of text, audio-visual information, etc.

The most important feature of the technologies of the sixth technological mode is their increasing knowledge intensity.

> *Knowledge intensity means* the share of knowledge applied in the production process.

There comes a point when the share of knowledge embedded in the technological process and its products begins to significantly exceed the material part itself.

The technologies of the sixth technological mode are characterised by the displacement of humans from direct participation in production activities.

All the features of the sixth technological mode open up the possibility of fully satisfying human needs. *However, the "Golden Age" of mankind is in no hurry to come around.* Examining the shifts that are taking place leads to the conclusion that the accumulation of new technological opportunities holds both *opportunities* and *threats.*

These threats began to emerge at earlier stages of technological development. The first to be realised was the threat of total annihilation of mankind in the event of the use of weapons of mass destruction: nuclear, chemical, biological. Then it became clear that the scale of industrial development of civilisation was putting a high strain on the natural environment. This was shown in a 1972 report to the Club of Rome (Meadows, et al, 1972).

The depletion of irreplaceable reserves of natural resources, the climate crisis due to changes in the composition of the atmosphere, the enormous scale of environmental pollution (mechanical, chemical, acoustic, electromagnetic), the loss of biodiversity, etc., all these put our civilisation on the threshold of self-destruction.

These threats are recognised, but are the risks that our production activities entail being mitigated? So far, the answer is disappointing.

The development of modern technologies leads simultaneously to the growth of crisis phenomena and to the formation of potential opportunities to overcome this crisis. The question is: will we be able to seize the opportunities or will we go down the path of increasing the accumulating problems? It depends on how the social structure of our life will evolve, where we will direct the forces created by our knowledge, but which we cannot manage wisely.

The immediacy of these problems was once again confirmed at the VII International Scientific Conference "Topical Issues of Global Studies: Global Development and Limits to Growth in the XXI Century" held on 15-18 June 2021. It presented the results of the interdisciplinary research project "Global Development and Limits to Growth in the XXI century: Modelling and Forecasting" under the leadership of the Rector of MSU, Academician V.A. Sadovnichy. This report rejects the concept of zero growth put forward in 1972. But, like the authors of the report to the Club of Rome, it assumes that a technological solution to the problems of conflict with the environment is possible only if appropriate societal goals are set for technological progress.[2]

The focus of this study is the problem of finding a path of social evolution that allows humanity to overcome the growing problems, as well as issues related to ensuring such evolution in the desired direction.

The analysis of trends and contradictions of the modern stage of economic development allows us to draw certain conclusions about the directions of its evolution. It is not a question of extrapolating established trends into the future, but of analyzing the accumulating problems and the emerging potential for their solution. This approach allows us to see in which direction the shifts in the socio-economic structure of society will take place. No one can guarantee that the development will go exactly in this direction, because it is impossible to exclude a negative scenario leading human civilisation to a dead end or catastrophe. But if we want to find a way out of the problems that beset us, we can identify ways right now.

Both the rise of risks and threats and the potential to prevent them lie in one and the same thing: *the development of technology, based on advances in our knowledge*. But whether we follow the path of increasing threats or the path of overcoming them depends not only on the technologies, but also on the social conditions under which we apply them.

The modern stage of technology development, which is characterised by the spread of the fifth technological mode and the emergence of the sixth technological mode, firstly is distinguished by the increasing share of knowledge (not just knowledge, but scientific knowledge) in the composition of production costs. Second, the application of these technologies is accompanied by an increasing withdrawal of humans from direct participation in the production process (Frank, Roehrig, Pring, 2017).

The consequence of these trends is reduction in consumption of materials, which leads to a significant predominance of the share of knowledge implemented in the finished product over the share of material costs. Does this mean the displacement of material production by "knowledge production"? No, because knowledge plays a key role in the development of new technologies and it cannot replace tangible products. *New knowledge in production is valuable only because it can be embodied in tangible technological processes and new tangible products, without which the development of the service sector is impossible.* Therefore, production at the new stage of development, while being highly knowledge-intensive, remains *material*. More than that, it remains *industrialised.* Despite the decline in the industrial sector share, it still plays the role of the engineering and manufacturing core for all other sectors of the economy. This conclusion is supported by empirical evidence on the role of industry in the US and European Union economies.[3]

Whatever steps technological development may allow us to take in increasing the efficiency of satisfying our needs, the key role is played by the nature of our needs, which determines them both quantitatively and qualitatively. *No efficiency will yield positive results if it is subordinated to the uncontrollable pursuit of increased consumption.* In the modern economy, the orientation of consumption towards an unlimited increase in its volume is aggravated by the tendency to increase illusory, false, irrational needs. This trend has been theoretically reflected in the social sciences in the works of Jean Baudrillard (Baudrillard, 1972, 1981) and Frederic Jameson (Jameson, 1991).

According to the concept of J. Baudrillard's concept, a significant part of consumption in modern capitalism is formed not by real useful things (use values), but only by signs of satisfaction of imaginary needs (simulacra). Indeed, many needs are formed artificially: under the influence of ideological processing of consumers, unnecessary or even harmful consumer goods are imposed on them through a variety of channels, and many useful things are attributed additional properties that simulate the satisfaction of needs. Thereby a hyper-reality is constructed that simulates real content (Huang, 2019). Simulative needs are inflated for the sake of seeking to expand markets through the production of simulacra. However, real resources are used to produce these simulacra, and the consumer gives up a portion of his income for them. Moreover, fake hyper-reality distorts the entire way of life and perceptions of the real world, shaping a world in which the pursuit of symbolic overconsumption becomes the highest value (Antony, Tramboo, 2020).

The consistent implementation of all the above trends embedded in the latest technologies is changing not only the production base, but also the entire way of life of society. It is possible to predict the beginning of society's transition to a new stage of development, which, following the tradition of J.K. Galbraith, is called the New Industrial Society (Galbraith, 1967). More precisely, in contrast to his "New Industrial State", we call it a New Industrial Society of the second generation (NIS.2) (Bodrunov, 2016a-b).

The transition to the NIS.2 stage opens up new opportunities for economic development and meeting people's needs. It's not just about the growth of need fulfilment along with productivity growth. Hybrid technologies based on the synergy of various technologies of the fifth and sixth technological modes relying on information and telecommunication technologies introduced in any technology, create products and services that allow simultaneously meeting a range of needs and significantly reducing the material intensity of production.

At the same time, the modern economy creates new material opportunities for the development of human personality. Information and communication technologies make the benefits of education and culture more accessible. There is a growing need for skilled labour in manufacturing, which requires high quality education and training. A high degree of satisfaction of main basic needs creates prerequisites for the development of higher-order needs. However, does a high level of needs satisfaction bring unambiguous progress, and does the formation of new technological possibilities for satisfying needs eliminate the problem of consumption? Far from being an automatic solution to our problems, it carries the potential to make them worse.

Modern economic and technological development is characterised by *increasing destructive pressure on the natural environment*. It's been talked about for decades. Recent research on this topic includes the work of William Connolly (Connolly, 2017, 2019). No less dangerous is the *increasing interference with human nature*. Such interference acts as a by-product of our consumption: the composition of the food we ingest, the air we breathe, the things we wear, the impact of the devices that surround us and that we use. One could mention the dramatically increased information load on human beings. The entire lifestyle of a modern person – at work, at home and at leisure – is permeated with a wide variety of influences of this kind, right up to the discrepancy between the rhythm of our life and our biological rhythms.

The current stage of human civilisation is characterised by the growth of threats associated with direct and targeted interference in human nature: whether it concerns experiments to modify the human genome, or the prospects of orthotics, or the use of electronic implants, or the development of diverse ways to manipulate our consciousness and psyche (Morris, 2021; Susser, Roessler, Nissenbaum, 2019; Reisach, 2021; Broudy, Arakaki, 2020).

As a result of increasing pressure on the natural balance, humanity is approaching a bifurcation point, a tipping point (Korotayev, LePoire, 2020). The decisions made will determine whether a "window of opportunity" opens for further development or whether humanity will have to struggle for survival in the face of the coming catastrophic consequences of the previous development pathway.

The technological capabilities on which these kinds of threats rely cannot themselves be characterised negatively. They may be used for good purposes: prolonging life, improving health, enhancing knowledge opportunities, mitigating social conflicts, and so on. These technologies are also expanding the range of our needs and our ability to meet them.

At this point, we face the most significant contradiction: an increase in the level of satisfaction of needs may result in such an increase in absorbed resources and produced waste (as well as side effects) that it can destroy our environment. Even the use of digital technologies and artificial intelligence can lead to an increasing burden on the environment due to increased energy consumption (Strubell, Ganesh, McCallum, 2019; Spelda, Stritecky, 2020). Thus, NIS.2, while raising society to a new level of satisfaction of needs and creating new opportunities for the development of the human personality, expanding the range of our knowledge, does not create guarantees for the reasonable use of these opportunities for the benefit rather than to the detriment of the individual. *If the system of economic relations that recognises as rational the growth of sales volumes of anything, as long as it brings profit and leads to growth in GDP (even if we are talking about simulated needs and the production of simulacra), is preserved, then no technological progress will save us from the thoughtless waste of resources.*

The solution to the problem lies in the mainstream of those social relations within the framework of which this new stage of production development functions. It is obvious that only a change in the social conditions of production, and along with the criteria, goals and motives of production activities, and the nature of the formation of our needs, can cope with the contradictions of development, with the growth of threats and obvious crisis phenomena.

This requires a gradual movement away from the focus on economic performance criteria, rather than private amendments and shifts in the current system of performance criteria. At one time, it was the development of economic rationality, the setting of production and consumption on the basis of the comparison of economic benefits and losses that served as the most powerful engine of progress.

Economic rationality made it possible to create powerful and ever-improving productive forces, to expand both the range of human needs and the possibilities of their satisfaction. It fostered, on the one hand, a spirit of enterprise, on the other hand, the habit of hard disciplined labour.

There comes a point, however, when human civilisation begins to pay too high a price for these achievements of economic society. The forces created by an economic society are used economically and rationally. But it turns out that this is not always reasonable in terms of their impact on the future of human civilisation. Economically rational behaviour relies on reason, on the knowledge of reality, but only on one side of it – on the side of the account of benefits and losses. Economic rationality does not cover by reasonable judgments the reality in its entirety and on the side of the whole complex of problems and contradictions of its development, including those created by economically rational actions.

We leave aside the theoretical limitations of the concept of rational and individual utility maximising the individual. It has long been clear that real people, including their economic relationships, are not walking calculators continuously calculating benefit-loss ratios, and that individual utility is almost always not the only factor in economic decision making (Conlisk, 1996). Therefore, the neoclassical concept of economic rationality has been criticised from the conceptual foundations of political economy (Heilbroner, 1988; Foley, 2004). It has also been criticised from philosophical positions that reject the productivity of the methodology of positivism on which the concept is based (Hollis, Nell, 1975). Criticism has also been come from methodological, empirical, sociological and psychological perspectives (Schram, Caterino, 2006; Green, Fox, 2007: 269-282; Bourdieu, 2005; McKinnon, 2013; Rubin, Capra, 2011). The theories of bounded rationality and the postulates of behavioural economics, which form part of this critique, are incorporated into modern neoclassical theory, which has made some concessions to reality.

Despite all these criticisms, economic rationality represents an essential fact of the modern economic system, albeit one that characterises this system in a simplistic and one-sided way. The pursuit of private interest and the desire for the most favourable ratio of benefits and losses have been and remain the leading factors of economic behaviour.

Such rationality as a criterion base for production and consumption decisions should be replaced by criteria that can more fully take into account the consequences of decisions: technological, environmental, social, etc. We can speak of replacing narrow criteria of economic rationality with broader and more universal criteria of reason. Thus, reasonable production goals and reasonable needs, based on the totality of knowledge of reality, should take the place of the main criteria for decision-making in the sphere of production. The place of economy should be taken by noonomy as a non-economic way of production and satisfaction of human needs (Bodrunov, 2018a).

How can we define those criteria of reasonableness that should replace narrow economic rationality? These criteria are determined (not only will be, but are partly determined already now) *by the richness of human culture.* The very change in the system of needs and objectives of production activities – from increasing consumption to the deployment of human potential – determines the criteria for achieving these goals. Since personality is formed by the sum of mastered cultural achievements of mankind, the criteria of reasonableness of human needs in the development of personality are also formed on the basis of these achievements. It is necessary to "connect technological power with the power of knowledge, with human reason embodied in the traditions of human culture" (Bodrunov, 2018a).

The mere desire to change social attitudes in this direction is not enough. What creates not only the necessity, but also the possibility of transition from economy to noonomy?

First, the opportunity is created by those technological advances that unfold at the NIS.2 stage and ensure, as the knowledge intensity of production grows significantly, a significant increase in the role of knowledge and people who possess knowledge. Thus, human creative activity comes to the fore as the leading factor in the development of production. The human transition to creativity is also created by the growth of labour productivity leading to an increase in free time, and by the displacement of the individual from the immediate process of production. This moves it into the realm of goal setting, management, research, development, etc.

Secondly, at the stage of NIS.2, such potential for satisfying human vital needs is created that can provide a sufficient level of saturation with vital benefits. This opens the way for the reorientation of needs from the provision of material conditions of human life to the development of the personality of the human itself. Contrary to the concept of Abraham Maslow and most of his critics, the change of predominant needs cannot be explained only from within the system of needs and motives of human behaviour through the construction of this or that scheme of their interaction (Maslow, 1954).

Empirical research shows that the actual hierarchy of needs is organised somewhat differently than Maslow believed.[4] Clayton Alderfer's theory attempts to resolve the apparent contradictions of Maslow's concept with reality through a more complex picture of interaction of hierarchically arranged levels of needs (Alderfer, 1969). Some critics see the solution to the relationship of needs as a revision of the ethical foundations of Maslow's concept (which he himself regarded as "humanistic psychology"), replacing them with "integral humanism" (Acevedo, 2018). Others feel the need to propose their own, more realistic construction of types and structure of needs (Desmet, Fokkinga, 2020). Maslow's views are subject to revision in terms of whether his views on human needs and drives are consistent with the Holy Scripture (McCleskey, Ruddell, 2020).

Those researchers who adopted Amartya Sen's concept of "capability approach" came somewhat closer to understanding the problem. Although this approach is used not to assess the ratio and interaction of needs but to assess the standard of living, it addresses the issue that the satisfaction of human needs depends not only on the amount of life goods consumed, but also on a person's ability to develop and the set of conditions that allow these abilities to be realised. As Amartya Sen emphasises, "These non-income variables point to opportunities that a person has excellent reason to value and that are not strictly linked with economic prosperity" (Sen, 1999). It was further concluded that the goods consumed are important not only in themselves but also as conditions for more or less successful human development (Levine, Abu Turab Rizvi, 2005). But the next step – to establish a connection not only between the realisation of human abilities and the level of consumption, but also between the development of the process of realisation of abilities and changes in the nature of needs themselves – has not been made.

The change in the predominant causes of human actions and needs cannot be explained solely on the basis of one or another approach to the sequence of saturation of needs or the interaction between high and low saturation. This also applies to the transition to the predominance of drivers and needs of self-development and self-realisation of a person. In reality, such a transition is not made possible by the very saturation of vital needs, which acts as a necessary prerequisite that allows a person to free himself from the daily struggle for "daily bread". The main driving force for changing the structure and hierarchy of needs is not the characteristics of consumption, but the characteristics of human production activity and its significant enrichment with creative functions. It is the development of these functions that brings the need for the development of the potential of human personality to the forefront.

Noonomy, while orienting production to meet the needs of personal development, is acting not only as a new way of organising production, but also as the basis of a new way of development of human society, or Noosociety.

The contradictions of social development, which create the impulse of movement towards noonomy, do not ensure automatic movement along this path of their resolution. I want to believe that humanity will make its way to a better future. But then that path may involve double bends, wandering, dead ends and finding a way out of them. Therefore, the movement towards noonomy should be based on the opportunities and prerequisites for its formation, which are already emerging now. The most important of these prerequisites is the possibility of conscious and purposeful improvement of social relations. In other words, *the movement to NIS.2 and through it to noonomy should be carried out as* ***a consciously calculated long-term strategic project****, implemented in stages.*

To date, the most fully developed concept of formation and implementation of such projects is the concept of strategising by Academician V.L. Kvint (Kvint, 2019, 2020).

In order to realise the movement towards ***noonomy as a strategic project,*** it is important to understand that in this case *the target of the strategy is not noonomy itself. The strategy is based on certain interests and key value orientations of society.*

Any development strategy aims to improve the quality of life of individuals and society. The difficulty in solving this problem is that it is necessary to determine the implementation of which specific interests and values at this stage will lead to an increase in the quality of life. They are specifically the basis for formulating the strategic priorities. But even that is not enough. It is necessary to identify which priorities we can implement to ensure the formation of advantages that will allow us to achieve significant progress, rather than wasting resources in pursuit of tempting, but utopian at this stage, goals (Kvint, 2018).

Quality of life acts not only as a general but also an abstract guideline, which does not fully reveal either the specific priorities of the strategy or the advantages that can be used to ensure them. The definition of quality of life will vary greatly across different social conditions and levels of economic development as well as the means of achieving this target will also differ.

The study of current objective trends allowing to conclude the evolution of society towards noonomy provides insight into significant interests and values, as well as to the advantages we can rely on to achieve our goals. The relevant priorities should also be refined in relation to the national characteristics of the strategising object. For Russia, for example, we are talking about the need for re-industrialisation as a necessary stage to ensure any subsequent strategic shifts.

The strategy of movement towards noonomy, which has an extremely distant prospect of realisation, assumes the achievement of *certain intermediate milestones,* to each of which a certain strategic project will lead. The realisation of the first strategic project always requires a change of strategy and the development of a new project leading to the next strategic milestone. As noted by V.L. Kvint, "even the most successful strategies reach a stage where a shift to a new strategy must begin due to changing conditions or needs" (Kvint, 2019). It can be tentatively determined that for our country the first such frontier will be re-industrialisation, then – the formation of NIS.2, and later – the movement directly to noonomy.

For each of these milestones, it is necessary to have a specific formulation of those interests and priorities, as well as those strategic advantages, which together will define *the concept of strategising for each stage of development.*

The concept of noonomy allows us to state unambiguously that, regardless of the specifics of each of the stages, their goals and priorities should be formulated taking into account the need to provide *conditions for the development of human personality*. At the same time, it must be recognised that we are still in an economic society and cannot immediately abandon economic criteria of rationality. This puts a strain on the interests and priorities of our society. In setting the task of limiting the obsessive drive to increase the volume of consumption, we cannot but take into account the fact that increased consumption is necessary because some members of society are not yet sufficiently provided with the basic survival needs. Simultaneously with the solution of this task, material and spiritual prerequisites should be formed in order to expand the possibilities of creative activity, mastering the wealth of culture and shifts towards reasonable criteria of consumption formed on this basis (Kvint, Bodrunov, 2021).

The benefits on which a strategy for moving towards noonomy can be based should be specified for each stage of this movement. Potential advantages for re-industrialisation lie in the ability to combine the income flow from fuel and commodity exports with existing capabilities in fundamental scientific research, extant engineering and design schools, and an industrial base in a number of high-tech industries. Moving to the NIS.2 stage will require adding to these benefits a significant expansion of human potential. As we move on from stage to stage, the benefits of unleashing the potential of a human person and nurturing the "cultural man" must be enhanced. This is seen not only as one of the most important development priorities, but also as a factor that provides significant advantages in this development.

At intermediate milestones, purely economic criteria of activity will play a significant role, and man will not yet completely lose the properties of "homo economicus". Only with the consolidation at the stage of NIS.2 will there be conditions for a gradual reduction in the role of those economic forms and relations that mediate and regulate human production activities. *Through the use of "technologies of trust" the sphere of economic intermediation will shrink, and the mass displacement of man from direct production will lead to the removal of the shell of production relations from social relations.* Only on this basis will it be possible to move away from economic rationality to a rationality based on the criteria of reason and culture.

The concept of noonomy focuses the strategy on the development of fundamentally new technologies, which are the result of breakthrough scientific research and are based on the use of highly developed human intelligence. These are the technologies that will reduce the resource intensity of production and move people from the direct process of production to the spheres of creative activity.

This kind of breakthrough research and the resulting technologies are critical to strategising. Their development and application can make it possible to achieve the strategic objectives formulated above at each stage of implementation of the strategy aimed at improving the quality of life in all its aspects. Therefore, the system of search and transfer of innovative developments is important to discover and use them to ensure the priorities of the strategy (Kvint, Khvorostyanaya, Sasaev, 2020).

Strategy development should not just capture current development trends in order to base itself upon them. It should forecast, identify potential impact, and incorporate into the strategy process trends that have not yet manifested themselves or have yet to emerge. Academician V.L. Kvint emphasises: "The most innovative and potentially successful strategies are based on the analysis of trends and patterns that are little known or not yet realised by the start of the strategy" (Kvint, 2015).

The study of modern trends in technological and socio-economic development allows us to state both the growth of opportunities to meet human needs and human development, and the growth of risks and threats. The load on the natural environment is increasing, the risks of uncontrolled development of the technosphere are growing, and fears of thoughtless or malicious interference in nature by man himself are becoming real. The growth of opportunities to satisfy needs is aimed at the formation of illusory needs and simulation of their fulfilment.

These problems can be solved on the basis of development of human perception of the surrounding world and application of the knowledge gained in technological processes. Technologies are becoming less resource-intensive, and the role of knowledge embedded in technologies and their products outweighs their material part. On this basis, humanity is approaching a new stage of its development – the New industrial society of the second generation (NIS.2).

However, the current focus on narrow criteria of economic rationality, where everything that brings economic benefits is rational, does not allow to abandon the unrestrained absorption of natural resources, accompanied by pollution of the natural environment, climatic shifts, loss of biodiversity and direct destruction of natural objects necessary for human existence.

The resolution of this contradiction is a change in the social structure of production and a change in the criteria for forming the goals of production and human needs. The basis for this is the increasing knowledge-intensity of production and the gradual displacement of people from the direct process of production into spheres of creative activity. The main goal of production is no longer the volume of consumption, but the development of the creative potential of a human personality. The place of economy is taken by noonomy, a non-economic way of satisfying needs based on the criteria of reason and culture.

To avoid conflicts and double bends along the way, it is necessary to make the movement towards noonomy manageable. It is necessary to develop a long-term strategy of gradual movement from frontier to frontier: through re-industrialisation to NIS.2 and then to noonomy.

The best theoretical and methodological basis for the development of such a long-term strategic project is the theory of strategising by Academician V.L. Kvint.

With regard to national development goals, it can be said that improving the quality of life and moving towards a society capable of creating living and working conditions worthy of human beings is the mission that should be at the root of a national development strategy. From the point of view of noonomy, the quality of life includes not only a rational (according to reasonable criteria) level of consumption, but also the conditions for the development of human personality and the elevation of its culture in the process of creative activity. On such a basis it will be possible to eliminate the risks associated with disruption of the reproduction of the natural environment.

The task of realising this mission can be considered as the main message that the strategy of movement towards noonomy addresses to our country and to all mankind.

Conjugation of the theory of noonomy and the theory of strategy yields important theoretical and practical results.

First, noonomy acts as the core objective of development, and strategising acts as the basic tool for achieving this goal.

Secondly, the theory of noonomy lays down a solid foundation for the start of strategising processes, substantiating the preceding forecasting work and goal setting.

However, it does not follow that the theory of noonomy is linked to the strategising process only at its starting and final "points". The closest connection between these theories occurs in the idea and rationale of the concept of nootransition, which, through the definition of the stages of global transformation and movement towards noosociety, determines the implementation of strategising processes, sets specific guidelines for them at each interval and allows for an intermediate assessment of the noodevelopment level achieved at a particular stage.

15.2. Strategy of Transition to Noosociety: Industrial Aspect

Contemporary transformation of economic and social system requires changes in approach to its analysis and management of its development. At the same time, it is not needed to keep the traditional approach based on the neoliberal theory and methodology. For Russia, the Chinese experience is more suitable, based on the closed and proportional combination of elements of market-based and planned models of economy management. It is precisely this approach that delivers sustainable technological, economic and social development, in process of which the tasks of qualitative renewal of all fields of public life are solved. And in addition, the central focus is made in the development of high-tech industries, which are becoming a core of an economic and social system being renewed. This requires top-priority development of fundamental science, culture and education, as well as the return of the state into a capitalist process, to the direct public administration of a number of development spheres, active support of state and public-private high-tech corporations. The basis of the development is technological advance. It also changes in new conditions. A new quality of industrialised production is observed. It is knowledge-intensive production, for which not only a speed-up is typical, but also a speed-up of technological development. Russia today is solving the tasks of not just industrialisation or re-industrialisation – these tasks will mostly be solved in the near future. It faces the challenge of laying the foundations for the New industrial society of the second generation (NIS.2), a knowledge-driven society. The latter means the priority of knowledge-intense production united with science and education. Hence, a necessity arises to integrate those three spheres within the frame of a united reproduction contour on all levels: micro-, meso- and macro-economics.

The transformation experienced by humanity in the XXI century is of a fundamental nature and covers all spheres of social life. We are witnessing that global threats may become the most important factor that necessitates a profound readjustment of the entire social life and, above all, of the economy. Unfolding under the banner of the "end of history" (Fukuyama, 2015), the neoliberal project generated a host of illusions, many of which were far from harmless. Some of the most ingrained in the public consciousness are the illusions of market fundamentalism and post-industrialism as the two pillars of the neoliberal model (Bell, 1999). They are still widespread among economists and politicians in the West.

However, there are other approaches and ***alternative development opportunities***. These are the ones that will be discussed in more detail.

For a number of decades, China has consistently pursued a policy of combining the principles of market and planning, private and public property within the framework of moving towards the development of socialism with Chinese specifics. This experience shows that this strategy produces globally recognised results. And it's not just the consistently high rates of economic growth. This is, first of all, technological, economic and social ***development***, in process of which the tasks of qualitative renewal of all fields of public life are solved.

Among the most striking achievements in moving in this direction, it is advisable to pay attention to the industrial aspect of this process, especially the transition from *labour-intensive* technologies, first to *capital-intensive*, and recently to *knowledge-intensive* technologies.

In present-day Russia, transformations are also beginning to take place, indicating a gradual shift away from neoliberal dogmatism. Among the most important of these changes is *the course on the development of high-tech production*. Its main areas cover both civilian and defence-industrial sectors.

The main results include the revival of a number of basic sectors of economy, such as the agrarian-industrial complex, which has already yielded visible results: from a net importer Russia has become a net exporter of agricultural products, and Russian agrarian machine building in a number of sub-branches has risen to a level of achievement in the quality of manufactured machines adequate for the current world level. Russian aviation and shipbuilding industries are developing. Russia has already overtaken the leading world powers in the production of a number of weapons. The space industry, nuclear industry and many other sectors are at the level of global achievement.

It is especially important to note that Russia is not only formally the legal successor of the USSR; our country has inherited the traditions of priority development of *fundamental science*, high *culture* and world-class education, of which the Soviet Union was deservedly proud. These achievements, despite many problems and difficulties, are generally alive in modern Russia and represent a powerful foundation for further development.

All this has become possible thanks to an important turn in the history of domestic economic development observed in recent years – *the return of the state to the investment process*, to direct management of a number of development areas, to the active progress of state and private-public high-tech corporations, i.e., thanks to the methods successfully used by China, which is becoming Russia's closest economic partner.

At the same time, the transformation of Russia, China, India and a number of other countries into active subjects of global *geopolitical* and economic development is no less, and perhaps even more significant. Today, humanity is witnessing that the world is moving towards a polycentric configuration. Moreover, as R. Desai emphasises (Bodrunov, Desai, Friman, 2022), the prospect can and should become *not a multipolar, but a pluripolar world* – a world in which different civilisations, different countries follow special development paths, and where this *diversity becomes the basis for unity and cooperation.*

Russia is not just a state. It is a special world, whose civilisational uniqueness as a bridge between Europe and Asia can serve as an important basis for dialogue and development of not just a *multi*polar, but a *pluri*polar world.

The basis of any development is *technological progress* (Bodrunov, 2018a; Glazyev, 2018). This generally recognised position was developed by the author to the conclusion about the transition to a *new quality* of *industrial* (I emphasise: exactly industrial!) production – *knowledge-intensive* production, which is characterised by not just acceleration, but *acceleration of technological development* (Bodrunov, 2016à).

This conclusion has a fundamentally important practical significance. It stipulates the necessity of orientation, firstly, on the priority development of breakthrough, *not catching up, but outrunning the world achievements* of technologies; secondly, in the conditions of accelerated acceleration of scientific and technological progress, the task is not so much to focus on the monopoly fixation of some, even advanced at the moment, technologies within the framework of one or another form of intellectual private property, but on *constant* advancement in the field of *innovation.*

However, for the progress of technology to become *continuous and accelerating, economic means* are needed to address the challenges highlighted above.

In this regard, it is strategically important for our country to choose the path of rethinking the experience – both its own and those of other countries, in particular, the experience of China in recent decades and the experience of the USSR during the N.E.P. era (Kvint, Bodrunov, 2021, 2023).

In both cases, these are examples of successful *experience of qualitative leaps* in solving the tasks of technological and socio-economic modernisation, industrialisation and accelerated social development in a mixed economy. These historical practices have demonstrated the effectiveness of combining market self-regulation and competition with active industrial policy and strategic planning, private business and a rapidly growing public sector.

But that's not enough today. Russia is already solving tasks not only in industrialisation or re-industrialisation: such tasks will be mostly solved anytime soon; but is also facing *the task of creating the basis of the New industrial society of the second generation (NIS.2)* – a society where *knowledge* takes the leading role.

The latter means the *priority* of knowledge-intensive production (sphere of knowledge *implementation*) in unity with science (sphere of knowledge generation) and education (sphere of formation of those who are able to generate and implement knowledge). Hence, the task of *integrating* these three spheres within a single reproductive contour at all levels: micro-, meso- and macroeconomics.

Let us repeat: to solve this problem, in turn, we need not only an *active industrial policy and strategic planning*, the activity of private capital and a focus on the public interests of the public sector, but also something more – ***the identification of priority areas of development and the creation of mechanisms for its regulation.***

First, the right *property relations strategy* is important today. This topic is hardly ignored by proponents of neoclassical economic theory. Meanwhile, here – and this is shown by the theory of institutionalism and political economy – lie the *foundations* of development, objective determinants of its content and focus. An important point is that if the main issue of the industrial economy was and remains the problem of the ratio of the private and public sector, then for knowledge-intensive production, characterised by accelerated acceleration of innovation, *the problem moves to another plane.*

To the constantly renewing technological content of production and, consequently, its configuration, structures and forms, there correspond more flexible, changeable, *"fluid" forms and rights of ownership*; moreover – *diffusion of ownership*, blurring of its boundaries, increasing transition to joint (not private and not public, but *joint, solidary*) use of it in the process of production and consumption (Bodrunov, 2021à).

The specific institutions of such sharing are already known in practice. These include the archaically fast-growing car-sharing (140-fold growth in the world in 2018–2020), the spaces of co-working and co-living, various forms of crowdsourcing and crowdfunding, etc. These forms are just being born today, but they are developing in an "accelerated acceleration" mode and will become dominant tomorrow.

Secondly, among the key problems of modern society, *social* problems are one of the most acute. In Russia in recent years much attention has been paid to solving the problems of poverty and social security of citizens in need. A confident course has been set for the creation of a socially-oriented state. Both practice and theory show that in order to move towards a new society, in which a person will not only be provided with material benefits, but also capable of *creativity*, there is no and cannot be progress of knowledge-intensive production in the mode of constant acceleration of innovative technological development.

This, in turn, requires a *process of socialisation of the economy and society*. In its focus on solving social problems, it is Russia that should and can in the future show the world a new direction of development – development based on a new industry, in which *the priorities are not only economic growth, but also social justice*, and even – let us make this imperative stricter – economic growth to ensure social justice.

Finally, third, a market economy is an economy the attributes of which are competition and individualism. They certainly motivate a person to elevate labour and entrepreneurial activity. But to move towards NIS.2, a society the main actor of which will be an innovation-oriented person, the necessary direction of development is the movement along the path of *solidarity*.

To summarise, it is advisable to turn to an allegory that the author has previously demonstrated (Bodrunov, 2021à): the image of "Apollo's quadriga", the ancient Greek carriage on whose four horses he, the god of beauty and reason, moves into the world of culture and humanism. We can theoretically and practically consider the conclusion about the necessity of forming such a "quadriga" of methods and means of moving towards the NIS.2 and the Noosociety to be justified. The "wheel-horse" of this quadriga, its main "horse" is scientific and technological progress. It is complemented by three other "horses": transformation of property relations (its diffusion), socialisation and solidarism.

Regarding the latter two – socialisation and solidarism – let us note that the Soviet experience has shown that *on the basis of relations of solidarity,* supplemented by a fair distribution of material benefits, it is possible to most effectively solve *breakthrough* tasks that ensure advancements in technological, economic and social development. This is how such gigantic projects as the electrification plan, the space and atomic programme, and the breakthrough to the world's best education were implemented in the USSR.

Based on these positions, combined with market incentives and government regulations, modern Russia has created many types of hypersonic missiles, anti-aircraft defense and missile defence systems and other defence systems that have no analogues in the world.

This quadriga directs us to a new society – a society in which the *economic man will become a cultural man, in which knowledge-intensive production will free man from routine labour and promote him to creative activity* – a society called ***noonomy***, a society, many features of which are recognisable in the strategic guidelines for the development of countries that form the core of the transformational process of transition to a new, "Integral" world economic mode of China, India, Russia (Bodrunov, Glazyev, 2023).

Humanity's advancement towards such a society – more harmonious than the current one – cannot be ensured without the active participation of China and Russia. The former leaders – the USA and the European Union and their satellites, professing neoliberal ideology, have led their economies into a crisis, which they themselves are already openly talking about (Schwab, 2016).

An alternative socio-economic and geopolitical course is offered to the world today by China, in practice promoting the ideas of the community with a shared future for mankind.[5] Russia's future also lies not on the path of market fundamentalism. There is *both historical experience and modern potential* to solve the tasks of breakthrough technological and socio-cultural development, using not only on national but also international scale economic and political institutions, the traditions and intents of development of which are the strongest in our country.

And these are the very *institutions* that the theory of NIS.2 and noonomy speaks about, as evidenced by the practices of our countries – institutions for the development of knowledge-intensive production: a) connecting basic science and experience in the implementation of its results; b) flexible, aimed at the implementation of not only private but also public interests of rights and forms of ownership; c) promoting the economy along the path of socialisation; d) solidarising society on the basis of common *interests and values.*

These are the main ***goals. The means*** for this should be *the mechanisms of active industrial policy and strategic planning* (Bodrunov, 2021b).

It is on this path that our country has a chance to become one of the leaders of global development, and geo-economic ties with partners within the SCO, BRICS and other formats – a factor in the formation of one of the basic centres of the new world economic mode of the XXI century (Glazyev, 2016a).

The conducted research has shown that today there is a paradigm shift in the paradigmatic ideas about the ways and direction of long-term civilisational development. The formation of a new world economy and the prospect of transition to a new society require the development of new strategies and long-term programmes in which, at least in the first stages, the industrial aspects of this transition should play a key role.

Representing a non-economic way of satisfying reasonable and conscious needs of people, noonomy will serve as a material basis for the formation and functionality of Noosociety, i.e., a material basis for the implementation and development of a promising humanitarian model of social order and a new world order (Bodrunov, 2021*) based on the development of appropriate prospective strategies and long-term programmes.

Notes

1 Prepared on the basis of the following materials: Bodrunov, 2021b, 2023a; Bodrunov, 2021*.

2 World development and "the Limits to Growth" in the XXI century: modelling and forecasting. URL: https://www.msu.ru/upload/pdf/2021/20210421-akaev.pdf (accessed: 13.09.2021).

3 Debunking the post-industrial myth. URL: https://www.industryweek.com/the-economy/public-policy/article/22007271/debunking-the-postindustrialmyth (accessed: 13.09.2021); Building a strong and modern European industry. URL: https://www.businesseurope.eu/

sites/buseur/files/media/reports_and_studies/building_a_strong_and_modern_european_industry_-_compressed_for_web_and_sending.pdf (accessed: 13.09.2021).

4 The three things employees really want: career, community, cause. URL: https://hbr.org/2018/02/people-want-3-things-from-work-but-most-companiesare-built-around-only-one (accessed: 13.09.2021).

5 Chinese traditional culture in the concept of "A Community with a Shared Future for Mankind". URL: https://russiancouncil.ru/blogs/zhengjielan/kitayskayatraditsionnaya-kultura-v-kontseptsii-soobshchestva-edinoy-s/ (accessed on 02.05.2023).

PART THREE

Global Social Transformation and Noosociety

The third part includes a direct analysis of the characteristics and "appearance" of noosociety and a noohuman. Looking into the distant future, science fiction writers often focus their attention on the appearance and external circumstances and living conditions of the descendants of modern humans: models of their appearance and transformation of some organs, options for constructing "habitats", etc., are known. We are interested in – just as this idea is expressed by the words of one of M.A. Bulgakov's heroes – "a much more important question": to what extent, under the condition of implementation of a positive scenario of their development, a human and society will change internally. The answer to this question is the subject of a whole set of the author's studies, the results of which are presented in this part of the book.

16

Noosociety and the Peak of Modern Social Development[1]

At present, Noosociety seems to us to be the peak of the evolution of modern society. Of course, with the conquest of this peak, social progress will not stop, and mankind will continue its development, but the contours of such a distant perspective and relevant forecasts are quite difficult to derive now. Therefore, we prefer in this paper to focus on a specific trajectory of social transformation and its end point – the achievement of a noo state by society.

The traditional concept of convergence considers the transition to convergence of different types of social structure (capitalism, socialism) as a certain gradual convergence of both types into a "uniform" society by "taking the best (what? what is the best? from what point of view? determined on the basis of what criteria?...) of each". The so-called "integral society", which in its basic concepts believes that "integration" should be defined along economic lines, is no better. Hence the ideas of "integration" (in economic terms, first of all) associations, singling out and establishing a certain "commonality/ integration" of interests (economic ones, of course) as almost the goals of universal development, etc.

These concepts, being viable (the concept of convergence – as a certain general philosophical message, the concept of integral society – as a "practical guide" at some intermediate stage on the way to the New industrial society of the second generation) and noting "integrating", "converging" trends in the development of society, nevertheless do not reveal the essence of the ongoing transformational processes in the development of civilisation, and the social system in particular.

Convergence of any currently existing variants of socio-political order, however, is realised not through political, administrative or economic convergence of different types of political or administrative systems or economic models, but through the gradual transition of individuals to a common understanding of basic values.

The formation of the criterion base of values, their structuring into a value core (and taking into account the gradual elevation of the content of values towards the general cultural-moral-ethical trend – we can talk about the "moral-value core" of social consciousness) occurs throughout the history of human evolution and the development of human civilisation.

At the heart of this process lies the phenomenon of a person's awareness of his or her needs. Maslow's hierarchy of needs (at the base, at the bottom of the hierarchy, there are the so-called vital needs, followed by more elevated needs: security, education, etc.) does not explain in essence why and how the higher-level needs in his hierarchy arose, revealing only the formation of their "lower" echelon – from the biological nature of man, abstracting from the fact that he also has a mind, comprehending knowledge, producing a deeper awareness of the world and allowing to realise and formulate needs other than vital ones.

Their gradual elevation is precisely based on the aforementioned process of realisation.

In this case, the realisation of a certain need by a person, becoming generally accepted (accepted by society, realised by it!), forms a value that requires, in turn, the inclusion of itself (it!) in the existing value nucleus, thus expanding it, as well as fixing it (the newly expanded nucleus) in the public consciousness – and, further, initiating the corresponding institutional fixation in the social order.

> *Values* are the main "regulator" of social relations, determining the creation and development/transformation of society's institutions.

Regulating social relations through the institutions of society, values, in their turn, require realisation by all people and goal-setting/subordination of people's activities to the established criterion base determined by values.

The value core is constantly evolving. And this development occurs "from bottom to top" according to Maslow's hierarchy, while not by narrowing the core (as in the "pyramid"), but on the contrary, by expanding it, i.e., it makes sense to speak (meaning dynamics, development) not of a pyramid, but, rather, of at least a "cylinder", or even a "truncated inverted pyramid", based on a minimum of "low", vital needs.

A standard pyramid (including a truncated pyramid) assumes stability when it rests on a wider base. Maslow's pyramid assumes as such a basis the vital needs of a person – they are depicted at the base of his hierarchy. However, with the gradual expansion of the nucleus of values (and more and more complete satisfaction of "lower" needs), the inclusion of higher-order values, the more exalted needs become more and more important for a person. That is, at a certain point there is a "reassessment of values" and higher-order values become the basis of absolutely prioritised needs. The pyramid is inverted – new values are placed at its base.

These new values, on the one hand, with man's deviation from simulative consumption, gravitate towards noo, the reasonable realisation by man of his mission as a bearer of reason, forming not just a new, broader base of values, but its noocriterial core ("noocore").

> *The value "noocore"* is a noocriterial universal moral and value core of an expanded base of values, formed by society during the nootransition and determining the gradual (as we move towards such a core) convergence of institutions and different strata of society, up to the formation of institutions that are unified/uniform in their functionality, uniting/integrating individuals (their interests, etc.) and social systems.

On the other hand, these values (exactly – noovalues!), by virtue of their nature, are universal as a manifestation of the universal mind. As universal, they become the basis for the formation of a homogeneous – in terms of value perception of existence – society. This is certainly not the identical views of the members of society on specific situations; no, it is a uniform (and – noo!) understanding of the values of life by people.

Noovalues on the basis of a universal noocore define the face of a new type of social structure – noosociety.

> *Noosociety* is an "integral" and "homogeneous" society that emerges on the basis of the formation of a single, universal, and at the same time noocriterial base of values (noocore of values).

The consequence of the transition to noosociety will be the elimination of the conflictogenity of civilisation development (not the elimination of contradictions – they will remain at least in the setting of tasks, the assessment of ways to achieve goals, the choice of means of such achievement, individual differences in the cognitive ability of individuals, and much more), since the interests of people-individuals, determined by a common base of values, will be close or coincide (perhaps it is worth paying attention to the fact that the conflict (non-compromise) way of resolving contradictions will not be preserved in the moral-value system).

The development of the value core will go not only in the direction of strengthening the qualities of the person-individual, but also along the "person-society" line; the development of solidarism and further socialisation of society are inextricably linked to the strengthening of the prioritisation of social values, which will become predominant (consciously on the part of the individual!).

Reaching consensus will become a priority way to develop solutions based on the core values; the main mechanism for reaching consensus will be not just a dialog of individuals, but a polylogue of society members.

> Polylogy within the framework of nootransition is a practical basis for the formation of public consciousness, harmonisation of interests of individuals on the basis of a core of values, in the structure of which public values reflecting the public interest and needs of society will prevail.

The noocore of values will become the basic "governing body" of the noosociety, forming its institutions, determining the goals and objectives of social development, the role and place of an individual in society, etc.

The noocore of values, thus forming a conglomerate of nooinstitutions (institutions of the noosociety) as a poststate (quite conventional, having lost the classical functions of coercion, violence, etc., and having developed into the function of regulating the procedures of coordinating noointerests and organising on this basis the satisfaction of public and individual nooneeds), will become the foundation of governance of the noosociety, determining the functions of nooinstitutions.

Notes

1 Prepared on the basis of Bodrunov, 2022c.

17

Harmony of Noopersonality: Noovalues and Creative Activity[1]

The noosociety will consist of harmonious noopersonalities, but how to achieve this inner and outer harmony and overcome the problems of human evolution? For answering these questions, it is inevitably necessary to understand the role of the existing system of interests and values in shaping the crisis of human civilisation. Meanwhile, it is necessary to understand how our values can (and should) change, for our getting out of the crisis, preserving our human race, and, moreover, taking a step forward in our development. The material basis of such development is transition to the new industrial society of the second generation, and the social conditions are created by transition from economy to noonomy. But what will happen to our interests and values in the course of this transition? Below, I will try to get closer to answers to these questions. Besides, creative activity and its development in the course of nootransition are of particular importance for a noopersonality, so further speculations will concern the formation of a detailed comprehension of the phenomenon of creativity.

17.1. Interests and Values

The interests of a modern person reflect the economic relations that the person enters into in the course of his/her life. The very word *interest* originally (in the Middle Ages) meant the amount of compensation for economic damages. Then it began indicating the amount of the loan use fee, that is, the amount of interest paid by the borrower. In English, the word *interest* is still used in this sense. Thus, even in terms of the word formation process, interests and economy are closely connected.

Of course, there are also non-economic interests, which sometimes are almost more important for a person's individual fate than the economic conditions of life and the economic interests determined by them. The interests to be generated by love, jealousy, desire for freedom, ambition or love of power can overshadow economic motives. However, in mass socio-historical processes, economic interests invariably come to the fore. "...In any society you are unlikely to find anything more shared by people than things separating them. In modern society one is unlikely to find anything more uniting people than economic differences separating them; it is unlikely that in modern society, there is a more 'universal' type of connection between people than *economy*, which is shared by people as a way of separating that promises both unity and autonomy at once" (Ashkerov, 2002: 78–79).

This is inevitable in a society, in which economy occupies a dominant position, determining fundamental conditions of human existence and the course of human daily life.

In modern philosophical science, understanding the correlation of interests and values falls into the wide range of interpretations, which is determined by the equally wide range of interpretations of the concept of "value" itself. Attempts to introduce greater certainty into the issue on fundamental theoretical foundations of this concept, which were made in philosophical science in the last third of the XX century, have not yielded tangible results. "Explorers of axiology state serious problems associated with its 'theoretical frameworks' and the methodological chaos reigning in definitions of the concept of "value" and in interpretations of value relations, not to mention attempts to localise axiology in the general structure of philosophical discourse" (Shokhin, 2010: 84). Delving into the essence of these disputes and developing our own position would require a separate article, and perhaps more than one. Meanwhile, there are some common points in the views of a significant part of philosophers in understanding values, and we will try to rely on these common points.

Interests may turn into social values when they begin to be shared by many people (Habermas, 2001: 166–167), become widespread, firmly entrenched in the public consciousness and begin determining our assessment of things and events, becoming also entrenched at the individual level. Value always acts as an ideal phenomenon, as a subjective estimate, assessment of an object by a subject (in which the subject's self-assessment is manifested as well), but such assessment that receives social meaning and significance (Baeva, 2003: 14). Nevertheless, gaining social meaning and significance, values take root and are consolidated only through a person's individual position, since any social phenomenon exists only through interaction of individuals, through relationship between them: "Every universally significant value becomes really significant only in an individual context" (Bakhtin, 1986: 108–109).

17.2. Values of Economic Society

In society, only values that support the functioning of the dominant system of economic relations, and allow an individual to realise his/her interests in the framework of this dominant system, can be fixed in moral norms.

"Speculations about morality in economic terms coincide with the proclamation of the debt problem as the centre of moral issues. The debt morality presents itself as nothing more than the *value legitimisation of exchange relations*" (Ashkerov, 2002: 79) (my italics – S.B.).

Modern values bear a deep imprint of economic rationality in its specific refraction for a market capitalist society. This society values appear in the undisguised form of the cash-at-any-cost morality. "Either bite everyone, or lie in the mud". It is pointless to moralise about this, just trying to contrast this morality with other values seeming superior for some reason. And what is more, the sermon on love for one's neighbour did not interfere in any way with slavery or robbery by feudal squads.

However, this is not the only vector of values of the market-capitalist society in particular and economic society in general. The other vector is recognising values of diligence and thrift. It is quite a logical addition, since for most people who are not engaged in business, it is diligence and thrift that can somehow, at least partially, compensate for their belittled economic and social status, as well as provide some individual well-being. For example, the fate of a medieval peasant who was not endowed with proper diligence was very unenviable.

Does this mean that there are no differently focused values in modern society? Of course, there are, and as much as you want: altruism, solidarity, creativity... Their social significance is very noticeable. However, within the framework of the current socio-economic order, they cannot take dominant positions.

And yet, this situation is not eternal. For changing this situation, there are objective prerequisites maturing within the economic society, which is reflected in the growing crisis of interests and values focused on monetary gain. This process was initiated by economic values themselves.

A long time ago, economic rationality was the strongest engine of social progress, generating the spirit of entrepreneurship and innovation, mixed up on realistic economic calculation, on the one hand, and the spirit of persistent, disciplined work, on the other hand. Society has advanced far in its development, having created powerful productive forces – both from the side of the latest technologies and from the side of human knowledge embodied in them.

New opportunities have arisen for human development, for changing conditions of human existence, for developing and satisfying diverse human needs. Capitalism has given us all this. It increased the speed of technical and scientific progress for the purpose of satisfying consumers' needs. The growth of consumption stands out almost as the most superior value. "In the value chain 'new technologies – economic growth – increased consumption', the last link is considered as the priority component. Explicitly or implicitly, all actors of globalisation accept this value chain as the expression of the universal human values" (Stepin, 2015: 163).

17.3. Expansion of Economic Values as Manifestation of their Crisis

Values of economic society, which grow out of economic interests, also affect values to be formed outside the properly economic sphere of society. Moral norms basing on economic relations "paint in their colours" those moral norms that regulate non-economic relations. Considerations of benefit, equivalence of exchange, and maximisation of consumption penetrate into the spheres of creativity, family ties, love and friendship, and religious beliefs.

However, since a certain point on, it is no longer just about influence. Of course, such phenomena as, for example, marriage of convenience, originated long ago. But, being quite widespread, they were still not of universal nature and were subjected to moral condemnation, albeit often quite hypocritical. producing children, parents thought about their supporting them in their old age. Standing with an easel in his hands, the artist was thinking, whether anyone would buy his painting, or did not start working without having an order. "Inspiration cannot be for sale, but one can sell the manuscript..."

Nevertheless, having a significant impact on people's behaviour, these economic motives could neither replace nor cancel other values that continued to exist along with the market ones. People continued to value emotional bondings, a sense of beauty, creative impulses, knowledge, etc., for their own sake, and not just for benefits they could bring. In public opinion, it was customary to separate these values from mercantile ones and even contrast one with another.

The situation has begun significantly changing in recent decades. No, non-economic values have not disappeared anywhere. But they began to be subjected to aggressive pressure from the very "public morality" that had previously opposed them to the thirst for profit, and now tries to subordinate them to this thirst both directly and indirectly, without hesitation.

All human feelings and generally all non-economic social phenomena begin to be measured by the standards of economic rationality. In the economic theory, the influential trend of "economic imperialism" has emerged and claims to explain all social processes according to the laws of economics. And what is more, all values that lie outside economy are declared conservative, outdated, and not meeting realities of the new world. What economic interests could be behind the ongoing attack, for example, on traditional family values? Directly – almost none. But the main thing is to blur any basic concepts of human culture and leave in place of this cultural desert only economic considerations that serve as a wrapper for the thirst for profit, to shake the moral foundations that serve as natural restraints of mercantilist expansion under the guise of expanding various "rights". And what is more, they are already trying hard to introduce "new values" into the field of legitimate institutions: for example, the recent proposal of a Dutch "human-rights activist" to recognise the rights of paedophiles at the level of European legislation, thereby turning children into a very specific commodity.

The criteria of love, goodness, beauty, and truth are declared to be unstable, conditional, relative, purely subjective, and eventually nonexistent. Only the criteria of benefit remain unconditional.

These attacks need to be unconditionally rebuffed not because it is necessary to adhere to "conservative values". It is not about conservative values, but about fundamental values developed by human culture throughout the civilisation development. Without relying on the criteria of culture, it is impossible to get away from the economy of cash and overconsumption, and transit to production based on satisfying reasonable needs. Economic rationality is now showing its aggressive pressure because it has to lose its public role. It has done its job, and it's time for rationality to leave the arena.

17.4. The Crisis of Economic Society

Today, we are challenged by the situation when, for moving along the path of progress of the "capitalist type", humanity has to pay an ever-increasing price, which threatens to become exorbitant. What's wrong with the goal of raising consumption levels?

Referring to the data of Erwin Laszlo (Laszlo, 2004: 70), V.S. Stepin notes that the current generation has consumed the same amount of goods and services (in value terms) over the past 50 years, as all the previous generations together. This leads to the conclusion that the principle "the more we consume, the better we live" acts as a path to the environmental catastrophe, therefore, new strategies for the civilisation development must be associated with rejection of this principle (Stepin, 2015: 164).

Indeed, reports on the catastrophic scale of pollution of the land and the oceans with various wastes, the threat of irreversible climatic shifts caused by the impact of growing man-made human activity, the progressive loss of biodiversity, etc., have become habitual. Why are humans ready to endanger their environment and their own existence, in pursuit of consumption growth?

Adam Smith's famous words are widely quoted, "It is not from the benevolence of the butcher, the brewer, or the baker that we expect our dinner, but from their regard to their own interests. We address ourselves, not to their humanity but to their self-love, and never talk to them about our own necessities but of their advantages" (Smith, 1962: 28). Usually this quotation is given as the proof of harmony of interests achieved on the basis of market benefits. Although Adam Smith himself did not think so flatly and simplistically, and this approach goes back rather to Jeremy Bentham, nevertheless, it is these words by Smith that are referred to as an argument. However, other conclusions can be drawn from these words.

Since our modern economic system strives for satisfying human needs and increasing consumption not for their own sake, but for the selfish economic interest of manufacturers and sellers, it cannot be excluded that they will encroach on our interests for the sake of these ones. In pursuit of profit, the baker will adulterate bread, the brewer will dilute beer, and the butcher will palm off stale meat. After all, the value for them is only their own benefit, but not our well-being. Of course, a buyer can turn away from a low-quality product and go to a competitor in a neighbouring bakery, and this serves as a strong enough incentive for not crossing a certain line, still providing goods and services of a sufficiently good quality.

But long gone are the days when people knew their baker by sight, and the economic interest to keep buyers was reinforced by interpersonal interaction with them. Now, we live in the era of mass production: for us, a manufacturer is just an abstract concept, indicated by small letters on the packaging of goods (or huge letters on advertising slogans). The buyer can no longer look into the manufacturer's eyes, and leaving one manufacturer for another will also change little, because in fact the buyer will meet exactly the same impersonal entity. Therefore, we have to rely not so much on the manufacturer's economic interests as on the state standardisation of products and on consumer-protection organisations.

However, it cannot be asserted that today manufacturers are not interested in consumer's needs. They are, and much more actively than they were, say, in the XIX century. But there are pitfalls in this attention, caused by the same economic interest.

An entrepreneur satisfies people's needs, pursuing the goal of making profits, and therefore gets primarily interested in the amounts of sales and the level of benefit. As a result, even at the initial stage of development of capitalism, business was ready to satisfy any whim, as long as it was profitable. And with the development of monopolistic tendencies, capital has got tools for manipulating consumers.

This was noted by Joseph Schumpeter, "... even in the most everyday matters, consumers' behaviour does not fully correspond to the postulates stated in economics textbooks. On the one hand, their desires are not so definite, and actions aimed at fulfilling desires are not so rational and fast. On the other hand, they are so susceptible to advertising and other methods of persuasion that manufacturers more often dictate terms, instead of being guided by consumers' desires" (Schumpeter, 1995: 339).

Now it has become commonplace, and guidelines for manipulating consumer preferences based on achievements of psychology and neuro-linguistics can be found on the shelves of bookstores (Dymshits, 2006) and on the Internet (Harris, 2016). Capacities of artificial intelligence to manipulate our choices are being explored (Dezfouli et al, 2020). Huge amounts of information are collected through social networks, making it possible to evaluate each individual's habitual reactions and pull these strings.

All these methods are aimed at forcing consumers to buy as much as possible, work harder to earn money for these purchases, get into debt and buy, buy, buy... Manipulating consumers can force them not only to buy more than necessary, but also to buy such goods that they do not need in principle, and even those, consumption of which can be harmful, not beneficial. In order for consumers to buy more and more, false and illusory needs are imposed on them, as well as goods that only simulate the opportunity for satisfying their needs are offered. The flow of these simulative goods (simulacra goods) and the process of imposing the respective simulative needs are growing. This trend took its shape long ago, but in the last few decades its scale in developed countries has become very impressive and the world of simulacra products began to attract the close attention of researchers (Baudrillard, 2003; Buzgalin, Kolganov, 2012a–b).

The illusion of satisfying simulative needs replaces development of the human personality, postpones settlement of social problems, and does not lead to real productivity growth. Moreover, increasing amounts of simulacra goods also distort the structure of needs, turning production and consumption towards the waste of natural resources.

Meanwhile, manufacturing simulacra goods is quite economically rational. Simulacra goods allow creating new markets by increasing the range of goods and services in addition to "ordinary" goods. And once simulacra goods are marketed, then their production makes a profit, increases the amount of GDP, i.e., it gives an economic effect. What else do you need? Thus, streams of spiritual gum called "mass culture", or really inactive cosmetics (at best giving a fleeting effect), or unhealthy foods that charm consumers through the use of flavours, etc., turn into visible evidence of efficient economic development and meet the economic interest.

As long as society is guided by such economic rationality and elevates the cult of consumption of anything to the supreme value, as long as this brings profit, our civilisation will move with increasing speed into a dead end of ecological and – perhaps even more importantly – spiritual crisis.

Individual noisy initiatives like "decarbonisation of economy" are not able to change the general trend. Let's ask ourselves: is it possible, within the framework of the current economic structure, the current economic model of formation and satisfaction of needs, not only to set, but also solve in practice the problem of transition to, say, the autotrophic production model (that is, production with the closed cycle of resource turnover)? Of course, it isn't, because this will lead to decreasing economic efficiency and, God forbid, to reducing consumption.

17.5. The Possibility of Going Beyond the Limits of Economic Rationality

However, there is a subtle difference between the amount of consumption and the extent to which an individual's needs are met. These values are not identical, and it is quite possible to increase the extent of satisfying needs, with reduction in consumption. Modern technologies demonstrate this possibility quite clearly. One modern smartphone, which weighs 110–120 grams (Smil, 2013: 127), meets the needs that 30–40 years ago would have required a phone, a radio, a TV set, a voice recorder, a video recorder, a camera, a watch, a computer, a notebook, maps, reference books and much more. The total weight of all these items and devices exceeds a smartphone weight by many tens of times. Thus, one may state *the possibility of increase in the level of satisfaction of needs with a sharp decrease in the amount of consumed material resources.*

The same can be said about the costs for producing the set of these items compared to the costs for producing a smartphone. This effect is achieved due to a sharp shift in the cost structure of the balance between the material costs and the cost of knowledge, intellectual resources, in favour of the latter. Production, without ceasing to be material, thereby turns into knowledge-intensive production, and its product becomes knowledge-intensive.

The latest technologies create the possibility of such changes in meeting the needs not only in the field of information and communication technologies, although here, this trend is most pronounced. In conventional branches of material production, significant reduction in material intensity of manufacturing a unit of product can be achieved by switching from distractive technologies (based on cutting, sawing, grinding material from a workpiece) to additive technologies (based on adding or combining initial materials). Such technologies have existed for quite a long time (for example, foundry or pottery), but with the advent of 3D printing, they have received a new lease of life. 3D printing allows to accurately reproduce items in accordance with a three-dimensional computer model by using various methods of connecting initial materials – layering, photopolymerisation, sintering, plasma spraying and many others. These methods are practically waste-free, providing significant savings in materials and energy (Prosvirnov, 2012; Greenwood, 2019).

Ultimately, modern technological platforms based on hybrid technologies of the sixth technological order make it possible to create unmanned production based on artificial intelligence, the industrial Internet of Things (Boyes et al., 2018) or even the Internet of Everything, processing large amounts of information coming from built-in sensors, etc. This results in projecting transition to "smart factories" and "Industry 4.0". The latter is designed to transform, on the basis of automation, not only the production process itself, but also the entire production organisation system: order formation and interaction with the customer, assignment of the production programme, cooperation with suppliers, subcontractors and outsourcers, the process of supplying materials and components, manufacturing products and delivering them to consumers, after-sales service.[2]

And all this also happens due to the development of knowledge-intensiveness of production. *A person exempt from participation in the direct production process reserves creative functions: research and development, goal setting, management.* All this opens up opportunities for reaching a new level of meeting needs – not only in terms of providing goods and services, but also in terms of expanding opportunities for personal development, creating the space of free time for the improvement of the person him/herself. All these shifts together will determine the face of the emerging new industrial society of the second generation and transition to noonomy (Bodrunov, 2021*).

As the person "leaves production", relationships referred to the direct production process also disappear, although social relations that determine goal-setting in the field of production (from research and development to assessment of development vectors) remain. Noonomy is based on non-economic criteria of production and consumption rationality, focusing not on profit or the amount of consumption, but on the real level of meeting reasonable needs (Bodrunov, 2018a: 258–259).

17.6. New Technologies and New Values

However, technologies only give people more opportunities. But how a person uses these opportunities depends on the values that have developed in society. The values that currently prevail can only turn new technological opportunities to further increasing amounts of goods consumed, and transforming growing free time into the time of thoughtless, wasteful, spiritually devastating consumption.

Can these values change? Yes, they can, and prerequisites for this change are also in new technological opportunities leading to the expansion of the range of employment in the areas with the growing share of creative activity. Participation in the process of cognition, inclusion in creative activities lead to generating appropriate motivations and value attitudes, among which increasing consumption is not in the first place.

However, new values are not formed automatically, and humanity is still very far from providing the entire contingent of employees with creative functions. *For its establishment, noonomy needs people to assimilate noovalues.* Therefore, it is necessary to transform the spiritual sphere and generally the entire sphere of human culture, which will be focused on people's rational attitude to their needs and to the natural environment, which will focus production activities not on unlimited growth, but on human development.

The criterion for the normal level of consumption will not be the amount of goods consumed, but satisfaction of particular reasonable needs.

But how can we shift to reasonable consumption, to nooconsumption? Neither externally determined restrictions nor the preaching of asceticism are able to solve the problem. This solution can only be provided by the *assimilation of internal cultural criteria.* It is on the basis of these cultural criteria that the person's self-identification as a reasonable person takes place. Identifying themselves in this way, these people separate themselves from unreasonable ones and *set limits to their own consumption according to the criteria of reason.*

That is why *human cultural development is no less important than scientific and technological progress.* Noovalues imply not only a reasonable attitude of a person to his/her needs and a careful approach to the natural environment. They suggest changing the nature of relations between people, focused on removing social conflicts. Therefore, the essential role in moving towards noonomy is given to the ideological environment focused not on the struggle of interests, but on joint actions to ensure them. In this sense, it is worth looking at the *ideology of solidarity.* Of course, in social systems with the discord of interests unfolding around the struggle for economic resources to be deeply rooted in their socio-economic foundations, the values of solidarity and cooperation based on mutual respect cannot gain predominant positions. But as social conflicts rooted in economic society based on the values of economic rationality are overcome and gradual transition to non-economic criteria of production is launched, the desire for joint actions in the common interests and in the interests of each person will increasingly pave its way and the wider acceptance of the values of cooperation will put an obstacle to conflicts.

17.7. The Path to the Affirmation of Noovalues

The prerequisites for this ideological orientation may begin taking shape right now. As I noted earlier (Bodrunov, 2021c), a person as a social being is not only a cast from social norms and stereotypes. People in their formation are socialised under the influence of a social environment; however, they simultaneously influence this social environment themselves, gradually changing accepted social norms and entrenched values.

New technologies and new production opportunities can neither revolutionise by themselves a person's social and individual consciousness, nor automatically create new moral values, although they generate necessary prerequisites for them. Therefore, without people's active position in the field of developing and disseminating culture, in the spiritual and moral sphere, without fighting for the transformation of values accepted in society in favour of noovalues, we risk falling into the gap between new opportunities created by technologies and the unreasonable use of these opportunities.

Of course, this will require appropriate "adaptation" of society to these new values, gradual transformation of its social institutions and adoption of relevant social norms necessary for creating favourable opportunities for shaping a "cultural person". This will make it possible to realise true value parameters of human existence, truly human attitude of people to each other and to nature.

It is not a coincidence that the adjective 'true' is used here. This is not just a turn of speech designed to emphasise the importance attached by the author to the values, on importance of which the author insists. No, it is about truth in the philosophical sense of the word and, through this, about values that meet the philosophical criterion of the truth. However, it is not about some universal, unchangeable, timeless true values. "If truth is abstract, then it is not truth" (Hegel, 1993: 88).

Social values are true when they correlate with the spirit and the truth of their time. But not its part that is turned to the past and clings to this past in a futile and at the same time pernicious effort to prevent development. True values that lead us into the future correlate with the truth to be born from social development, from necessary historical moving forward. In the words of Christ, conveyed to us by the evangelist John, Jesus just symbolises unification of the concept of truth with the concepts of life and development. Thus the truth appears both alive and developing: "I am the way, the truth, and the life" (John 14:6).

True values are born out of necessity and opportunity to preserve and affirm in a person, first of all, his/her human nature. These are the values that prevent a person from embarking on the path of self-destruction – whether through mutual extermination with weapons of mass destruction, through destruction of our natural environment where we live, or through such interference in our own nature that will destroy the human in us. It is about not only physical or biological intervention, but also a spiritual one – from manipulating consciousness to replacing the values of human culture by rejecting all values, and the criteria of reason and culture (which in fact makes economic interest the only measure of all values). That is why it is so important for us to fight for true values, that is, for those values that lead us to the path of elevation of the human personality – through developing reason, through knowledge, through culture, through harmonisation of mutual relations.

I insist again and again that these noovalues cannot be established by preaching. They grow out of the needs generated by developing objective conditions of human life. But they grow not as a weed, but as a cultivated plant, cultivated by our efforts, perceived as an absolute necessity, applied, including to ourselves, through the awareness of our responsibility to the world. Only by assimilating these values will we be able to get out of the impasse of contradictions, into which our civilisation is sinking. *Only moving along this way, one can get away from the predominance of atavistic, "animal", "zoo" traits in a person and come to the triumph of a truly human being.* This is exactly the essence of moving from "zoo" to "noo", as I discussed in the first article of this series (Bodrunov, 2018b).

17.8. Creative Activity as an Open Problem: The Approach of Noonomy as a Meta-Theory

The phenomenon of creativity is a complex problem that humanity has been struggling to solve for thousands of years. The works of philosophers, psychologists, theologians, and economists are dedicated to researching it. The tasks of our research do not include the analysis of all this heritage. The subject will be, at first glance, a narrower problem, which our colleague Alan Freeman talks about. This is an *economic* view on creativity, close to real problems of the market economy. Meanwhile, the range of sciences considering this phenomenon emphasises the need to study it not only by narrowly focused methods, but also comprehensively, within the framework of the meta-theoretical approach.

The first aspect, *creativity as a phenomenon of the market economy*, is considered in modern literature mainly through the prism of rather boring and trivial issues of *creative business* and *creative industries*, which focus on the fields classified as such in international statistics. This is a variety of spheres of show business, fashion industry, games, design, etc.

Is such a statement of the question sufficient? I don't think so. Even without addressing fundamental problems of the meta-theoretical discourse, in which the phenomenon of creativity should be considered, and remaining at the level of analyzing practices, we should note that the largest areas, in which *work* can be (and partly is) of *creative nature*, are not only art (moreover, in its market segment), but also science, education and production (to the extent that it becomes knowledge-intensive within the framework of transition to NIS.2). And this is the minimum. This aspect of the analysis is important.

This theme is discussed separately at the annual congresses on "Production, Science, Education" devoted to researching problems of development and integration of production, science and education, where the potential of these spheres as subspaces of creative activity is analyzed. At the same time, it is emphasised that under the domination of the neoliberal model of capitalism, their creative nature *is deformed* by the processes of commercialisation and bureaucratisation. But that's not all. A person is a demiurge, a creator by nature, and all the person's activities are inextricably linked with creation. Including the economic activity, where it is present in different proportions in various spheres, even occupying the main place in some of them.

Richard Florida, one of the recognised leaders in the sociological study of the phenomenon of creativity, showed in a series of works devoted to researching the "creative class" that the living space of this class in developed countries accounts for about 40 per cent of the employed.

But creative activity, even in economy, is not limited to "creative industries". Alan Freeman, in fact, also does not reduce the problem of creativity in economy to these "creative industries". Although we should note that a lot of his efforts were given to researching theoretical and practical issues of the latter, and he received significant results, and not only scientific ones (we should note our colleague's job as an adviser to the government of Greater London on these issues, which indicates his deep knowledge of the subject).

The phenomenon of creativity in the modern economy is not exotic, but a central issue of the future development of production and society. As mentioned above, modern production becomes *knowledge-intensive*. But what implements knowledge into production? Creative activity does.

Firstly, in the process of ***creating*** *technologies of production itself, and knowledge-intensive production*, creativity is both R&D and know-how, and, above all, fundamental science; secondly, creativity is an indispensable component of *the knowledge-intensive production* ***management*** *process*; thirdly, creativity directly in the production process as the ***labour*** of highly qualified people with ***knowledge*** *of the subject and* ***knowledge of the use of knowledge***, i.e., *the creative capacities* of specialists.

This crucial observation can be found in Professor Freeman's views, as well. Speaking about the creative product, he notes that its "distinctive feature ... is the *qualified* nature of the work involved in its creation". And then he adds, "That's where the added value comes from...". Thus, Professor Freeman actually recognises *coherence of the creative and knowledge components of labour* – with one component increasing, the other grows too, and with the degradation of the amount of knowledge involved in labour in manufacturing a product, the creative element of the labour process also decreases.

And here, there is no contradiction with the concepts of knowledge-intensive product, knowledge-intensive production, where the amount of labour decreases, since speaking about labour, we mean exclusively a special component of production – human labour. A machine that replaces human labour does not replace labour as *a kind of activity*, but only *substitutes* human labour with the work of a technical device. Thus, we clearly separate human labour from the mechanical devices that substitute it: the first contains a creative element, the second does not.

The opponents may ask, "Is there no place for creativity in other spheres of human activities?" Freeman writes about this. Of course, there is. But it is the *development* of industrial, material production, transition to higher-level technologies that *increase the knowledge-intensiveness* of social production and *ensure the increasing role of knowledge as a factor of production*, becoming its main factor (!), the main resource, that is the basic distinguishing feature of the new quality of industry of the era of NIS.2. Herewith, the creative process is not just inseparable from the process of discovery, processing, and implementation of knowledge into technology and other components of production, including labour – *creativity is the creation, awareness and mastering of new knowledge, meta-knowledge*, – these processes become the main factors in increasing the share of the *creative industry* in the modern economy.

For clarifying our position on the issue of applying knowledge in production, we will make one remark. Professor Freeman writes in one of his articles, "Summing up, we note that knowledge cannot be 'applied' as an external factor to the production process, but even before production begins, it is 'embedded' in materials, tools and labour that unites them. Therefore, Bodrunov is approaching the true state of affairs when writing that the development of the technosphere currently is not due to the tools of production and their qualified use, but to the power of knowledge included in these tools and underlying the capability to apply them and increase production efficiency.

All he had to do was to remove the word 'currently'. What is changing in modern economy is neither the presence of mental content nor the 'addition' of something that has actually always been there, but the way in which this mental content relates to production" (Freeman, 2021: 214–215).

It is strange for Alan Freeman to reproach me for what I have repeatedly declared. And what is more, look at the "Bodrunov's cross": that's exactly what he means! Another thing is that I have always emphasised what Professor Freeman (like many other researchers) missed: the viewpoint at industrial development based on changes in technological modes, or development paradigms (according to K. Perez) leads to the question: what is their boundary, a new quality, etc.?

The current stage is a transitional one, and although Knowledge is an integral part of all components of production, it *is "there"*, and it has *always* been so; and what is more, the share of knowledge (and the creative component) has been *continuously* growing, but it is *now* when Knowledge becomes the *key factor* in developing production; and it is Knowledge, not availability of raw materials, materials, energy, etc., that really starts prevailing in this development *now*. Hence the noticeable increase in the role of the creative element in labour hence – in economy, as well. Growth has *always* been there. The growth spurt is *today*, now, at the current stage. This is what is emphasised.

Thus, we absolutely agree with Professor Freeman on this issue, as well as on a number of other ones, where he also interprets ideas of noonomy in his own way. As for his criticism of my ideas, which he drew from the relatively small amount of material presented in "Noonomy", I will say: the problem is either the lack of details in the theses in the book itself, or nuances of translation, or "scattering" of my theses across several hundred articles and dozens of other works. I accept the criticism gratefully.

One more quotation from Freeman. Criticising post-industrialists, he writes, "...labour irreplaceable by machines does not mean 'labour without machines', this is new relationships with machines in the broadest sense of the word". What a wonderful observation! The only remark is that post-industrialists mean the "post-industrial" society, believing that it will remain economic. In the theory of noonomy, we convincingly prove that, following the path of achieving a *new quality* of industry, including a gradual decrease in the share of *human labour* (in the political-economic sense) in social production, with the simultaneous *qualitative* transformation of the *nature of labour* into knowledge-intensive and predominantly creative, turning into *non-labour activities*, social development moves towards post-economic, non-economic society that remains industrial in terms of providing for human needs, but based on *conscious* creative and qualified human participation in monitoring and developing the industrial process (i.e., based on the very "special relationships with machines" that our colleague Professor Freeman talks about, calling the process not "the end of industry", but "a new type of industry").

We are currently watching the conceptual generalisation in the theory of noonomy of these profound changes affecting all spheres of society under conditions of high-tech development and transition from *reproductive labour* to predominantly *creative activity* (changes not only in production, science, education, etc., but also in socioeconomic relations, institutions, culture). Over 10 years ago, the theory of New Industrial Society of the Second Generation (NIS.2) was proposed in INID as the conceptual generalisation of changes taking place.

The NIS.2 theory gave answers to the questions posed by high-tech development, partially addressing the problem of place and role of creative labour in this process. However, it is *insufficient* to respond to many of the larger challenges of theory and practice. We mean challenges associated, among other things, with the phenomenon of creativity as the subject not only and not so much of economic as of socio-philosophical research.

Let's return to Alan Freeman's ideas and his fundamental works on the problem of creativity. In this case, we will focus on two very important features of creativity, which our colleague gives: 1 – on the feature of creativity as a "non-mechanised activity"; 2 – on activities, in which "mental objects" are present.

Recognising the depth of representation of the phenomenon of creativity in terms of these definitions, I would like to give my own vision. The first feature raises the least objections. Indeed, since the time of Karl Marx and his colleagues, and perhaps even earlier, almost from Leonardo da Vinci's reflections, it is known that in future, society must reach such a level of development when machines will perform all functions of reproductive, non-creative labour, and people will develop in the space of the "kingdom of freedom" located, in Marx's words, "on the other side of proper material production". Of course, we accept that. In the theory of noonomy, we talk about the *self-acting industrial system* under human control.

However, let's look at the problem of creativity more broadly: if creativity is "non-machinised" labour, then it must have certain attributes that qualitatively distinguish it from "machinised" labour. Which ones exactly? Without anticipating the analysis of the "mental objects" concept, we note that in the works of our and foreign philosophers, sociologists, and economists of the second half of the XX century, *self-motivation* is mentioned as the most important feature of creative labour. In the creative space, motivation for labour is *labour itself*: labour as such becomes a need. And what is more, in non-economic society, where the self-acting production system is to become its material basis for satisfying needs and *with labour as an economic phenomenon and an element of production to be transformed into activity, and creative labour – into creative activity, self-motivation will become the only type of motivation for such activity.*

This description reverses, throws off the chessboard of history all usual axiomatics of modern economics, at least its neoclassical version – the mainstream. Let's recall that within the framework of the latter (with rare exceptions specifically stipulated by behavioural economics), labour is *a burden, and money is the value*. In our case (gradual progress towards "smart" production and creative activity as the dominant one) everything changes: labour becomes more creative and gradually loses its economic meaning, turning into non-labour creative activity! It increasingly becomes the *non-economic* need for creating, and utilitarian goods turn into means of developing an individual as a creative person, a cultural person. This is how transition to the new, post-economic way of meeting needs is carried out, and it is from this that the new *post-economic reality* is born. This is how we move into the space of *noonomy genesis* – a qualitatively new world, in which the *post-economic way of human existence* replaces the economic one.

Let's focus on the concept of "non-mechanised labour". This definition of creative activity, in our opinion, is very "productive" for describing this specific type of labour activity in *economic* society. It echoes classical definitions of creative labour in the works of scientists of the XX century and even with the features of the world of future in the Programme for Building the Material Base of Communism, adopted at the 22nd Congress of the Communist Party of the Soviet Union in 1961, as well as numerous "presentations" of this world in the works of Soviet futurist writers, primarily the famous scientist, Professor Ivan Efremov. It is relevant in the light of ideas of the great scientist Christopher Freeman (Alan's father), one of the pillars of science (along with Schumpeter, Schmitt, Kondratiev, John Galbraith and Sergey Glazyev), whose ideas formed the *foundation of the theory of noonomy*. Finally, this concept is consonant with the features of high-tech production given by scientists of the XXI century.

We use the terms *smart manufacturing*, in which the decisive role is given to knowledge, and *knowledge-intensive production of a knowledge-intensive product* as an integral attribute of the new industrial society of the second generation. These are not questions of taste and choice of terms: the task of replacing human labour with machine labour, with the simultaneous increase in the role and share of "non-mechanised" labour, can be solved *only as the consequence of transition to NIS.2* in the whole range of its parameters, and in no other way. And it is by choosing the term "knowledge-intensive production" that we give not just the expanded understanding of this type of labour as a *creative process* within the *industrial process*, but we link together the key factors that ensure this process: knowledge, the process of its development and implementation, and – most importantly – the "migration" of the creative element of activity into the machinised one!

Creativity as a phenomenon has special "objectification", "manifestation" in human existence. As far as we understand, Professor Freeman agrees with this, speaking about *materialisation of mental objects*.

The creative process *cannot be machinised*. We adhere to this point of view, unlike those who are ready to claim that artificial intelligence is capable of being a creator! But creative labour allows making a completely *uncreative* product. And what is more, *any product is initially the result of a creative act*, a chain of creative acts, a creative process aimed at transforming reality. And then, this process of creating a product and scaling it in its development becomes *machinised*. Let us note in passing that a machine is not God's creation, but a creation of humans, the result of material embodiment of the same creative act! There is an elusive line, a threshold, crossing which *the non-machinised creative process migrates into the machinised one*.

It is necessary to know production well (and here again we will refer colleagues to the legacy of C. Freeman): any innovation as a result of creative mastering of reality gradually, with development of technologies and other production processes (again – through creative comprehension of this reality), *can be machinised*, but thereby opening up some new space for a person *to comprehend new knowledge and a new act of creativity*.

In this regard, let us discuss the concept of a *mental object*, which is given great importance in Alan Freeman's works, as well as the phenomenon (and the corresponding concept) of *mental economics*. Moreover, in our dialogues, Alan suggested that I should use it instead of the *noonomy* concept, since in both cases it is about the mind.

These concepts are really based on the nooconcept of human existence and activity, of the transformation of the world outside a person through knowledge. *However, mental economics and noonomy essentially differ from each other, they coincide neither in content nor in amount*.

The phenomenon of the mental object remains largely undefined. Professor Freeman defines it as "...a reproducible entity manifested in various physical forms, with recognisable identity independent of these physical forms", and, moreover, "...the physical form of a mental object can be transformed from one kind into another", and a "mental object itself becomes a part of the form existence" (Freeman, 2021: 209).

A mental object is a kind of product of the mind, if you like, the result of a creative act, and exists in the space of the mind, and, as it can be assumed, transforms into other objects that have their objective existence in the process of human activity. In any case, this concept can be interpreted this way in the language of social philosophy. This concept captures some important aspect of creative activity, probably its result, in some way. But it can hardly claim to be a systemic quality of creative activity, which is not limited to "production of mental objects". And what is more, as far as we understand, a mental object is not even an unconditional attribute of creative activity, creativity as a phenomenon.

Let us emphasise that we proceed from the primacy of production, from qualitative changes in its content due to the increase in its knowledge-intensiveness, and neither from some properties of the human mind capable of creating and generating "mental objects", nor from respective changes in the content of labour, which is only one of many components of the process of social production, and *the very change of its content is only a consequence of the growth of its knowledge-intensiveness.* Therefore, we agree that the term "mental object" is very useful for studying the phenomenon of creative activity, and studies of this phenomenon are useful for researching qualitative changes in society that are currently experienced by us. But the *holistic* description of these changes *cannot be reduced* to any of these concepts – neither to mental objects, nor to creative activity.

A *comprehensive description* that could combine systematically various facets and aspects of transformations to be experienced is required. It is this approach, this meta-theory that we discuss, putting forward the concept of *noonomy genesis* on the basis of developing the new industrial society of the second generation, which makes it possible to conceptualise and generalise particular features of the changes described in the works of domestic and foreign scientists, including the works of Professor Freeman.

It should be noted that our esteemed colleague from China, President of WAPE and member of the Chinese Academy of Sciences, Professor Cheng Enfu, in our joint book *A(O)ntology of Noonomy* (Cheng, Gao, 2021), bluntly said that the "Concept of *Intellectual Economy*" being developed by him and his Chinese colleagues, which is based on the idea of intellectualisation and improvement of the creative level of labour, *is included in the ideological framework of the theory of noonomy.*

Moreover, we *cannot agree with the identification of the concepts of "mental economy" and "noonomy"*. Firstly, noonomy is *no longer economy, this is a post-economic way of meeting social needs.* Secondly, noonomy is *smartnomics.* This is not just a post-economic world, in which all aspects of social existence change. We have just noted that production changes in it, becoming knowledge-intensive. But the main thing is that *a person also changes,* turning from an economic person into a cultural person, a creative person – a creator. Humanity as a whole is moving from the ZOO-era to the NOO-era (Bodrunov, 2018b). And this era, including the era of creativity, endless creativity, is based on infinite Knowledge. Thirdly, these transformations cause changes *in the system of public relations and institutions*, mediating the transition to post-economic reality.

The noonomy genesis presupposes the unity of four processes: *technological progress, diffusion of property, socialisation of economy and society, and development of solidarity.* In the process of promoting its elements, this "quadriga of noonomy" presupposes the *presence of phenomena* that we talked about today, but it fundamentally *cannot be reduced* to the progress of non-mechanised labour and the economy of mental objects.

The description of fundamental differences can be continued, but in this case it is important to emphasise that the concept of transition to NIS.2 and further progress towards noonomy is not an academic game of concepts, but *theoretical representation of humanity's global choice between NOO and ZOO.* And this choice is not speculative, but purely practical. The global financial and economic crisis of 2008–2010, the COVID-19 pandemic, aggravation of political conflicts beyond the usual, escalation of geopolitical economic processes, fundamentally investigated by Professor R. Desai, – all this puts us on the brink of survival. Our civilisation is approaching a turning point in its development, the point of bifurcation, which we talked about many years ago. And it is possible to choose positive development, rather than chaos and regression, only having a holistic scientific worldview of objective trends of progress.

In our opinion, the concept of noonomy, various aspects of which we discuss, can submit this objective worldview. And I am sincerely grateful to everyone who contributes to this worldview, adding their own colours!

NOTES

1 Prepared on the basis of Bodrunov, 2022d, 2023b.

2 GTAI (2018). Germany Trade&Invest. Industrie 4.0, URL: https://www.gtai.de/resource/blob/64500/8b7afcaa0cce1ebd42b178b4430edc82/industrie4-0-germany-market-outlook-progress-report-endata.pdf; FY (2014). Summary of the White Paper on Manufacturing Industries (Monodzukuri). URL: http://www.meti.go.jp/english/press/2015/pdf/0609_01a.pdf.

18

Nooneeds as "the Screw on Which Everything Turns"[1]

Transition to the new industrial society of the second generation based on the growth of knowledge-intensive production makes it possible to expand meeting human needs while simultaneously reducing the burden on the natural environment. But for this to happen, there must be shifts in people's motivation, withdrawal from the pursuit of consumption of material goods, driven by economic rationality, and satisfaction of fake needs inflated by the market, transition to the non-economic mode of production – noonomy. This shift is certainly possible on the basis of not "persuasion" or coercion to asceticism, but of objective changes in the conditions of human existence: people's exit from direct material production, their transition to creative activity, expansion (on the material basis of the production system of the next generation) of opportunities for meeting their reasonable needs. People themselves will set limits to their needs, focusing them not on consuming the largest possible amount of goods, but on conditions of their self-realisation. It is on this path that it is possible to solve urgent problems of development – of both civilisation and human personality – and mitigate social conflicts on the basis of objectively increasing socialisation of society and on the ideological platform of solidarity, as well as eliminate their causes in the long term.

In this block of research, we attach special importance to the category of "needs" (and nooneeds), the changes in which will be decisive and most important for the nootransition.

The trend towards simulating needs, developing especially in recent decades, creates significant threats to civilisation development, leading to unlimited increase in consumption and the burden on the natural environment. Meanwhile, many vital needs of the majority of the world's population are far from being met, despite the achieved potential of technological progress. This trend is largely determined by those economic criteria of rationality that are characteristic of the modern social structure. For overcoming the negative trends of simulating needs, it is necessary to solve three inter-related tasks. Firstly, it is required to remove the simulation burden imposed on the existing needs. Secondly, society should be focused on fostering truly human needs in the development of human qualities. Thirdly, it is necessary to change the mechanism of needs formation itself, subordinating it to the criteria of reason and culture, and thereby forming nooneeds.

18.1. Back to the Issue of Global Challenges: Civilisation in the Face of Problems

Modern civilisation is obviously increasingly challenged, to which human society has not yet given an effective answer. These challenges are poverty and misery of hundreds of millions, unprecedented inequality not only of individual strata of the population, but also of entire countries in access to public goods, artificial inhibition of developing human personality, instability of the global economy induced by shocks of various etiologies, and much more in this series. Besides, these are environmental problems, large-scaled environmental pollution, and so far not too noticeable to the uninitiated, but increasingly rapidly developing (and already rising to the level of drama, according to experts) loss of biodiversity, and the risk of using weapons of mass destruction, and threats associated with interference in biological and cognitive nature of people themselves. We can also recall the spiritual crisis: the "big narratives" are destroyed, people lose their ideological and spiritual guidelines, the established categories of truth, personal progress, goodness, and beauty. A whole range of man-made problems entails the approaching new stage of technological progress, which changes material conditions of production and the entire way of life of a person. And implementation of a new technological revolution is in itself a significant problem, as well.

It is obvious that the current state of human social existence cannot provide an adequate response to all these challenges. Human civilisation is about to transform into some new state, and it has already partially entered into this objectively inevitable transition process – chaotically, fragmentally, mostly unconsciously. However, people will have to change along with changes in both the material and social conditions of human life.

Is human socioeconomic behaviour reasonable, in the presence of so many increasingly escalating man-made problems? Modern people, historically subordinated to economic necessity in the struggle for a living are now focusing mainly on economic rationality in their behaviour and social practices, *homo economicus* species in their essence, if they are going to survive and develop as human beings, must inevitably go into the past. A person is changing, (s)he cannot help but change towards the state when it will be possible for them to be called, finally, a fully sensible person, a true *homo sapiens*. And what is more, changing a person also changes the social component of existence by socialising society, forming and strengthening the noocriterial base of existence, its moral and value core.

We intend to outline the reasons, conditions, opportunities and content of this transition.

The subject of our analysis is the changes that we can observe in economy and society, issues of "designing" the positive future economic and social structure, as well as discussion of the tools for minimally conflictual and effective transformation to this future state, including the most important element – "human transformation", and on this basis – transition to a more just and reasonable arrangement of people's lives.

The modern global socioeconomic system and its components – economy, society, and person – are in a systemic crisis. With the complication of the global economic system, which is associated not least with the observed transition to the new technological and world economic order, the uncertainty of the future and chaotisation of economic relations and ties sharply increase, at all levels, the prospects for not even development, but the very existence of humans and civilisation are becoming worse. The problem of sustainability of social development has become so weighty and obvious that it has brought to life the well-known UN documents on achieving the Sustainable

Development Goals, multiple discussions at various levels – from Davos to Beijing, from summits of G7 and G20 to direct consultations of world leaders.

The coronavirus pandemic, which became not the cause, but a kind of indicator and trigger for many components of the current and accelerator of many significant trends in the future state of the global socioeconomic system, sharply highlighted a number of already known problems of our civilisation development and accelerated moving along some previously identified trends.

It is obvious that the crisis that has begun is all-encompassing. It fully affected the totality of industrial relations and economic institutions. Market mechanisms of self-regulation, the basis of the current socioeconomic system, fail more and more often. The "invisible hand of the market", the further the more, points towards financial speculations and predatory exploitation of resources, including not only natural and material ones, but also labour and intellectual resources, and not at all towards developing human qualities and solving social problems.

The conflict between the need for joint actions to combat common threats and the economic selfishness that prevents this, on which the modern socio-economic system is built, has also become obvious. Historical futility of the ongoing struggle for global dominance has been exposed, and tendencies towards de-globalisation have intensified as a response to these attempts, which, in turn, creates risks of splitting the world into fiercely opposing blocs. Global economic and political interactions are in crisis; the geopolitical-economic configuration of the world is in a state of a global breakdown, and trajectories of the starting changes are dark and contradictory (Desai, 2020).

The situation is no better with institutions of state and democracy: in some countries, results of their elections are questioned, in others these results are known long before the elections, etc. Freedom, on the one hand, increasingly turns into an explosive mixture of permissiveness with indifference; on the other hand, it is trampled by corporate, mass media and ideological manipulations.

The trends of the increasing reactive development of new-generation technologies and industries are obvious. Movement has accelerated along such trends as digitalisation of economic relations, transition to distance employment and online education, robotisation and the use of artificial intelligence. However, man-made risks have increased, while extremely unequal distribution of opportunities to positively take advantage of these technological advances has been revealed. It turned out to be impossible for the poor and the bulk of those working in industry and in the service sector to use modern digital technologies for organising distant work. Meanwhile, managers, financial market specialists, and most other categories of office workers have received this opportunity (Schwab, Malleret, 2020). Thus, the entirety of new technological trends allows a person to follow the path of leaving direct participation in the production process and expands the space of free time, although they simultaneously create prerequisites for deepening people's social alienation, within the framework of the archaic modern socio-economic system.

The growing "substitution" of real human communication with a virtual one is also alarming. Of course, the virtual world creates some additional space for a person's development and self-realisation, for expanding people's communication. But at the same time, it generates problems related to identifying people, communicating infantilism of perception of the virtual world (which is transferred to the real world), establishing "hate groups" (Bondarenko, 2009: 220–221) and even "death groups", displacing attempts to solve real-life problems exclusively in the virtual world, transforming people into consumers of virtual reality, and not preserving them as researchers and creators (Sorotskii, 2012: 230).

The growing attempts to organise total digital control by both states and major corporations are also alarming (Kleimenova, 2020).

It is clear that it would be ridiculous to call for resisting new technological opportunities from the standpoint of something like "digital luddism". People's new way of life and activity, new forms of society arrangement, the emergence of which was accelerated, among other things, by the coronavirus pandemic, are inevitable. Remote (distant) employment, online communication and online education, additional incentives to use robotics and unmanned technologies in production – all of them have already become a new reality. And it depends on the person how to respond to such changes. Will a person become more humane, relying on solidarity and socially responsible behaviour both in the field of manufacturing a public product, and in everyday life, at home, in society? Or will economic selfishness and universal alienation prevail in the competition for all kinds of benefits? Results of this choice will not only directly affect the lives of people living now and future generations, but also determine vectors and pace of transition to the qualitatively new state of society.

18.2. Towards the Idea of Qualitative Nootransition and Social Development Evolution: The New Industrial Society of the Second Generation (NIS.2)

The achieved current level of global social production, reflecting realities and achievements of modern scientific and technological progress, allows to begin solving most of the above-mentioned problems right now. However, "the cart is still upon the self-same spot". This is a global contradiction of modernity, and it is aggravated by the progress of technology while maintaining (and this is precisely what the efforts of global actors of the world economy are aimed at) the current outdated economic models, regressing towards conservatism and fetishisation of the market, in which achievements of technological progress do not serve for the resolution and reduction of the accumulated problems, but rather, on the contrary, their acceleration.

In fairness, it should be noted that many experts have long been talking about the need for moving away from the one-sided vision of the model of human development, closely linked to the idealistically understood market concept of management, when market relations penetrate everywhere and are consolidated in all spheres of human activities: culture, art, healthcare, science, sports, law, public administration, etc. The economy in its current version began turning from the important, key sphere, the semantic task of which is creating material conditions for people to live, the rational mechanism for meeting their needs, into a decisive sphere and even claiming a self-sufficient role in society, through increasing financialisation destroying and deforming those areas that are inherently partially commercialisable or even not commercialisable at all without fundamental deformations of human consciousness and exclusion of its inalienable prerogatives from the accessible public space. The last clear example of this kind is the recent attempt of the European "grandees" of football to create the so-called Super League supposed to dramatically increase commercialisation of sports (exactly sports in general, and not just football, since this step is nothing more than a model for such initiatives in any kind of sports), with the actual exclusion of "underdeveloped" football teams and most countries from the media space, depriving them of incentives to develop sports in "failed" countries, and the sports community of these countries – of the opportunity for their teams to take part in the most advanced matches of top competitions.

The escalation of the above-mentioned basic contradiction of modernity is fraught with multiple global risks that are well known and repeatedly analyzed in scientific literature.

The burden of problems that increasingly threaten humanity raises the question of further evolution of the human civilisation to a certain new stage, at which it will be feasible to expand and consolidate opportunities created by new technologies, and use these opportunities for overcoming the aforementioned contradiction, which is a result of the lag in the development of socioeconomic relations from the pace of progress set by acceleration of developing knowledge-intensive industry and new technologies changing people's way of life, and the mechanisms for meeting their needs, and people themselves. It is about transition to the next generation of the New Industrial Society. The New Industrial Society described by John Kenneth Galbraith (Galbraith, 1967) in his time has largely stayed behind. The march into the post-industrial future, proclaimed in the last third of the XX century, did not take place, although post-industrial theorists guessed many features of the changes correctly (Bell, 1973; Sakaiya, 1991; Smart, 2011). However, despite the significant increase in the share of the service sector in developed countries' economies, industrial material production has remained the technological core of economy. The increasing role of knowledge has led not to substituting material production with it, but to forming a new stage of it – knowledge of intensive material production, which acts as the basis for transition to the new industrial society of the second generation, NIS.2 (Bodrunov, 2016à).

Transition to NIS.2 creates a set of prerequisites both in the sphere of production (in all its elements) and in the sphere of respective organisation of society, for moving towards the formation of a non-economic way of meeting human needs, towards noonomy (Bodrunov, 2018a).

18.3. New Opportunities for Meeting Needs and New Risks

Modern economy has already created material prerequisites and technological capabilities to meet human needs at a much higher level than before. However, are these opportunities always used for meeting real human needs? The capitalist market economy has demonstrated huge opportunities for increasing production and consumption. But the growth of production and consumption in the pursuit of profit results in manufacturers' indifference to the nature of the needs being satisfied, they just want to ensure expansion of sales of goods and services. And in this pursuit of profit, capital is not averse to forming and inflating all sorts of illusory, simulated needs, playing on any human weaknesses.

The pursuit of status symbols by some consumer groups instead of real benefits was described in the early XX century by Thorstein Veblen (Veblen, 1899). The disproportionately great importance gained by the phenomenon of simulative needs and simulative benefits in the last third of the 20th century caused the need for philosophical comprehension of the nature and significance of this phenomenon. The analysis of simulacra benefits was carried out in the works of the famous French postmodernist Jean Baudrillard (Baudrillard, 1972, 1981) and the American philosopher and literary critic Fredrik Jameson (Jameson, 1991).

It's not just about the needs that are irrational. *There is nothing but illusions behind simulative needs and simulacra products that "satisfy" them. Simulacra act as just signs of meeting imaginary needs (although this simulative component is often related to a very real useful product, inflating its price due to additional imaginary value in consumers' eyes).*

As the result, not just a "consumer society" is being formed, which does not know when to stop increasing the amount of goods consumed, but *the economic machine for inflating imaginary needs and means of their equally imaginary satisfaction, for which, however, rather real resources are spent.* This leads to the growth of both the amount of consumed natural resources and the waste from their processing, which then comes into nature.

Up to certain limits, the Earth's ecosystem coped with the consequences of the natural balance disturbed by man. However, in recent years, the threshold of the ecosystem's capacity to ensure resumption of spent natural resources has already been significantly exceeded.[2]

But the loss of the ability to resume natural resources is not the only danger posed by economic pressure on the natural environment. The impact on it of various types of pollution – mechanical, chemical, electromagnetic, acoustic, etc., – increases. This leads to disrupting functions of the biosphere and the living conditions of people themselves, to violating the climatic balance, losing biological diversity and many other consequences, perhaps not yet fully realised.

The rate of extinction of species of living beings, for example, has already many times exceeded the rate of the natural process of species extinction. We emphasise that every day the planet loses 72 species on the average. If we take the highest estimate of the number of species of living beings on the Earth – 100 million, then 263 species per million die out per year, with the natural rate of extinction of one species per million per year[3] (Knight, 2012).

Meanwhile, spontaneous growth of the technosphere, determined by the criteria of economic rationality, i.e., the pursuit of "market efficiency", thereby leads to dangerous, poorly controlled consequences. The number of technetic (i.e., man-made technocenoses (Kudrin, 1980)) species rapidly overtakes the biodiversity of nature, reaching one billion (Zalasiewicz, Williams et al., 2017). In fact, technocenoses created by man suppress biocenoses, and technetic species of creatures displace biological ones, not only overtaking, but also reducing biodiversity.[4]

The paradigm of unrestrained growth of production and consumption leads to this impasse threatening the existence of people themselves, it has turned into the paradigm of growth in production of anything and consumption of anything, as long as, in accordance with the meaning of chremastics, sales and profits grow. Obviously, it is hardly possible to talk about sensibility of this approach to organising human life; this was established by Aristotle already.

This problem has been recognised for long, scientists and public figures have been sounding the alarm since the sensational report to the Rome Club on the limits of growth in 1972 (Meadows et al, 1972), green movements around the world support this concern, and at the international level, the problem of sustainable development has not been off the agenda for many years, starting with the Stockholm (1972) United Nations Conference on the Environment, then creation in 1983 of the United Nations Commission on the Environment ("Brundtland Commission") and the UN World Summit held in 2002. A number of climate agreements have been concluded. Under the new President, the USA, which until recently rejected the problem of climate change and the impact of human economic activity on the climate, on the contrary, now tries to lead global efforts in solving it.[5]

However, all these concerns and all the decisions taken so far have not led to any significant practical steps to prevent the environmental crisis. And what is more, even now, the proposed measures are of a distinctly pragmatic "merchant" nature, which is due to attempts to solve these problems by applying familiar economic mechanisms, which, with a high degree of probability, do not have a perspective that ensures their solution.

A minority of humanity has provided themselves with the opportunity for isolating themselves from epidemic troubles, and continue to increase their incomes within the framework of the paradigms "feast during the plague" or "war makes some people rich", to continue the thoughtless growth of consumption, which turns into an increasing plunder of natural resources. Meanwhile, for the majority of the world's population, the pursuit of material accumulation turns into vulnerability to health threats and at the same time unavailability of the most basic benefits: sufficient nutrition, clean water, housing, education, etc.

18.4. The New Look of Production – the New Goals and Needs

This situation is inevitable in the world where the problems of the human civilisation development are solved only to the extent of achieving economic success criteria. It is impossible to resolve this global contradiction without gradually moving away from the primacy of these criteria, and bringing to the fore truly human criteria that determine achievement of specific goals of human development. We need transition to such social relations, in which economic activity that meets human needs will be determined primarily by non-economic criteria. This becomes objectively possible insofar as vital needs become saturated, other needs that gain a non-economic form come to the fore. First of all, it is about the development of *culture benefits, rise of human personality and human mind, as well as the development of human abilities for self-realisation on this basis.*

Replacing economic criteria for satisfying needs with criteria of *genuine sensibility* turns us to the well-known concept of noosphere, the sphere of the human mind domination (Vernadsky, 1944). Formation of the noosphere by itself does not ensure the arrival of the "kingdom of goodness". And what is more, the presence of the noosphere immediately raises the question of which exactly imperatives of reason will prevail in it, and how reason will be used: as a tool of development or as a tool of destruction? The concept of noosphere does not provide answers to these key questions.

Humanity's transition to the NIS.2 stage means increasing opportunities for a person to get out of direct participation in the production process and thereby expanding the space of free time. However, the presence of these opportunities in itself does not either guarantee that free time will become the space for human development, and not the time of idleness and thoughtless consumerism. Indeed, along with increasing material opportunities, wide spaces for more and more complete satisfaction of human needs open up. Do not think that the "Maslow pyramid" will automatically ensure transition to higher needs as the lower needs become saturated.

This problem cannot be solved, moving along the path of simple enlightenment and propaganda of certain lofty ideals. The key to solving the issue is not so much in the extent of saturation of needs (although this is one of necessary prerequisites), as in changing the nature of a person's main activity: transition from economically determined labour for the sake of obtaining "daily bread" to free creative activity requiring development and mobilisation of various human abilities.

Transition to this activity becomes possible as a person, having left the direct production process during developing knowledge-intensive production, turns into the force monitoring and guiding the development of the relatively autonomous technosphere. Of course, the prerequisite for this is the saturation of human vital needs in conditions of decreasing the time required for labour.

One should not think that even if all these conditions are present, the structure of human needs formed in economic society that brought up *homo economicus* will be able to change the situation easily and simply. Let us recall that Hannah Arendt was generally afraid that this might not happen and as the result, all objects of the world, so-called cultural objects, along with objects of consumption, will fall victim of devouring and destructing (Arendt, 2000: 171).

These fears are quite justified, given the reality that Arendt observed around her, in the world that we still live in, that is, in the world of capitalism and market, most people's behaviour is exactly like this. And prolongation of these conditions may well allow the famous philosopher's apocalyptic forecast to come true. Exhausting work for the sake of earning leaves people free time only for them to consume, consume and consume – both for recovering their strength and starting to work again, and for having time to consume the mass of goods and services to be supplied to the market. Everything produced must be bought, and the whole machine of marketing, advertising, fooling people and cultivating sinister needs and pseudo-progressive values of mass culture, fostering "exemplary consumers" of modern education, functions to form a lifestyle, in which people strive for consuming as much as possible and working for this purpose as much as possible, to earn money again and consume again. Most people live in this vicious circle, not seeing a way out of it and not even imagining that there could be a way out at all. And what is more, they consider this order to be natural and... reasonable!

"The human individual appears to be completely immersed in the all-dominating non-human and anti-human world of things-objects, where there is not and cannot be a place for one's true sovereignty as a subject-creator" (Batishchev, 2015: 199). How can a person break out of this vicious circle created by him/herself?

As shown by various millennial attempts, neither preaching asceticism, nor striving for limiting consumption by various kinds of coercive barriers, nor appealing to ideals of altruism, communism, etc., are actually a solution, because they are not based on objective development trends. Of course, explanatory and educational measures, introduction into consciousness of the understanding of the need for being careful about shaping the range of one's own needs, are also necessary, but only if they are based on objective prerequisites.

There are objective prerequisites that can change the structure of preferences and the set of human needs. First of all, this is changing the nature of the main human activity.

Men are what they do. "The subject cannot be reduced only to the subject of consciousness and will, but there is a subject of activity that forms the entire cultural world of a public person, human reality" (Batishchev, 2015: 200). When the activities of people begin meaning the conscious creation of their own cultural world for them, then both the imperatives of culture and the noocriteria of the structure of existence will become the most important elements of the criteria base for them, on the basis of which they will take any decisions, including those on production and consumption, their reasonable boundaries.

Herewith, in NIS.2, objective processes of developing knowledge-intensive production will increasingly free up people's time for self-development, education, and creativity. And what is more, the creative component will inevitably increase in the very reducing work activity. In case when people's activities become primarily creative, their preferences will gradually shift from the pursuit of amounts of material goods and services to the self-realisation of personality in the process of creative activity.

For noopeople, the main values will be means and conditions for developing their creative potential.

Another prerequisite, together with knowledge-intensive production, is the development at the NIS.2 stage of human activity in cognising the world and oneself as a part of the world, and consequently, awareness of one's true, unsimulative needs, acceptance of this knowledge and, on this basis, loss of value imperatives of simulative or irrational consumption. Thus, a person will make significant progress in understanding what restrictions are imposed on both production and consumption by the reasonable approach.

The third prerequisite *is in the sphere of consumption itself.* Saturation of human vital needs (on the basis of developing knowledge-intensive production), providing the escape from the struggle for existence, from the fear of underconsumption in the face of the threat of malnutrition, diseases, etc., creates conditions for such needs not to occupy a primary place in people's lives, becoming increasingly secondary, due to progressive opportunities of their resolution.

The important factor is *the increasing socialisation of society* – a social component of human development as a personality and as a social being.

Technological progress and growing changes in economic institutions (in particular, the objective process of steady transformation of the economic way of satisfying needs into a predominantly non-economic one, including the process of property diffusion, also due to the development of technologies of the new technological order (Bodrunov, 2021a), pave the way for the socialisation of society and development of human-personality's nooqualities. With the development of society, people are forced to gain (and gain, it cannot be denied, partly unconsciously, partly consciously) the increasing social responsibility, becoming more and more "social", more and more responding to general cultural imperatives of life, more and more involved in fulfilling their social mission, advancing, as we have already written (Bodrunov, 2018b) from "zoo" to "noo", both in relation to shaping the type of their social behaviour (a person is "socialised"), and in relation to shaping the criterial base of this behaviour, motives, moral and value cores. Meanwhile, it is required to pay attention to the reverse side of human socialisation: a socialising person, accepting more socially advanced norms of society, its attitudes, morals, etc., provides, in turn, a respective – socialising – impact on economic, political and other institutions of society, introducing their own, sometimes different ones at a specific stage from the ideas of others, personal ideas and formats of social existence, expands its existing criterial base.

A person socialises society. The increasingly socialising person brings new values and motives of life and actions into the social existence and into the public consciousness, thereby transforming socio-political and economic institutions towards "noo". And these updated institutions, in turn, will have a respective reverse effect on the person, on the community of individuals, intensifying the human nootransformation.

Thus, all four of these factors create the basis for combining the awareness of the need and the realisation of the opportunity for reasonable ***self-limitation*** *of quantitative increase in consumption.*

Herewith, the term "self-limitation" does not fully, but too narrowly, reflect the definition of that shift in people's attitude to their reasonable needs, which becomes necessary in the face of global problems and at the same time possible due to the development of material, technological prerequisites for transition to the new stage of production development.

Rather, we should talk *about a person's self-determination as a reasonable, truly reasonable person, who is aware and establishes for him/herself, by the power of reason, boundaries and levels of satisfaction of his/her needs (including those in personal consumption), going beyond which means entering the sphere of the unreasonable, that is, already "inhuman", which does not meet the sapiens criterion.* This self-determination cannot be based on any external compulsion (even purely spiritual or ideological one) aimed at limiting consumption. A person will have *to rethink the criteria of rationality of production and consumption by him/herself,* so that they could correspond to the tasks of human development and preservation of the natural, bio- and techno-environment, in which the person exists and can meet his/her nooneeds.

18.5. Reducing Conflicts and New Inequality

It is this type of person who is able to get rid of the pursuit of consumption of material goods, the mirage of false needs imposed on them by the market, and turn to developing truly human qualities. Accordingly, such development creates prerequisites for reducing conflictogenicity in human development.

We agree with the well-known philosophical paradigm, according to which development cannot take place at all without removal and reproduction of contradictions. However, if we keep in mind the current level of global contradictions, we must realise that the situation now is completely different from any other historical epochs of the human civilisation development: *the level of modern technologies no longer allows us to hope on its survival, if they are used to resolve the contradictions.*

Is it possible to prevent such a development of the situation? Of course, it is; the current socioeconomic system inevitably generates political, economic, and social conflicts, and going beyond it is also unlikely to be conflict-free. And still, both the current state of the process of cognising social reality and the level of development of production make it possible to anticipate, prevent, or at least mitigate social conflicts. The achieved potential to meet human needs allows finding social compromises instead of the uncompromising struggle for a living, which was inevitable when this struggle was largely identical to the struggle for survival.

It is obvious that adherence to old stereotypes meets certain private interests of those who get economic benefits or social preferences from exploiting the weaknesses of *homo economicus*, imposing on them the model of unlimited inflating of needs, including simulative ones. *It is the pursuit of these private interests, misunderstood as certainly reasonable, that underlies the rise of modern global problems, which were discussed above. Therefore, elimination of social conflicts is possible if changes are ensured not only in the technological capabilities of production, but also in the social structure of economic activity, moving away from purely economic rationality.*

One of the steps may be the development of productive and consciously aimed at promoting nooprocesses in society methods of regulating social production, which are free from bureaucratic centralisation and are based, for example, on the involvement of purposeful planned and joint activities of all stakeholders in the processes. This would make it possible to focus production not only on the criterion of economic rationality, but also – more and more, step by step – on achieving specific goals determined by the criteria of reason and the goals of cultural development. In future, when people transit from the economic way of meeting their needs to noonomy (Bodrunov, 2018a, 2019, 2020a), where meeting needs will be based on the interaction of humans and the relatively autonomous technosphere, there will be no place for market exchanges and economic relations at all, while the same planned regulation of the technosphere functioning in the interests of creating conditions for self-realisation of each person will take its proper place in the structure of organisation of social production.

It should be borne in mind that the path to mitigating conflicts will not be easy, because the inertia of just economic stereotypes in human behaviour cannot be overcome automatically and immediately, even with expanding opportunities for knowledge-intensive production to meet human needs, as well as with an increasing creative content in human activities. All the more important is the formation of the ideological platform of society focused not on the principles of social Darwinism, but on the ideology of solidarity (Bodrunov, 2021a; Leroux, 1840; Bourgeois, 1896).

However, mitigating and then removing social conflicts does not mean eliminating social contradictions as such. However, if now, *deep economic inequality* lies at the heart of social contradictions (Bodrunov, Galbraith, 2017), based essentially on the tradition of struggling for a living, which for some people turns into the struggle for survival in the face of starvation, and for others – the struggle for consuming as much material resources as possible, the nature of future inequality will be different. It will be determined by basic features of the new social structure of production based on the principles of noonomy.

Since the main goal of production and simultaneously its main factor in noonomy is a person's creative self-realisation, *the new inequality will be based on the person's ability to master the means of this self-realisation.* There will no longer be economic barriers to obtaining knowledge, information, all the benefits of culture, for training and advanced training.

However, differences based on people's various individual inclinations will remain. Herewith, it is clear that these differences can also be mitigated through the development of cognitive technologies, but differences in human personality will still remain, including those in people's abilities to master various types of activities.

Thus, there will be inequality based on differences within the extent of development of a person's creative abilities, which will stimulate the desire for mastering benefits of culture and education, increasing self-realisation, but it will not form the basis for property privileges and for the polarisation of society into opposing social groups and classes; in turn, a person of the noosociety, a true homo sapiens, will live in the society of high-level socialisation, the basic values of which will include the idea of unconditional social responsibility and the need for conscious and joint efforts to overcome social and personal contradictions.

18.6. On the Issue of Imperatives of Shaping Noosociety: Desimulatisation of Needs

The analysis of the mechanism of shaping and establishing noosociety, "design"/structure of the future noosocial organisation requires identification of appropriate imperatives that fundamentally and objectively determine the trajectory of progress towards the noosociety. These imperatives include, but are not limited to those mentioned below, the following essential processes: a) desimulatisation of human and social needs; b) gradual transition to the noocriterial base of values and respective attitudes and development goals; c) continuous clarification and definition (at each stage of development) of ethical boundaries of cognition (opportunities of which, due to the specifics of Knowledge, are unlimited); and finally, d) emergence/formation of the nooperson. Let us explain the situation in terms of the existence of prerequisites for emerging one of the above imperatives – the necessity for *desimulatisation of needs.*

In recent decades, the so-called process of simulatisation of needs has manifested itself more and more vividly, acting as one of the most important components of the trend towards the universal simulatisation of reality and human manipulation (Volodenkov, 2022; Grachev, Melnik, 1999). A number of important factors contribute to this.

Firstly, in the current economic development paradigm, within the framework of today's social structure, there is the priority for using achievements of scientific and technological progress (STP) in the version, when, based on currently accepted criteria of "economic rationality" and normality of "rational selfishness", the trend for increasing the mass of consumed resources and goods/services (ceasing to be benefits when being simulated and turning into anti-benefits for society) is expanding, and that ultimately threatens to create and sublimate many imbalances both in the development of the person him/herself and the human habitat, in particular, for example, the already quite obvious problem of irreversible disruption of the ecological balance, with devastating consequences of such predatory human intervention in nature (including in own nature). In fact, society spending immensely on natural resources for achieving fruitless illusions, turns them into waste, reducing its people's life period and quality of life. Indeed (and indisputably), the depletion of available exhaustible resources leads to economic and political conflicts, their escalation with severe consequences, and even wars over the sources of resources. And, in addition, in the inextricable combination of economic logic, wars for new markets for simulacra goods, despite the presence of globally dangerous real hunger problems in a number of countries and regions of the globe (Bodrunov, 2019: 251-252).

For achieving this "antisocial" state, society also needs to be "educated" accordingly (which, in an economic actor's logic, is much more productive than fighting competitors, since "there will be enough buyers for everyone" then), and *secondly*, such "education" goes on, increases and strengthens;

but, obviously, it is of negative nature, which does not stop either the process itself or its participants at all.

We can give one of its most progressing ways of influencing a person as an example – the obsessive belief in what and how to consume, and obsessive promotion of a simulative product through the mass media. As a result, the person, sometimes without noticing what is happening to him/her, as if under hypnosis, voluntarily begins to consider a fake need as real, unnecessary goods or services as useful, stupid rhetoric as reflection of progressive thought. And then he/she goes where modern storytellers lead him/her, like children to the tune in the famous story by the Brothers Grimm about the Pied Piper of Hamelin. For the object of manipulation, the line between the reality imposed on the person and the actual world is blurred (Marcuse, 2002: 94).

Thirdly, society must "mature" for solving these problems, for realising and determining the choice of its path of development; this "maturation" occurs in the course of accumulating knowledge and satisfying needs (here we can agree with those who believe that the Russian word "sozret'" ("mature") derives from the ancient Slavic meaning of "zret'" ("see", "behold", "notice", "understand", "realise" and "be ripe", having enlightened and accumulated knowledge...). It is obvious, however, that the current society has not yet "matured" to the level of "enlightenment", which ensures, on the ongoing basis, the positive development of technological progress and the use of its achievements, inter alia due to the presence of countries and regions that cannot yet have enough benefits to meet real needs; this problem, quite solvable at the current level of STP and technology, remains because of specifics of economy as the mechanism for meeting needs (Bodrunov, 2021c: 22; Bodrunov, 2022e), still extremely relevant due to the existence of the economic method of appropriating goods.

Fourthly, one of the most important sources of "fuelling" simulatisation of needs is the current stage of global economy, which is characterised by its financialisation on a scale that was unthinkable 20–30 years ago; financial capital is running the show. With the current development of STP, it is given the opportunity not only to "consume" positive results of technological progress, but also to reproduce itself and expand immensely through the redistribution of income in its favour, and not to overflow into production capital or other forms, the priority of which is to meet the real needs of people and society. Thus, financial capital secures world domination for itself and takes over all social processes (increasingly striving for subjugating people's minds) on a scale not even dreamed of by any conqueror who raved about getting the "sword of Caesar" and power over all "kingdoms on the Earth".

Economic society, under the laws of which the current world still lives, retains the generic sign of human natural existence: it "knows" (or does it not want to know?) no "measure", no "limit". Once, the financial system did provide many benefits to society: for example, it ensured the accumulation of resources for consumption and production, and separation of financial capital from production capital contributed to the concentration of monetary resources and their efficient use for productive investments, rapid overflow into the fastest growing industries and advanced technologies. However, with the development of financial institutions, markets, financial instruments, etc., it is no longer the interests and needs of people and society that are at the forefront, but interests of financial capital itself, aimed at self-growth, with the resulting disregard and suppression of the importance of real tasks of developing human civilisation, i.e., ***simulative interests of financial capital, creating simulatisational chains of influence on real needs.*** Hence its connection with the process of simulatisation of the needs of people and society in conditions of limited exhaustible resources and their high cost and development of the phenomenon of financialisation.

Let's note that production capital is directly related to the category "limit": for example, it faces market saturation, limited demand and the maximum level of satisfaction of people's specific needs in the product manufactured, etc., which cannot be said about financial capital: it is "fixated" solely on cash flow, and people are considered in this case only as a means of expanding it. This is especially prominently demonstrated in the humiliating, but widely used concept of "human capital" in the mainstream of modern (subordinated to financial capital) economy. The system of "crooked mirrors" develops and grows here in "magnificent colour": for example, fake "pseudo-innovations" replace real innovations, pulling over large-scale financial resources, and, more importantly, false human needs are interpreted as true; simplifying needs; reducing them to sinister ones requires focusing on the priority of one's "zoo" (it's not for nothing that there are advertising slogans like: "Awaken the beast in yourself!", "Don't think – buy! It doesn't matter what to buy, it's already been decided for you what you need. Hold out your 'rake hands'!"). Thus, in fact, the main goal for financial capital in this process is actually to reduce a person to the level of a "subhuman".

The most developed countries and regions come under special attack from financial capital, since fake needs are easier and more economically profitable to form where the extent of satisfaction of natural real needs and the level of STP that allows to satisfy them are higher. Thus, financial capital turned out to be able to "paint" achievements of STP in "gloomy colours", and lead human civilisation to disaster by creating the contradiction between its immeasurable growth (its unlimited simulative need for self-development) and waste of exhaustive resources to satisfy simulative needs of society, which cannot be saturated.

Finally, it is worth noting that the process of simulatisation of needs is "fuelled" by myths about so-called "post-industrial" economy and "happiness of deindustrialisation", which today, under the pressure of irrefutable evidence of their fallacy, gradually begin dispelling. Objecting to provisions of the paradigm of the "end of history" and the "post-industrial" mode of production, which became popular on the border of the XX–XXI centuries, we argue that after the industry of the fifth-sixth technological modes (TM), no "post-industrial" economy emerges, but the completely industrial economy retains, with all its features inherent in the industrial way of meeting needs; another thing is that the nature of this industry is different. Knowledge-intensive industrial production is being formed (Bodrunov, 2018a: 68). This happens in strict accordance with the provisions of the theory of changing the TM (Lvov, Glazyev, 1985; Glazyev, 2010): the previous TM is replaced by a new, coming one, the main resource of which is Knowledge and new, more knowledge-intensive and, consequently, more highly penetrative technologies formed on the basis of the new space of open/accumulated knowledge (Bodrunov, 2019: 141–152), which, penetrating into the "body" of industry, change its appearance (so radically that the uninitiated had to come up with the concept of post-industrialism, for the purpose of explaining what was happening...).

The most important question is about the role of financial capital as an accumulator of "reserve". Indeed, it was this function of it (together with the ease of overflow) that, at the initial stage, gave rise to its special role in economy and just ensured the transformation of "intermediary capital" (recall the formula: "G – M – G") into an all-powerful master ("M – G – M!", and even "M – M!"...). This "basic" function of it will disappear with the development of nooproduction, which will entail the exhaustion of financial capital itself; the phenomenon of financial capital will be erased by noonomy from the face of history. *In noosociety, due to nooproduction, the role of "reserve" will be given to the factor of complete and obligatory satisfaction of true, real needs of a person and society by the autonomously functioning production system, which will entail corresponding changes in the criterial base that determines the behaviour of an individual and the "correctness" of one's actions.*

The basic imperative here is precisely "***desimulatisation of needs***", the process involving the "moving" along three different but interrelated trends: a) transformation of simulative needs into non-simulative ones and/or removal of the "simulative burden" from a number of goods/services; b) displacement of simulative needs due to gradual prioritisation of natural, real needs for a person and society (given the achieved level of satisfaction of needs); c) formation of nooneeds.

It is STP that is destined to play one of the main roles in this process. In the process of developing the technological space, not only does the law of increasing needs, including simulative ones, operate, but also the law of partially transforming simulative needs into non-simulative ones, along the following "trajectory": "simulative need! 'development of knowledge and technologies that embody this knowledge, making it possible and rational to satisfy the analyzed need'! transition of the simulative need into the category of non-simulative ones" (Bodrunov, 2018a: 203–204). Thus, a simulative need can gradually turn first into an excess, and then into a normal or ordinary need, that is, what seemed excessive at one level of development becomes the norm at a higher one, while what was considered necessary at one level of development becomes excessive at another level (Bodrunov, 2018a: 203–207). The reason is that progress in the discovery of new knowledge and STP (as embodied knowledge) leads to progress in productive forces that create both new needs and new opportunities for meeting needs.

Thus, it cannot be argued that simulative needs can be considered exclusively with a non-positive connotation. Obviously, this does not apply to all and any simulacra. In this regard, it might be worth researching this issue further.

At the same time, in general, simulative needs, given their negative side (in particular, stimulation of the economy's desire for unrestrained consumption of resources), must be rationally limited (taking into account their potential "dynamics of transformations"), so that, on the one hand, not to slow down STP and the progress of society's development, and, on the other hand, not to harm the development of the human beings changed by satisfying their needs. ***This essential contradiction must also be resolved through knowledge, which in this case is the search and awareness of the edge, measure, "limit" or boundary***, beyond which, at each specific stage, simulative needs begin, entailing the irrational tension of the system.

Thus, there is an imperative: the vital for human civilisation need for reasonable limiting of "unreasonable" needs, desimulatisation of needs.

Processes ensuring socialisation of society are rather important for the desimulatisation of the space of needs (Bodrunov, 2022a, 2022f).

There is a gradual increase in both the importance in public consciousness and the realised "amount" of unsimulative, real needs within the framework of these processes, with the gradual displacement of simulacra from the life of society.

And finally, the most important factor in the desimulatisation of needs is the *formation of nooneeds*, or needs determined by the criteria of the human mind and based on other cultural imperatives relying on the rational level of satisfaction of real needs and characterised by the increasing role of "higher" needs.

All cognition presupposes both the freedom of choice and the acceptance of limitations – as two recognised necessities. It is Knowledge that can show a person which need is false and which is true. Thus, *it is objective knowledge that negates simulative needs.*

NOTES

1 Prepared on the basis of Bodrunov, 2021c, 2022a. The title contains a quote from L.N. Tolstoy.

2 Calculating Earth Overshoot Day 2020: Estimates Point to August 22 [June 5, 2020. Global Footprint Network]. URL: https://www.overshootday.org/content/uploads/2020/

06/Earth-Overshoot-Day2020-Calculation-Research-Report.pdf.

3 UN Report: Nature's Dangerous Decline 'Unprecedented'; Species Extinction Rates 'Accelerating' (May 6, 2019). URL: https://www.un.org/sustainabledevelopment/blog/2019/05/nature-decline-unprecedented-report/; IPBES (2019): Global assessment report on biodiversity and ecosystem services of the Intergovernmental Science-Policy Platform on Biodiversity and Ecosystem Services. E.S. Brondizio, J. Settele, S. Díaz, and H.T. Ngo (editors). IPBES secretariat, Bonn, Germany. URL: https://www.ipbes.net/globalassessment

4 UN Report: Nature's Dangerous Decline 'Unprecedented'; Species Extinction Rates 'Accelerating' (May 6, 2019). URL: https://www.un.org/sustainabledevelopment/blog/2019/05/nature-decline-unprecedented-report/

5 Leaders' Summit on Climate Summary of Proceedings, The White House (April 23, 2021). URL: https://www.whitehouse.gov/briefing-room/statements-releases/2021/04/23/leaders-summit-on-climatesummary-of-proceedings/

19

Noosocialisation of the Economy and Modern Society[1]

The problem of transition to the new structure of society and transformation of the economy into noonomy is one of the urgent problems of modern holistic social knowledge. The further trajectory of human development largely depends on the ways of solving it. That is why research in this area is one of the main priorities.

The problems of the noonomy genesis are diverse and have various dimensions. The aim of this chapter is theoretical analysis of the socialisation process, the objective course of which creates prerequisites for the genesis towards "noo".

19.1. Socialisation of Society and the Noonomy Genesis: The Problem Statement

Socialisation is a complex phenomenon (Giddens, 1999; Lukov, 2014; Giddings, 1897). It is usually understood as the person's development, self-change in the broadest sense in the process of assimilation, reproduction of social norms and rules of behaviour, culture. This development and self-change happen permanently and continuously. However, there is another facet of this process: socialisation can be interpreted as the process of making personal contribution to the development of culture and social norms by a person, an individual. There is a third facet as well. The phenomenon in question occurs in interaction with external living conditions, and cannot be considered in isolation from them. Finally, the fourth: this interaction happens both with spontaneous and purposefully created living conditions.

In terms of socialisation, it is important to emphasise *the dualism of human existence.* On the one hand, a person is a product of this process, because it is through socialisation that personality formation takes place, a person gains human (noo) qualities and transforms from a bio(zoo)-being into a *human being, a social being, a personality. Personality cannot be formed without socialisation*; for proving this conclusion, it is enough to recall examples of "Mowgli people".

With society development, a person grows as a "noo". Let's fix this conclusion. On the other hand, according to K. Marx, a person is not only a product, but also a creator of social relations, a creator of history, and in this case, society is a product of joint creativity (co-creativity) of individuals.

The term "socialisation" can also be used to denote a person's fixed state ("the person is socialised" is said if the person is ready to live in the current society, general culture level and norms of social behaviour), and in this case, we are speaking about the level of socialisation achieved by the person at a particular moment.

Let's expand the concept of socialisation and approach it from the other side.

> *"Socialisation of society"* [the term is ours – *the author's note*] as a kind of state is the currently achieved level of social organisation of society, culture, norms, etc., accepted by the majority of individuals. Changing this level is the process of socialisation of society, i.e., it is the process of creating living conditions for people in society. This is a permanent reconfiguration of institutions, life support, upbringing, culture, and other living conditions of an individual in society.

By *"increasing socialisation of society"* we mean exactly this – *creating much more comfortable conditions for developing human properties of individuals in society.* And at this point we must turn to the theory of noonomy, noosociety, and nooperson, because a person in this kind of society is a non-economic one. There is a transition to the state when a person living with unsimulative needs and values takes the place of an economic person with his/her properties of a rational, selfish market actor. Thus, the term "socialisation" gains a new and particular certainty:

> *In terms of the theory of noonomy, socialisation* means increasing human nooproperties that occurs in the course of educating personal properties of the progressive nature (humanity, solidarity, awareness of the self-restriction need, etc.), as well as a person's creative properties.

The theory of noonomy means precisely this (Bodrunov, 2018a) – the need for transition to a new state of society, as well as the formation of human nooproperties, noopersonality.

Each time, the state of society (defined by such criteria) describes the level of its socialisation. Therefore, whenever we consider noonomy as a kind of conceptual platform, we mean that *the highest goal of developing society (in terms of moving towards "noo") is shaping the person as a personality and existence of the personality in this noospace, socialised according to noocriteria.*

19.2. A Person Is Not a "Zoo" by Definition

Having published a number of monographs (Bodrunov, 2016a, 2018a) and a series of subsequent articles, the author often has to face the objection: a person allegedly is an imperfect being, cut according to certain patterns – the patterns of egoism. And the person is not so easy or even impossible to "be re-made" and be turned into a being that will be guided by the criteria of moving towards noosociety.

Critics of the author's concept often emphasise that a person is a biological being, which means that (s)he is characterised by the principles of zoological existence: competition, promotion of one's own interests as special ones, as opposed to the interests of other members of society, opposition of one's own interests to the interests of both society and nature, the priority of selfish interests, etc. Of course, this may result in increasing conflictogenicity and not harmonisation of social interactions in the course of transition to further stages of the civilisation existence. This criticism is worth analyzing separately.

The theory of noonomy precisely dwells on the capacity of harmonising social relations, bearing in mind, of course, the existence of a person in the period after the approaching "bifurcation point" of civilisational development, if the person manages to pass it while maintaining the positive development trend. It is this that the theory of noonomy means as the opportunity (given the level of modern scientific and technical equipment and production) for reducing conflictogenicity when conscious correct ways and tools for such development are chosen.

But it also means the capacity for implementing the negative development scenario.

Ultimately, if the current situation is not changed, it may result in catastrophic consequences, given the paradigm of economic existence that is currently witnessed. Let us briefly recall its main features: strengthening the role of financial capital; absorbing interests of people, society, and "interests" of nature by financial capital; aggravating global challenges (the topical example of them is the coronavirus pandemic, which humanity cannot cope with no matter the efforts), etc.

Moreover, we are told that there is no way of forming a human being as a *noobeing*, that there are no other principles of existence, except zoological ones. We have partially answered this (Bodrunov, 2018b). We have shown how a person gradually, as (s)he becomes a personality, increasingly *gains the character of a being of nootype*, a humanistic being who takes into account not only one's own interests, but also – more and more fully – the interests of the surrounding space, society, environment, and other people. This moving from "zoo" to "noo" is historically proven.

Quite another matter is how does this happen and how can we ensure the priority of this moving, increase the pace of the moving towards "noo" and, conversely, slow down the negative processes reducing people and society to "zoo"?

Answering this question, we emphasise that it is worth taking a closer look at the process of socialisation of society. For ensuring the mentioned priority, it is necessary to strengthen the human awareness of that part of the socio-scientific space, which is determined by social sciences. They are part of the general layer of human cognition and norms of behaviour, which is simultaneously formed on their basis; this is *general culture of a person, society*. We see that this layer constantly grows and develops. Of course, there are opposite situations; nevertheless, we understand that the level of general culture of modern society is significantly higher than it was thousands of years ago.

Many features of "primitive" attitude to life are preserved in that part of people who have not sufficiently entered this cultural space.

People have entered the cultural space differently; some individuals (or their communities) are more sensitive to the layer of knowledge called "culture", which leads to developing human nooneeds, forming his/her attitude to life as a *noobeing*, and some are less sensitive. We can observe numerous examples of the current society's "flaws" in this regard. *Moreover, we can often see the purposeful creation of the system building restrictions on a person's entry into the cultural space, preventing him/her from forming as a person, stupefying a person.* This is not done by chance, because restricting a person's access to culture is a prerequisite for manipulating him/her. For example, financial capital and its satellites are engaged in this. Its satellites are its derivatives, its "siblings, children and grandchildren": poverty, inequality, limited access to consumption of cultural phenomena and education, etc., – everything that leads to *the shortfall by a person of the arsenal of knowledge, cultural benefits to form a nooperson.*

All this is also used to justify the theses about a person as an animal-like creature, to justify speculation about the impossibility, in principle, of getting rid of the "zoo". We strongly object to this. Every person, an individual, is endowed with promises of "noo" from birth. Inclinations, as you know, do not determine abilities; they are prerequisites for their formation and development. And what influences their formation? In the language of social psychology, the mechanism of such formation is generalisation and consolidation in the individual's activities of the entire range of mental processes, which, in turn, are the reflection – let's switch to the language of philosophers – of the external world, its impact on the individual, which forms, among other things, his/her worldview, fixing in his/her mind "codes" and values, allowing him/her to be aware of the world and society, as well as to position him/herself within the framework of such values.

19.3. The Mechanism of Influence of Society on a Personality and the Personality on Society

Socialisation is a two-way process. A person is characterised by the process of entering a society as the awareness of his/her place in it, his/her role, interests, and not only one's own, but also other people's interests that are transformed into social needs. And this happens precisely in the course of socialisation. In this sense, we can say that socialisation is the process of human adaptation to public spaces, norms, requirements, rules of behaviour, ideology, attitudes, etc.

However, society also affects the personality. But, let us specifically note, this is only one plane of the two-sidedness of this process. There is also another plane – the personality's impact on society. If the individual is strong and powerful, (s)he gives some new attitudes, ideas, concepts, sets norms of behaviour by "expanding" these norms. All of them affect society, and, in return, when it requires to adapt other individuals to itself, society affects the formation of these individuals' inner worldview, already "taking into account" the updated norms.

Thus, a person can (of course, if there are objective conditions for this) change institutions and rules of the game in economy, politics, and the social sphere, directly or through technological progress (when the person affects technological progress).

But, by influencing society, an individual creates conditions for that society to influence the individual. Herewith, we should remember that it looks as if we mean the same individual, when saying "individual". In fact, it is about interaction of society and many individuals.

19.4. Socialisation and the Genesis of Noonomy: From Theory to Practice

Let's move on to the practice in this matter. Two things are important here: the first thing is strengthening the scientific and technological progress; the second one is the advanced stimulation of human development through knowledge of that part of the world, with which social knowledge "operates". It is given to us by social science, shaping a person's general culture through ecumenical knowledge. We live in the world in which scientific, scientific-technical and technological types of progress are combined with the progress of social knowledge, cognition of person, society, and its special features.

Social research began later than scientific, technological and technical studies, although the earliest area of general development has been represented in philosophical treatises and ideas for more than two thousand years already.

But studying man as a social being, as an individual in society, began actively and purposefully together with the development of psychological and social sciences at around the end of the XIX century and continued throughout the XX century, gaining recognition as the field of social sciences in the second half of the XX – early XXI centuries.

Developing these studies gives its results. In particular, the concept of "socialisation" put forward by social sciences allows us to understand that a) combination in the theory of noonomy of our approach related to technological development with the idea of advanced human cognition of social knowledge, formation of the social structure through the mechanism of socialisation, and b) step-by-step moving towards a new person (in terms of his/her adaptation in society, as well as adaptation of society "to self", to real needs), moving towards self-restraint, etc., are the points to be paid attention to in practical activities of institutions (both state and public ones).

This approach shows how to look for a solution of the above problem. We can involve a practically untapped layer of sociology and social psychology, the emerging theory of cognitive human states, etc., considering their impact on developing society, using the obtained results in purposeful social design, since these ideas explain and show how we influence society, and that society affects us.

Being in society, an individual is "encoded" by the society, taking as a "code" in the process of socialisation the moral and value core that currently makes up social essence of the society and is determined by the criterial base of values inherent in the society at that moment. The individual is being socialised.

Influencing society, the individual also "socialises" it by changing its moral and value core. The task is for this core to be changing under the influence of the noocriterial base. And the discovery, expansion of the developmental area of this knowledge, inclusion of it in the moral and value core of a modern and promising society is an important aspect for increasing the level of a society's socialisation; "making" it more "social", non-individualistic (in the "malicious" sense of the word "individualism"), more comfortable to the individual, more noooriented.

In case of adding to this the process of human cognition of their needs, i.e., combining processes of obtaining knowledge of one type and knowledge of another type into a single whole, we will be able to get the key to solving the problem basing on this – how to move along the path towards a nooperson. This means that we will get the key to "doing", creating not just a non-economic person (in terms of not using economic mechanisms for solving the problem of satisfying their needs), but a person who will consciously improve him/herself and do everything necessary "in self" and in the society in order for him/her to have, on the one hand, a sufficient level of well-being (social, material, mental, spiritual), comprehended and accepted by him/her, and, on the other hand, to have no need (namely, a need, a real need) for expanding production of something, which is impossible to obtain at this stage of development without harming society, the outside world and other people.

Of course, it is important to find approaches to solving the set tasks of social development, and many social design methods have already been used actively today for promoting various social programmes. And here, there is a room for the broad application of platforms from other fields of knowledge with more extensive coverage and approaches. As an example, let's consider the theory of strategising (Kvint, 2019), which is aimed at creating and implementing strategies. This well-developed theoretical basis for implementing hopeful practices combined with ideas of the theory of noonomy (synthesis of both ones) makes it possible to obtain a new property of the latter – strengthening the aspect of its practical implementation.

On the one hand, we get the explanation of applicability of strategising for the strategic planning of processes of developing public institutions towards noonomy. On the other hand, the theory of noonomy allows us to understand where to move and what to do at each stage, as well as to offer mechanisms necessary for moving towards this goal, i.e., it allows filling the strategising of social development with new content. As the result, we can get a concept of "what is needed and how to achieve it".

The civilisation development towards noonomy is fundamentally predetermined, since it is objective, because there is an objective need in this kind of development. Quite another matter is how specifically society is being "noocivilised", how exactly it will move and is moving (and whether it is moving at all) along this path. This need can (and sometimes we observe it) be realised directly, with step-by-step development. And sometimes it happens that, under the influence of fluctuational factors, the development trajectory, in spite of all objectivity of "direct" trends, "bends", changes by either "bouncing sideways", or coming back, or something else occurs. History also provides such examples, twists and loops of civilisational moving.

This is the very room for applying both new methods and traditional ones, but interpreted in a new way. For applying, for example, strategising, which will make it possible to "straighten" the development path, preventing the slide into recession, considering fluctuations and mutual influence of various parameters, forming certain practical steps aimed at changing certain things – from the formulation of the concept – through the methodology – to practice.

Through the use of actually tested social, socio-prognostic and socio-project tools, through comprehending the need for not only considering the dual nature of the socialisation process (formation of a person by society and of the society by the person), but also actively, consciously influencing this process, using opportunities that open up, it is possible to develop theoretical and practical solutions contributing to both sides of the socialisation process to lead us towards the nooworld, straightening barriers of historical development.

19.5. Socialisation of the Economy: Priorities of Modern Development of Russia

At the beginning of 2022, the consensus forecast of both our and foreign experts assumed that our country's GDP would slowly but surely recover after two pandemic years. But the new reality to emerge in March of that year made its own adjustments: the Russian economy has been unprecedentedly challenged. In the new conditions, the sharp drop in our GDP seemed inevitable; many analysts, especially foreign ones, predicted that the emerging foreign trade restrictions, as well as the ongoing and increasing sanctions pressure, would paralyze the key sectors of our economy. However, this did not happen. According to the Rosstat, Russia's GDP fell by 0.4 per cent in the first half of 2022 (as compared with the first half of 2021). In the second quarter, the Rosstat estimated the decrease in GDP by 4.1 per cent. You should agree that the figures are not devastating. There were worse times. Herewith, already in the third quarter, the negative peak smoothing began, and by the end of the year, the country's economy will decrease, as calculations show, by 2.8...2.9 per cent. This was the assessment given by the President of Russia, speaking at the final plenary session of the Valdai International Discussion Club. The Central Bank predicts a slightly stronger, but a fairly close decline in GDP. According to its updated forecast, the decline may amount to 3...3.5 per cent. International financial and economic institutions "improve" their forecasts of the dynamics of the Russian economy (despite the understandable bias). So, the International Monetary Fund expects the decline in Russia's GDP by 3.4 per cent by the end of 2022. The dynamics of its forecasts is interesting: in April, the IMF predicted minus 8.5 per cent, in July – minus 6 per cent, and here is a new forecast, which is twice as good as a quarter ago. The World Bank calls a close figure: minus 4.5 per cent, though it also predicted a drop down to 8.9 per cent.

Thus, the Russian economy has clearly demonstrated ***stability*** unexpected by many foreign forecasters. What particularly stands out? In this country, agricultural production increases (according to the Rosstat, in January–September of 2022, the growth was 5.2 per cent compared to the same period in 2021, and this year grain harvested a record over 150 million metric tons). Thus, we are completely independent in food. Further, housing construction grows (in January–September of 2022, the increase was 26.5 per cent compared to the same period in 2021, according to the Rosstat).

I have given the figures for the mentioned industries only for the purpose of emphasising that the course towards human-focused economy and construction of a welfare state in our country has not been curtailed, in spite of everything.

However, there is no reason for calming down, much less for resting on our laurels. The situation concerning the citizens' welfare cannot but be alarming. According to the Rosstat, in the second quarter of this year, domestic end demand decreased by 6.4 per cent compared to the same period in 2021. Russians began to spend money by 5.5 per cent less. The share of wages in GDP decreased by 1.5 per cent in the first half of the year, real wages fell similarly, and real disposable incomes fell by 0.8 per cent again, as a few years ago. Meanwhile, according to the forecast of the Central Bank, at the end of this year, consumer inflation will amount to 12...13 per cent.

It is clear that the inflation is the effect of sanctions, but not only this; it is largely imported by our economy: colossal inflation has become a sign of the new geo-economic reality in many countries of the world. I will provide some data for 2022. So, in October, annual inflation in Europe reached a new record, exceeding 10.7 per cent, and in a number of European countries, their inflation exceeded ours by one and a half to two times, as it follows from preliminary data submitted by the Eurostat. Of the BRICS countries, only China holds out (their inflation is 2.2 per cent). All market economies are currently challenged by the inflationary problem: in India and Brazil – 8 per cent, in South Africa – over 7.5 per cent.

It is necessary to bear global trends in mind, see problems and learn from them, there is no doubt about it. However, Russia, Russian society ***must and are able** to form their own socio-economic path* of development (and many experts say this), and we, economists (scientists and practical workers), shall offer our vision of the key milestones along this path.

The few figures that I have given, the results of numerous discussions in the Free Economic Society of Russia and the International Union of Economists, and finally, the political maxims voiced in recent months by the President of Russia suggest that the "message" traditionally presented from year to year by the All-Russian Economic Assembly, should not be so much economic, but of a ***social*** nature.

Of course, it is hard to separate one from the other: in our country, 50 per cent of GDP is generated by household consumption, i.e., the economy directly depends on peoples purchasing power. And this "power" is still quite far from that of the economic leaders: there is a falling behind in the provision of Russians with housing, durable goods (including high-tech), and high-quality services.

Unresolved social issues, coupled with insufficient incomes of the population, lead to the fact that most of the expenses of 50 per cent of Russian households are for food and mandatory payments. Moreover, in the current reality, the problems in the structure of consumption, which slow down the economy development, may worsen. So, the demand for household appliances and cars has declined. The share of cheaper food products and other goods in the population's consumption structure grows again.

All these facts point to the need to strengthen the socialisation of our economy.

The head of the state indicated *the priority of* ***social*** *tasks*, which are aimed at solving all the national development goals of the country, in October at the plenary session of the Valdai International Discussion Club, as well as at the special meeting on this occasion. It is extremely important that socialisation of our society must be carried out on the basis of traditional Russian spiritual and moral values, superior universal human values (I would call them "noovalues"), as written in Presidential Edict No. 809 dated November 9, 2022; many practical measures and decisions of the Government of the Russian Federation are aimed at this. I think that at the Scientific Expert Session our colleagues will analyze these decisions in detail.

However, the efforts of one State are not sufficient for solving these problems. Today, more than ever, consolidation and concentration of forces of all strata of the population is needed for overcoming crisis phenomena and solving the tasks of the country's socioeconomic development. The problems of the current period concern everyone. In this regard, I would like to remind you about one of the provisions of the Basic Law of the Russian Federation – our Constitution, which was very timely supplemented by Article 75.1. For the first time in the country's modern history, the principles – I would say, the ideology, – of the country's socioeconomic development are included in it. "The Russian Federation creates conditions for the country's sustainable economic growth and the citizens' welfare improvement, for mutual trust between the state and the society, protection of the citizens' dignity and respect for human labour are guaranteed, the balance of rights and duties of a citizen, *social partnership, economic, political and* ***social solidarity*** *are ensured"*.

Social partnership, economic and social solidarity are not just words! Social solidarity is what unites us into a single whole, makes our society cohesive, a "tough nut to crack" for unfriendly "teeth", which have long been trying to "crack" us, split us and, sorry, swallow us piece by piece. However, it is also extremely important for solving the problems that have arisen during the global transformation of the world. At present, the world is in the state of transition, according to academician S.Yu. Glazyev, towards a new world economic mode – the new social and economic order. Scientists, major economists of the globe have been talking about this for a long time. And we will have to build this order, this new world, we have no other choice. Moreover, to build together we have no right to divide into "membership clubs", since it is only solidarity that *can ensure the sustainability of social and economic development.*

In conclusion, I'll recall the words from the Gospel of Matthew (Chapter 12, Verse 25): "Every kingdom divided against itself will be ruined, and every city or household divided against itself will not stand". May this message from the depths of time become a testament to us. Not Old, but New one!

NOTES

1 Prepared on the basis of Bodrunov, 2020h, 2022f.

2 * – here and after – means that Dr. Bodrunov's material is in English.

Epilogue. On Noonomy as a Theory of the Future

To conclude, this work proposes the author's version of the trajectory of social transformation based on the application of the nooapproach we are developing.

It should be noted that Noonomy is a relatively young direction of research on a qualitatively new system of social relations. Despite the fact that this theory already has quite a lot of supporters and has managed to gain recognition in the domestic and foreign expert communities in a fairly short period of time, it is still at the stage of its formation and rapid development, which is also associated with increased criticism of a number of its provisions. In particular, this concerns finding the trajectory of social transformation or a special type of optimistic very-long-term forecast (up to the seventh technological mode).

Thus, in his major works, the author has to occasionally revert to explanation and interpretation of the nooapproach used by him, including for the purposes to prove its usefulness and eligibility for practical application.

To this end, in this note which concludes the book, we will give a very unexpected example, drawing a parallel between our theory and Russian Futurism ("creation of the future") as one of the largest movements in the literature and art of the "Silver Age".

Although the future has always occupied the minds of "living and wise humans", in Russia the outbreak of futurism occurred in the 1910s and is associated with the activities of famous Russian poets: V. Khlebnikov, V. Mayakovsky and others. Thus, the beginning of the XX century became a favoured time for the emergence of new threads in intellectual life – both in literature and art, and in science.

Let us recall that, for example, within futurism, the "new tribe" of poets considered their main objective "at the turn of eras" to create literature of the future, including the idea to embody technological progress in art.

A similar task, whereas global transformation has begun as part of modern science development, has been set before the author of the Noonomy theory as a "theory of the future".

At the same time, note that one of the principles of Russian Futurism was the call to abandon classical literary traditions and the expression of non-confidence – both towards the past and towards the "vulgarity of the present" – its adherents boldly demonstrate a "slap in the face of public taste" to those accustomed to archaizing traditions. However, there is a very subtle aspect here: despite this call to destroy deeply-rooted traditions, the Futurists were faced with the need to "re-evaluate values" and divide "traditions" into "harmful" and "useful".

But – let us not further immerse our esteemed reader in the details of Russian Futurism of the early XX century – a special cultural phenomenon that, however, gave impetus to the "re-evaluation" and "denial" of many dogmas and ideas in science that had been well-established by that time.

Let us just say once again – just about the same thing is happening with Noonomy in the XXI century. In the theory of Noonomy, the author also contrasts his ideas with the current "mainstream economics", which has literally enthralled and shackled modern economic thought. Further, following the philosophical Hegelian tradition, we "deny those who have renounced" the ideas of many predecessors – we rely on the classical works of Aristotle, Marx, Vernadsky, Galbraith and other thinkers, developing their best research traditions. At the same time, studies on Noonomy often emphasise the tension of the current stage of global socio-economic development, its crisis and suppression of the best human qualities. In this vein, the nooapproach can also be called a symbolic "slap in the face" to all who have embarked on the path of cultivating "zoo".

And yet, there are a couple more parallels between Noonomy and the phenomenon of Russian Futurism.

Futurism was rightly considered the art of the enlightened. In Noonomy, the central concept is knowledge. There is something behind that. It is knowledge, cognition that reveals the future to us.

And finally, the Futurists, not finding the necessary terms to explain new ideas in their contemporary world, vigorously constructed a "new language".

In the theory of Noonomy we face the same challenge. So, we follow the same logic, introducing new concepts: Noonomy, noosociety, Quadriga of Noonomy, diffusion of ownership, noovalues, acceleration of acceleration, readiness-penetration process, socialisation of society, noointegration, nooapproach and many others.

"Every man is the architect of his own fortune", said the Roman poet Publius Ovidius Naso back in the first century AD. "And of his own future", we would add.

What will it be like?

Will it be bloody? Full of conflicts? Hungry?

Or bright and reasonable?

It depends on us. First of all, it depends on scientists and scholars, reflecting and responsible humans. Those, who are equipped with deeply grounded, fundamental, theoretical knowledge and useful practices. Those having clear development goals based on a system of values that ensure positive development. Those able to devise social solutions on this basis. Those able to do good.

Of course, in citing the above-mentioned example, we are far from equating Russian Futurism of the early XX century and the theory of Noonomy of the XXI century. This is about something else.

Like Russian Futurism, the theory of Noonomy "constructs" a new world order. We are theorists of the future. Or are we rather its demiurges?

Bibliography

Acevedo A. (2018). A personalistic appraisal of Maslow's needs theory of motivation: From "humanistic" psychology to integral humanism // *Journal of Business Ethics,* 148 (4): 741–763.

Agaev V. (2017). Man, woman, intersex / *Ogonyek*, 49. URL: https://www.kommersant.ru/doc/3486805 [In Russian].

Agonnude, B.V.F. and Glebov, V. (2023). Perspektivi rasshireniya BRICS (Prospects for BRICS expansion) // *The International Affairs*, 4 [In Russian]. URL: https://interaffairs.ru/jauthor/material/2813?ysclid=lt3yap5m8q289964535.

Alderfer C.P. (1969). An empirical test of a new theory of human needs // *Organizational Behaviour and Human Performance*, 4(2): 142–175.

Amin S. (1973). *Le Developpement Inegal: Essai Sur Les Formations Sociales Du Capitalisme Peripherique.* Paris: Les Editions De Minuit.

Amin S. (1976). *Unequal Development: An Essay on the Social Formations of Peripheral Capitalism*. New York: Monthly Review Press.

Amin S. (2016). *Russia and the Long Transition from Capitalism to Socialism.* New York: Monthly Review.

Antony S. and Tramboo I.A. (2020). Hyperreality in media and literature: An overview of Jean Baudrillard's Simulacra and Simulation // *European Journal of Molecular and Clinical Medicine*, 07(10): 3314–3318.

Arapova Å. and Lissovolik Y. (2022). BRICS+: The Global South Responds to New Challenges (in the Context of China's BRICS Chairmanship) / Valdai Papers 118. URL: https://valdaiclub.com/files/38432/?ysclid=lty1evhemr292740487.

Arendt H. (1958). *The Human Condition*. Chicago: University of Chicago Press.

Àrkhipova V.V. (2023). Integration Processes in the World Economy: a Nooapproach and Development of Eurasian Space // *Ekonomicheskoye vozrozhdeniye Rossii, 1(75):* 35-49 [In Russian].

Arthur W.B. (1996). Increasing returns and the new world of business // *Harvard Business Review*. 74, no. 4, Jul-Aug: 100–109.

Ashkerov A. Yu. (2002). Morality, Reason, Globalization (On Some Aspects of the Socio-political Theory of Jurgen Habermas) // *Russian Sociological Review*, 2 (2): 69–84 [In Russian].

Babaev K.V., Lavrov S.V. (2023). Both in breadth and depth. Ways to strengthen the BRICS institutional framework [I v shir, i v glub. Puti ukrepleniya institutsionalnoy osnovi BRICS] // *Rossiya v globalnoy politike*, 21(5): 69-81 [In Russian]. URL: https://globalaffairs.ru/articles/vglub-i-vshir-brics/?ysclid=lt3yfcrdt633526118.

Baeva L.V. (2003). *The Value Bases of Individual Existence. The Experience of Existential Axiology.* Moscow: Prometey [in Russian].

Bakhtin M.M. (1986). Philosophy of Action / Philosophiya i sotsiologiya nauki i tekhniki. Moscow: Nauka, pp. 84–157 [In Russian].

Balandin R.K. (1978). *Geological Activity of Mankind. Technogenesis*. Minsk: High School.

Batishchev G.S. (1969). *The Active Essence of Man as a Philosophical Principle* / in *The Problem of Man in Modern Philosophy.* Moscow: Nauka.

Batyschev H.S. (2015). Active Essence of Human as Philosophical Principle / Izbranniye proizvedeniya. Almaty: Institut philosophii, politologii i religiovedeniya KN MON RK [In Russian].

Baudrillard J. (1972). *Pour une critique di l'économie politique du signe*. Paris: Gallimard.

Baudrillard J. (1981). *Simulacres et simulation.* Paris: Galilee.

Baudrillard J. (1981). *For a Critique of the Political Economy of the Sign.* Candor, NY: Telos Press.

Baudrillard J. (2003). *Pour une critique di l'economie politique du signe*. Moscow: Biblion – Russkaya kniga [In Russian].

Bauer E.S. (1935). *Theoretical Biology*. M.: VIEM [In Russian].

Bell D. (1967). Notes on the Post-Industrial Society (II) // The Public Interest, 7.

Bell D. (1973). *The Coming of Post-Industrial Society: A Venture in Social Forecasting.* New York: Basic Books.

Bell D. (1996). *The Coming of Post-Industrial Society. A Venture in Social Forecasting.* N.Y.: Harper/Collins.

Bell D. (1999). *The coming of post-industrial society: A venture of social forecasting.* Moscow: Academia Publ. [In Russian].

Bergson A. (1907). *L'évolution créatrice*. Paris: Felix Alcan.

Berle A.A., Means G.C. (1963 [1932]). *The Modern Corporation and Private Property*. New York: Harcourt, Brace & World.

Bidwai P. (2003). A Great Movement Is Born: Global Justice Movement Finds Fertile Ground at the Asia Social Forum / Focus on the Global South, January 28. URL: https://focusweb.org/a-great-movement-is-born-global-justicemovement-finds-fertile-ground-at-the-asia-social-forum/

Blaug M. (1986). *Great Economists before Keynes: An Introduction to the Lives & Works of One Hundred Great Economists of the Past*. Brighton, Sussex: Wheatsheaf Books.

Bodrunov S.D. (2013). *Formirovaniye strategii reindustrializatsii Rossii [Formation of the Strategy of Reindustrialization of Russia]*. St. Petersburg: S.Y. Witte Institute for New Industrial Development (INID) [In Russian].

Bodrunov S.D. (2015a). *Formirovaniye strategii reindustrializatsii Rossii [Formation of the Strategy of Reindustrialization of Russia]*. In 2 parts. St. Petersburg: S.Y. Witte Institute for New Industrial Development (INID) [In Russian].

Bodrunov S.D. (2015b). Integratsiya proizvodstva, nauki i obrazovanija kak osnova reindustrializatsii rossijskoj ekonomiki [Integration of Production, Science and Education as the Basis for the Reindustrialization of the Russian Economy] // *Economic Revival of Russia*, 1 [In Russian].

Bodrunov S.D. (2016a). *Gryaduscheye. Nonoye industrialnoye obschestvo: perezagruzka [The Future. The New Industrial Society: Reset]*. St. Petersburg: S.Y. Witte Institute for New Industrial Development (INID) [In Russian].

Bodrunov S.D. (2016b). Novoye industrialnoye obschestvo. Proizvodstvo. Ekonomika. Instituti [New Industrial Society. Production. Economy. Institutions] // *Economic Revival of Russia*, 48(2) [In Russian].

Bodrunov S.D. (2017). Vozvrascheniye industrializatsii – vozvrascheniye Gelbrejta: ot NIO.2 k noospheroj tsivilizatsii [Return of Industrialization – Return of Galbraith: From NIS.2 to Noospheric Civilization] // *Economic Revival of Russia*, 2(52): 17-21.

Bodrunov S.D. (2018a). *Noonomika [Noonomy]*. Moscow; St. Petersburg; London: Kulturnaya revolutsiya [In Russian].

Bodrunov S.D. (2018b). Ot ZOO k NOO: chelovek, obschestvo i proizvodstvo v usloviyakh novoj tekhnologicheskoj revolyutsii [From ZOO to NOO: Man, Society and Production in the Conditions of a New Technological Revolution] // *Voprosy Filosofii*, Vol. 7: 109–118 [In Russian].

Bodrunov S.D. (2019). *Obschaya teoriya noonomiki [General Theory of Noonomy].* Moscow: Kulturnaya revolutsiya [In Russian].

Bodrunov S.D. (2020à). K voprosu o sravnitelnom analize teorii noonomiki i sotsializma [On Comparative Analysis of Noonomy and Socialism Theories] // *Problems in Political Economy,* Vol. 3: 52–66 [In Russian].

Bodrunov S.D. (2020b). *Noonomika: trayektoriya globalnoj transformatrii [Noonomy: the Trajectory of Global Transformation].* Moscow: S.Y. Witte Institute for New Industrial Development (INID); Kulturnaya revolutsiya [In Russian].

Bodrunov S.D. (2020ñ). Sotsializatsiya: ternistij put k noonomike [Socialization: thorny path towards the noonomy] / In Materials of International scientific seminar of S.Y. Witte Institute for New Industrial Development (INID) "Socialozation of economy: human as the product and active subject of historical process" (October 26, 2020) // *Economic Revival of Russia*, 4(66): 5-12 [In Russian].

Bodrunov S. (2021). *Chto takoye noonomika?* [*What is noonomy?*] / In Bodrunov S.D. (Ed.). (2021). A(O)Ontology of Noonomy: the Fourth Technological Revolution and Its Economic, Social and Humanitarian Consequences. St. Petersburg: S.Y. Witte Institute for New Industrial Development (INID), pp. 19-92 [In Russian].

Bodrunov S. (2021*[2]). Noonomy as the Material Basis for a Prospective Humanitarian Model of Public Order // *Sustainability.* 13. 1454. https://doi.org/10.3390/su13031454.

Bodrunov S.D. (2021à). Genezis noonomiki: NTP, diffuziya sobstvennosti, sotsializatsiya obschestva, solidarizm [Genesis of Noonomy: Scientific and Technological Progress, Diffusion of Ownership, Socialization of Society, Solidarism] // Economic Revival of Russia, 1(67): 5–14 [In Russian].

Bodrunov S.D. (2021b). Noonomika kak strategicheskij proekt [Noonomy as a Strategical Project] // *Strategizing: Theory and Practice*, 1(2): 136–150 [In Russian].

Bodrunov S.D. (2021c). Ot homo ekonomikus – k homo sapiens [From Homo Economicus – to Homo Sapiens] // *Voprosy Filosofii*, 12: 18-31 [In Russian].

Bodrunov S.D. (2022a). K voprosu ob imperativakh formirovaniya nooobschestva: desimulyatsizatsiya potrebnostej [Questioning the imperatives of the noosociety formation: de-simulation of wants] // *Noonomy and Noosociety. Almanac of Scientific Works of the S.Y. Witte INID,* 1(4): 13-20) [In Russian].

Bodrunov S.D. (2022b). Noonomika i noosphera: vzaimosvyaz i razlichiya kontseptsij [Noonomy and Noosphere: Interrelation and Differences of Concepts] // *Vestnik Instituta ekonomiki Rossijskoj akademii nauk,* 1: 7-31 [In Russian].

Bodrunov S.D. (2022c). Nooobschestvo: integralnoye odnorodnoye obschestvo na baze nootsennostej, polilogiya i postgosudarstvo (tezisi k kollokviumu Instituta novogo industrialnogo razvitiya im. S.Yu. Vitte, 02 dekabrya 2021 g.) [Noosociety: an integral homogeneous society based on noovalues, polylogy and poststate (abstracts to the colloquium of S.Y. Witte Institute for New Industrial Development (INID), December 2, 2021)] // *Noonomy and Noosociety. Almanac of Scientific Works of the S.Y. Witte INID*, 1(2): 148-151 [In Russian].

Bodrunov S.D. (2022d). Ot ekonomicheskikh interesov – k nootsennostyam [From Economic Interests – to NooValues] // *Voprosy Filosofii*, 7: 15-26 [In Russian].

Bodrunov S.D. (2022e). Ot noonomiki – k noosphere? [From noonomy to noosphere?] // *Noonomy and Noosociety. Almanac of Scientific Works of the S.Y. Witte INID,* 1(3): 36-47 [In Russian].

Bodrunov S.D. (2022f). Sotsializatsiya ekonomiki: prioriteti sovremennogo razvitiya Rossii (dpklad na Vserossijskom ekonomicheskom sobranii, 11.11.2022 g.) [Socialization of the economy: priorities of modern development of Russia (Speech for National Economic Assembly, November 11, 2022)] // *Economic Revival of Russia,* 4(74): 5-8 [In Russian].

Bodrunov S.D. (2022g). Sovremennij tekhnologicheskij perekhod i yego sotsialno-ekonomicheskiye posledstviya [Modern technological shift and its socio-economic aftermaths] // *Economic Revival of Russia,* 2(72): 35-43 [In Russian].

Bodrunov S. (2023*). *Noonomy: the Trajectory of Global Transformation.* Boston: Academic Studies Press.

Bodrunov S.D. (2023a). Strategiya perekhoda k novomu mirokhozyajstvennomu ukladu i nooobschestvu: industrialnij aspekt [Strategy of transition to a new world economic order and noosociety: industrial aspect] // *Russian Journal of Industrial Economics*, 16(2): 135–140 [In Russian].

Bodrunov S.D. (2023b). Tvorcheskaya deyatelnost kak otkritaya problema: podkhod noonomiki kak metateorii [Creative activity as an open problem: Noonomy Approach as a metatheory] // *Noonomy and Noosociety. Almanac of Scientific Works of the S.Y. Witte INID*, 2(1): 25-34 [In Russian].

Bodrunov S.D. (Ed.). (2015). Integratsiya proizvodstva, nauki i obrazovanija i reindustrializatsija rossijskoj ekonomiki [Integration of Production, Science and Education and Reindustrialization of the Russian Economy]. Proceedings of the International Congress "Revival of Production, Science and Education in Russia: Challenges and Solutions". Moscow: LENAND [In Russian].

Bodrunov S.D. (Ed). (2019). New Industrial Society: origins, reality, future. Noonomy. Vol. III. (Selected materials of seminars, publications and events of the S.Y. Witte Institute for New Industrial Development (INID) on the topic of the concept of new industrial society of the second generation and nooindustrial development of society). (2019). / Collection of scientific works. St. Petersburg: S.Y. Witte Institute for New Industrial Development (INID). (In Russian).

Bodrunov S.D. and Arkhipova, V.V. (2024). *The role of BRICS in the process of global nootransition* / Scientific report. St. Petersburg: S.Y. Witte Institute for New Industrial Development (INID) [In Russian].

Bodrunov S.D., Desai R. and Freeman A. (2022). *On the other side of the global crisis: Noonomy, creativity, geopolitical economy.* St. Petersburg: S.Y. Witte Institute for New Industrial Development [In Russian].

Bodrunov S.D. and Galbraith J.K. (2017). *New Industrial Revolution and Inequality Issues: Study guide.* Moscow: Plekhanov Russian University of Economics.

Bodrunov S.D. and Glazyev S.Yu. (2023). *Regularities of the Noonomy Foundations Formation as Future Social Order: To Know and Operate.* St. Petersburg: S.Y. Witte Institute for New Industrial Development (INID); Moscow: Centercatalog [In Russian].

Bodrunov S.D. and Lopatin V.N. (2014). *Strategy and Policy of Reindustrialization for Innovative Development of Russia.* Moscow, St. Petersburg: S.Y. Witte Institute for New Industrial Development (INID) [In Russian].

Bondarenko T.A. (2009). Communication in Virtual World of Internet // *Vestnik DGTU,* Vol. 9, 4(43): 728-735 [In Russian].

Bourdieu P. (2005). *The social structures of the economy.* Malden: Polity.

Bourgeois L. (1896). *Solidarité.* Paris: Colin.

Boyes H., Hallaq B., Cunningham J. and Watson T. (2018). The industrial internet of things (IIoT): An analysis framework // *Computers in Industry,* Vol. 101, October: 1–12.

Brandenburger A.M. and Nalebuff B.J. (1996). *Co-opetition.* New York: Doubleday.

Broudy D. and Arakaki M. (2020). Who wants to be a slave? The technocratic convergence of humans and data // *Frontiers in Communication*, 5(37).

Burnham J. (1941). *The Managerial Revolution: What Is Happening in the World.* New York: John Day Company.

Butorina Î.V. (Ed). (2011). *European Integration: textbook [Evropejskaya integratsiya: uchebnik].* Moscow: Izdatelskij dom "Delovaya literatura" [In Russian].

Buzgalin A.V. (1996). *The future of communism.* Moscow: OLMA-PRESS [In Russian].

Buzgalin A.V. and Kolganov A.I. (1990). *On the other side of alienation (collection of political economic hypotheses).* Moscow: Lomonosov Moscow State University Moscow [In Russian].

Buzgalin A.V. and Kolganov A.I. (2012a). The Market of Simulacra: a Look Through the Prism of Classical Political Economy // *Philosophy of Economy*, 2–3.

Buzgalin A.V. and Kolganov A.I. (2012b). The Market of Simulacra: a Look Through the Prism of Classical Political Economy // *Alternatives*, No. 2: 65-91.

Chase S. (1932). *A New Deal.* New York: The Macmillan Company.

Cheng Enfu and Gao Siyang (2021). Knowledge-Based Economy as a form of noonomy and its socio-economic impact. In Bodrunov S.D. (Ed.). (2021). A(O)Ontology of Noonomy: the Fourth Technological Revolution and Its Economic, Social and Humanitarian Consequences. St. Petersburg: S.Y. Witte Institute for New Industrial Development (INID), pp. 178–203 [In Russian].

Clayton P.A. (1969). An empirical test of a new theory of human needs // *Organizational Behavior and Human Performance*, 4(2): 142–75.

Conlisk J. (1996). Why bounded rationality? // *Journal of Economic Literature*, 34(2): 669–700.

Connolly W. (2017). *Facing the planetary: Entangled humanism and the politics of swarming.* Durham, London: Duke University Press.

Connolly W. (2019). *Climate machines, fascist drives, and truth.* Durham: Duke University Press.

Correspondence of Vernadsky V.I and Florensky P.A. (1989) // *New World*, no. 2: 194–203 [In Russian].

Dana J.D. (1863). *Manual of Geology: Treating of the Principles of the Science, with Special Reference to American Geological History.* Philadelphia: Theodore Bliss & Co; London: Trübner & Co.

Desai R. (2013). *Geopolitical Economy: After US Hegemony, Globalization and Empire*. London: Pluto Press.

Desai R. (2013). Geopolitical Economy: After US Hegemony, Globalization and Empire, Pluto Press, London [Russian Translation 2020].

Desmet P. and Fokkinga S. (2020). Beyond Maslow's pyramid: Introducing a typology of thirteen fundamental needs for human-centered design // *Multimodal Technologies and Interaction,* 4(3). https://doi.org/10.3390/mti4030038.

Dezfouli A., Nock R. and Dayan P. (2020). Adversarial Vulnerabilities of Human Decision-making // *PNAS*. Vol. 117(46): 29221–29228. URL: https://doi.org/10.1073/pnas.2016921117

Drucker P. (1969). *The Age of Discontinuity; Guidelines to Our Changing Society*. New York: Harper and Row.

Drucker P.F. (2011). *Post-Capitalist Society*. New York: Routledge.

Dymshits M. (2006). Buyer Manipulation. Moscow: Omega-L [In Russian].

Fersman A.E. (1934). *Geochemistry*, Vol. 2. Leningrad: Publ. Academy of Sciences of the USSR [In Russian].

Foley D.K. (2004). Rationality and ideology in economics // *Social Research,* 71(2): 329–342.

Frank M., Roehrig P. and Pring B. (2017). *What to do when machines do everything: How to get ahead in a world of AI, algorithms, bots, and big data.* Hoboken: Wiley.

Freeman A. (2021). Mental Objects as a Productive Force: Towards a Critique of Noonomy. In Bodrunov S.D. (Ed.). (2021). A(O)Ontology of Noonomy: the Fourth Technological Revolution and Its Economic, Social and Humanitarian Consequences. St. Petersburg: S.Y. Witte Institute for New Industrial Development (INID), pp. 207–265 [In Russian].

Fukuyama F. (2015). *The end of history and the last man*. Moscow: AST Publ. [In Russian].

Galbraith J.K. (1967). *The new industrial state.* Boston: Houghton Mifflin.

Galbraith J.K. (1967). *The New Industrial State*. London: Hamish Hamilton.

Galbraith J.K. (2017). *New Industrial Revolution and Inequality Issues: Study guide*. Moscow: Plekhanov Russian University of Economics.

Giddings F.H. (1897). *The Theory of Socialization: A Syllabus of Sociological Principles for the Use of College and University Classes.* New York: The Macmillan Company.

Giddens A. (1999). *Sociology.* Moscow: Editorial URSS [In Russian].

Glazyev S.Yu. (2010). The Prospects of Becoming the World's New VI Technological Mode // *MIR (Modernizatsiya. Innovatsii. Razvitiye)*, 1(2): 4-10 [In Russian].

Glazyev S.Yu. (2016a). National economy structures in the global economic development // *Economics and Mathematical Methods*, 52(2): 3–29 [In Russian].

Glazyev S.Yu. (2016b). *The Last World War. The U.S. to Move and Lose* ("The Izborsk Club Collection"). Moscow: Knizhny Mir Publ.

Glazyev S.Yu. (2018). *The Burst into the Future. Russia in the New Technological and World Economic Modes*. Moscow: Knizhnij Mir [In Russian].

Glazyev S.Yu. (2021). *Beyond the Horizon of the End of History*. Moscow: Prospekt Publ. [In Russian].

Glazyev S.Yu. and Kharitonov V.V. (Eds.). (2009). *Nanotechnologies as a Key to a New Technological Mode of the Economy*. Moscow: Trovant [In Russian].

Grachev G. and Melnik I. (1999). *Personality Manipulation: Organization, Methods and Technologies of Information and Psychological Impact*. M.: RAS Institute of Philosophy [In Russian].

Green D.P. and Fox J. (2007). *Rational choice theory / The SAGE handbook of social science methodology* / Editors W. Outhwaite and S.P. Turner. London: Sage.

Grinberg R.S. (2016). Smart Factories Need Smart People and Smart Economy // *Economic Revival of Russia*, 4(50).

Greenwood M. (2019). 2018 Was a Strong Year for the Global 3D Printer Market. URL: https://www.engineering.com/AdvancedManufacturing/ArticleID/18279/2018-Was-a-Strong-Year-for-theGlobal-3D-Printer-Market.aspx

Habermas J. (2001). *Die Einbeziehung des Anderen: Studien zur politischen Theorie*. St. Petersburg: Nauka [In Russian].

Hamilton C. and Grinevald J. (2015). Was the Anthropocene anticipated? // *The Anthropocene Review*. Vol. 2. Issue 1: 59-72.

Haria R. (2017). Europe's First 3D Printed Pre-Fab House Completed by AMTSPETSAVIA // 3D Printing Industry: The Authority on Additive Manufacturing, October 25. URL: https://3dprintingindustry.com/news/europes-first-3d-printed-pre-fab-housecompleted-russias-amt-spetsavia-123245/

Harris T. (2016). How Technology is Hijacking Your Mind – from a Magician and Google Design Ethicist // *Medium. Thrive Global*. URL: https://

medium.com/thrive-global/howtechnology-hijacks-peoples-minds-from-a-magician-and-google-s-design-ethicist-56d62ef5edf3#.4mpjo1tw.

Hegel G. (1993). *Lectures on the History of Philosophy (1833).* Vol. 1. St. Petersburg: Nauka [In Russian].

Heilbroner R. (1988). *Behind the veil of economics: Essays in the worldly philosophy.* New York: W.W. Norton.

Hollis Ì. and Nell E.J. (1975). *Rational economic man: A philosophical critique of neo-classical economics.* London, New York: Cambridge University Press.

Huang Y. (2019). The construction of hyper-reality of advertisement in consumption culture // *Journal of Asian Research*, 3(2): 190–205.

Humboldt A. (1889). Ansichten der Natur / Alexander von Humboldt. Gesammelte Werke. Band 11. Stuttgart: Verlag der J.G. Cotta'schen Buchhandlung Nachfolger.

Immerman G. (2020). Emerging Industry 4.0 Technologies with Real-World Examples. Machinemetrics, Industry 4.0. URL: https://www.machinemetrics.com/blog/industry-4-0-technologies

Inozemtsev V.L. (1998). Outside of the economic society: Post-industrial theories and post-economic trends in the modern world. Moscow: Academia: Nauka [In Russian].

Inozemtsev V.L. (2020). Post-industrial Society / Humanitarian Encyclopedia: Concepts / Center for Humanitarian Technologies, 2002-2020. URL: https://gtmarket.ru/concepts/7368)/

Issberner L.-R., Léna P. (2018). Anthropocene: the vital challenges of a scientific debate / The UNESCO Courier 2. URL: https://en.unesco.org/courier/2018-2/anthropocene-vital-challenges-scientific-debate

Jameson F. (1991). *Postmodernism or the cultural logic of late capitalism.* Durham: Duke University Press.

Karlovich I.A. (2004). Regularities in Technogenesis Development in the Structure of Geographical Shell and Its Geological Consequences / PhD thesis. Vladimir State Pedagogical University.

Keynes M. (2009). Economic opportunities of our grandchildren // *Issue of Economics*, No. 6 [In Russian].

Kheyfets B.A. (2023). À new model of international economic integration / Scientific report. M.: Institute of Economics of the Russian Academy of Sciences [In Russian].

Kleimenova L. (2020). The New York Times: kak kompanii sledyat za nashej zhiznyu cherez prilozheniya [The New York Times: how companies monitor our lives through apps] / RBK. URL: https://trends.rbc.ru/trends/industry/5e1888919a79472a692abf75 [In Russian].

Knight R. (2012). Biodiversity loss: How accurate are the numbers? / BBC News. URL: https://www.bbc.com/news/magazine-17826898

Korogodin V.I. and Korogodina V.L. (2000). *Information as the basis of life. Dubna:* Phoenix Publishing Center [In Russian].

Konotopov M.V. (2008). *Economic History of the World*: In 6 Volumes. Vol. 1. M.: KNORUS Publ. [In Russian].

Korotayev A. and LePoire D.J. (2020). *The 21st century singularity and global futures: A big history perspective.* Cham: Springer.

Kovalchuk M.V. (2011). Convergence of Science and Technology – a Breakthrough in the Future // *Nanotechnologies in Russia*, Vol. 6, No. 1–2.

Kovalchuk M.V., Naraikin O.S. and Yatsishina E.B. (2011). Convergence of Science and Technology and Creation of New Noosphere // *Nanotechnologies in Russia*, Vol. 6, No. 9–10.

Kudrin B.I. (1981). Studies of Technical Systems as Communities of Technocenosis Pieces / in System Studies. Methodological Issues. Annals 1980. Moscow: Nauka.

Kudrin B.I. (1980). Scientific and technical progress and the formation of technocenoses // *ECO*, 8: 15–28 [In Russian].

Kudrin B.I. (2003). *Technogenesis* / in Mazur I.I., Chumakov A.N. (Eds.). (2003). Global Studies Encyclopedia. Moscow: Raduga Publishers.

Kvint V.L. (2015). Development of strategy: Scanning and forecasting of external and internal environments // *Administrative Consulting*, 79(7): 6–11 [In Russian].

Kvint V.L. (2018). To the analysis of the formation of a strategy as a science // *Vestnik TSEHMI [Bulletin of the Central Institute of Economics and Mathematics]*, 1 [In Russian].

Kvint V.L. (2019). *The concept of strategizing.* Vol. 1. St. Petersburg: SZIU RANKhiGS [In Russian].

Kvint V.L. (2020). *The concept of strategizing*. Vol. 2. St. Petersburg: SZIU RANKhiGS [In Russian].

Kvint V.L. and Bodrunov S.D. (2021). *Strategirovanie transformatsii obshchestva: znanie, tekhnologii, noonomika [Strategic transformation of society: knowledge, technology, and noonomy]*. St. Petersburg: INIR im. S.Yu. Vitte [In Russian].

Kvint V.L. and Bodrunov S.D. (2023). *Strategizing societal transformation: Knowledge, technologies, and noonomy.* Oakville, MO: Apple Academic Press.

Kvint V.L., Khvorostyanaya A.S. and Sasaev N.I. (2020). Advanced technologies in strategizing // *Economics and Management*, 26(11): 1170–1179 [In Russian].

Lamarck J.-B. (1820). *Système analytique des connaissances positives de l'homme.* Paris: Belin.

Laszlo E. (2002). Macroshift: Navigating the Transformation to a Sustainable World. San Francisco: Berrett-Koehler Publishers [Russian Translation].

Le Conte J. (1877). On Critical Periods in the History of the Earth, and Their Relation to Evolution; on the Quaternary as Such a Period // *American Naturalist.* Vol. 11. No. 9: 540–557.

Lenin V.I. (1961). Notes on Plekhanov's Second Draft Programme / in *Collected Works*, Vol. 6. Moscow: Progress Publishers.

Leontiev A.N. (1975). *Activity, Consciousness and Personality*. Moscow: Politizdat.

Le Roy E. (1927). *L'exigence idé aliste et le fait de l'é volution.* Paris: Boivin & Cie.

Leroux P. (1840). *De L'humanité de son Principe, et de son Avenir ou se Trouve Exposée, la Vraie Définition de la Religion et ou l'on Explique le Sens, la Suite, et L'enchaînement du Mosaisme et du Christianisme. Tome 1.* Paris: Perrotin, Éditeur-Libraire.

Levine D.P. and Abu Turab Rizvi S. (2005). *Poverty, work, and freedom: Political economy and the moral order.* Cambridge: Cambridge University Press.

Levit G.S. (2000). The Biosphere and the Noosphere. Theories of V. I. Vernadsky and P. Teilhard de Chardin: A methodological essay // *Archives Internationales d'Histoire des Sciences*. Vol. 50. No. 144: 160–177.

Libman A.M. and Kheyfets B.A. (2011). *Modeli regionalnoy integratsii* (*Models of regional integration*). Moscow: Ekonomika [In Russian].

Lukov V.A. (2014). On the theory of socialization of Franklin Giddings / Information humanitarian portal "Knowledge. Understanding. Skill". 3 (May–June). URL: http://www.zpu-journal.ru/e-zpu/2014/3/Lukovs_Theory-Socialization-Giddings].

Lvov D.S. and Glazyev S.Y. (1986). Theoretical and Application Aspects of the STP Management // *Economics and Mathematical Methods*, 5.

Machlup F. (1962). *The Production and Distribution of Knowledge in the United States*. Princeton: Princeton University Press.

Malakooti B. (2013). *Operations and Production Systems with Multiple Objectives.* New York: Wiley.

Marcuse H. (2002). *Eros and Civilization. One-Dimensional Man: Studies in the Ideology of Advanced Industrial Society.* M.: AST Publ. [In Russian].

Mareev S.N. and Mareeva E.V. (2003). *History of Philosophy* (General Course): Textbook. Moscow: Academic Project Publ. [In Russain].

Marx Ê. (1954). Economic manuscripts 1857-1859 / Marx K., Engels F. Writings. Vol. 46. Issue II. Moscow: Politizdat.

Marx K. (1955). *Manifesto of the Communist Party* / Marx K., Engels F., Vol. 4. M.: Gosudarstvennoye Izdatelstvo politicheskoj literaturi [In Russian].

Marx K. (1978). *Critique of the Gotha Program* / in Tucker R.C. (Ed.). (1978).The Marx-Engels Reader, 2nd edn. New York: Norton.

Marx K. (1982). *Capital: A Critique of Political Economy*. Vol. 1. New York: Penguin Books.

Marx K. (1993). *Grundrisse*. London: Penguin.

Marx K. (2011). A Contribution to the Critique of Political Economy. Marx, Engels – creators of scientific socialism. Moscow: LIBROKOM. 176 P. [In Russian].

Marx K. and Engels F. (1955). *German ideology*. Vol. 3. Moscow: Gospolitizdat [In Russian].

Marx K. and Engels F. (1974). *The German Ideology*. London: Lawrence & Wishart.

Marx K. and Engels F. (1978). *Manifesto of the Communist Party* / in Tucker R.C. (Ed.). (1978).The Marx-Engels Reader, 2nd edn. New York: Norton.

Maslow A.H. (1943). A Theory of Human Motivation // *Psychological Review*, 50: 370–396.

Maslow A.H. (1954). *Motivation and personality*. New York: Harper and Brothers.

Masuda Y. (1981). *The Information Society as Post-Industrial Society*. Washington, DC: World Future Society.

McCleskey J.A. and Ruddell L. (2020). Taking a step back – Maslow's theory of motivation: A Christian critical perspective // *Journal of Biblical Integration in Business*, 23(1): 6–16.

McKinnon A.M. (2013). Ideology and the market metaphor in rational choice theory of religion: A rhetorical critique of "religious economies" // *Critical Sociology*, 39(4): 529–543.

Meadows D.H. et al. (1972). *The limits to growth: A report for the Club of Rome's project on the predicament of mankind*. New York: Universe Books.

Medvedev Yu. (2017). A life of six letters. The first bacterium with synthetic DNA has been created / *Rossiyskaya Gazeta* – Federal Issue No.7448 (282).

Mensch G. (1975). *Das technologische Patt: Innovationen überwinden die Depression*. Frankfurt a. M.: Umschau Verlag Breidenstein.

Menshikov S.M. and Klimenko L.A. (2014). *Long Waves in the Economy: When Society Changes Its Skin*. Moscow: LENAND.

Menshutkin V.V. and Levchenko V.F. (2017). A Stochastic Cellular Automata-Based Model of Evolution of the Anthroposphere // *Biosfera*, 9(4): 275–285 [In Russian].

Mironov V.V. (2011). Philosophy: Textbook. M.: Prospect Publ. [In Russian].

Momdzhyan K.Kh. (2019). On the role of material production // *Economic Revival of Russia*, 4, pp. 37-43 [In Russian].

Morris J. (2021). Simulacra in the age of social media: Baudrillard as the prophet of fake news // *Journal of Communication Inquiry*, 45(4): 319–336.

Murray J. (1912). *The depths of the ocean.* London: Macmillan.

Murray J. (1923). *The Depths of the Ocean.* Odessa: Gosizdat Ukrainy [In Russian].

Novikov Y.Y., Rezhabek B.G. (2017). The Contribution of E. Le Roy and P. Teilhard de Chardin to the Development of the Concept of the Noosphere. URL: http://www.nffedorov.ru/w/images/3/36/Lerua.pdf.

Ohno T. and Mito S. (1988). *Just-In-Time for Today and Tomorrow*. New York: Productivity Press.

Perez C. (2002). *Technological Revolutions and Financial Capital: The Dynamics of Bubbles and Golden Ages.* Northhampton, MA: E. Elgar Pub.

Perkins J. (2007). *The secret story of the American empire*. NY: Dutton.

Platonov S. (1989). *After communism*. Moscow: Molodaya Gvardiya [In Russian].

Podolinsky S. (1880). Le Socialisme et l'unité des forces physiques // *La Revue Socialiste.* Vol. 8: 353–365.

Pride V. and Medvedev D.A. (2022). Phenomenon of NBIC-Convergency: Reality and Expectations. Russian Transhumanist Movement. URL: http://transhumanism-russia.ru/content/view/498/110/ (accessed October 15, 2022).

Prosvirinov A. (2012). New Technological Revolution Is Sweeping Past Us / PRoAtom, December 11. URL: http://proatom.ru/modules.php?name=News&file=article& sid=4189.

Prozorov L.L. (2012). Whether There Was the Vernadsky's Concept on 'Noosphere'? (A Brief Historical Analysis) // *Prostranstvo i Vremya*, 4(10): 223–229 [In Russian].

Richter F. (2014). The Rise of the Sharing Economy // *Statista.* URL: https://www.statista.com/chart/2323/the-rise-of-the-sharing-economy/.

Reisach U. (2021). The responsibility of social media in times of societal and political manipulation // *European Journal of Operational Research*, 291(3): 906–917.

Rezhabek B.G. (2015). The Doctrine of the Noosphere for a Wide Range of Readers. Moscow: INRI Publ. [In Russian].

Roco M. and Bainbridge W. (Eds.). (2003). Converging Technologies for Improving Human Performance: Nanotechnology, Biotechnology, Information Technology and Cognitive Science. Dordrecht: Springer.

Rubin P.H. and Capra C.M. (2011). The evolutionary psychology of economics / Applied evolutionary psychology / Editor: S.C. Roberts. New York: Oxford University Press. https://doi.org/10.1093/acprof:oso/9780199586073.003.0002.

Rubinstein A.A. (2011). Theory of Patronized Goods: Inefficient and Efficient Equilibria // *Voprosy Ekonomiki*, 3: 65-87 [In Russian]. https://doi.org/10.32609/0042-8736-2011-3-65-87.

Rumyantsev A.M. (Ed.) (1985). *Political Economy. Textbook.* Moscow: Politizdat [In Russian].

Sakaiya T. (1991). *The Knowledge-Value Revolution or a History of the Future.* Tokyo, New York: Kodansha International.

Schmitt C. (2006). *The Nomos of the Earth in the International Law of Jus Publicum Europaeum.* Candor, NY: Telos Press.

Schram S.F. and Caterino B. (2006). *Making political science matter: Debating knowledge, research, and method.* New York, London: New York University Press.

Schumpeter J.A. (1939). *Business Cycles: A Theoretical, Historical and Statistical Analysis of the Capitalist Process.* New York – Toronto – London: McGraw-Hill Book Company.

Schumpeter J.A. (1995). *Capitalism, Socialism, and Democracy.* Moscow: Ekonomika [In Russian].

Schumpeter J.A. (2017). *The Theory of Economic Development.* New York: Routledge.

Schwab K. (2016). *The Fourth Industrial Revolution.* Geneva: World Economic Forum.

Schwab K. and Malleret T. (2020). Covid-19: The Great Reset. World Economic Forum, Geneva. URL: http://reparti.free.fr/schwab2020.pdf.

Sen A. (1999). *Development as freedom.* New York: Alfred A. Knopf.

Shaheen S., Cohen A. and Jaffee M. (2018). Innovative Mobility: Carsharing Outlook / Berkeley University of California. Institute of Transportation

Studies at UC Berkeley, UC Berkeley Transportation Sustainability Research Center. URL: https://escholarship.org/uc/item/49j961wb.

Shokhin V.K. (2010). Axiology / The New Philosophical Encyclopedia in 4 volumes. Vol. 1. Moscow: Mysl, pp. 62–67 [In Russian].

Simic S. (2007). Need, not greed / *The Guardian*, January 25. URL: https://www.theguardian.com/commentisfree/2007/jan/25/post997.

Skobeeva V. (2016). The Sixth Great Extinction / *Vokrug sveta*. URL: http://www.vokrugsveta.ru/article/233607/

Smart B. (Ed.). (2011). *Post Industrial Society* / Four-Volume Set edition. London: SAGE Publications.

Smil V. (2013). *Making the Modern World: Materials and Dematerialization.* Hoboken: Wiley.

Smith A. (1962). *An Inquiry into the Nature and Causes of the Wealth of Nations.* Moscow: Sotsyekgiz [In Russian].

Smith K. (2002). What is the 'Knowledge Economy'? Knowledge Intensity and Distributed Knowledge Bases / United Nations University Institute for New Technologies Discussion Paper Series #20026, June.

Sorokin A.V. (2009) *Theory of Social Wealth. The Foundations of Micro- and Macroeconomics. Textbook.* Moscow: Economics [In Russian].

Sorokin A.V. (2020). On developing the concept of new industrial society of the second generation and noonomy // *Economic Revival of Russia,* 3(65): 33-45 [In Russian].

Sorotskii M.S. (2012). Virtual Communication: Social Networks – Loneliness or Frankness? // *Nauchnye Vedomosti BelGU, Seriya Filosofiya, Sotsiologiya, Pravo,* 14(133), Issue 12: 227–232 [In Russian].

Spelda P. and Stritecky V. (2020). The future of human-artificial intelligence nexus and its environmental costs // *Futures.* Vol. 117. https://doi.org/10.1016/j.futures.2020.102531

Spohrer J. (2003). NBICS (Nano-Bio-Info-Cogno-Socio) Convergence to Improve Human Performance: Opportunities and Challenges / in: Roco M., Bainbridge W. (Eds.). (2003). *Converging Technologies for Improving Human Performance: Nanotechnology, Biotechnology, Information Technology and Cognitive Science.* Dordrecht: Springer.

Stepin V.S. (2015). Rational Interests and Universal Values: The Problem of Globalization Strategies / Modern Global Challenges and National Interests: XV International Likhachev Scientific Readings. St. Petersburg: SPGUP, pp. 162–165 [In Russian].

Stoppani A. (1873). *The Anthropozoic Era: Excerpts from Corso di Geologia.* Miliano: G. Ber-nardoni E. G. Brigola. http://www.scapegoatjournal.org/docs/05/SG_Excess_346-353_P_STOPPANI.pdf

Strubell E., Ganesh A. and McCallum A. (2019). Energy and policy considerations for deep learning in NLP / Proceedings of the 57th Annual Meeting of the Association for Computational Linguistics. Florence. pp. 3645–3650.

Suess E. (1875). *Die Entstehung der Alpen.* Wien: Wilhelm Braumüller.

Susser D., Roessler B. and Nissenbaum H. (2019). Technology, autonomy, and manipulation // *Internet Policy Review*, 8(2).

Svegander M. (2019). The Carsharing Telematics Market – 3rd Edition. Product Sheet // *Berg Insight.* M2M Research Series. URL: http://www.berginsight.com/ReportPDF/ProductSheet/bi-carsharing3-ps.pdf.

Sziebig G. and Korondi P. (2015). Effect of Robot Revolution Initiative in Europe – Cooperation Possibilities for Japan and Europe / IFAC-PapersOnLine 48.19.

Taleb N.N. (2007). The Black Swan: The Impact of the Highly Improbable. New York, Random House.

Tapscott D. and Tapscott A. (2018). *Blockchain Revolution: How the Technology behind Bitcoin and Other Cryptocurrencies Is Changing the World.* New York: Portfolio.

Tarde J.-G. (1890). *Les Lois de l'imitation: étude sociologique.* Paris: Félix Alcan.

Tavrovsky Y. (2023). BRICS – startup that has become successful [BRICS – startap, stavshiy uspekhom] / Izborsky club [In Russian]. URL: https://izborsk-club.ru/24650?ysclid=lt41rmd5xu974705646.

Teilhard de Chardin Pierre (1925, 1957). L'Hominisation. Introduction à une étude scientifique du Phénomène humain, in: Pierre Teilhard de Chardin Oeuvres, t. 3: La vision du passé. Paris: Du Seuil, pp. 75–111.

Tillema S. and van der Steen M. (2015). Co-Existing Concepts of Management Control: The Containment of Tensions Due to the Implementation of Lean Production // *Management Accounting Research*, 27, June.

Toffler A. (2003) Powershift: Knowledge, Wealth, and Violence at the Edge of the 21st Century. Moscow: AST [In Russian].

Toffler E. (2003). *Metamorphoses of power.* Moscow: AST [In Russian].

Toloraya G.D., Borzova A.Yu., Dezhina I.G., Reinhardt R.O., Nikolskaya M.V. and Krasnova G.A. (2023). Promising areas of scientific cooperation: BRICS countries [Perspectivnyiye napravleniya nauchnogo sotrudnichestva: strani BRICS] / Report No. 90/2023. Moscow: NP RSMD [In Russian].

Trubetskova I.L. (2010). From biosphere to noosphere: Vladimir Vernadsky's theoretical system as a conceptual framework for universal sustainability education. University of New Hampshire, Durham. Doctoral Dissertations. 612. URL: https://scholars.unh.edu/dissertation/612.

Tsagolov N.A. (Ed.) (1974). *Course of Political Economy*. In 2 V. Vol. 2. Socialism. Textbook. Moscow: Economics [In Russian].

Tsvetkova M., Yasseri T., Meyer E.T., Pickering J.B., Engen V., Walland P., Luders M., Følstad A. and Bravos G. (2015). Understanding Human Machine Networks: A Cross-Disciplinary Survey // *E-Print*. Cornell University Library / ACM Computing Surveys 50, no. 1: 1–35.

Umov N.A. (1916). *Physical and mechanical model of living matter* / Umov N.A. Collected Works. Vol. 3. M.: Moscow Society of Naturalists, pp. 184–200 [In Russian].

Ushkalova D.I. (2016). Models of economic integration and their typology // *Vestnik IE RAN*, 3: 158-170 [In Russian].

Usselman S.W. (2013). Research and Development in the United States since 1900: An Interpretive History // Economic History Workshop, Yale University, November 11.

Veblen T. (1899). *The Theory of the Leisure Class: An Economic Study of Institutions*. New York: Macmillan.

Veblen T. (1936 [1921]). *The Engineers and the Price System*. New York: Viking.

Veile J.W., Kiel D., Müller J.M. and Voigt K.-I. (2020). Lessons learned from Industry 4.0 implementation in the German manufacturing industry // *Journal of Manufacturing Technology Management*, 31(5): 977–997.

Vernadsky V.I. (1924). *La Géochimie*. Paris: Librairie Félix Alcan.

Vernadsky V.I. (1927). Ideas on the modern value of the history of knowledge. Paper read at the first meeting of the Commission on the History of Knowledge. Proceedings of the Commission on the History of Knowledge. L.: AN SSSR [In Russian].

Vernadsky V.I. (1939). On the fundamental material and energy difference between living and inert natural bodies of the biosphere / Problems of biogeochemistry, issue II. L.: AN SSSR [In Russian].

Vernadsky V.I. (1944). A Few Words about Noosphere // *Uspekhi sovremennoi biologii*, 18(2): 113–120 [In Russian].

Vernadsky V.I. (1991). *Scientific Thought as a Planetary Phenomenon*. M.: Nauka [In Russian].

Vernadsky V.I. (1997). *Scientific Thought as a Planetary Phenomenon*. Moscow: Nongovernmental Ecological V.I. Vernadsky Foundation.

Volodenkov S.V. (2022). The World Around Us as a Simulated Reality: On the Issue of the Contemporary Worldview's Communication Foundations // *Zhurnal politicheskikh issledovaniy*, 6(3): 20-40. DOI: 10.12737/2587-6295-2022-6-3-20-40 [In Russian].

Waddell W.H. and Bodek N. (2005). *Rebirth of American Industry*. Vancouver: PCS Press.

Wallerstein I. (1982). *World-Systems Analysis: Theory and Methodology*. Beverly Hills: Sage.

Wallenstein J. and Shelat U. (2017). Hopping Aboard the Sharing Economy / Boston Consulting Group, Henderson Institute. URL: http://image-src.bcg.com/Images/BCG-Hopping-Aboard-the-Sharing-Economy-Aug-2017_tcm104-168558.pdf.

Wyatt I.D. and Hecker D.E. (2006.). Occupational Changes during the 20th Century // *Monthly Labor Review*, 129(3): 35–57.

Yadgarov Y.S. (2007). *History of Economic Thought*: Textbook. Moscow: INFRA-M Publ. [In Russian].

Yang F. and Gu S. (2021). Industry 4.0, a revolution that requires technology and national strategies // *Complex & Intelligent Systems*. Vol. 7: 1311–1325.

Yashin A.A. (2015). *Phenomenology of the Noosphere: Thematic Encyclopedia. Living Matter and Phenomenology of the Noosphere: Encyclopedic volume*. Tula: TulGU Publishing House [In Russian].

Zalasiewicz J., Williams M., Waters C.N., etc. (2017). Scale and diversity of the physical technosphere: A geological perspective // *The Anthropocene Review*, 4(1), April.

Zudilina N.V. (2020). *Fundamentals of the Doctrine of the Noosphere*. Simferopol: Publisher N.V. Zudilina [In Russian].

Index